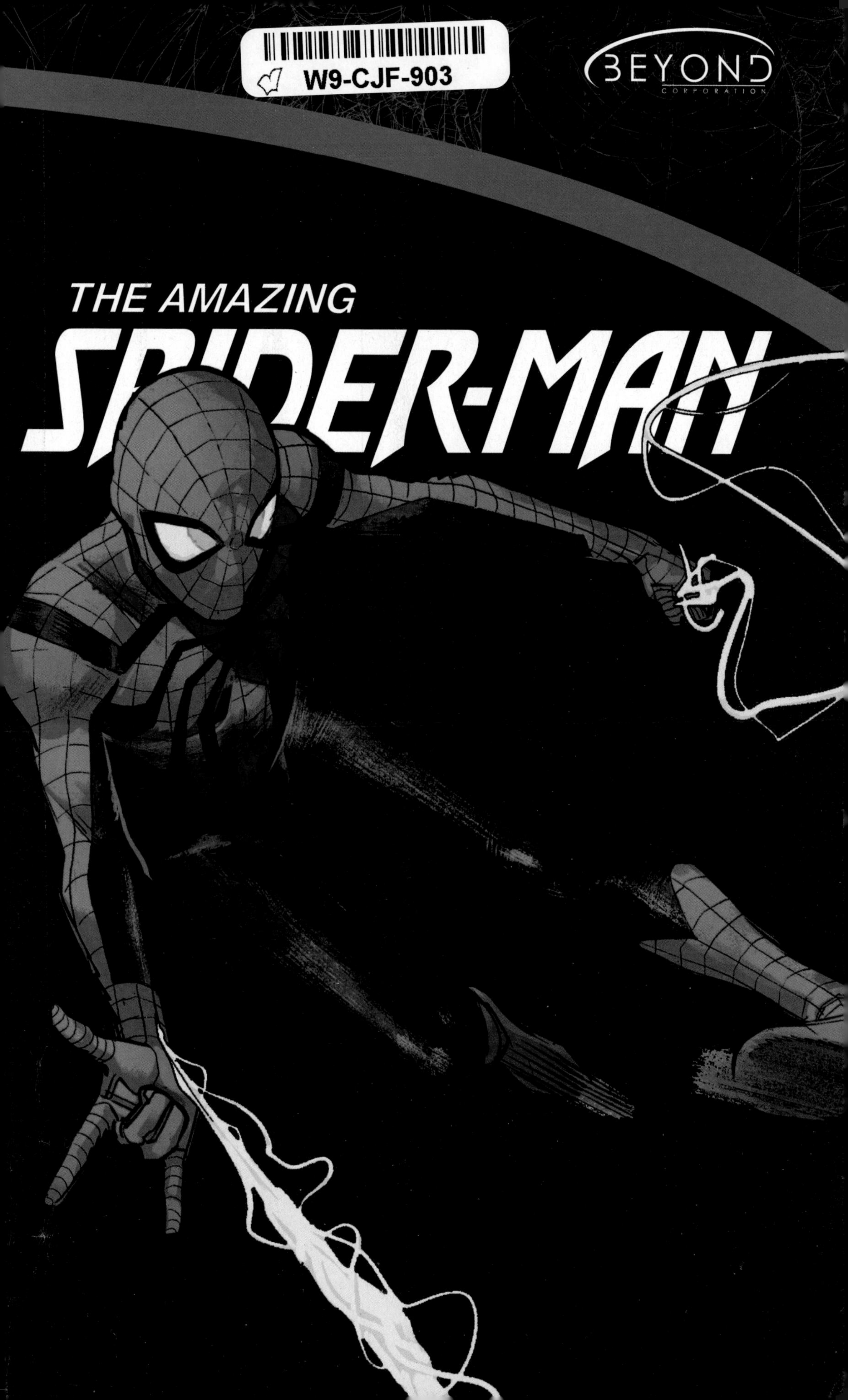
BEYOND
CORPORATION
THE AMAZING
SPIDER-MAN

BEYOND CORPORATION

PETER PARKER was bitten by a radioactive spider and gained the proportional speed, strength, and agility of a SPIDER, adhesive fingertips and toes, and the unique precognitive awareness of danger called "SPIDER-SENSE"! After the tragic death of his UNCLE BEN, Peter understood that with great power there must also come great responsibility. He became the crimefighting super hero called...

THE AMAZING SPID

AMAZING SPIDER-MAN #75-76

ZEB WELLS/WRITER
PATRICK GLEASON/ARTIST
MARCIO MENYZ/COLOR ARTIST

"JANINE"

ZEB WELLS/WRITER
IVAN FIORELLI/ARTIST
DEE CUNNIFFE/COLOR ARTIST

"KAFKA"

ZEB WELLS/WRITER
IVAN FIORELLI/ARTIST
EDGAR DELGADO/COLOR ARTIST

"LOVE AND MONSTERS"

KELLY THOMPSON/WRITER
TRAVEL FOREMAN/ARTIST
JIM CAMPBELL/COLOR ARTIST

AMAZING SPIDER-MAN #77-78

KELLY THOMPSON/WRITER
SARA PICHELLI
WITH **JIM TOWE** (#78)/ARTISTS
NOLAN WOODARD WITH
RACHELLE ROSENBERG (#78)/COLOR ARTISTS

AMAZING SPIDER-MAN #78.BEY

JED MacKAY/WRITER
ELEONORA CARLINI/ARTIST
FEDERICO BLEE/COLOR ARTIST

AMAZING SPIDER-MAN #79-80

CODY ZIGLAR/WRITER
MICHAEL DOWLING/ARTIST
JESUS ABURTOV WITH
ERICK ARCINIEGA (#80)/COLOR ARTISTS

Peter Parker has just been through hell. A SINISTER WAR and the most harrowing fight of his life has left Peter very scathed and left Peter's best friend since college, HARRY OSBORN, very dead. Peter's gone through intense situations before but has always bounced back. He'll do it again this time, right?

ER-MAN

VC'S **JOE CARAMAGNA**/LETTERER

ARTHUR ADAMS &
ALEJANDRO SÁNCHEZ (#75-80),

PATRICK GLEASON &
ALEJANDRO SÁNCHEZ
(FREE COMIC BOOK DAY 2021)

AND **LEINIL FRANCIS YU** &
SUNNY GHO (#78.BEY)/COVER ART

**KELLY THOMPSON,
CODY ZIGLAR,
SALADIN AHMED,
PATRICK GLEASON** &
ZEB WELLS/BEYOND BOARD

LINDSEY COHICK &
KAEDEN McGAHEY/ASSISTANT EDITORS

NICK LOWE/EDITOR

SPECIAL THANKS TO
DEVIN LEWIS & **DANNY KHAZEM**

SPIDER-MAN CREATED BY
STAN LEE & **STEVE DITKO**

JENNIFER GRÜNWALD/COLLECTION EDITOR
DANIEL KIRCHHOFFER/ASSISTANT EDITOR
MAIA LOY/ASSISTANT MANAGING EDITOR
LISA MONTALBANO/ASSOCIATE MANAGER, TALENT RELATIONS
JEFF YOUNGQUIST/VP PRODUCTION & SPECIAL PROJECTS
DAVID GABRIEL/SVP PRINT, SALES & MARKETING
JAY BOWEN &
ANTHONY GAMBINO/BOOK DESIGNERS
C.B. CEBULSKI/EDITOR IN CHIEF

AMAZING SPIDER-MAN: BEYOND VOL. 1. Contains material originally published in magazine form as AMAZING SPIDER-MAN (2018) #74-80 and #78.BEY and FREE COMIC BOOK DAY 2021 SPIDER-MAN/VENOM #1. Second printing 2022. ISBN 978-1-302-93211-4. Published by MARVEL WORLDWIDE, INC., a subsidiary of MARVEL ENTERTAINMENT, LLC. OFFICE OF PUBLICATION: 1290 Avenue of the Americas, New York, NY 10104. © 2021 MARVEL. No similarity between any of the names, characters, persons, and/or institutions in this book with those of any living or dead person or institution is intended, and any such similarity which may exist is purely coincidental. **Printed in Canada.** KEVIN FEIGE, Chief Creative Officer; DAN BUCKLEY, President, Marvel Entertainment; JOE QUESADA, EVP & Creative Director; DAVID BOGART, Associate Publisher & SVP of Talent Affairs; TOM BREVOORT, VP, Executive Editor; NICK LOWE, Executive Editor, VP of Content, Digital Publishing; DAVID GABRIEL, VP of Print & Digital Publishing; SVEN LARSEN, VP of Licensed Publishing; MARK ANNUNZIATO, VP of Planning & Forecasting; JEFF YOUNGQUIST, VP of Production & Special Projects; ALEX MORALES, Director of Publishing Operations; DAN EDINGTON, Director of Editorial Operations; RICKEY PURDIN, Director of Talent Relations; JENNIFER GRÜNWALD, Director of Production & Special Projects; SUSAN CRESPI, Production Manager; STAN LEE, Chairman Emeritus. For information regarding advertising in Marvel Comics or on Marvel.com, please contact Vit DeBellis, Custom Solutions & Integrated Advertising Manager, at vdebellis@marvel.com. For Marvel subscription inquiries, please call 888-511-5480. **Manufactured between 6/10/2022 and 7/12/2022 by SOLISCO PRINTERS, SCOTT, QC, CANADA.**

10 9 8 7 6 5 4 3 2 1

BEYOND #75

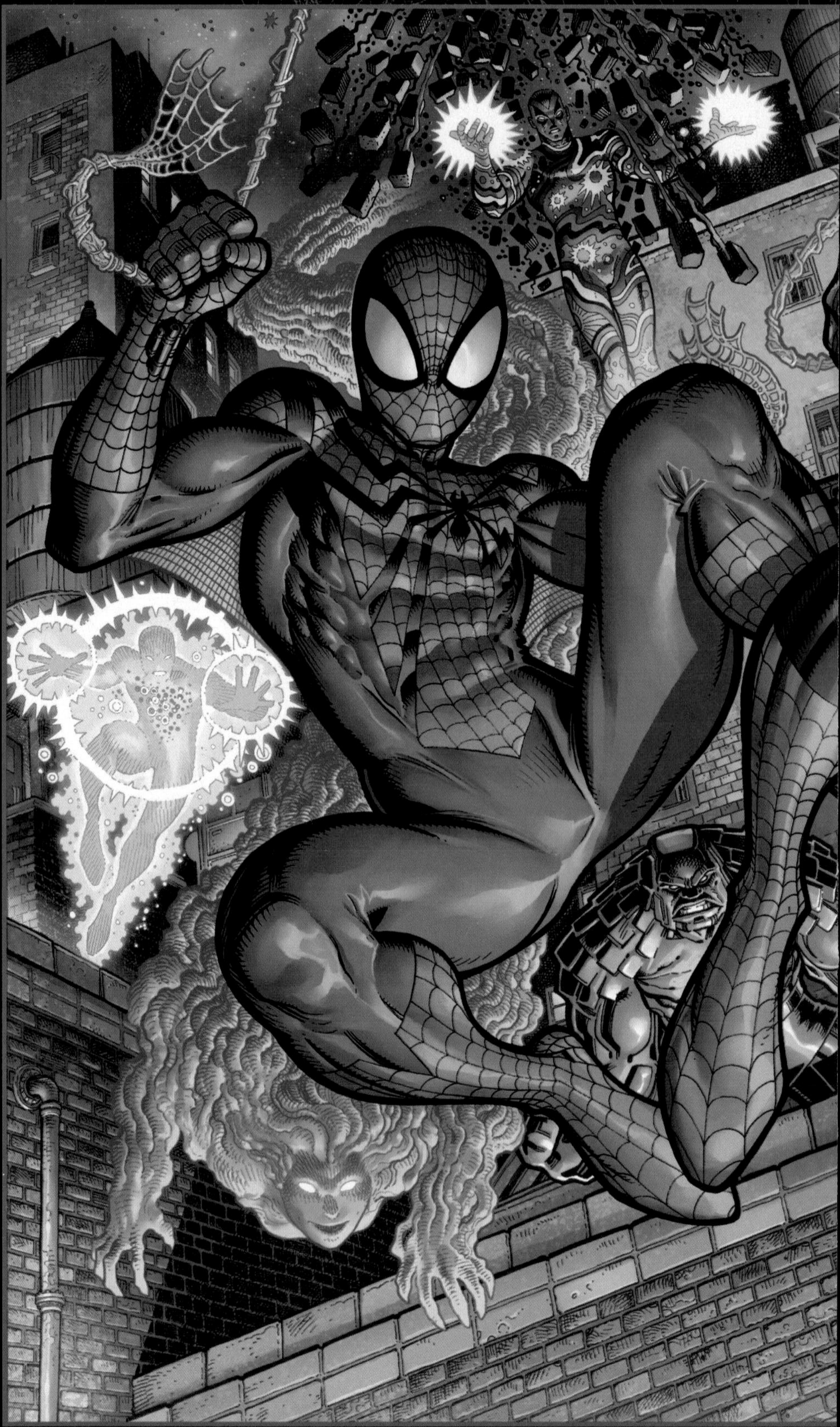

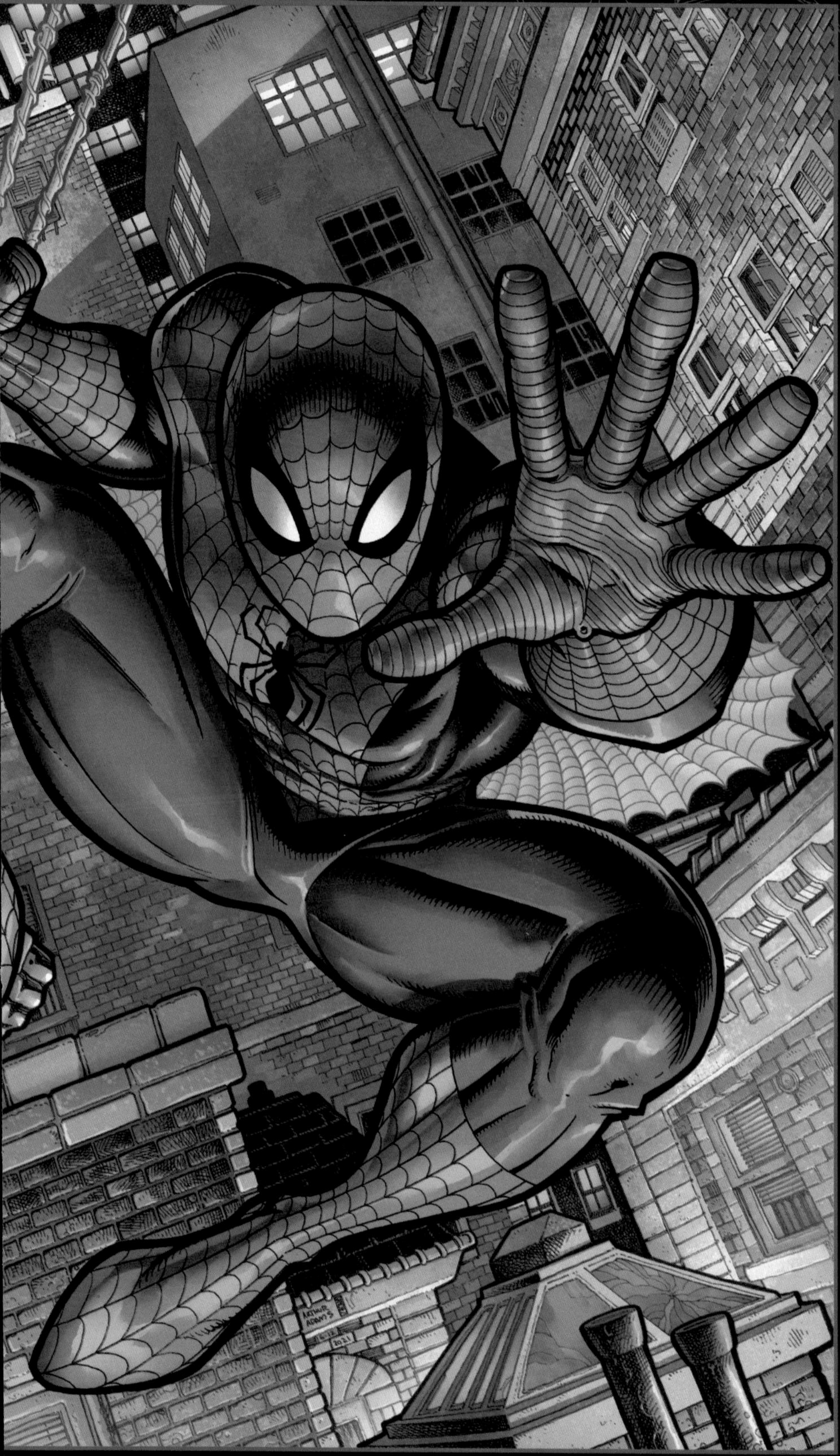

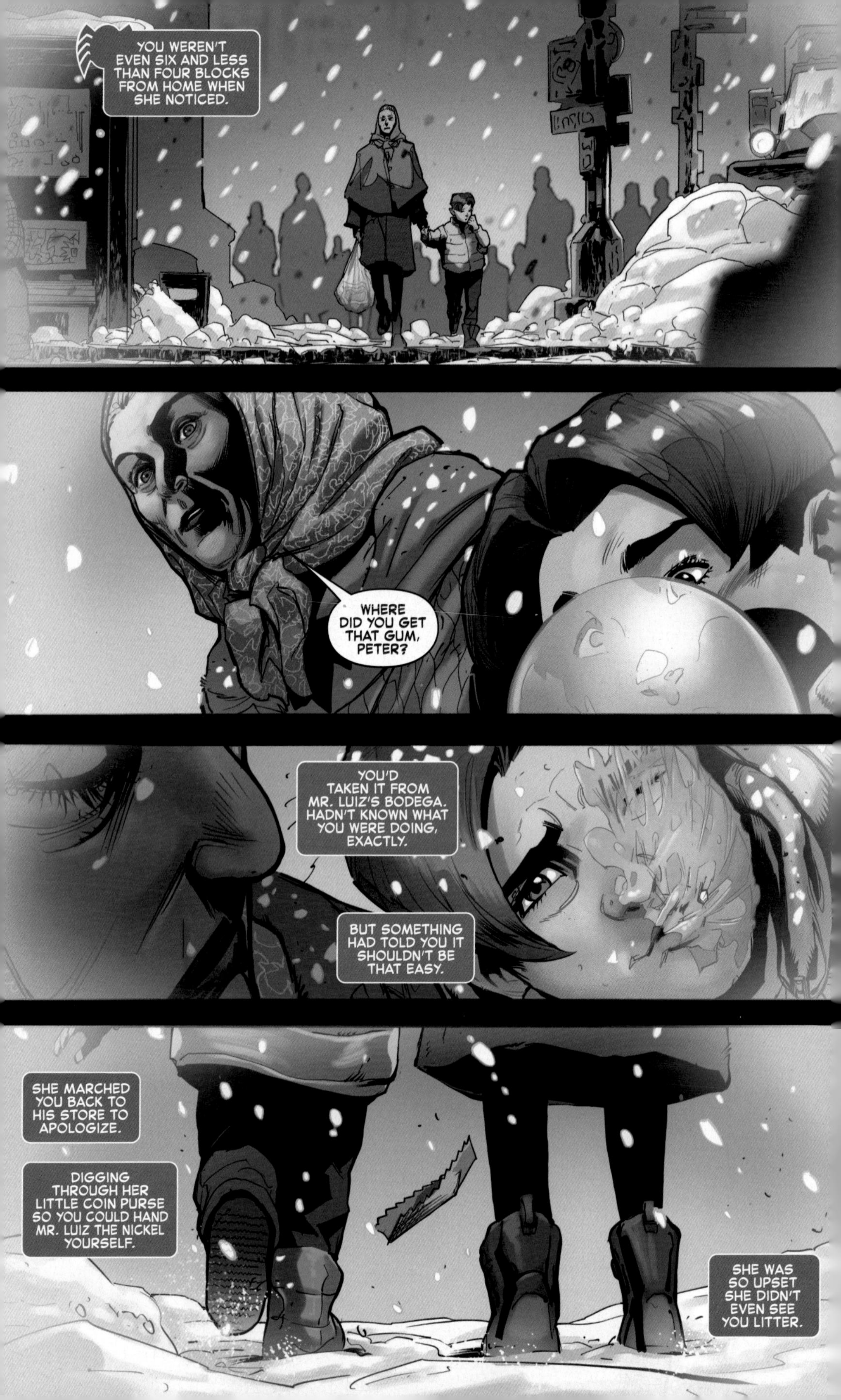
YOU WEREN'T EVEN SIX AND LESS THAN FOUR BLOCKS FROM HOME WHEN SHE NOTICED.
WHERE DID YOU GET THAT GUM, PETER?
YOU'D TAKEN IT FROM MR. LUIZ'S BODEGA. HADN'T KNOWN WHAT YOU WERE DOING, EXACTLY.
BUT SOMETHING HAD TOLD YOU IT SHOULDN'T BE THAT EASY.
SHE MARCHED YOU BACK TO HIS STORE TO APOLOGIZE.
DIGGING THROUGH HER LITTLE COIN PURSE SO YOU COULD HAND MR. LUIZ THE NICKEL YOURSELF.
SHE WAS SO UPSET SHE DIDN'T EVEN SEE YOU LITTER.

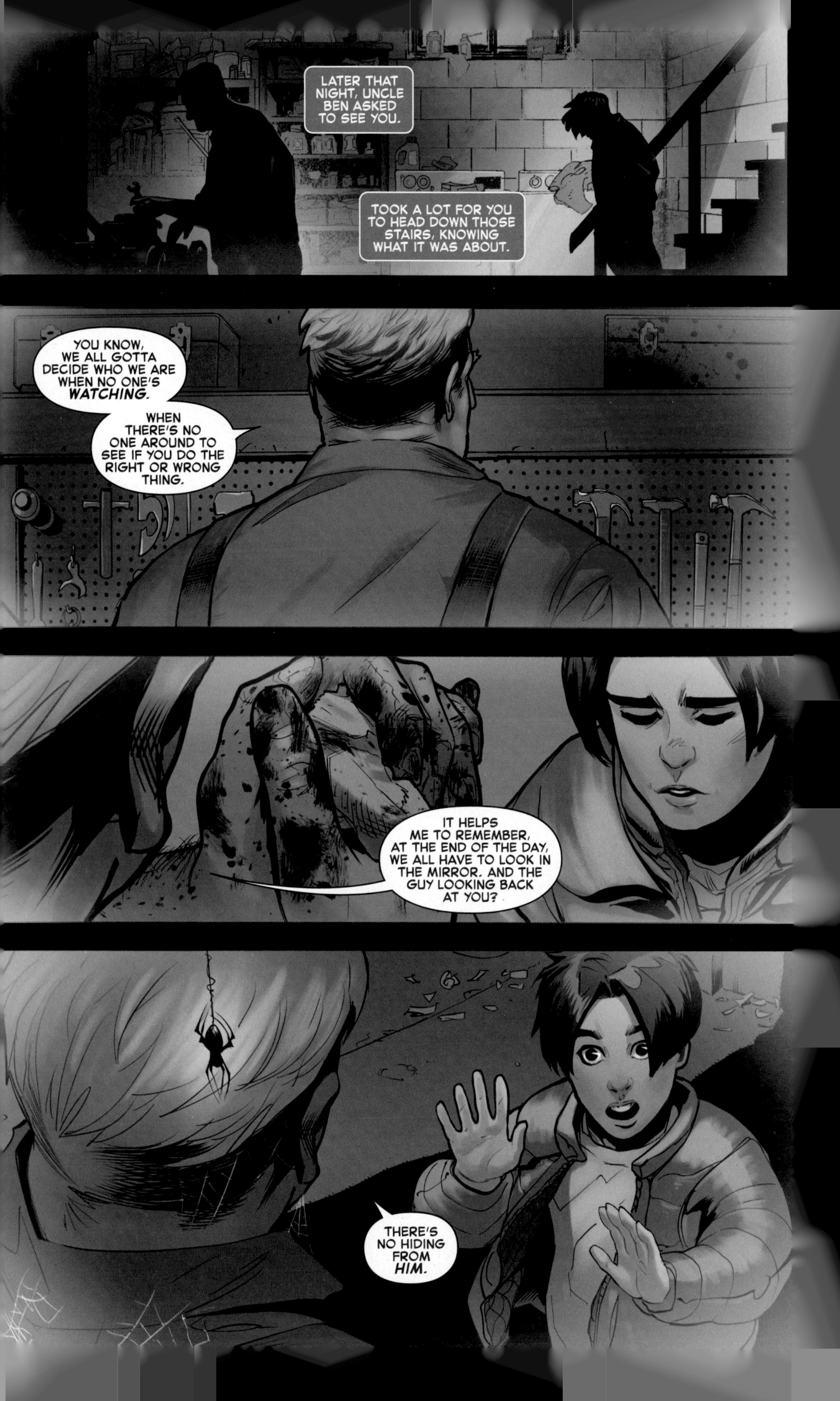
LATER THAT NIGHT, UNCLE BEN ASKED TO SEE YOU.
TOOK A LOT FOR YOU TO HEAD DOWN THOSE STAIRS, KNOWING WHAT IT WAS ABOUT.
YOU KNOW, WE ALL GOTTA DECIDE WHO WE ARE WHEN NO ONE'S *WATCHING.*
WHEN THERE'S NO ONE AROUND TO SEE IF YOU DO THE RIGHT OR WRONG THING.
IT HELPS ME TO REMEMBER, AT THE END OF THE DAY, WE ALL HAVE TO LOOK IN THE MIRROR. AND THE GUY LOOKING BACK AT YOU?
THERE'S NO HIDING FROM *HIM.*

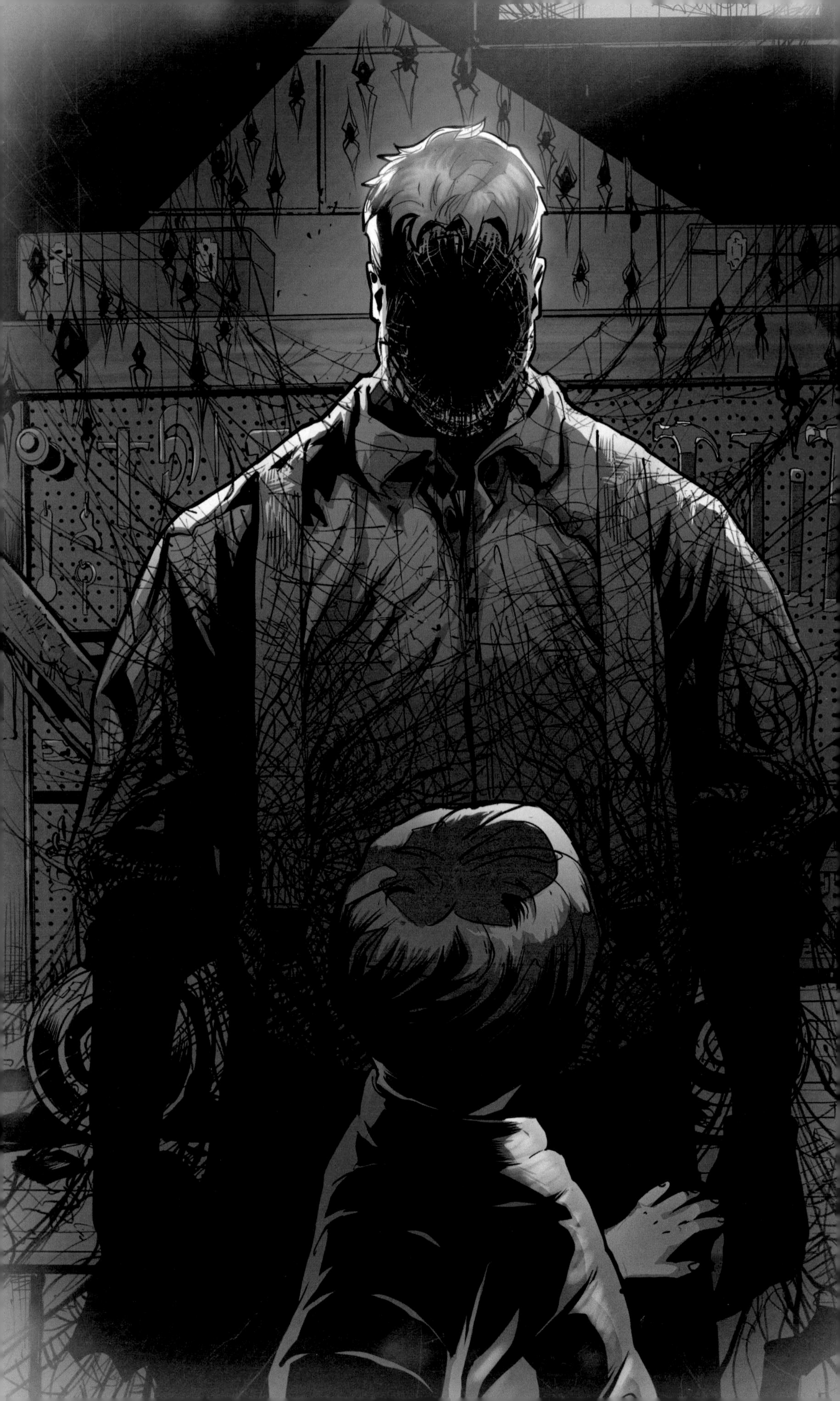

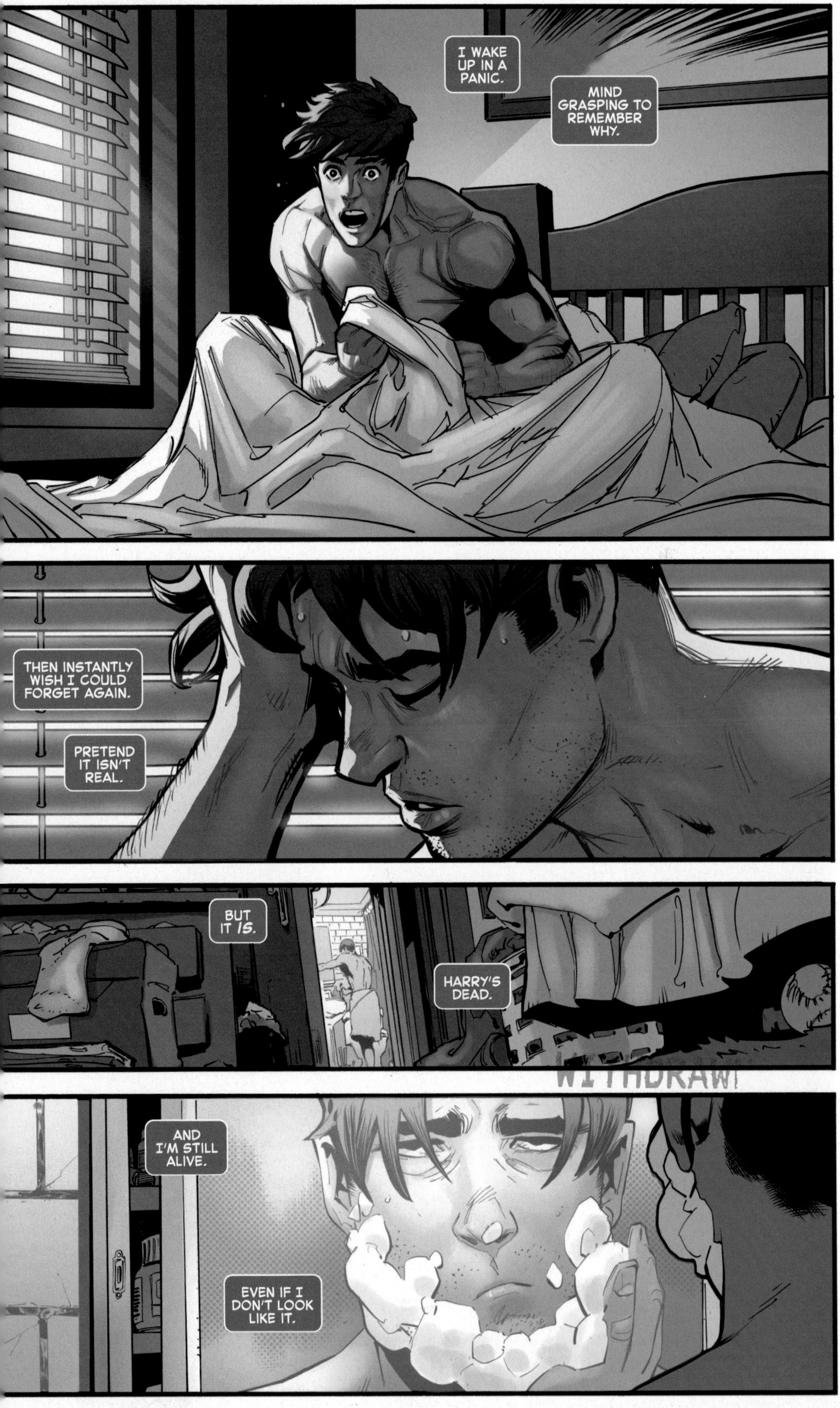
I WAKE UP IN A PANIC.
MIND GRASPING TO REMEMBER WHY.
THEN INSTANTLY WISH I COULD FORGET AGAIN.
PRETEND IT ISN'T REAL.
BUT IT *IS*.
HARRY'S DEAD.
AND I'M STILL ALIVE.
EVEN IF I DON'T LOOK LIKE IT.

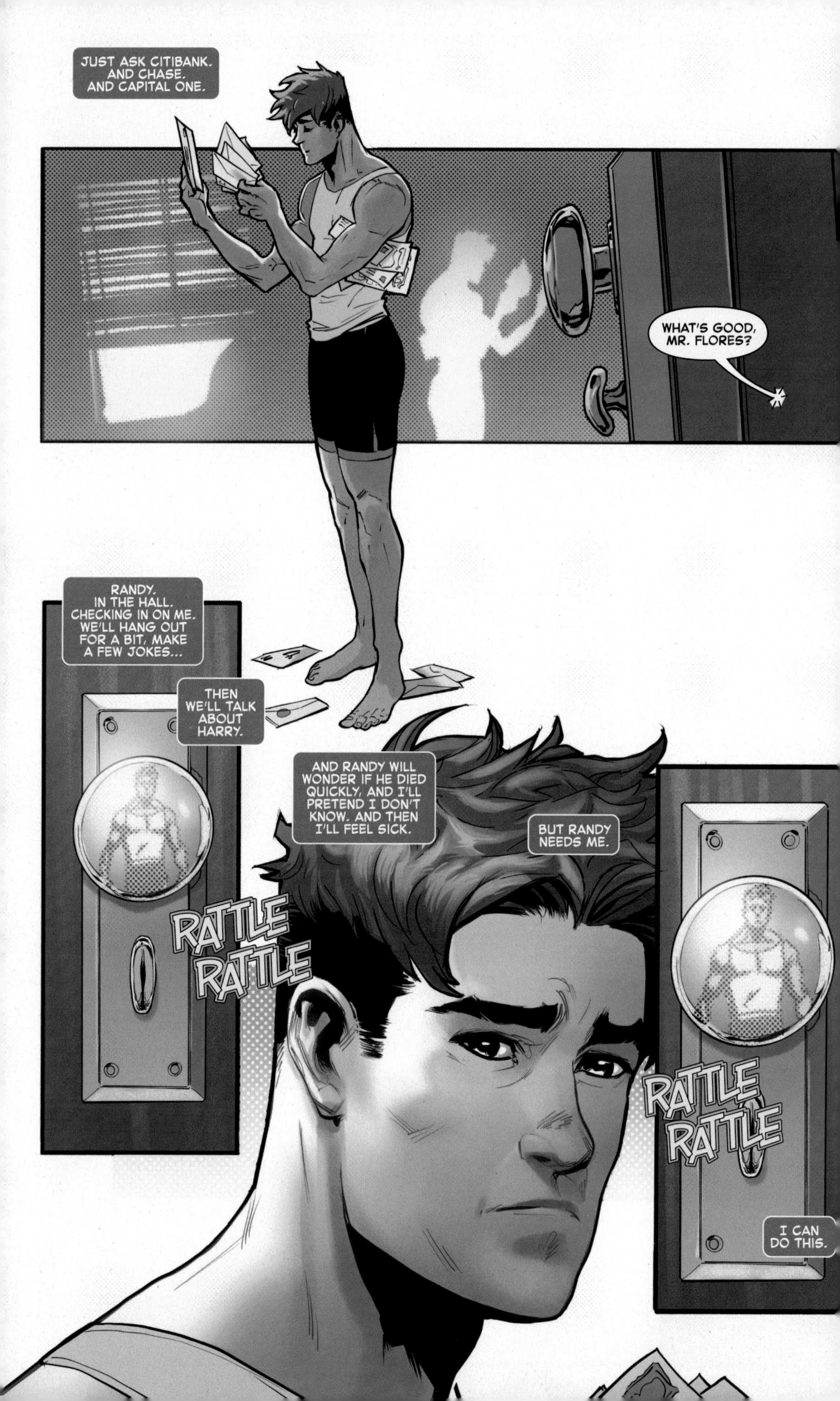
JUST ASK CITIBANK. AND CHASE. AND CAPITAL ONE.
WHAT'S GOOD, MR. FLORES?
RANDY. IN THE HALL. CHECKING IN ON ME. WE'LL HANG OUT FOR A BIT, MAKE A FEW JOKES...
THEN WE'LL TALK ABOUT HARRY.
AND RANDY WILL WONDER IF HE DIED QUICKLY, AND I'LL PRETEND I DON'T KNOW. AND THEN I'LL FEEL SICK.
BUT RANDY NEEDS ME.
RATTLE RATTLE
RATTLE RATTLE
I CAN DO THIS.

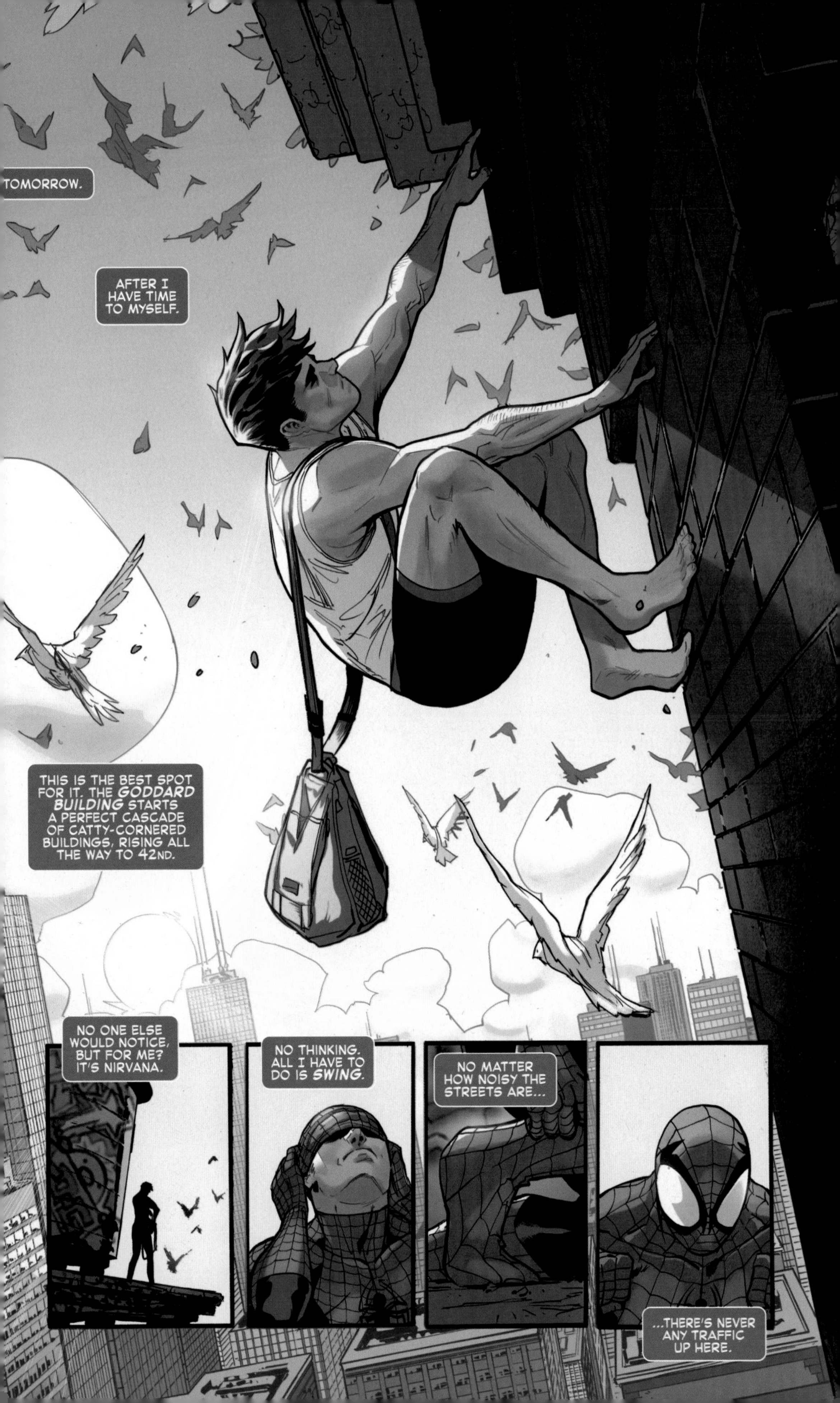
TOMORROW.
AFTER I HAVE TIME TO MYSELF.
THIS IS THE BEST SPOT FOR IT. THE GODDARD BUILDING STARTS A PERFECT CASCADE OF CATTY-CORNERED BUILDINGS, RISING ALL THE WAY TO 42ND.
NO ONE ELSE WOULD NOTICE, BUT FOR ME? IT'S NIRVANA.
NO THINKING. ALL I HAVE TO DO IS SWING.
NO MATTER HOW NOISY THE STREETS ARE...
...THERE'S NEVER ANY TRAFFIC UP HERE.

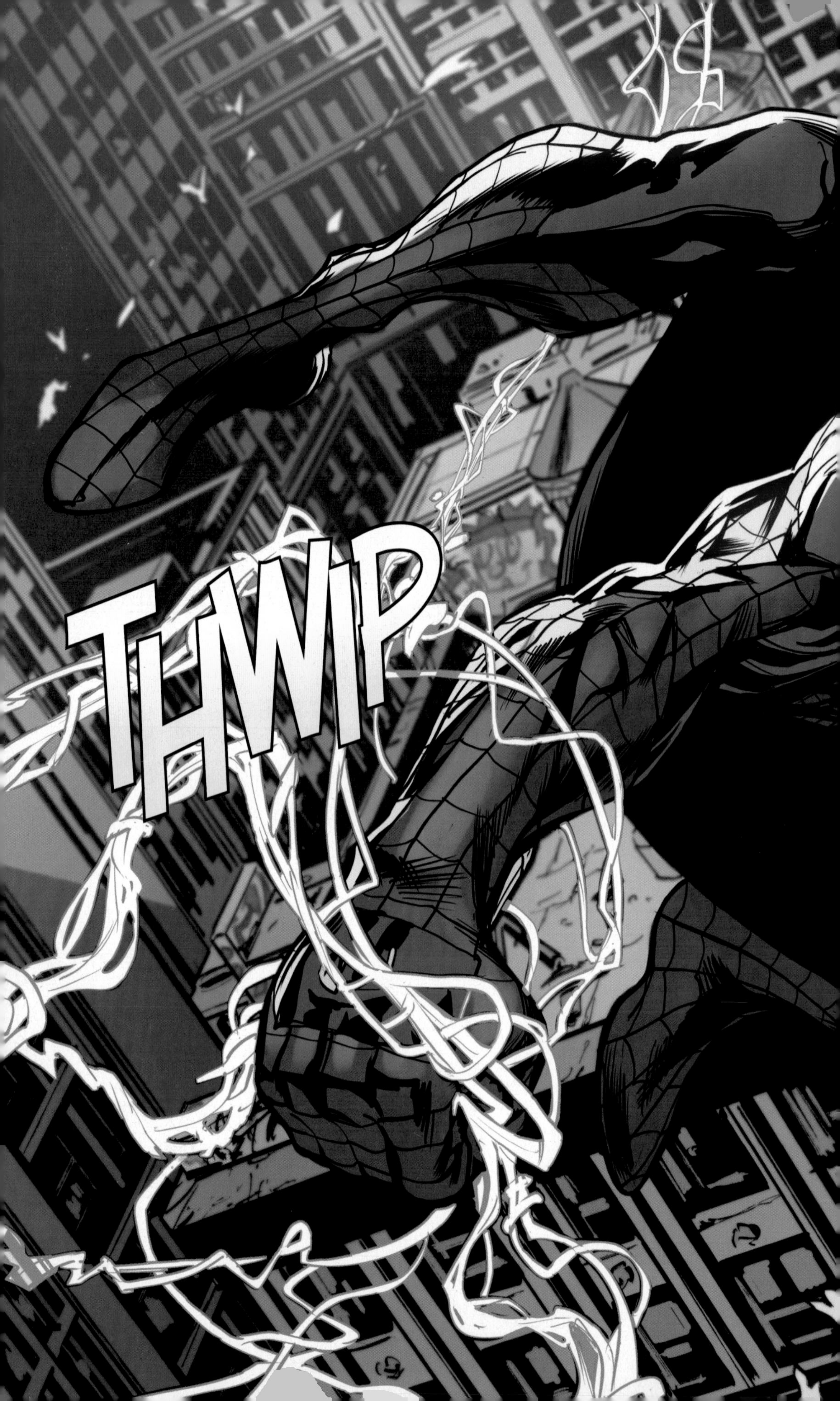
THWIP

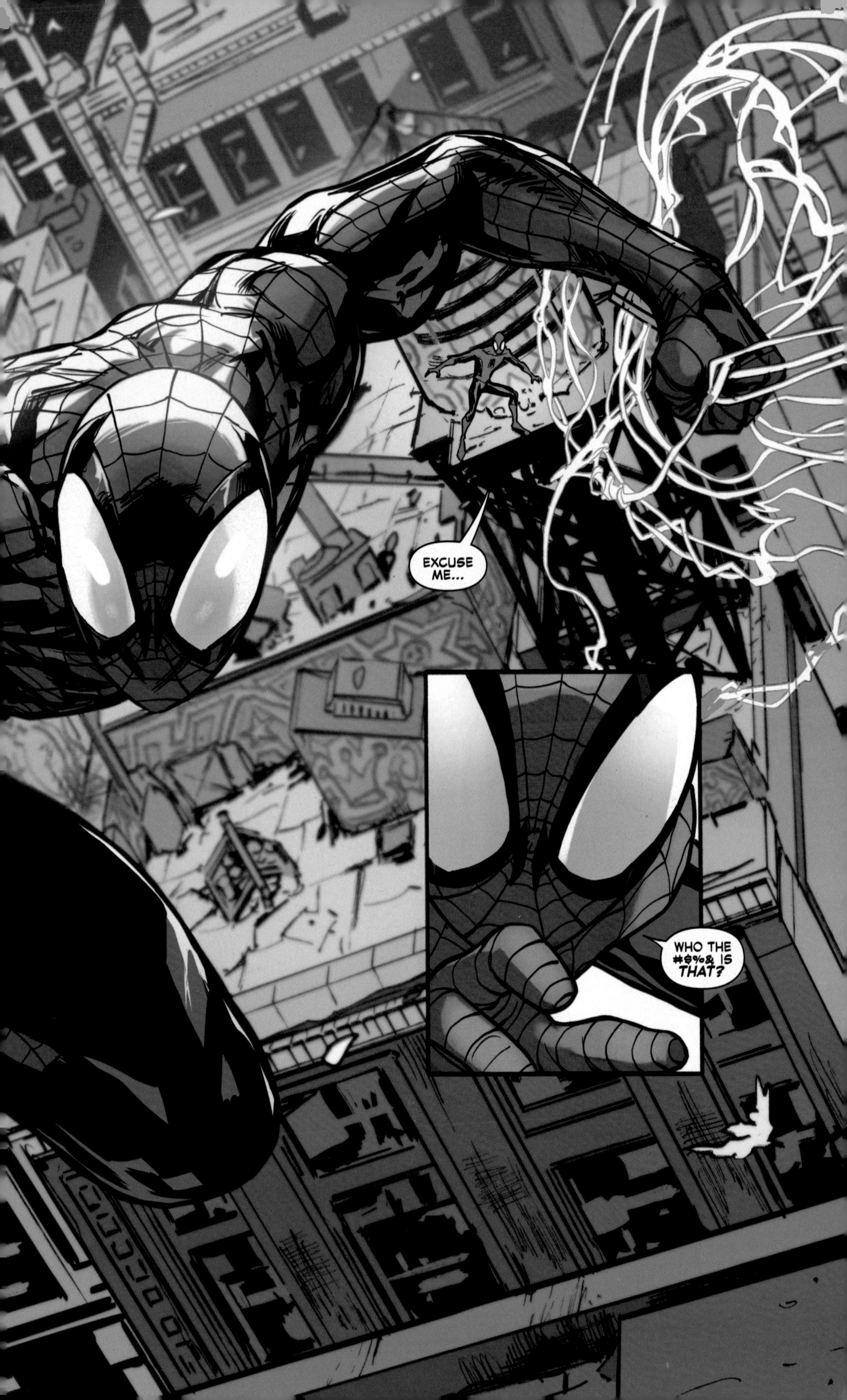
EXCUSE ME...
WHO THE #$%& IS *THAT?*

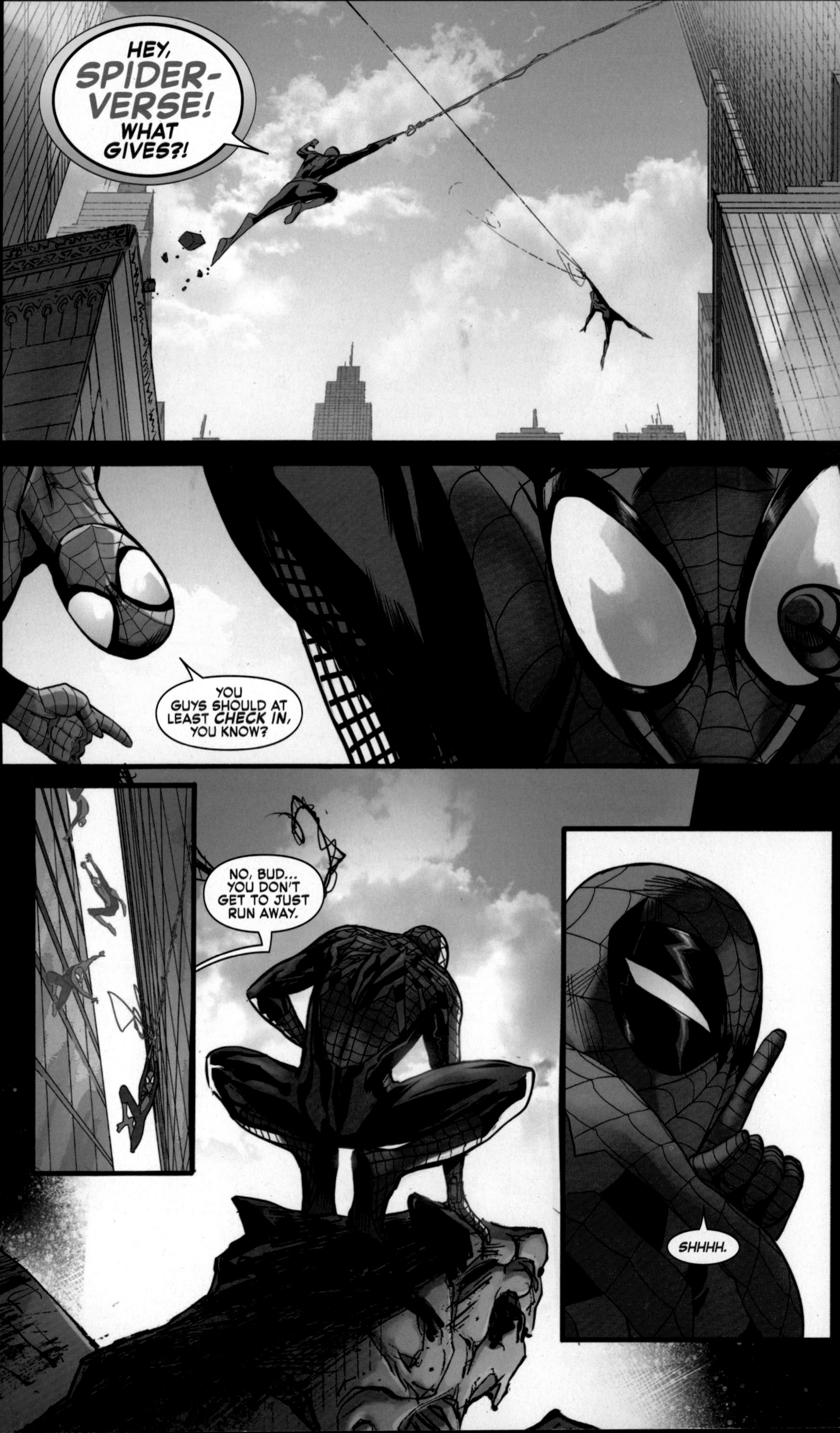
HEY, SPIDER-VERSE! WHAT GIVES?!
YOU GUYS SHOULD AT LEAST CHECK IN, YOU KNOW?
NO, BUD... YOU DON'T GET TO JUST RUN AWAY.
SHHHH.

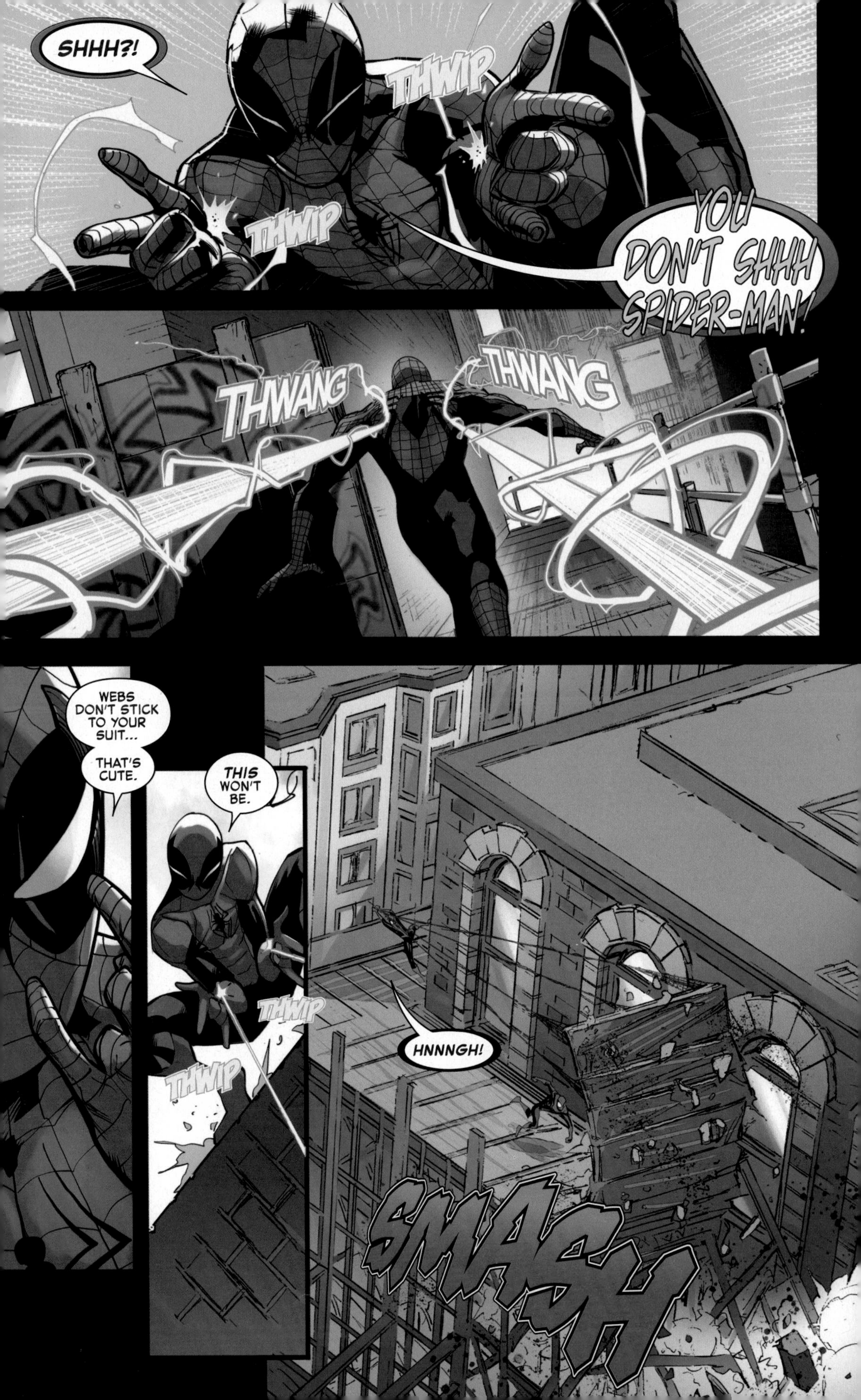
SHHH?!
THWIP
THWIP
YOU DON'T SHHH SPIDER-MAN!
THWANG
THWANG
WEBS DON'T STICK TO YOUR SUIT...
THAT'S CUTE.
THIS WON'T BE.
THWIP
THWIP
HNNNGH!
SMASH

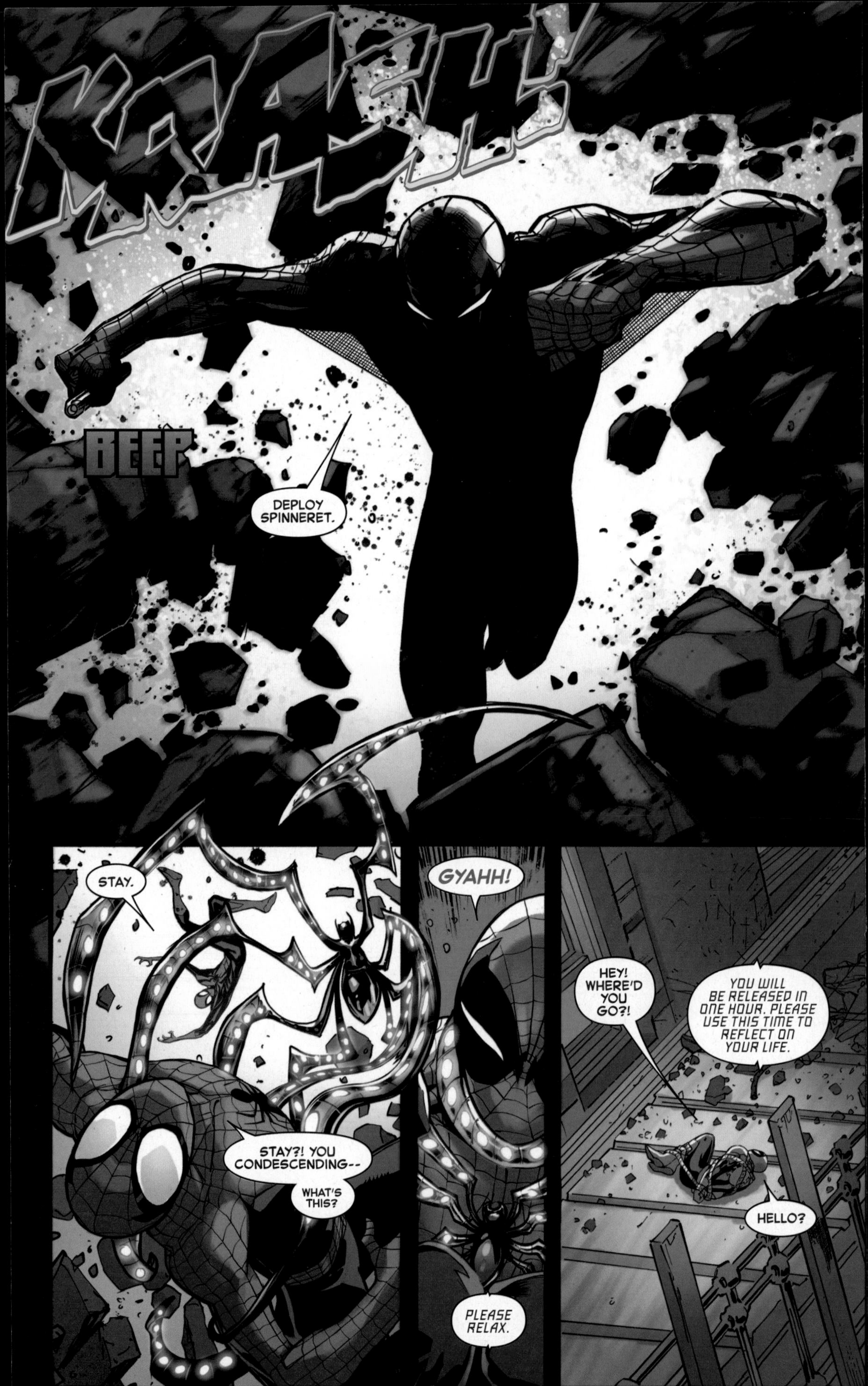
KRASH
BEEP
DEPLOY SPINNERET.
STAY.
STAY?! YOU CONDESCENDING--
WHAT'S THIS?
GYAHH!
PLEASE RELAX.
HEY! WHERE'D YOU GO?!
YOU WILL BE RELEASED IN ONE HOUR. PLEASE USE THIS TIME TO REFLECT ON YOUR LIFE.
HELLO?

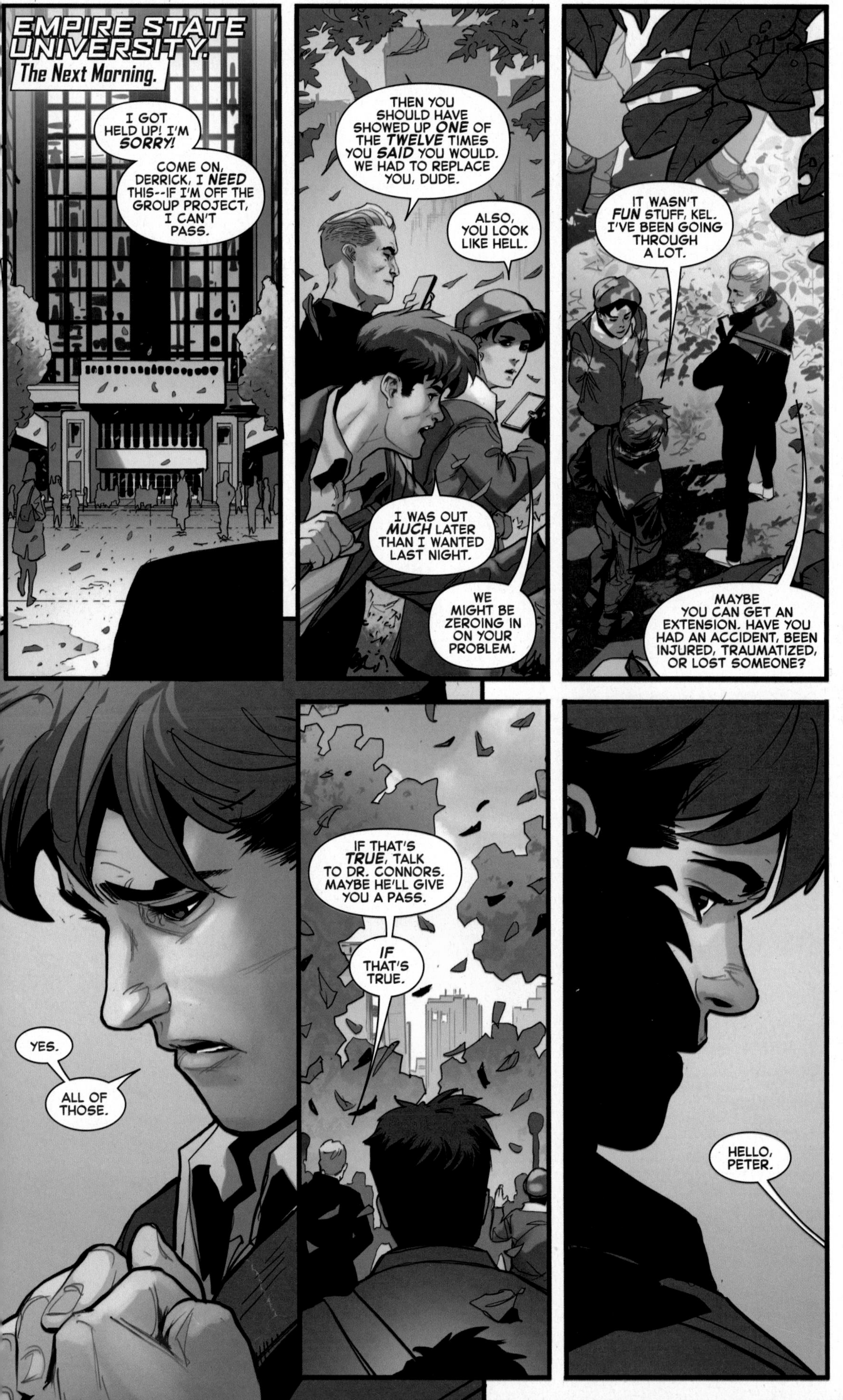
EMPIRE STATE UNIVERSITY.
The Next Morning.
I GOT HELD UP! I'M SORRY!
COME ON, DERRICK, I NEED THIS--IF I'M OFF THE GROUP PROJECT, I CAN'T PASS.
THEN YOU SHOULD HAVE SHOWED UP ONE OF THE TWELVE TIMES YOU SAID YOU WOULD. WE HAD TO REPLACE YOU, DUDE.
ALSO, YOU LOOK LIKE HELL.
I WAS OUT MUCH LATER THAN I WANTED LAST NIGHT.
WE MIGHT BE ZEROING IN ON YOUR PROBLEM.
IT WASN'T FUN STUFF, KEL. I'VE BEEN GOING THROUGH A LOT.
MAYBE YOU CAN GET AN EXTENSION. HAVE YOU HAD AN ACCIDENT, BEEN INJURED, TRAUMATIZED, OR LOST SOMEONE?
YES.
ALL OF THOSE.
IF THAT'S TRUE, TALK TO DR. CONNORS. MAYBE HE'LL GIVE YOU A PASS.
IF THAT'S TRUE.
HELLO, PETER.

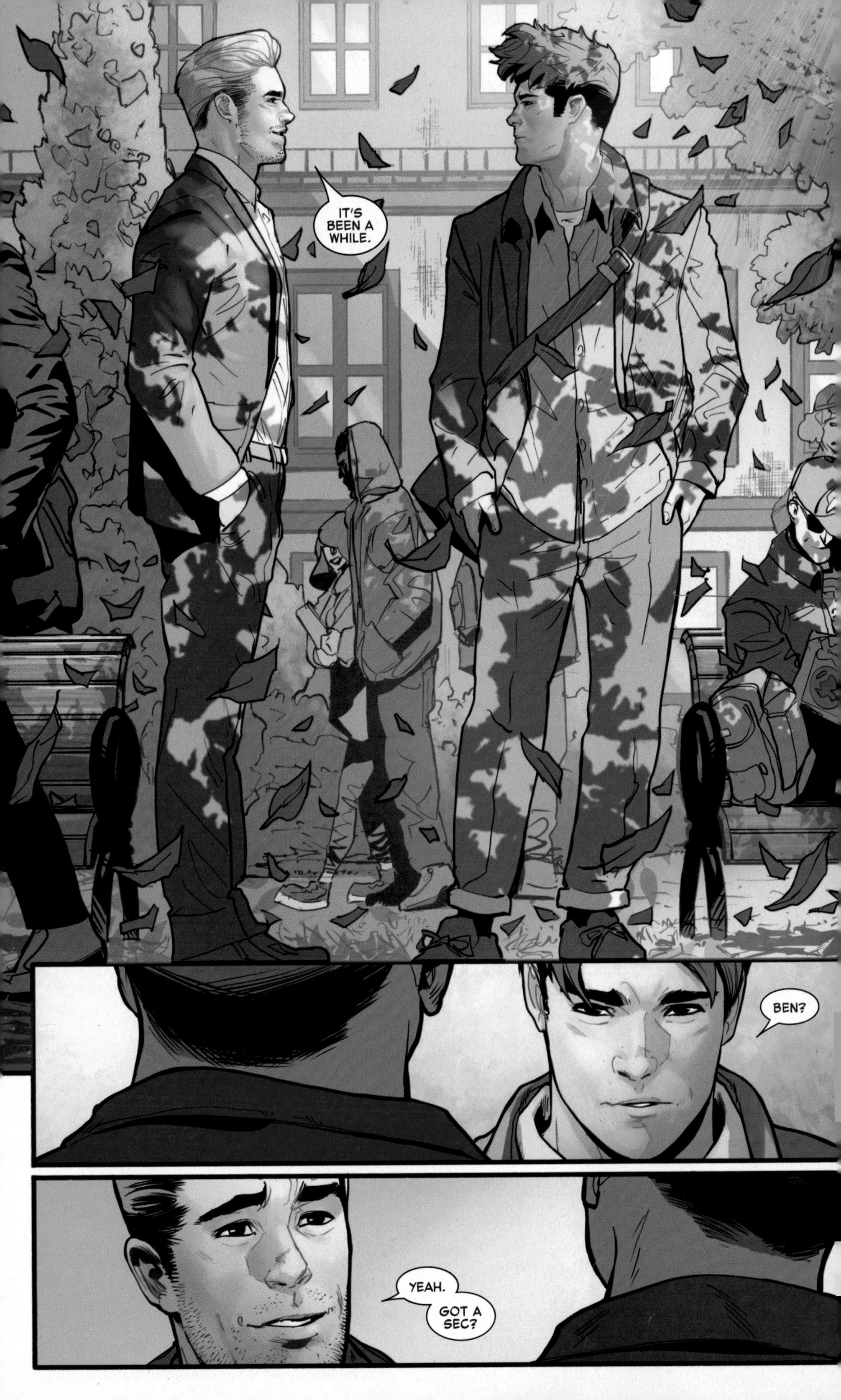
IT'S BEEN A WHILE.
BEN?
YEAH.
GOT A SEC?

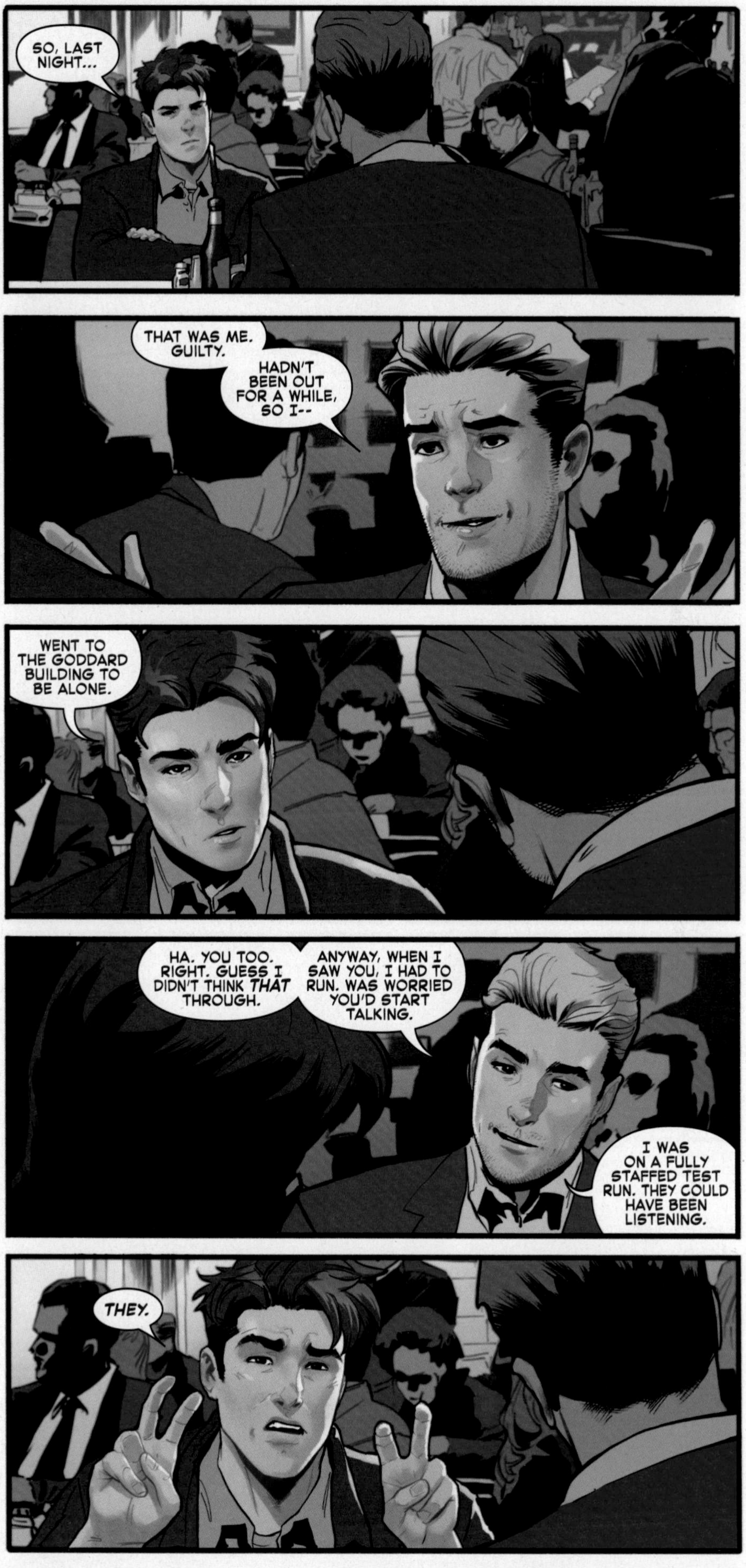
SO, LAST NIGHT...
THAT WAS ME. GUILTY.
HADN'T BEEN OUT FOR A WHILE, SO I--
WENT TO THE GODDARD BUILDING TO BE ALONE.
HA. YOU TOO. RIGHT. GUESS I DIDN'T THINK *THAT* THROUGH.
ANYWAY, WHEN I SAW YOU, I HAD TO RUN. WAS WORRIED YOU'D START TALKING.
I WAS ON A FULLY STAFFED TEST RUN. THEY COULD HAVE BEEN LISTENING.
THEY.

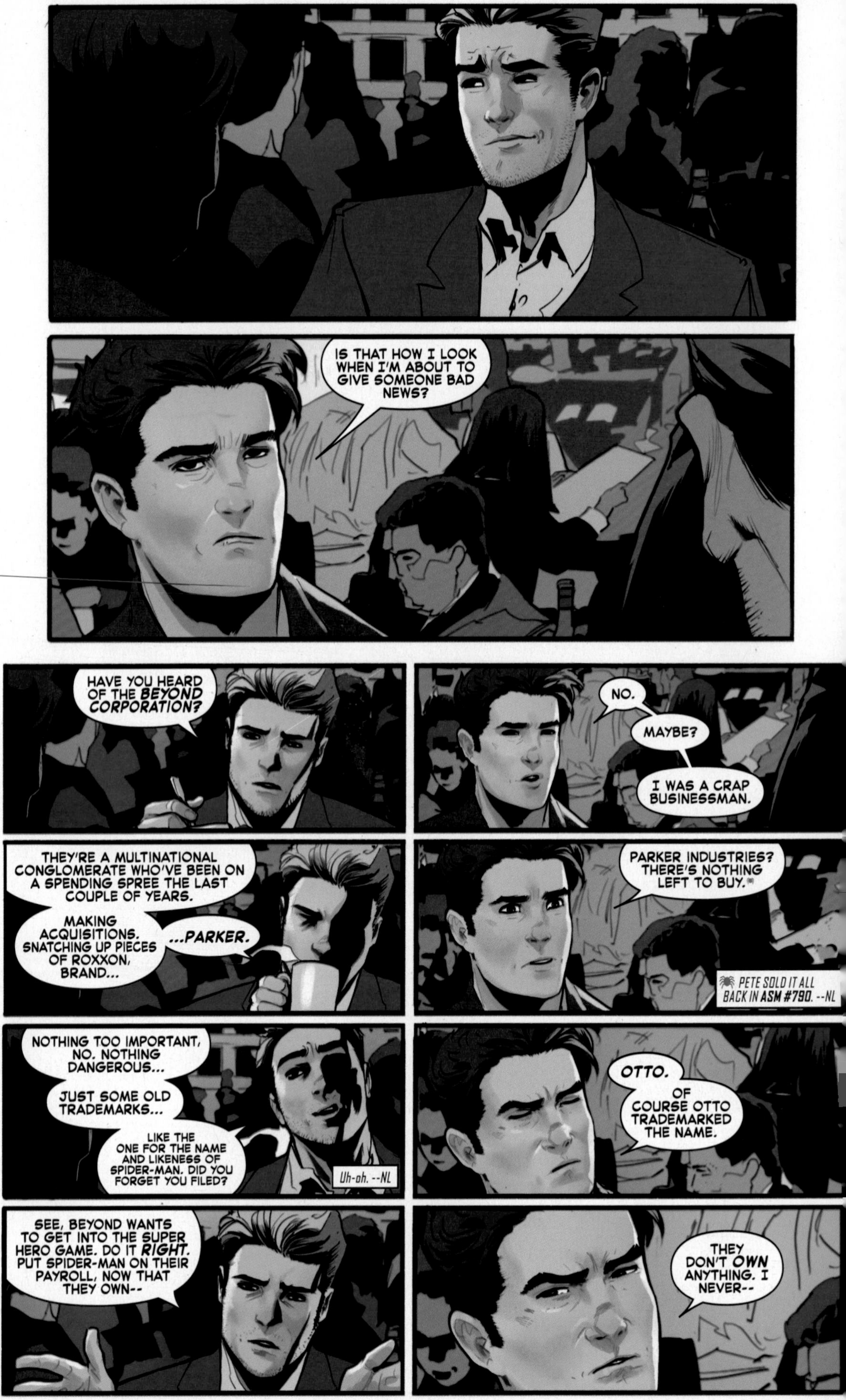
IS THAT HOW I LOOK WHEN I'M ABOUT TO GIVE SOMEONE BAD NEWS?
HAVE YOU HEARD OF THE BEYOND CORPORATION?
NO.
MAYBE?
I WAS A CRAP BUSINESSMAN.
THEY'RE A MULTINATIONAL CONGLOMERATE WHO'VE BEEN ON A SPENDING SPREE THE LAST COUPLE OF YEARS.
MAKING ACQUISITIONS. SNATCHING UP PIECES OF ROXXON, BRAND...
...PARKER.
PARKER INDUSTRIES? THERE'S NOTHING LEFT TO BUY.
PETE SOLD IT ALL BACK IN ASM #790. --NL
NOTHING TOO IMPORTANT, NO. NOTHING DANGEROUS...
JUST SOME OLD TRADEMARKS...
LIKE THE ONE FOR THE NAME AND LIKENESS OF SPIDER-MAN. DID YOU FORGET YOU FILED?
Uh-oh. --NL
OTTO.
OF COURSE OTTO TRADEMARKED THE NAME.
SEE, BEYOND WANTS TO GET INTO THE SUPER HERO GAME. DO IT RIGHT. PUT SPIDER-MAN ON THEIR PAYROLL, NOW THAT THEY OWN--
THEY DON'T OWN ANYTHING. I NEVER--

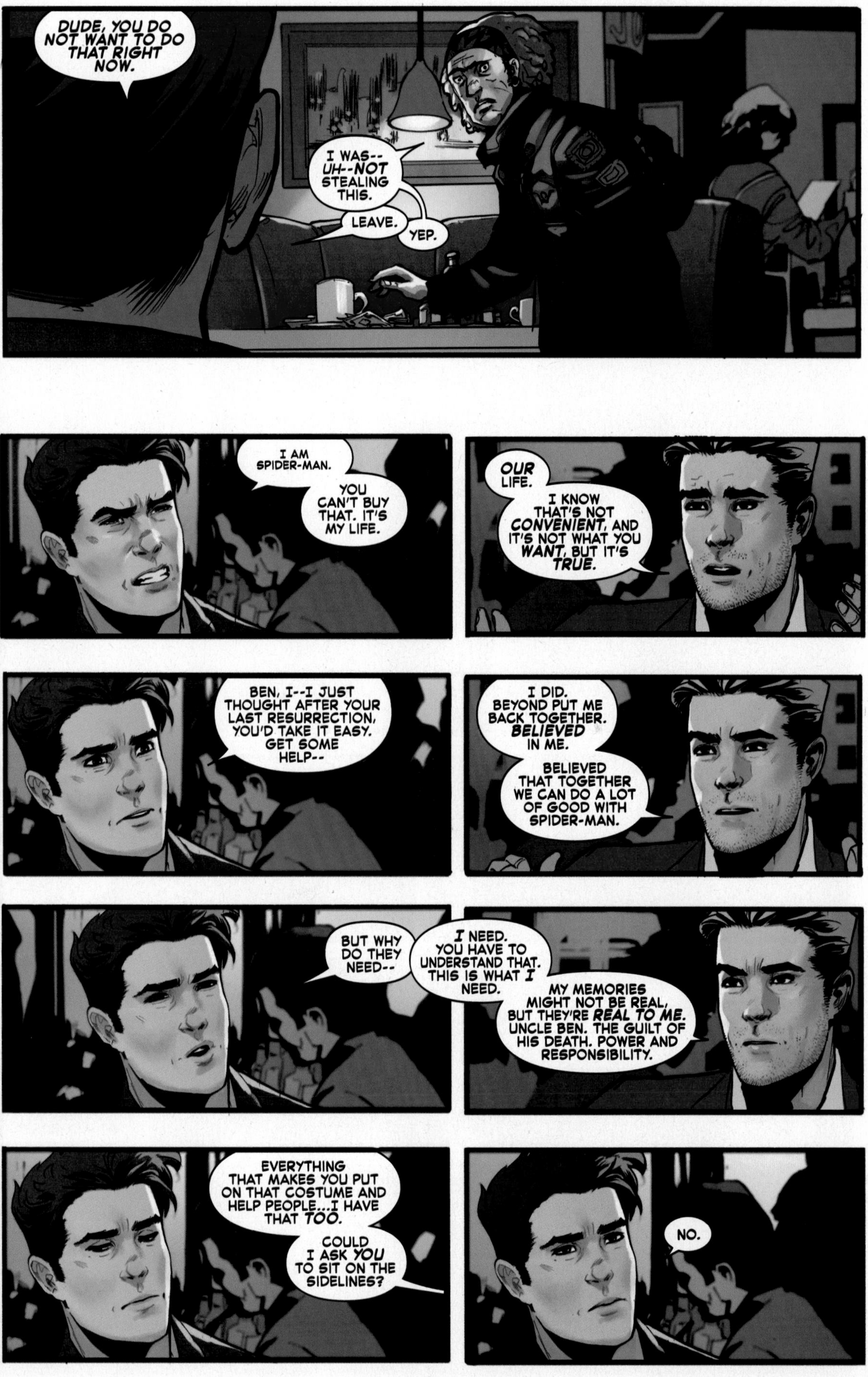
DUDE, YOU DO NOT WANT TO DO THAT RIGHT NOW.
I WAS-- UH--NOT STEALING THIS.
LEAVE.
YEP.
I AM SPIDER-MAN.
YOU CAN'T BUY THAT. IT'S MY LIFE.
OUR LIFE.
I KNOW THAT'S NOT CONVENIENT, AND IT'S NOT WHAT YOU WANT, BUT IT'S TRUE.
BEN, I--I JUST THOUGHT AFTER YOUR LAST RESURRECTION, YOU'D TAKE IT EASY. GET SOME HELP--
I DID. BEYOND PUT ME BACK TOGETHER. BELIEVED IN ME.
BELIEVED THAT TOGETHER WE CAN DO A LOT OF GOOD WITH SPIDER-MAN.
BUT WHY DO THEY NEED--
I NEED. YOU HAVE TO UNDERSTAND THAT. THIS IS WHAT I NEED.
MY MEMORIES MIGHT NOT BE REAL, BUT THEY'RE REAL TO ME. UNCLE BEN. THE GUILT OF HIS DEATH. POWER AND RESPONSIBILITY.
EVERYTHING THAT MAKES YOU PUT ON THAT COSTUME AND HELP PEOPLE...I HAVE THAT TOO.
COULD I ASK YOU TO SIT ON THE SIDELINES?
NO.

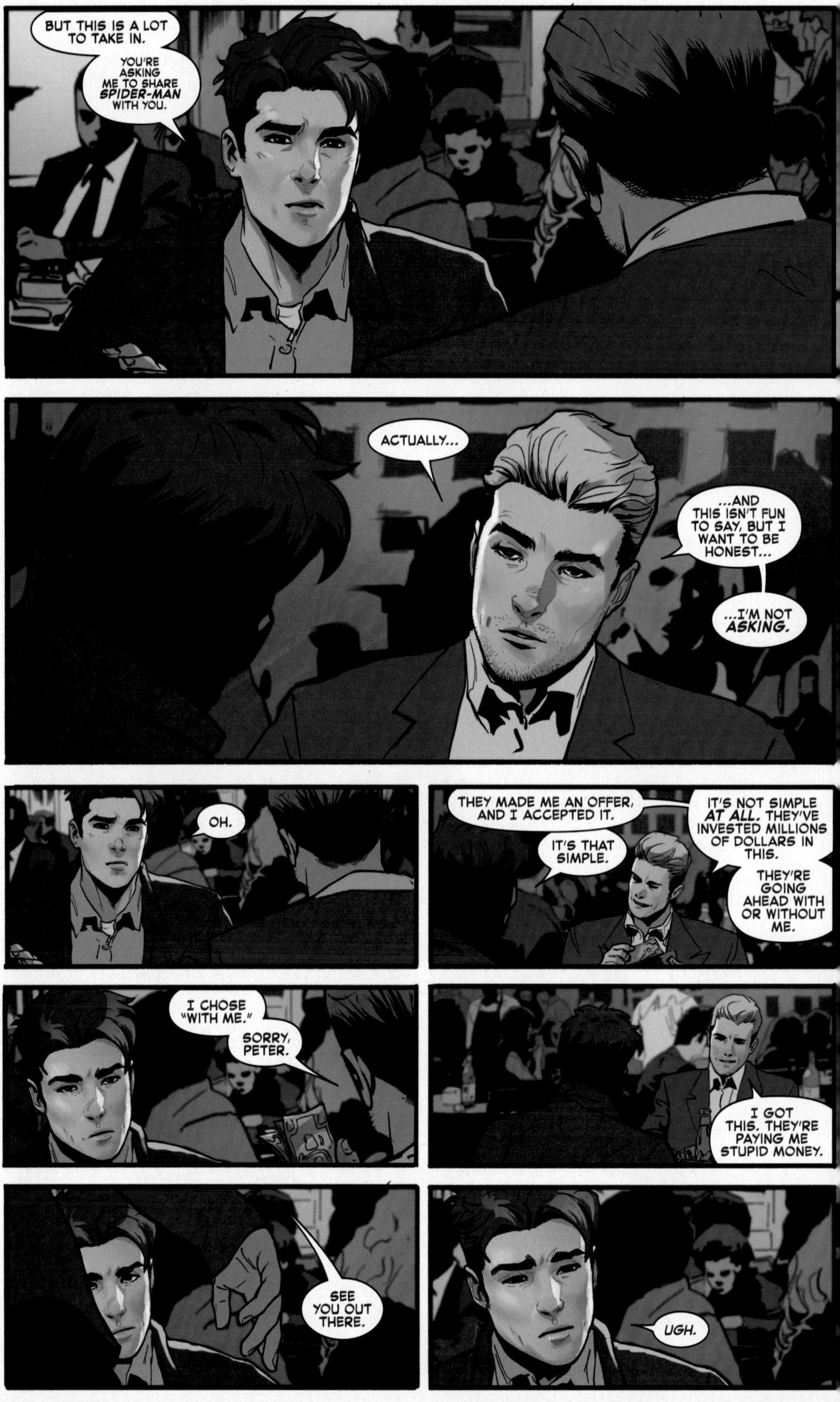

BUT THIS IS A LOT TO TAKE IN.
YOU'RE ASKING ME TO SHARE SPIDER-MAN WITH YOU.
ACTUALLY...
...AND THIS ISN'T FUN TO SAY, BUT I WANT TO BE HONEST...
...I'M NOT ASKING.
OH.
THEY MADE ME AN OFFER, AND I ACCEPTED IT.
IT'S THAT SIMPLE.
IT'S NOT SIMPLE AT ALL. THEY'VE INVESTED MILLIONS OF DOLLARS IN THIS.
THEY'RE GOING AHEAD WITH OR WITHOUT ME.
I CHOSE "WITH ME."
SORRY, PETER.
I GOT THIS. THEY'RE PAYING ME STUPID MONEY.
SEE YOU OUT THERE.
UGH.

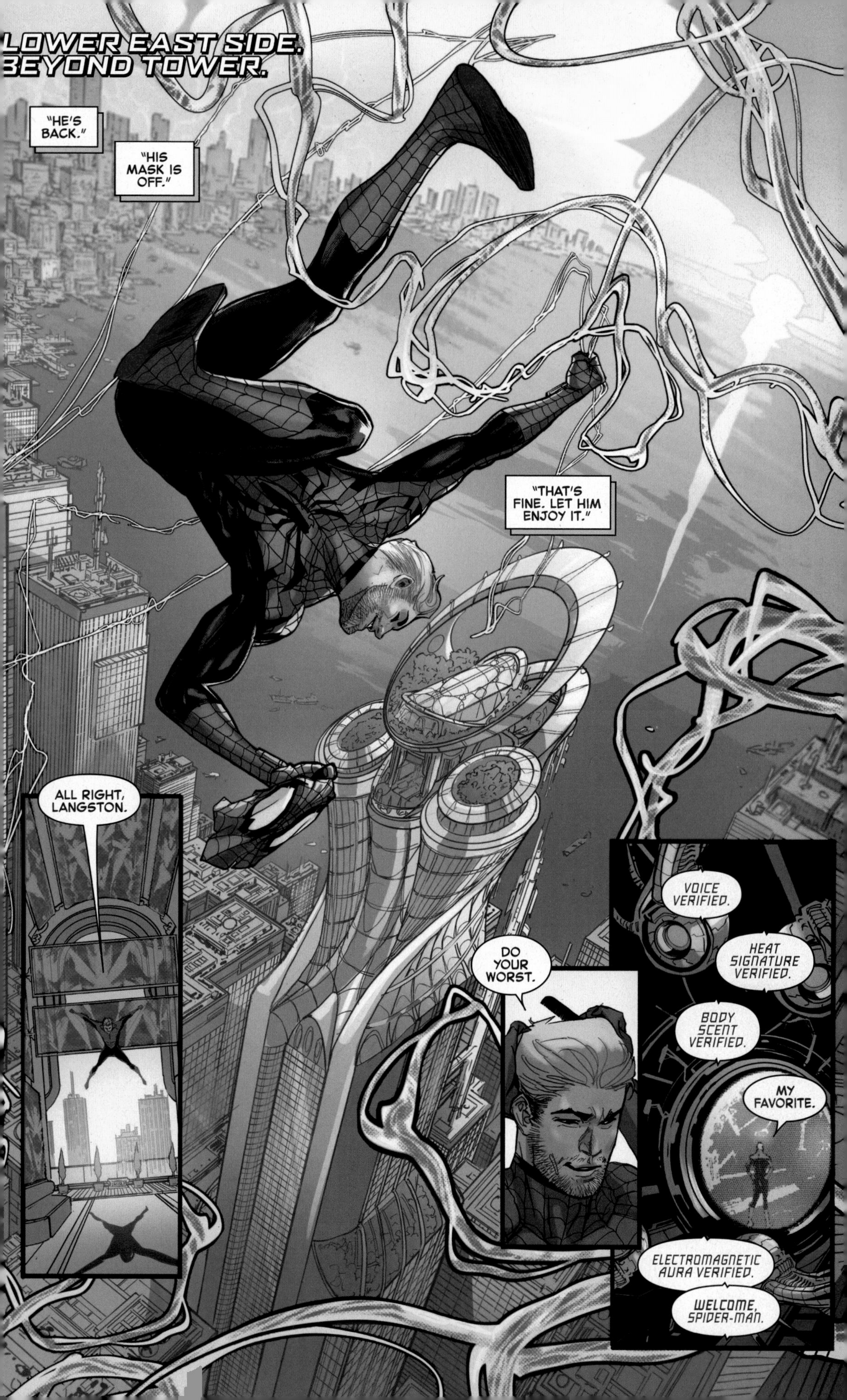
LOWER EAST SIDE.
BEYOND TOWER.
"HE'S BACK."
"HIS MASK IS OFF."
"THAT'S FINE. LET HIM ENJOY IT."
ALL RIGHT, LANGSTON.
VOICE VERIFIED.
DO YOUR WORST.
HEAT SIGNATURE VERIFIED.
BODY SCENT VERIFIED.
MY FAVORITE.
ELECTROMAGNETIC AURA VERIFIED.
WELCOME, SPIDER-MAN.

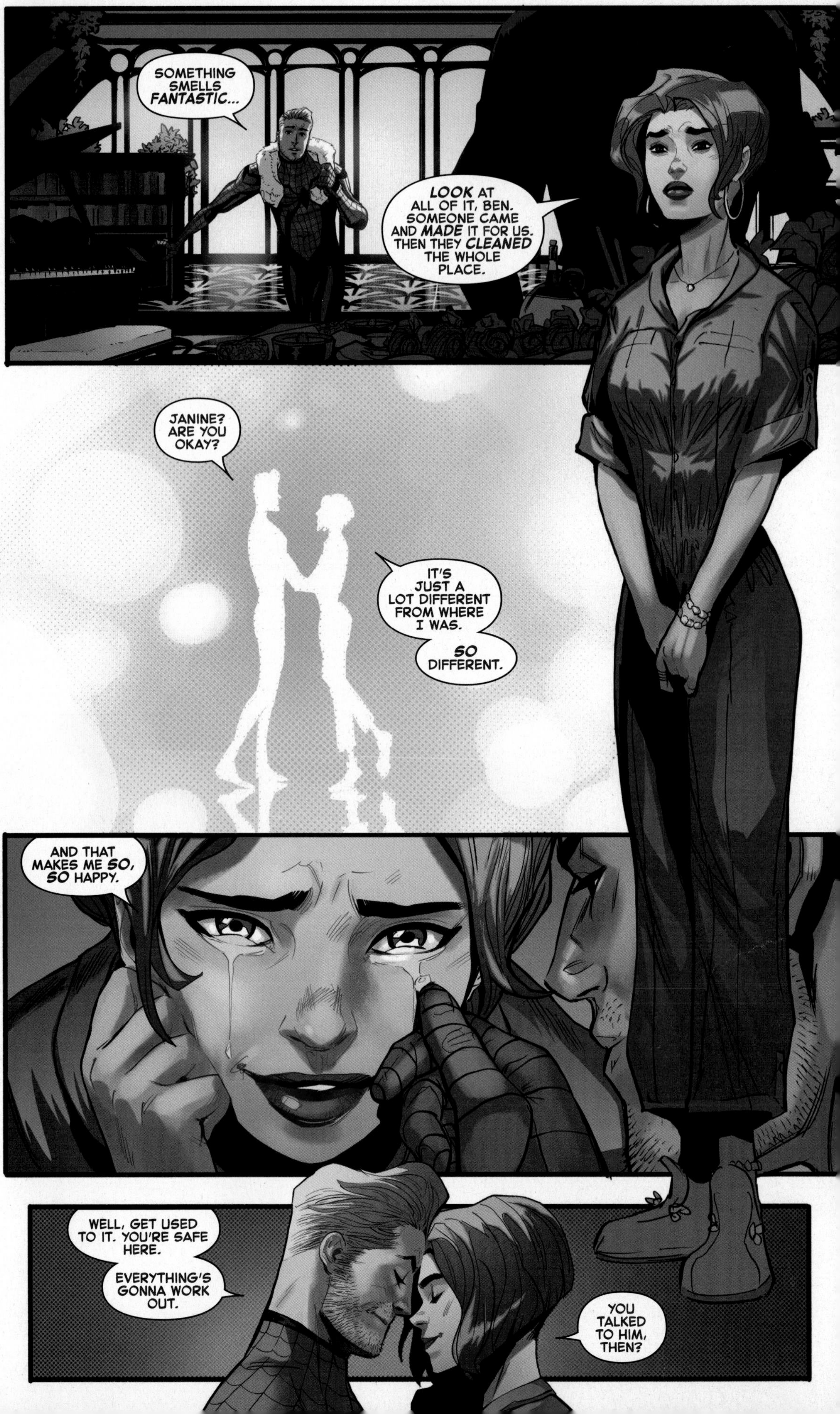
SOMETHING SMELLS FANTASTIC...
LOOK AT ALL OF IT, BEN. SOMEONE CAME AND MADE IT FOR US. THEN THEY CLEANED THE WHOLE PLACE.
JANINE? ARE YOU OKAY?
IT'S JUST A LOT DIFFERENT FROM WHERE I WAS.
SO DIFFERENT.
AND THAT MAKES ME SO, SO HAPPY.
WELL, GET USED TO IT. YOU'RE SAFE HERE.
EVERYTHING'S GONNA WORK OUT.
YOU TALKED TO HIM, THEN?

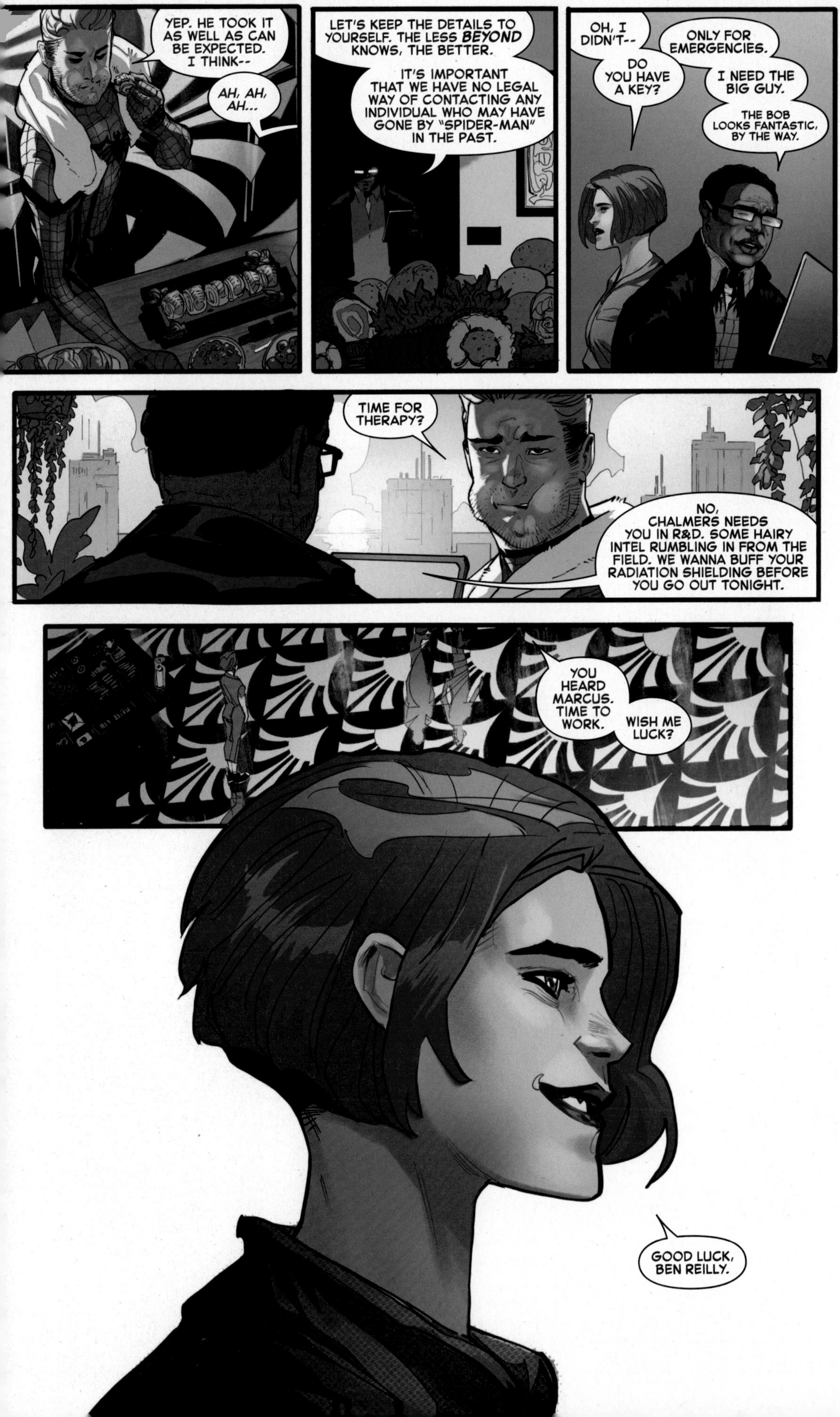
YEP. HE TOOK IT AS WELL AS CAN BE EXPECTED. I THINK--
AH, AH, AH...
LET'S KEEP THE DETAILS TO YOURSELF. THE LESS BEYOND KNOWS, THE BETTER.
IT'S IMPORTANT THAT WE HAVE NO LEGAL WAY OF CONTACTING ANY INDIVIDUAL WHO MAY HAVE GONE BY "SPIDER-MAN" IN THE PAST.
OH, I DIDN'T--
ONLY FOR EMERGENCIES.
DO YOU HAVE A KEY?
I NEED THE BIG GUY.
THE BOB LOOKS FANTASTIC, BY THE WAY.
TIME FOR THERAPY?
NO, CHALMERS NEEDS YOU IN R&D. SOME HAIRY INTEL RUMBLING IN FROM THE FIELD. WE WANNA BUFF YOUR RADIATION SHIELDING BEFORE YOU GO OUT TONIGHT.
YOU HEARD MARCUS. TIME TO WORK.
WISH ME LUCK?
GOOD LUCK, BEN REILLY.

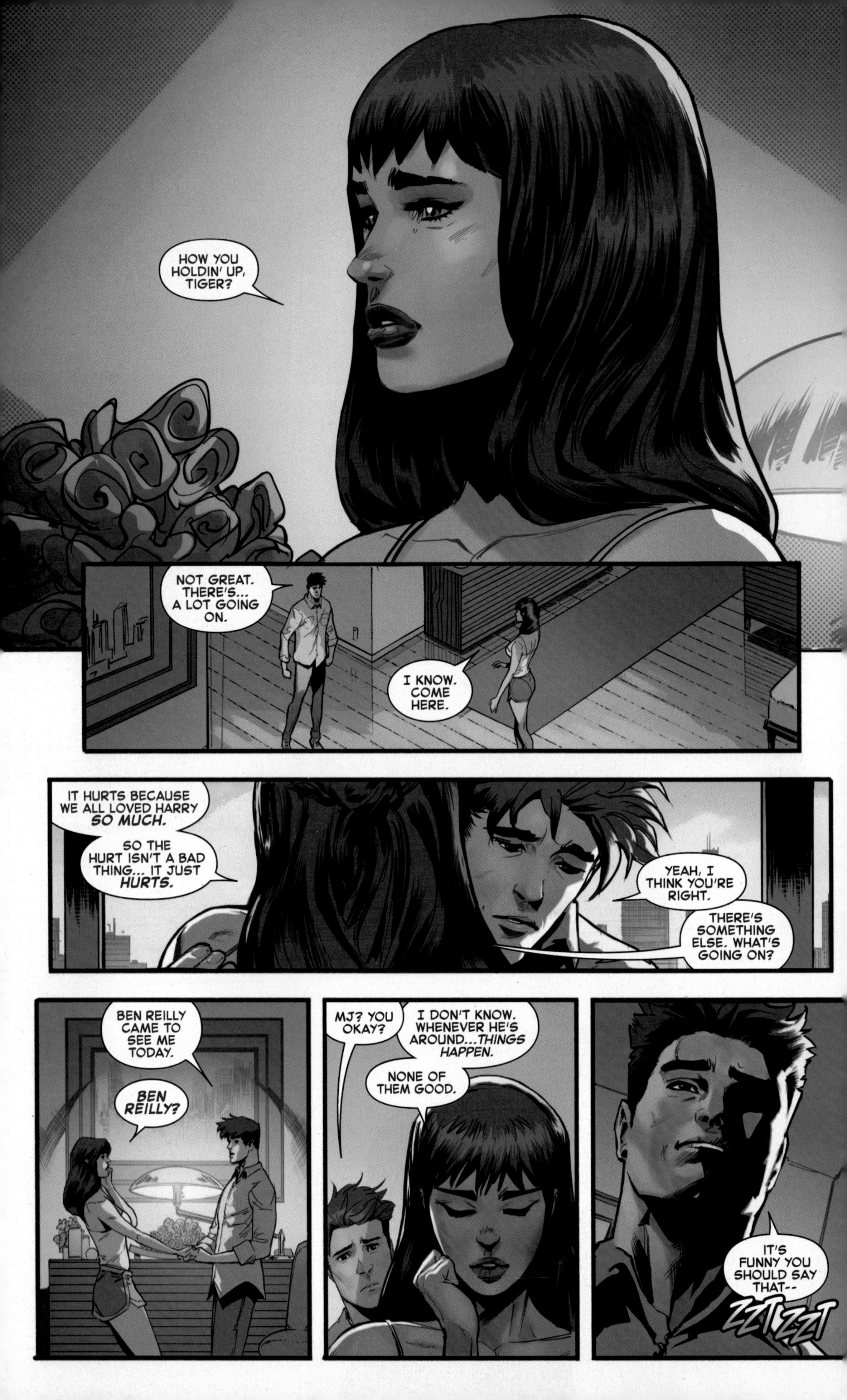
HOW YOU HOLDIN' UP, TIGER?
NOT GREAT. THERE'S... A LOT GOING ON.
I KNOW. COME HERE.
IT HURTS BECAUSE WE ALL LOVED HARRY SO MUCH.
SO THE HURT ISN'T A BAD THING... IT JUST HURTS.
YEAH, I THINK YOU'RE RIGHT.
THERE'S SOMETHING ELSE. WHAT'S GOING ON?
BEN REILLY CAME TO SEE ME TODAY.
BEN REILLY?
MJ? YOU OKAY?
I DON'T KNOW. WHENEVER HE'S AROUND...THINGS HAPPEN.
NONE OF THEM GOOD.
IT'S FUNNY YOU SHOULD SAY THAT--
ZZT ZZT

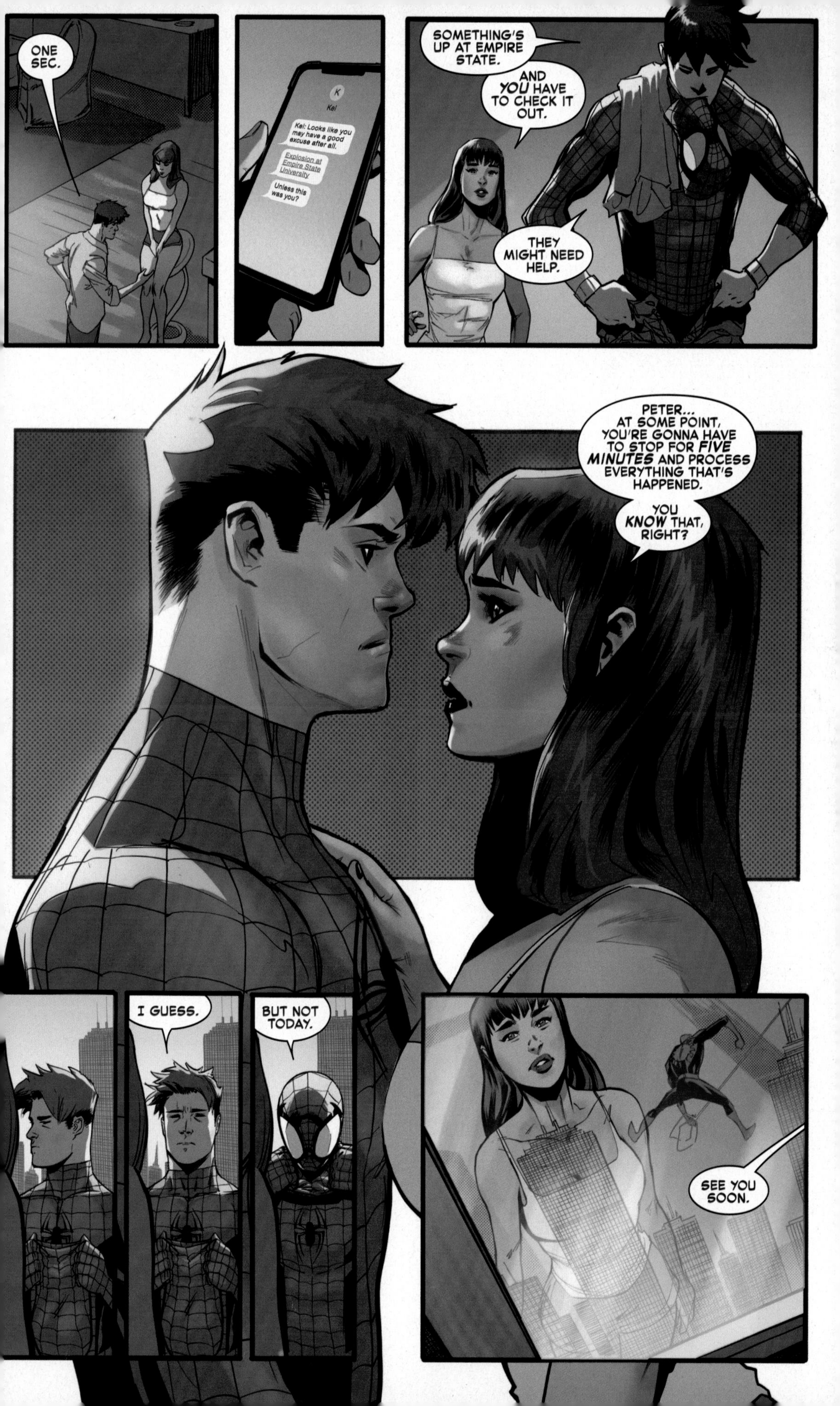
ONE SEC.
K
Kel
Kel: Looks like you may have a good excuse after all.
Explosion at Empire State University
Unless this was you?
SOMETHING'S UP AT EMPIRE STATE.
AND YOU HAVE TO CHECK IT OUT.
THEY MIGHT NEED HELP.
PETER... AT SOME POINT, YOU'RE GONNA HAVE TO STOP FOR FIVE MINUTES AND PROCESS EVERYTHING THAT'S HAPPENED.
YOU KNOW THAT, RIGHT?
I GUESS.
BUT NOT TODAY.
SEE YOU SOON.

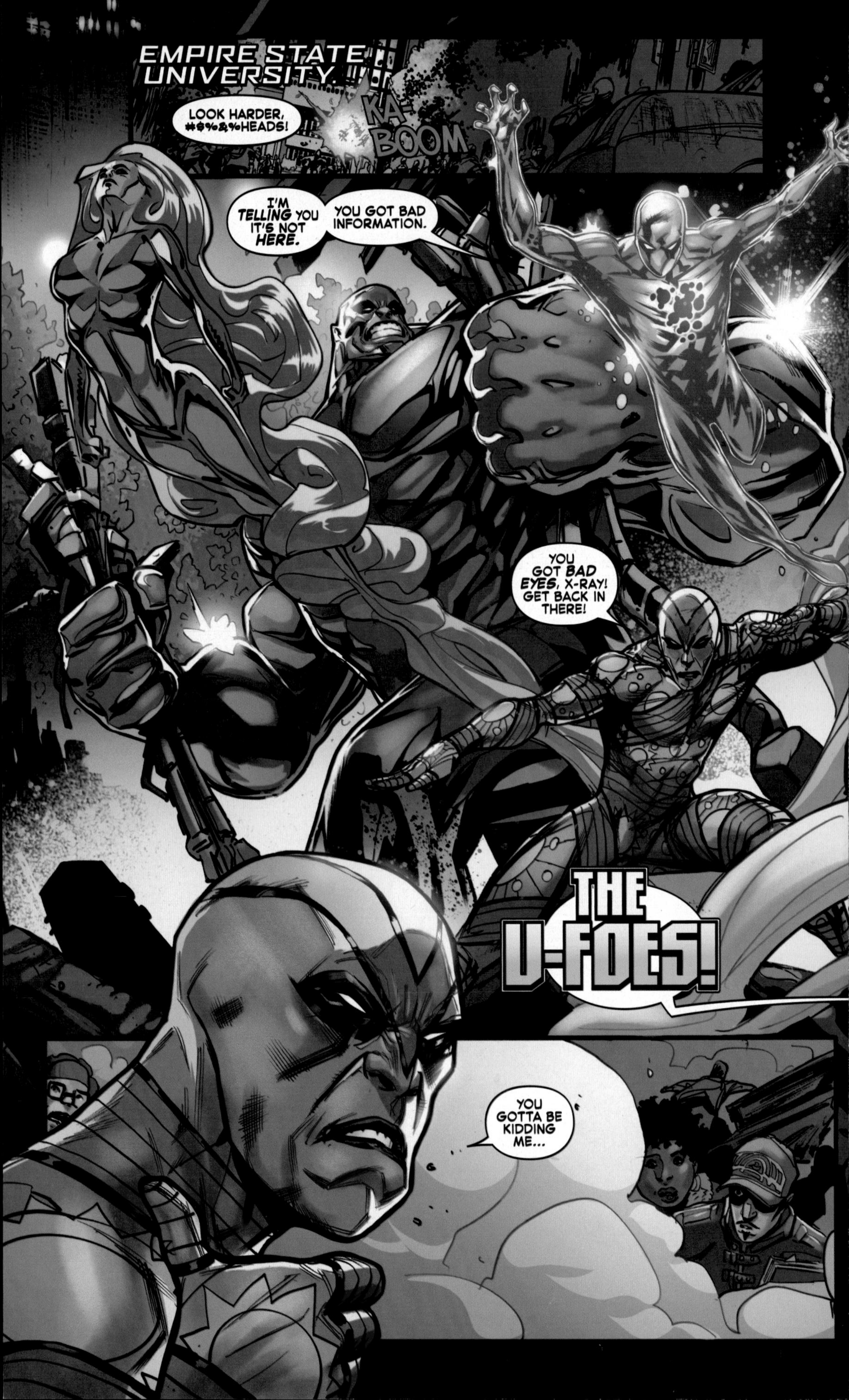
EMPIRE STATE UNIVERSITY.
LOOK HARDER, #$%&%HEADS!
KA-BOOM
I'M TELLING YOU IT'S NOT HERE.
YOU GOT BAD INFORMATION.
YOU GOT BAD EYES, X-RAY! GET BACK IN THERE!
THE U-FOES!
YOU GOTTA BE KIDDING ME...

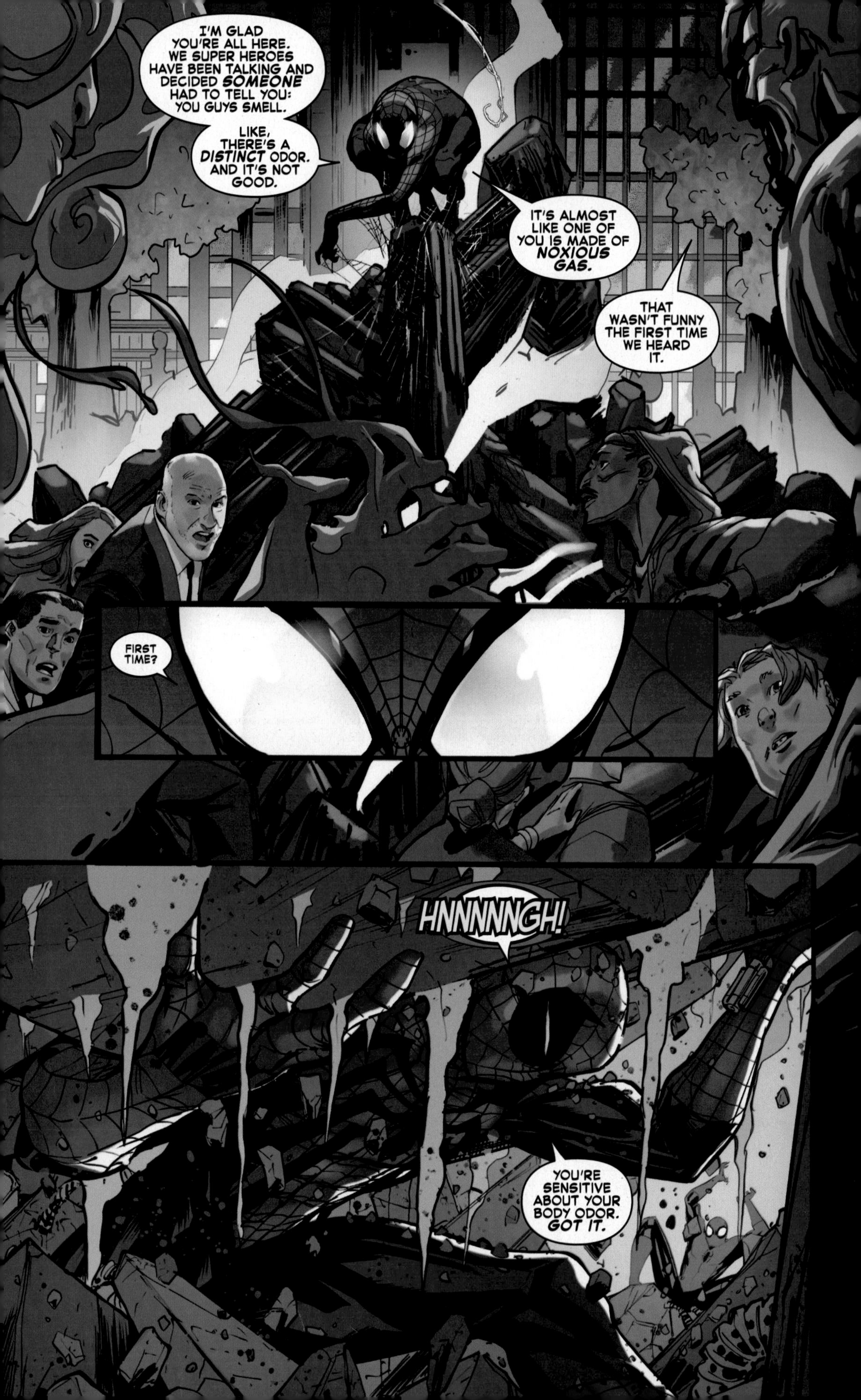
I'M GLAD YOU'RE ALL HERE. WE SUPER HEROES HAVE BEEN TALKING AND DECIDED SOMEONE HAD TO TELL YOU: YOU GUYS SMELL.
LIKE, THERE'S A DISTINCT ODOR. AND IT'S NOT GOOD.
IT'S ALMOST LIKE ONE OF YOU IS MADE OF NOXIOUS GAS.
THAT WASN'T FUNNY THE FIRST TIME WE HEARD IT.
FIRST TIME?
HNNNNNGH!
YOU'RE SENSITIVE ABOUT YOUR BODY ODOR. GOT IT.

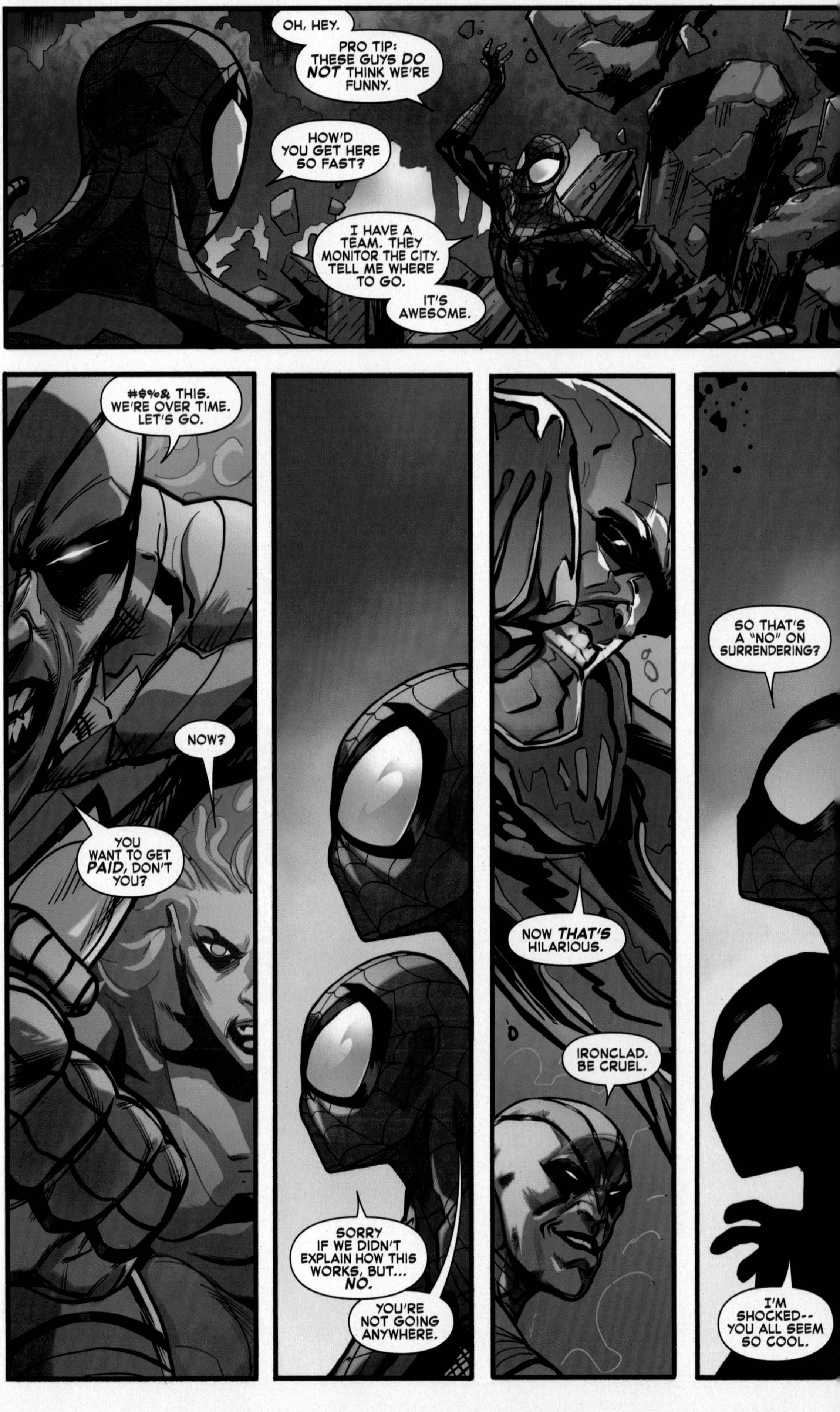
OH, HEY.
PRO TIP: THESE GUYS DO NOT THINK WE'RE FUNNY.
HOW'D YOU GET HERE SO FAST?
I HAVE A TEAM. THEY MONITOR THE CITY. TELL ME WHERE TO GO.
IT'S AWESOME.
#$%& THIS. WE'RE OVER TIME. LET'S GO.
NOW?
YOU WANT TO GET PAID, DON'T YOU?
SORRY IF WE DIDN'T EXPLAIN HOW THIS WORKS, BUT... NO.
YOU'RE NOT GOING ANYWHERE.
NOW THAT'S HILARIOUS.
IRONCLAD. BE CRUEL.
SO THAT'S A "NO" ON SURRENDERING?
I'M SHOCKED-- YOU ALL SEEM SO COOL.

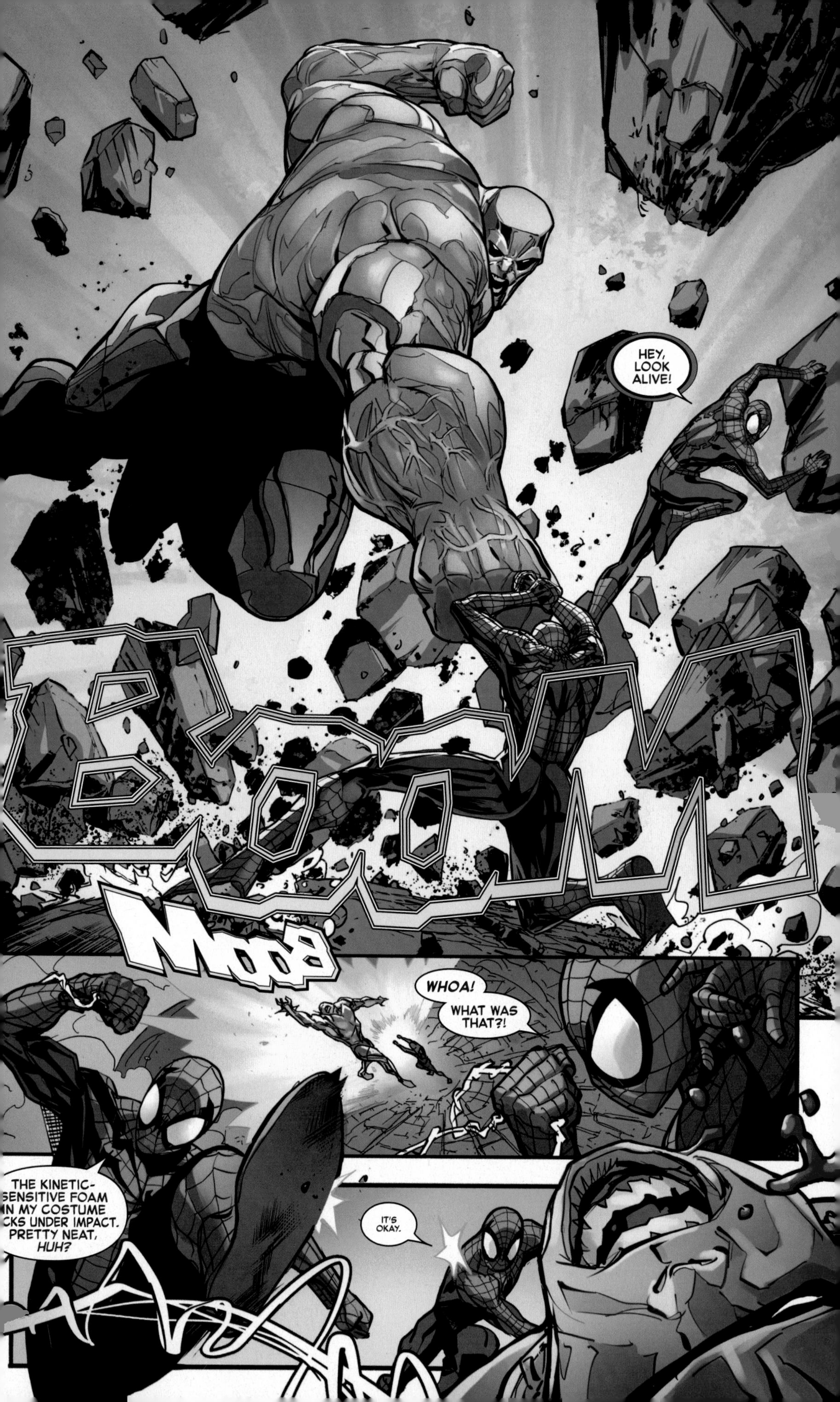
HEY, LOOK ALIVE!
BOOM
WHOA!
WHAT WAS THAT?!
THE KINETIC-SENSITIVE FOAM N MY COSTUME CKS UNDER IMPACT. PRETTY NEAT, HUH?
IT'S OKAY.

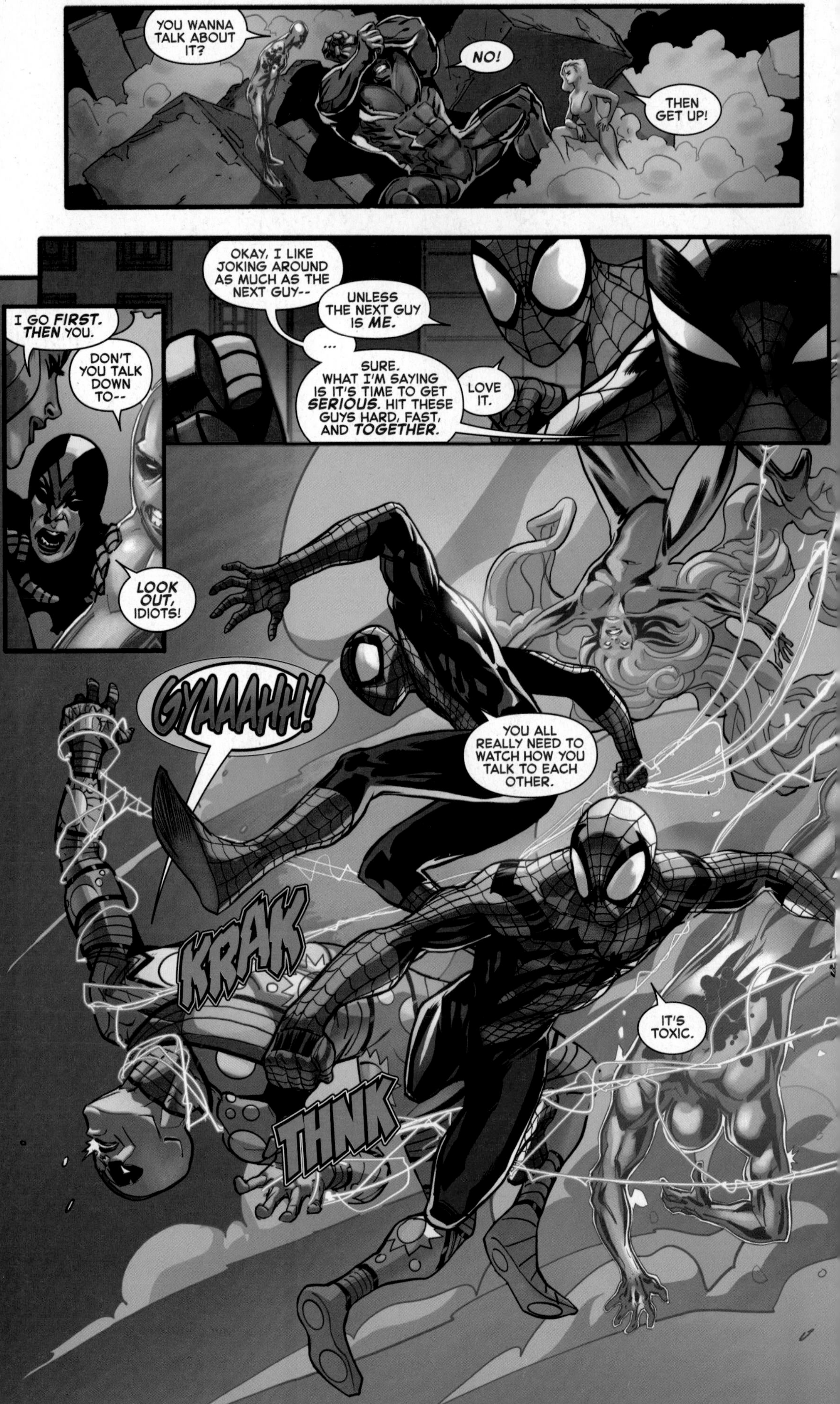

YOU WANNA TALK ABOUT IT?
NO!
THEN GET UP!
OKAY, I LIKE JOKING AROUND AS MUCH AS THE NEXT GUY--
UNLESS THE NEXT GUY IS ME.
...
SURE. WHAT I'M SAYING IS IT'S TIME TO GET SERIOUS. HIT THESE GUYS HARD, FAST, AND TOGETHER.
LOVE IT.
I GO FIRST. THEN YOU.
DON'T YOU TALK DOWN TO--
LOOK OUT, IDIOTS!
GYAAAHH!
YOU ALL REALLY NEED TO WATCH HOW YOU TALK TO EACH OTHER.
KRAK
THNK
IT'S TOXIC.

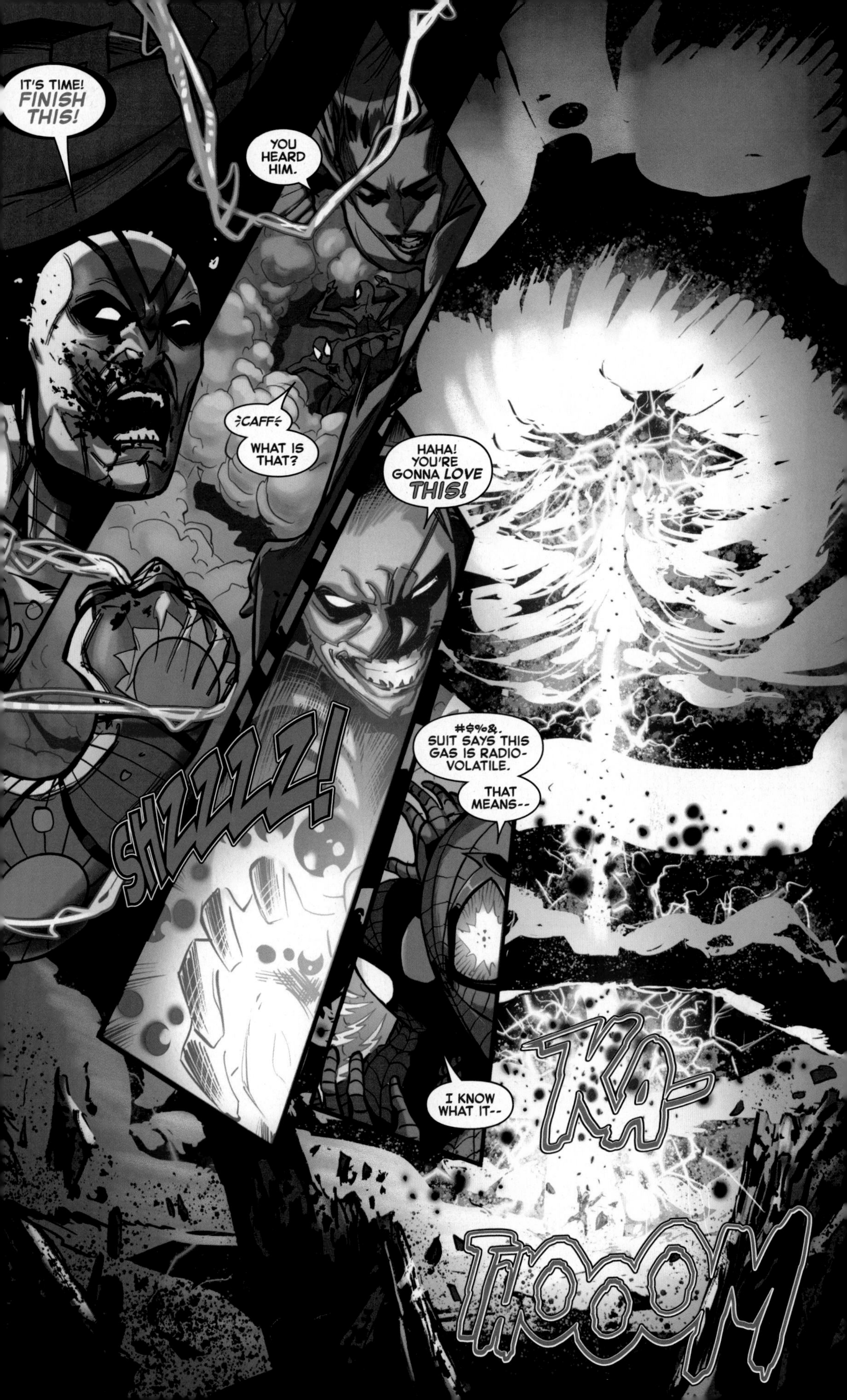
IT'S TIME! FINISH THIS!
YOU HEARD HIM.
≠CAFF≠
WHAT IS THAT?
HAHA! YOU'RE GONNA LOVE THIS!
SHZZZZZ!
#$%&. SUIT SAYS THIS GAS IS RADIO-VOLATILE.
THAT MEANS--
I KNOW WHAT IT--
KA
THOOOM

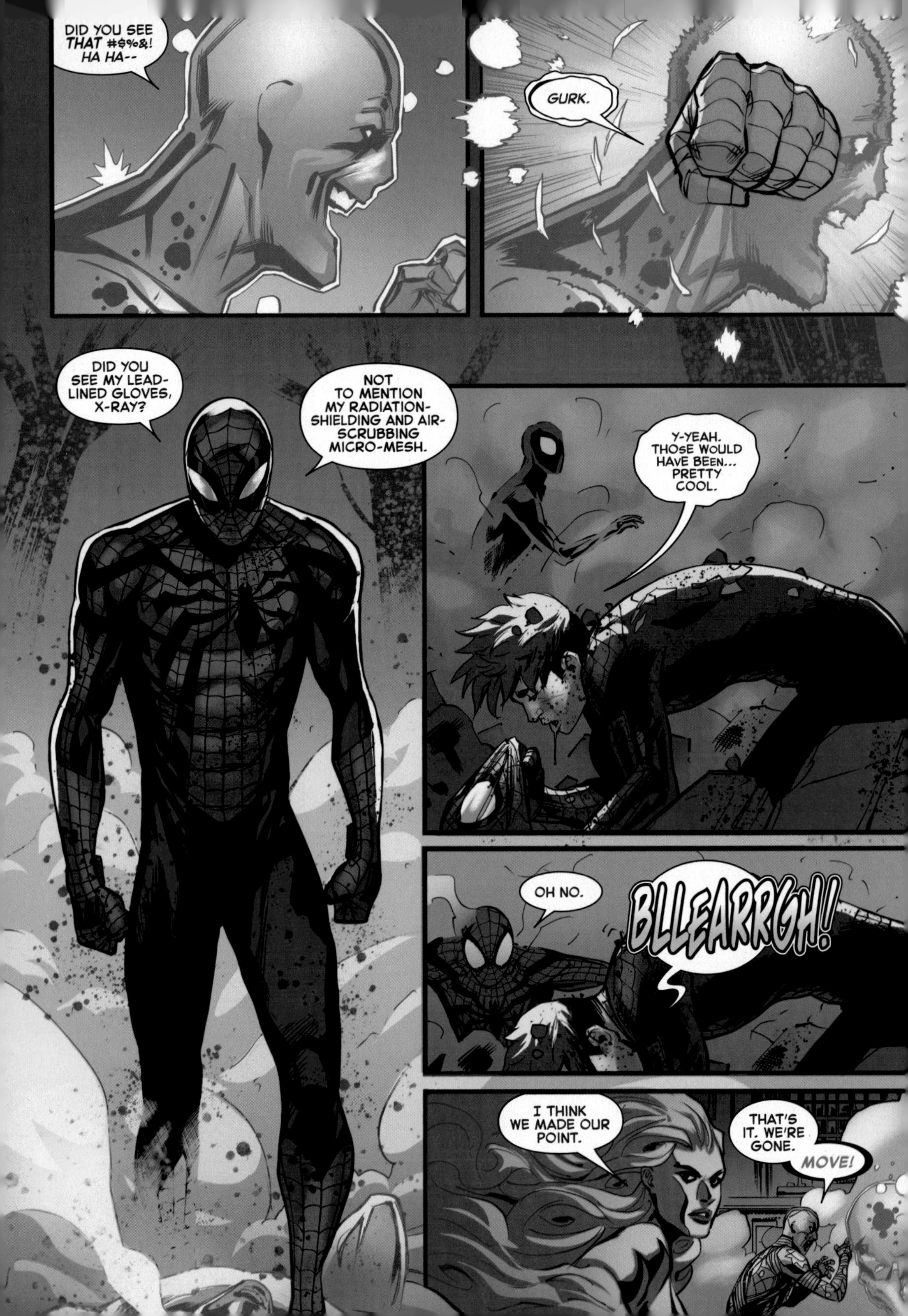
DID YOU SEE THAT #$%&! HA HA--
GURK.
DID YOU SEE MY LEAD-LINED GLOVES, X-RAY?
NOT TO MENTION MY RADIATION-SHIELDING AND AIR-SCRUBBING MICRO-MESH.
Y-YEAH. THOSE WOULD HAVE BEEN... PRETTY COOL.
OH NO.
BLLEARRGH!
I THINK WE MADE OUR POINT.
THAT'S IT. WE'RE GONE.
MOVE!

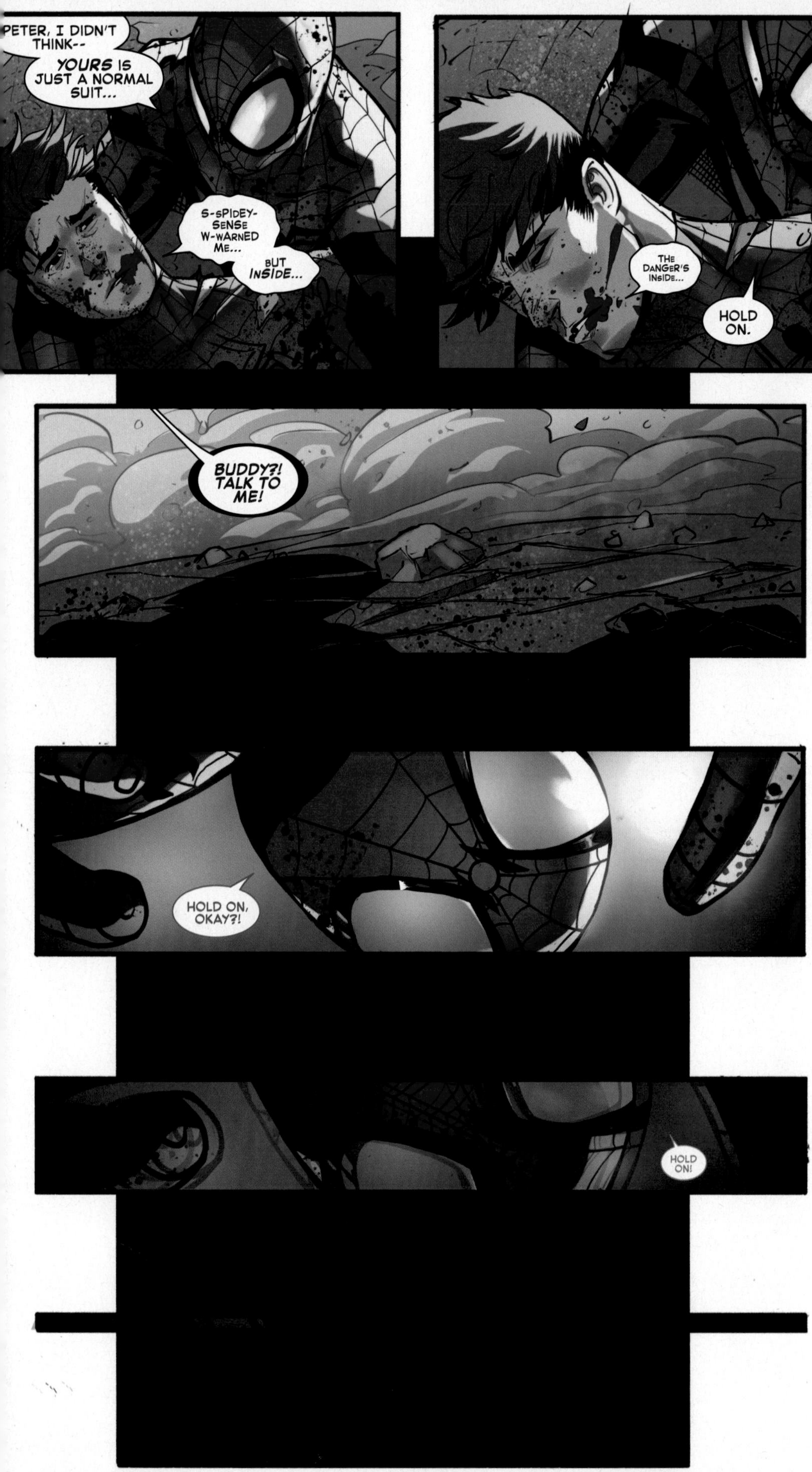
PETER, I DIDN'T THINK-- YOURS IS JUST A NORMAL SUIT...
S-SPIDEY-SENSE W-WARNED ME...
BUT INSIDE...
THE DANGER'S INSIDE...
HOLD ON.
BUDDY?! TALK TO ME!
HOLD ON, OKAY?!
HOLD ON!

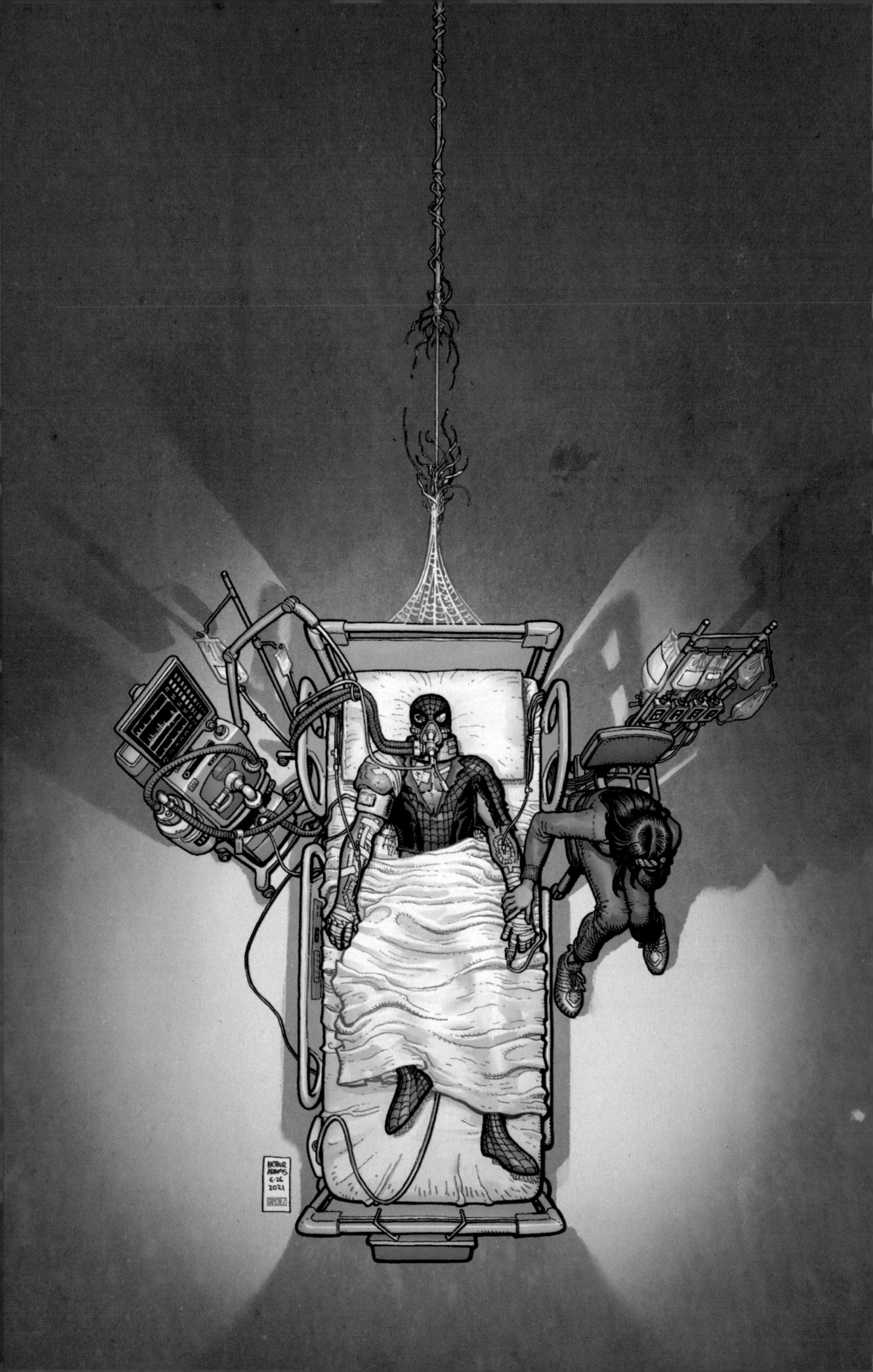
ARTHUR ADAMS
6-26
2021
SANCHEZ

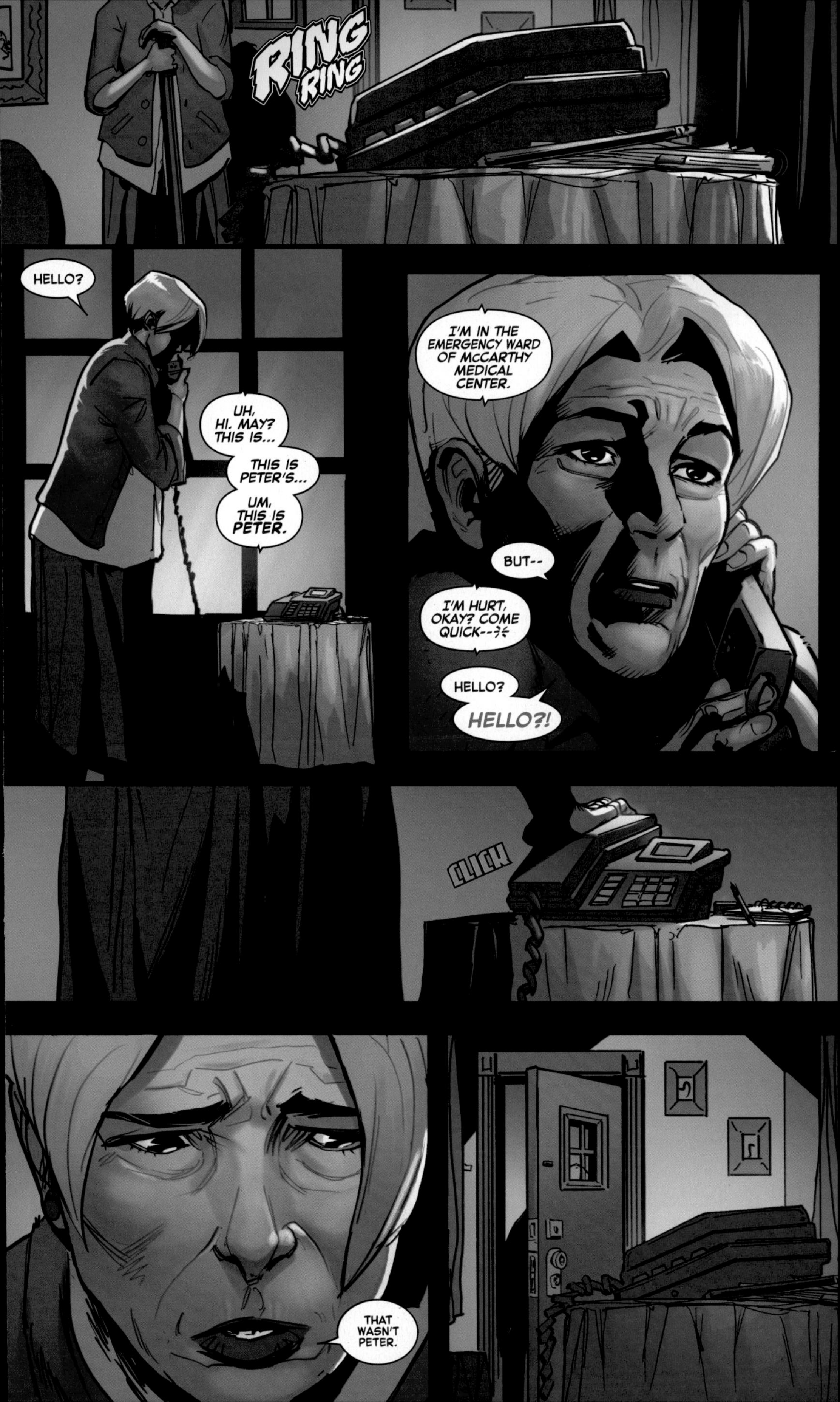
RING RING
HELLO?
UH, HI. MAY? THIS IS...
THIS IS PETER'S...
UM, THIS IS PETER.
I'M IN THE EMERGENCY WARD OF McCARTHY MEDICAL CENTER.
BUT--
I'M HURT, OKAY? COME QUICK--
HELLO?
HELLO?!
CLICK
THAT WASN'T PETER.

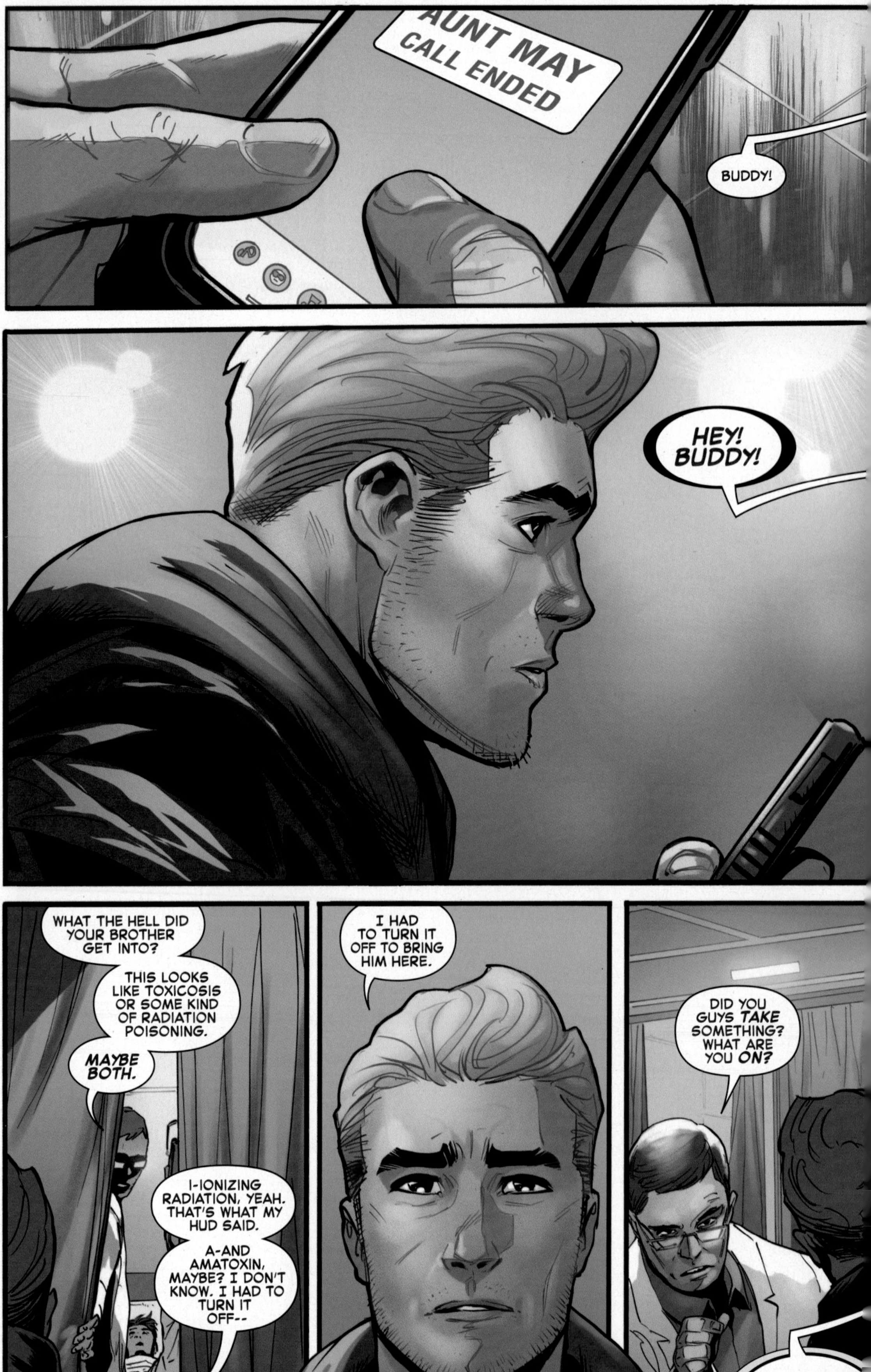
AUNT MAY
CALL ENDED
BUDDY!
HEY! BUDDY!
WHAT THE HELL DID YOUR BROTHER GET INTO?
THIS LOOKS LIKE TOXICOSIS OR SOME KIND OF RADIATION POISONING.
MAYBE BOTH.
I-IONIZING RADIATION, YEAH. THAT'S WHAT MY HUD SAID.
A-AND AMATOXIN, MAYBE? I DON'T KNOW. I HAD TO TURN IT OFF--
I HAD TO TURN IT OFF TO BRING HIM HERE.
DID YOU GUYS TAKE SOMETHING? WHAT ARE YOU ON?
WHERE IS HE?!

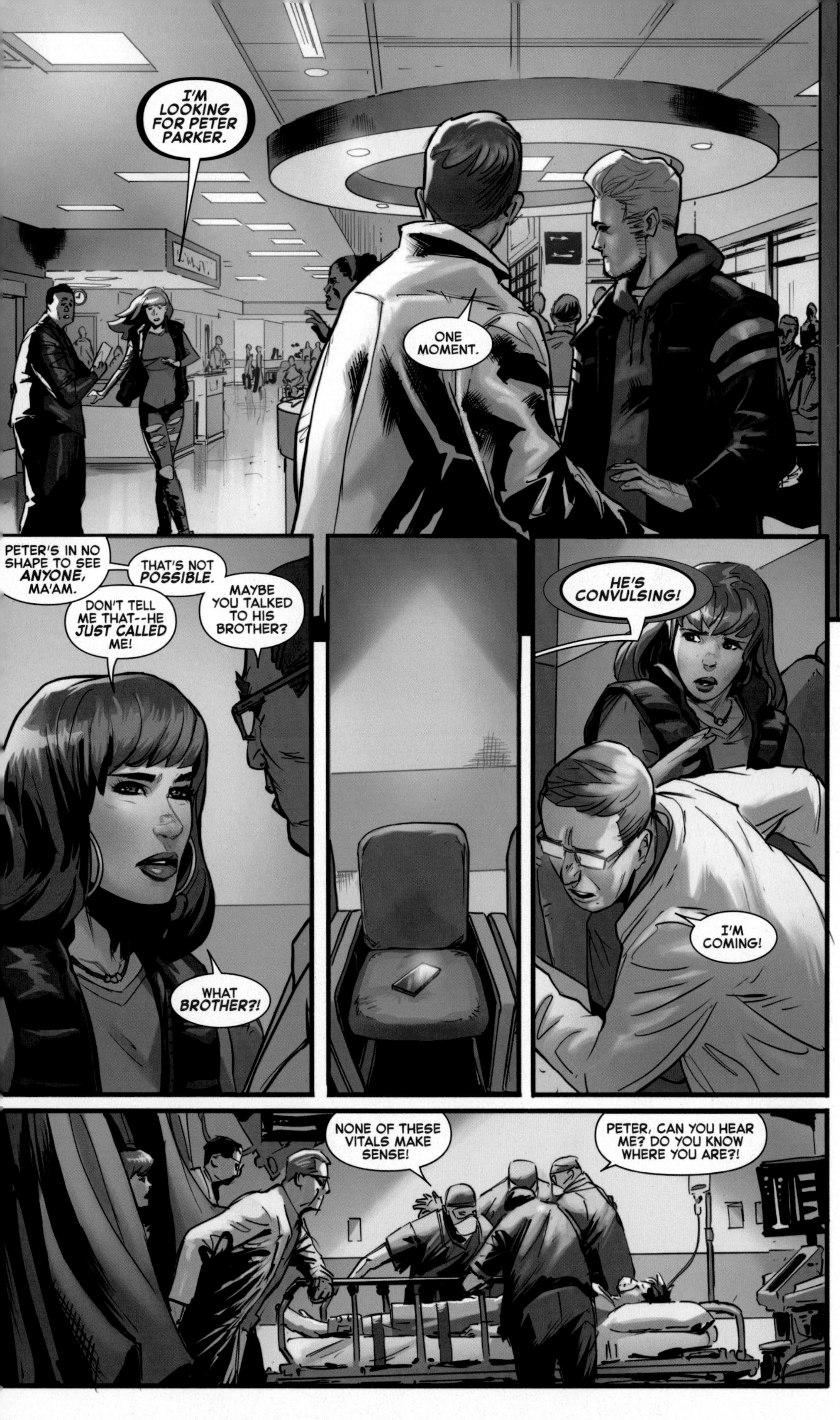
I'M LOOKING FOR PETER PARKER.
ONE MOMENT.
PETER'S IN NO SHAPE TO SEE ANYONE, MA'AM.
THAT'S NOT POSSIBLE.
DON'T TELL ME THAT--HE JUST CALLED ME!
MAYBE YOU TALKED TO HIS BROTHER?
WHAT BROTHER?!
HE'S CONVULSING!
I'M COMING!
NONE OF THESE VITALS MAKE SENSE!
PETER, CAN YOU HEAR ME? DO YOU KNOW WHERE YOU ARE?!

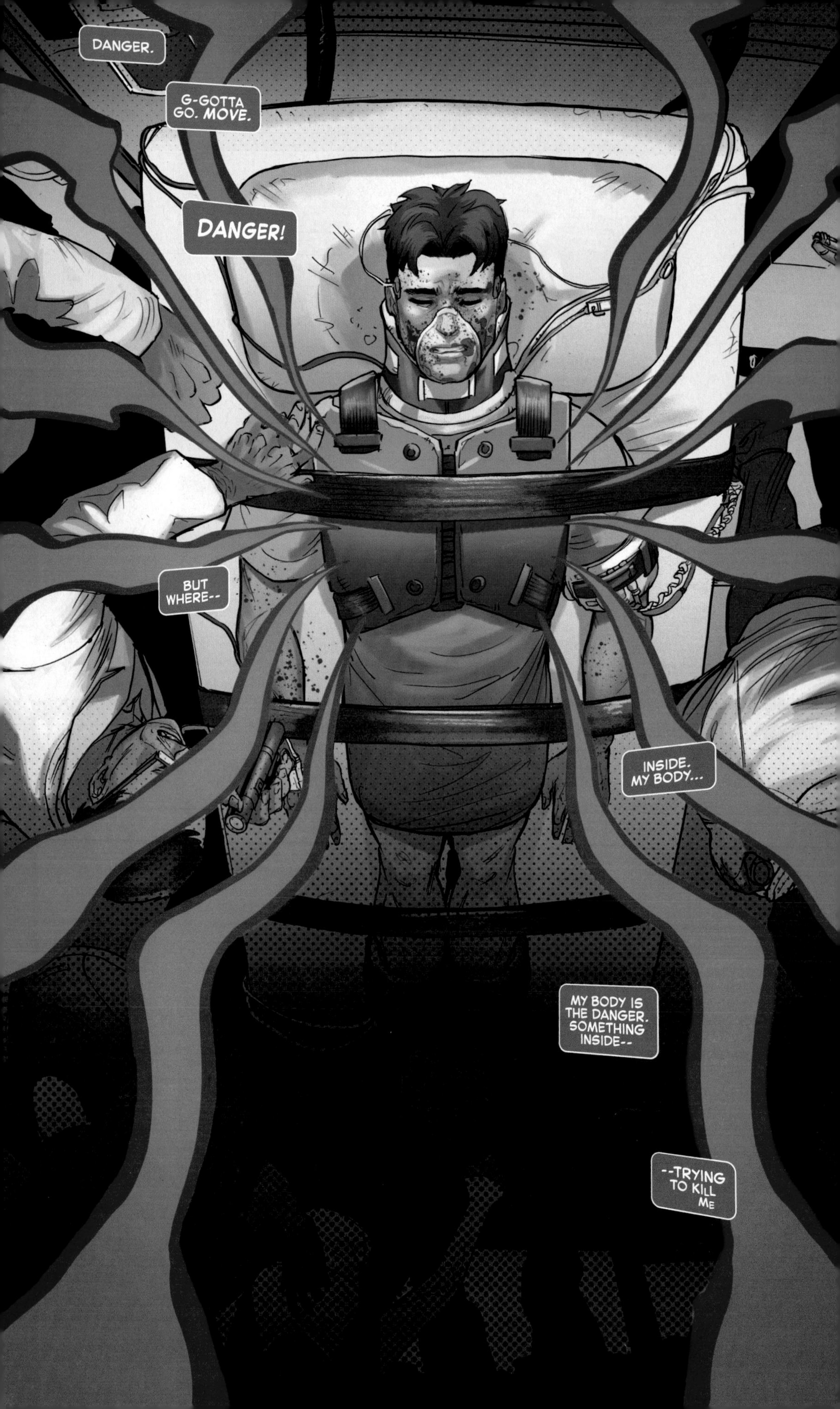
DANGER.
G-GOTTA GO. MOVE.
DANGER!
BUT WHERE--
INSIDE. MY BODY...
MY BODY IS THE DANGER. SOMETHING INSIDE--
--TRYING TO KILL ME

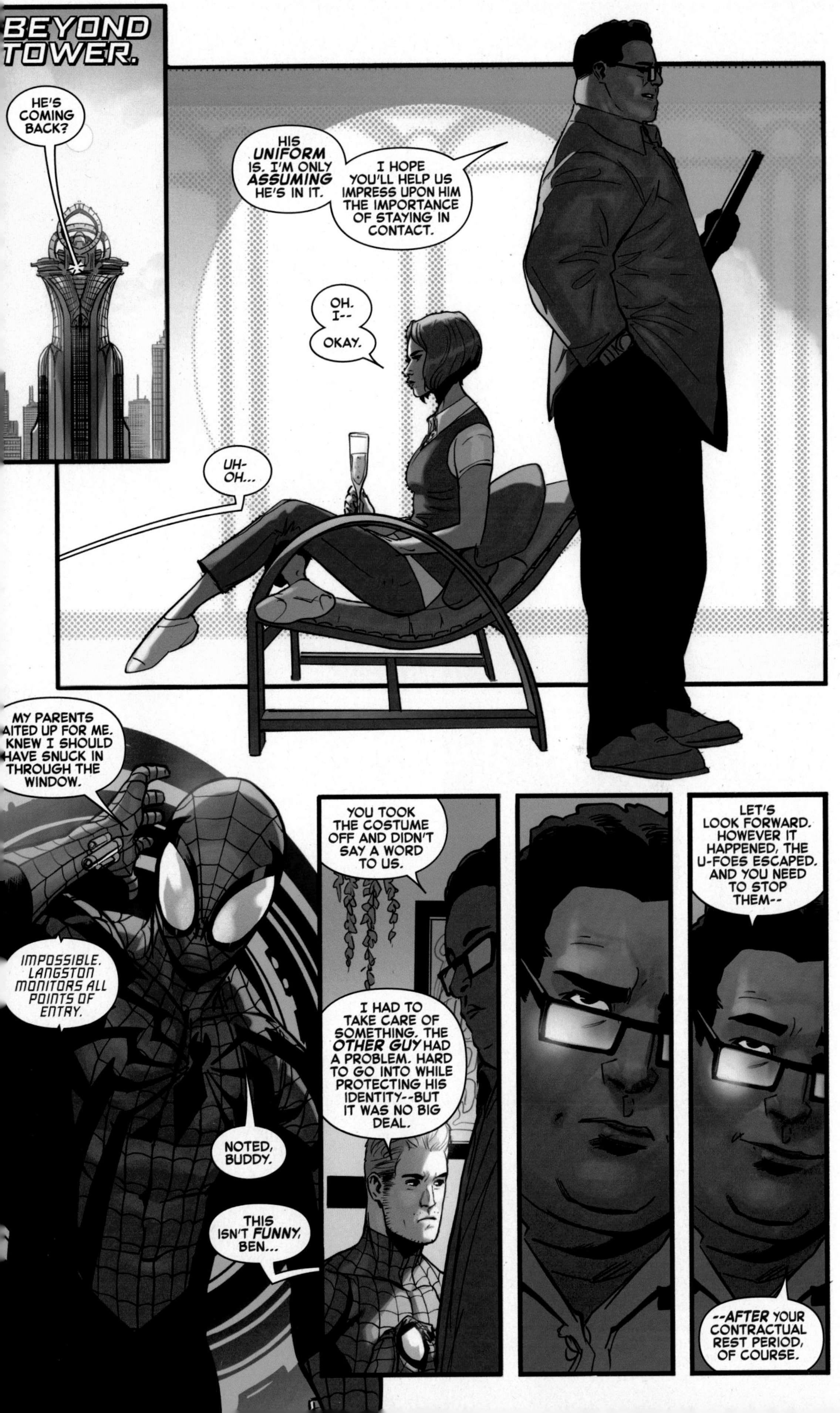
BEYOND TOWER.
HE'S COMING BACK?
HIS UNIFORM IS. I'M ONLY ASSUMING HE'S IN IT.
I HOPE YOU'LL HELP US IMPRESS UPON HIM THE IMPORTANCE OF STAYING IN CONTACT.
OH. I--
OKAY.
UH-OH...
MY PARENTS AITED UP FOR ME. KNEW I SHOULD HAVE SNUCK IN THROUGH THE WINDOW.
IMPOSSIBLE. LANGSTON MONITORS ALL POINTS OF ENTRY.
NOTED, BUDDY.
THIS ISN'T FUNNY, BEN...
YOU TOOK THE COSTUME OFF AND DIDN'T SAY A WORD TO US.
I HAD TO TAKE CARE OF SOMETHING. THE OTHER GUY HAD A PROBLEM. HARD TO GO INTO WHILE PROTECTING HIS IDENTITY--BUT IT WAS NO BIG DEAL.
LET'S LOOK FORWARD. HOWEVER IT HAPPENED, THE U-FOES ESCAPED. AND YOU NEED TO STOP THEM--
--AFTER YOUR CONTRACTUAL REST PERIOD, OF COURSE.

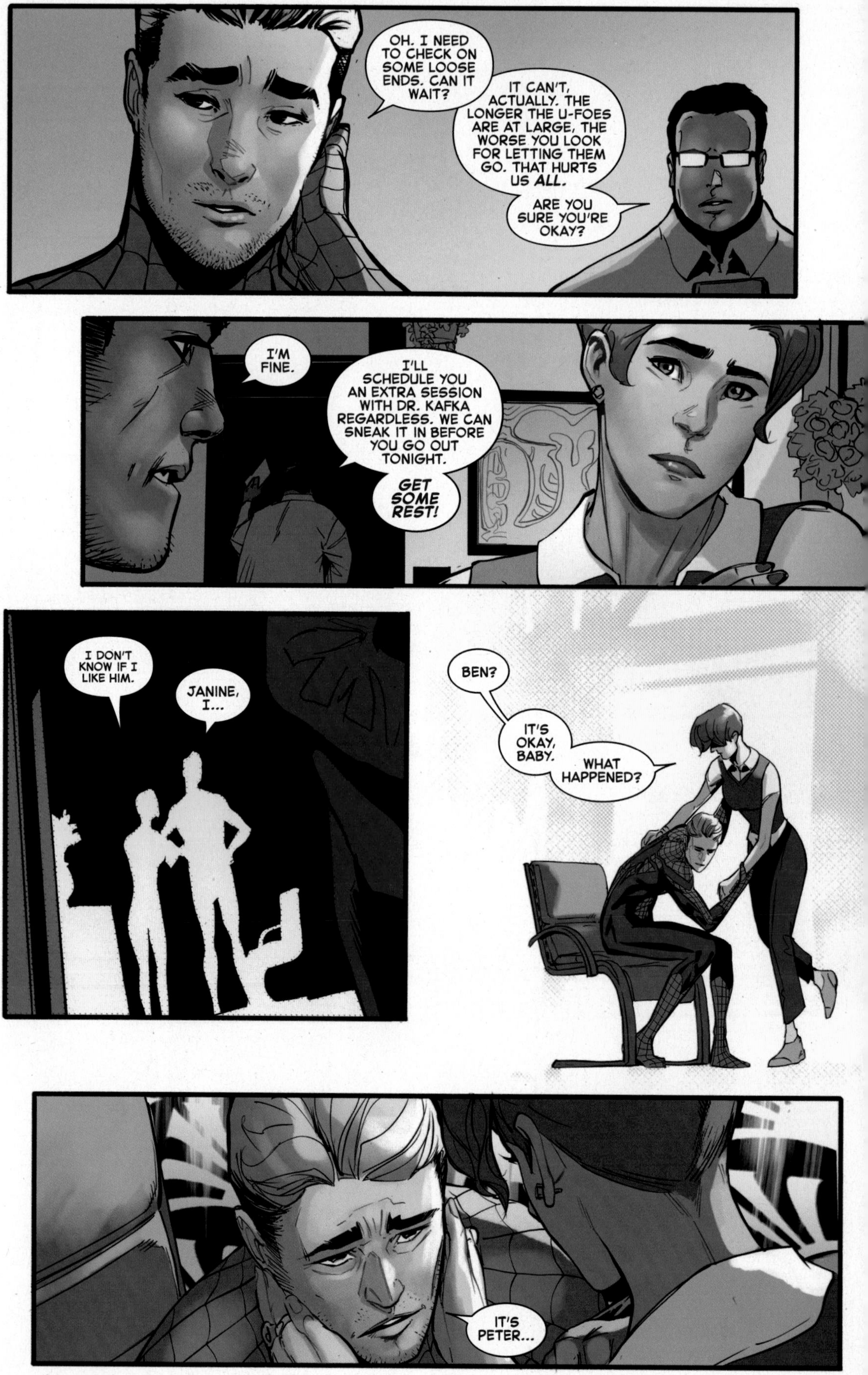
OH. I NEED TO CHECK ON SOME LOOSE ENDS. CAN IT WAIT?
IT CAN'T, ACTUALLY. THE LONGER THE U-FOES ARE AT LARGE, THE WORSE YOU LOOK FOR LETTING THEM GO. THAT HURTS US ALL.
ARE YOU SURE YOU'RE OKAY?
I'M FINE.
I'LL SCHEDULE YOU AN EXTRA SESSION WITH DR. KAFKA REGARDLESS. WE CAN SNEAK IT IN BEFORE YOU GO OUT TONIGHT.
GET SOME REST!
I DON'T KNOW IF I LIKE HIM.
JANINE, I...
BEN?
IT'S OKAY, BABY.
WHAT HAPPENED?
IT'S PETER...

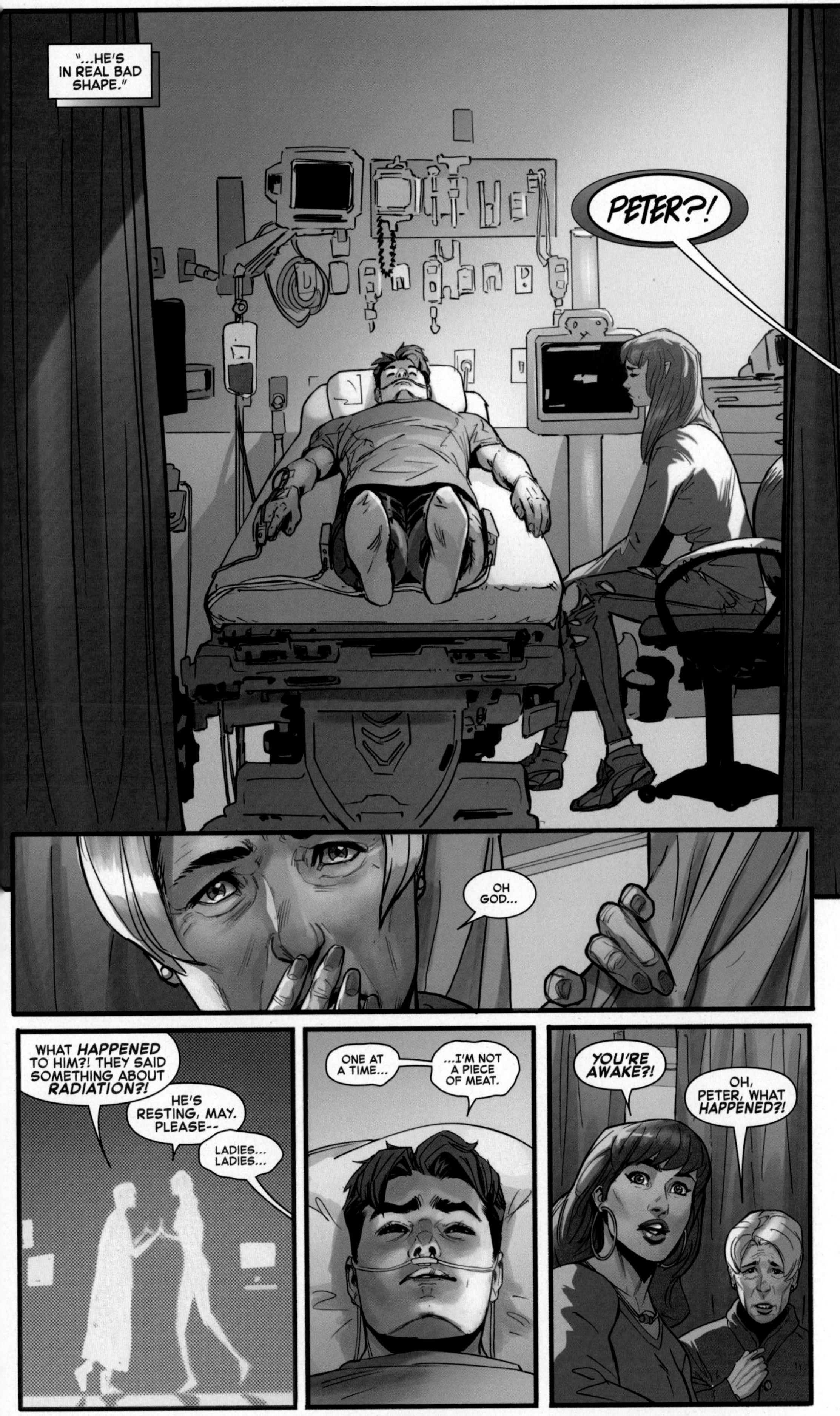
"...HE'S IN REAL BAD SHAPE."
PETER?!
OH GOD...
WHAT HAPPENED TO HIM?! THEY SAID SOMETHING ABOUT RADIATION?!
HE'S RESTING, MAY. PLEASE--
LADIES... LADIES...
ONE AT A TIME...
...I'M NOT A PIECE OF MEAT.
YOU'RE AWAKE?!
OH, PETER, WHAT HAPPENED?!

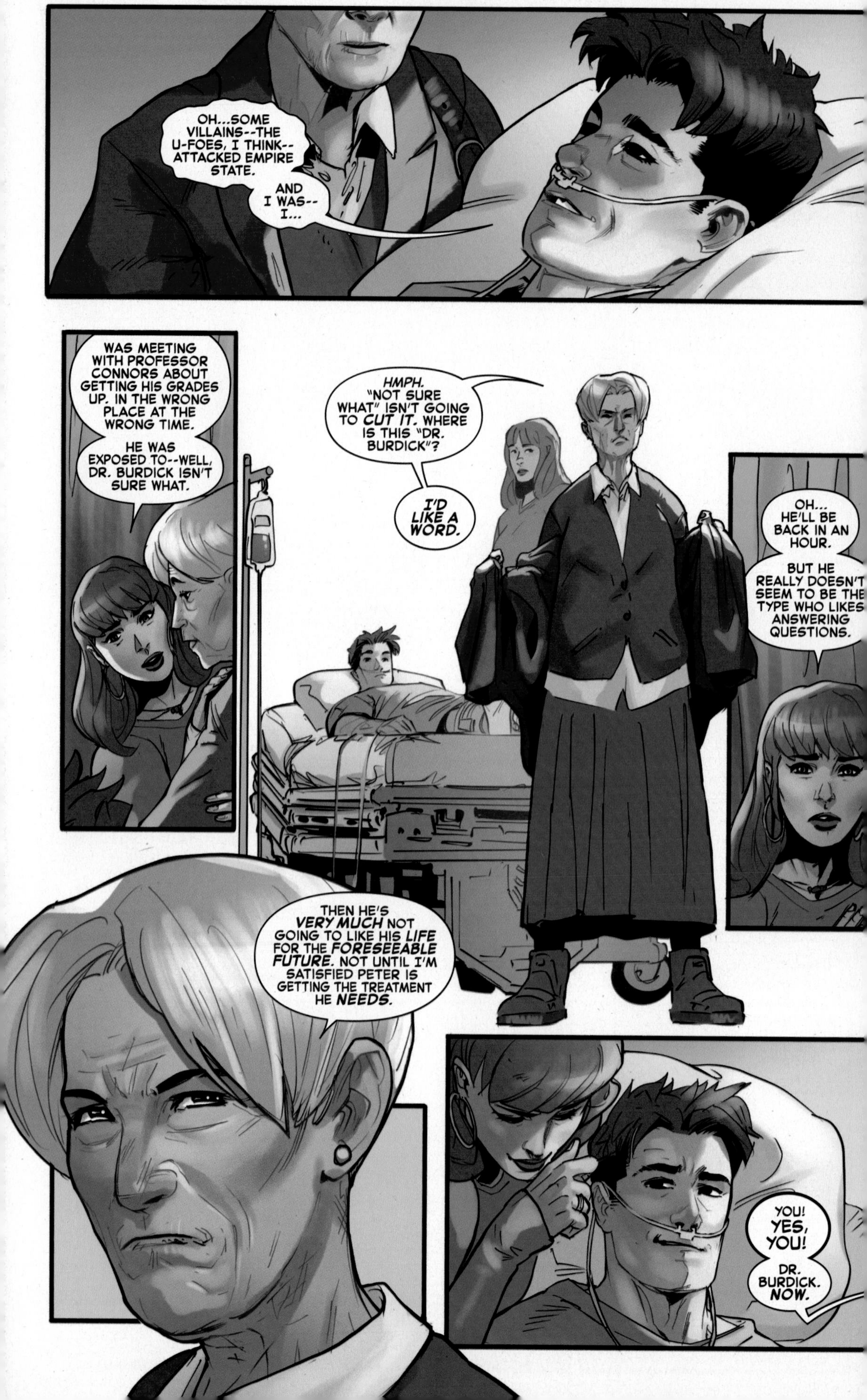

OH...SOME VILLAINS--THE U-FOES, I THINK--ATTACKED EMPIRE STATE.
AND I WAS-- I...
WAS MEETING WITH PROFESSOR CONNORS ABOUT GETTING HIS GRADES UP. IN THE WRONG PLACE AT THE WRONG TIME.
HE WAS EXPOSED TO--WELL, DR. BURDICK ISN'T SURE WHAT.
HMPH. "NOT SURE WHAT" ISN'T GOING TO CUT IT. WHERE IS THIS "DR. BURDICK"?
I'D LIKE A WORD.
OH... HE'LL BE BACK IN AN HOUR.
BUT HE REALLY DOESN'T SEEM TO BE THE TYPE WHO LIKES ANSWERING QUESTIONS.
THEN HE'S VERY MUCH NOT GOING TO LIKE HIS LIFE FOR THE FORESEEABLE FUTURE. NOT UNTIL I'M SATISFIED PETER IS GETTING THE TREATMENT HE NEEDS.
YOU! YES, YOU!
DR. BURDICK. NOW.

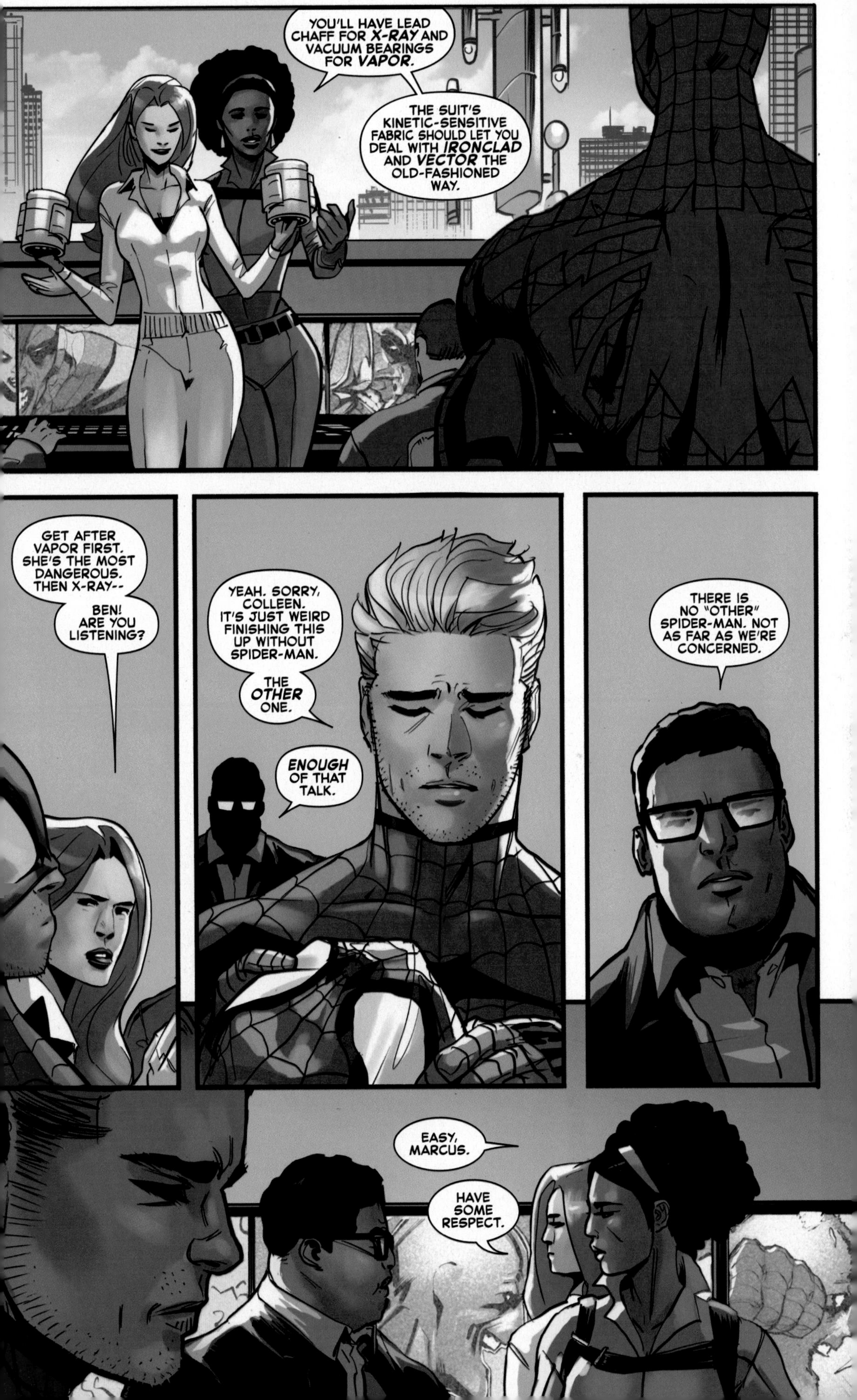

YOU'LL HAVE LEAD CHAFF FOR X-RAY AND VACUUM BEARINGS FOR VAPOR.
THE SUIT'S KINETIC-SENSITIVE FABRIC SHOULD LET YOU DEAL WITH IRONCLAD AND VECTOR THE OLD-FASHIONED WAY.
GET AFTER VAPOR FIRST. SHE'S THE MOST DANGEROUS. THEN X-RAY--
BEN! ARE YOU LISTENING?
YEAH. SORRY, COLLEEN. IT'S JUST WEIRD FINISHING THIS UP WITHOUT SPIDER-MAN.
THE OTHER ONE.
ENOUGH OF THAT TALK.
THERE IS NO "OTHER" SPIDER-MAN. NOT AS FAR AS WE'RE CONCERNED.
EASY, MARCUS.
HAVE SOME RESPECT.

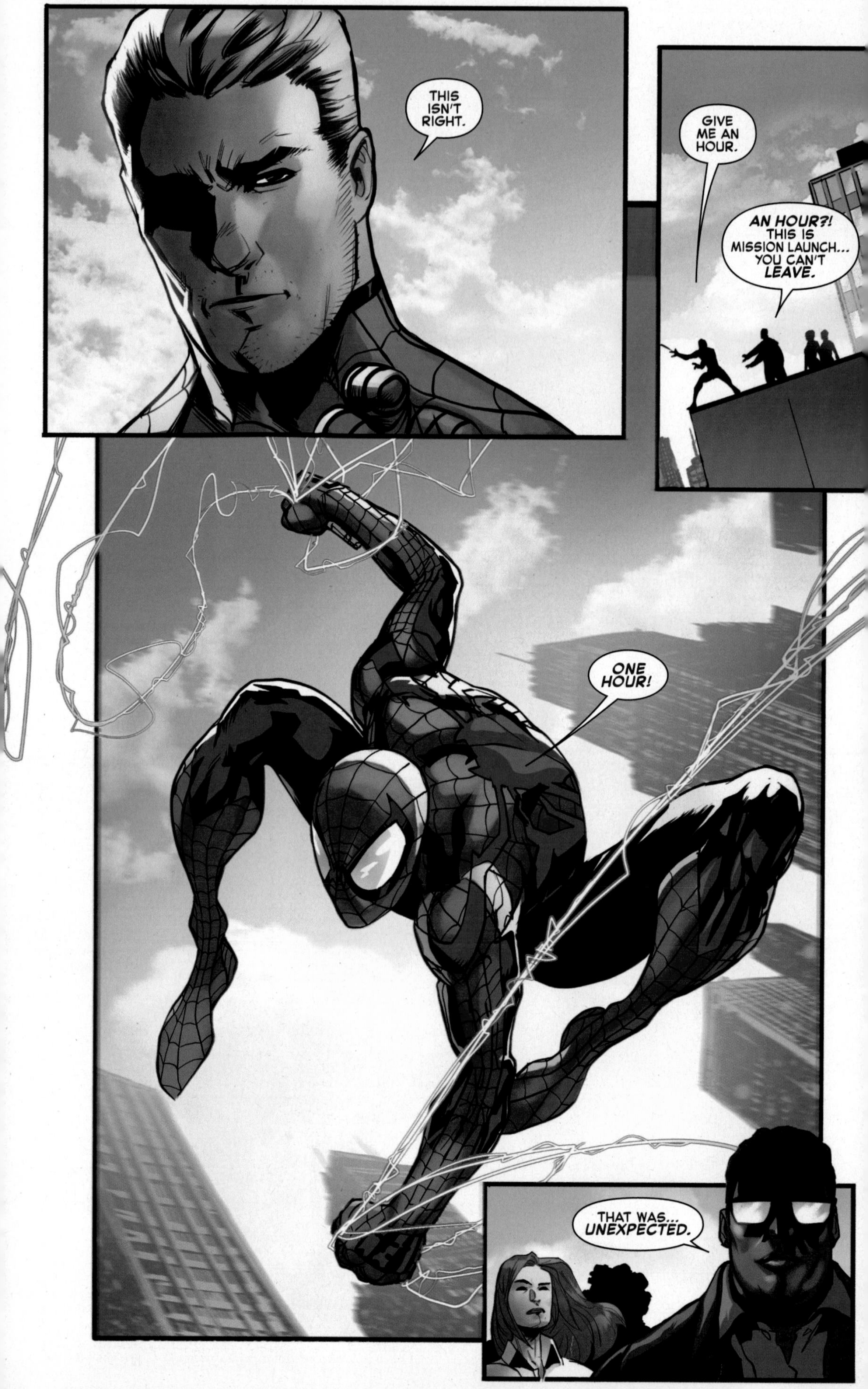
THIS ISN'T RIGHT.
GIVE ME AN HOUR.
AN HOUR?! THIS IS MISSION LAUNCH... YOU CAN'T LEAVE.
ONE HOUR!
THAT WAS... UNEXPECTED.

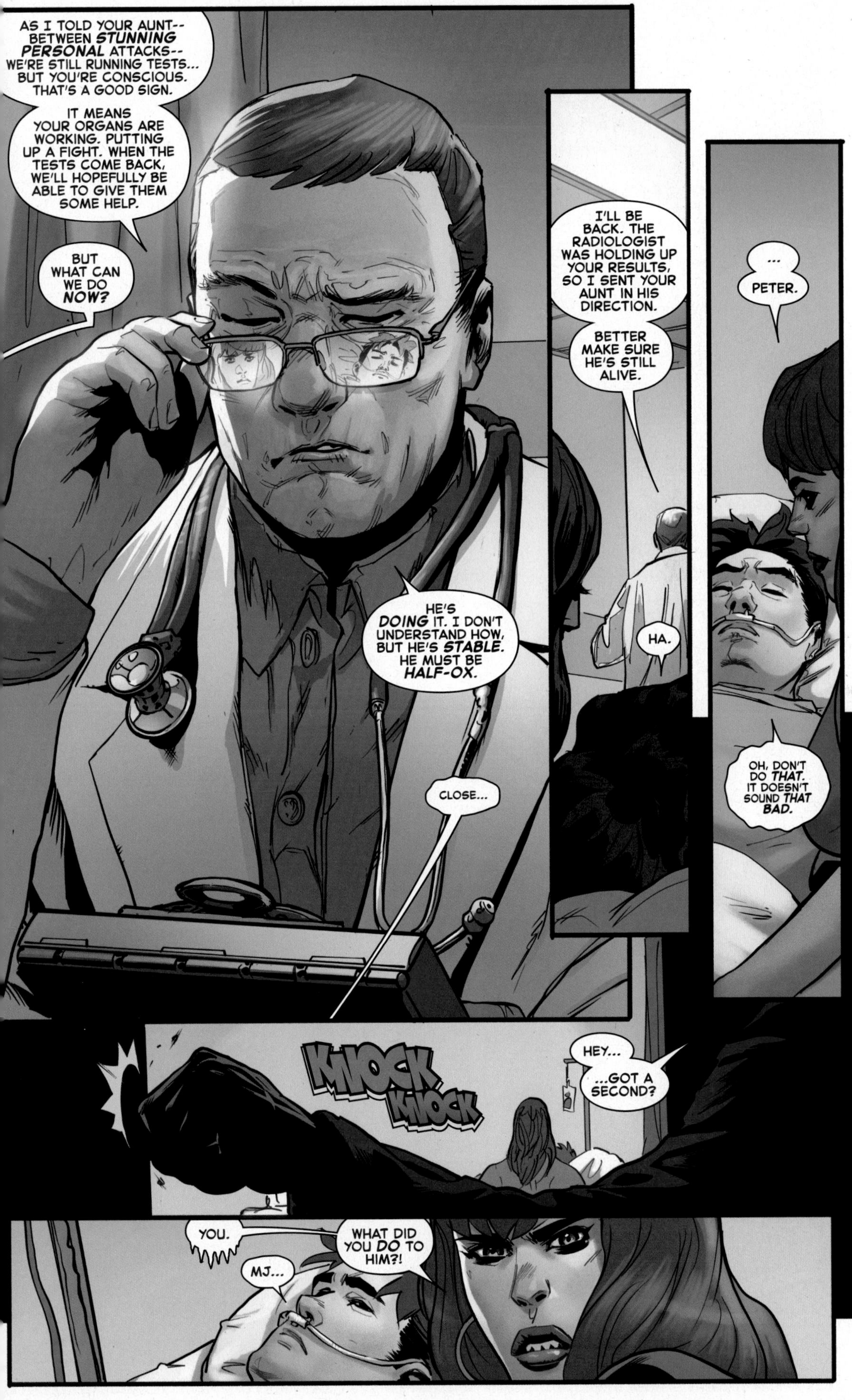
AS I TOLD YOUR AUNT-- BETWEEN STUNNING PERSONAL ATTACKS-- WE'RE STILL RUNNING TESTS... BUT YOU'RE CONSCIOUS. THAT'S A GOOD SIGN.
IT MEANS YOUR ORGANS ARE WORKING. PUTTING UP A FIGHT. WHEN THE TESTS COME BACK, WE'LL HOPEFULLY BE ABLE TO GIVE THEM SOME HELP.
BUT WHAT CAN WE DO NOW?
HE'S DOING IT. I DON'T UNDERSTAND HOW, BUT HE'S STABLE. HE MUST BE HALF-OX.
CLOSE...
I'LL BE BACK. THE RADIOLOGIST WAS HOLDING UP YOUR RESULTS, SO I SENT YOUR AUNT IN HIS DIRECTION.
BETTER MAKE SURE HE'S STILL ALIVE.
HA.
... PETER.
OH, DON'T DO THAT. IT DOESN'T SOUND THAT BAD.
KNOCK KNOCK
HEY...
...GOT A SECOND?
YOU.
WHAT DID YOU DO TO HIM?!
MJ...

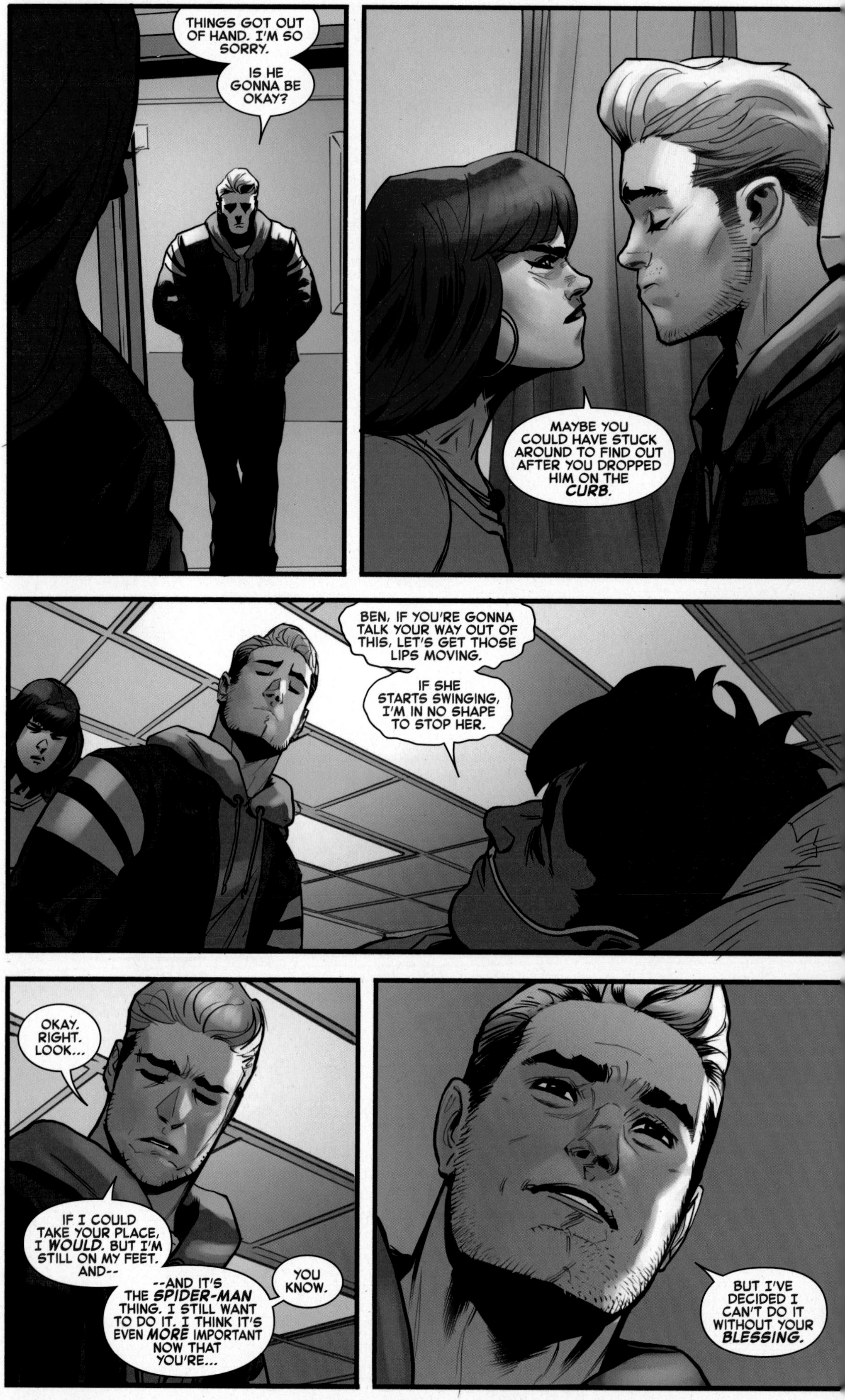
THINGS GOT OUT OF HAND. I'M SO SORRY.
IS HE GONNA BE OKAY?
MAYBE YOU COULD HAVE STUCK AROUND TO FIND OUT AFTER YOU DROPPED HIM ON THE CURB.
BEN, IF YOU'RE GONNA TALK YOUR WAY OUT OF THIS, LET'S GET THOSE LIPS MOVING.
IF SHE STARTS SWINGING, I'M IN NO SHAPE TO STOP HER.
OKAY. RIGHT. LOOK...
IF I COULD TAKE YOUR PLACE, I WOULD. BUT I'M STILL ON MY FEET. AND--
YOU KNOW.
--AND IT'S THE SPIDER-MAN THING. I STILL WANT TO DO IT. I THINK IT'S EVEN MORE IMPORTANT NOW THAT YOU'RE...
BUT I'VE DECIDED I CAN'T DO IT WITHOUT YOUR BLESSING.

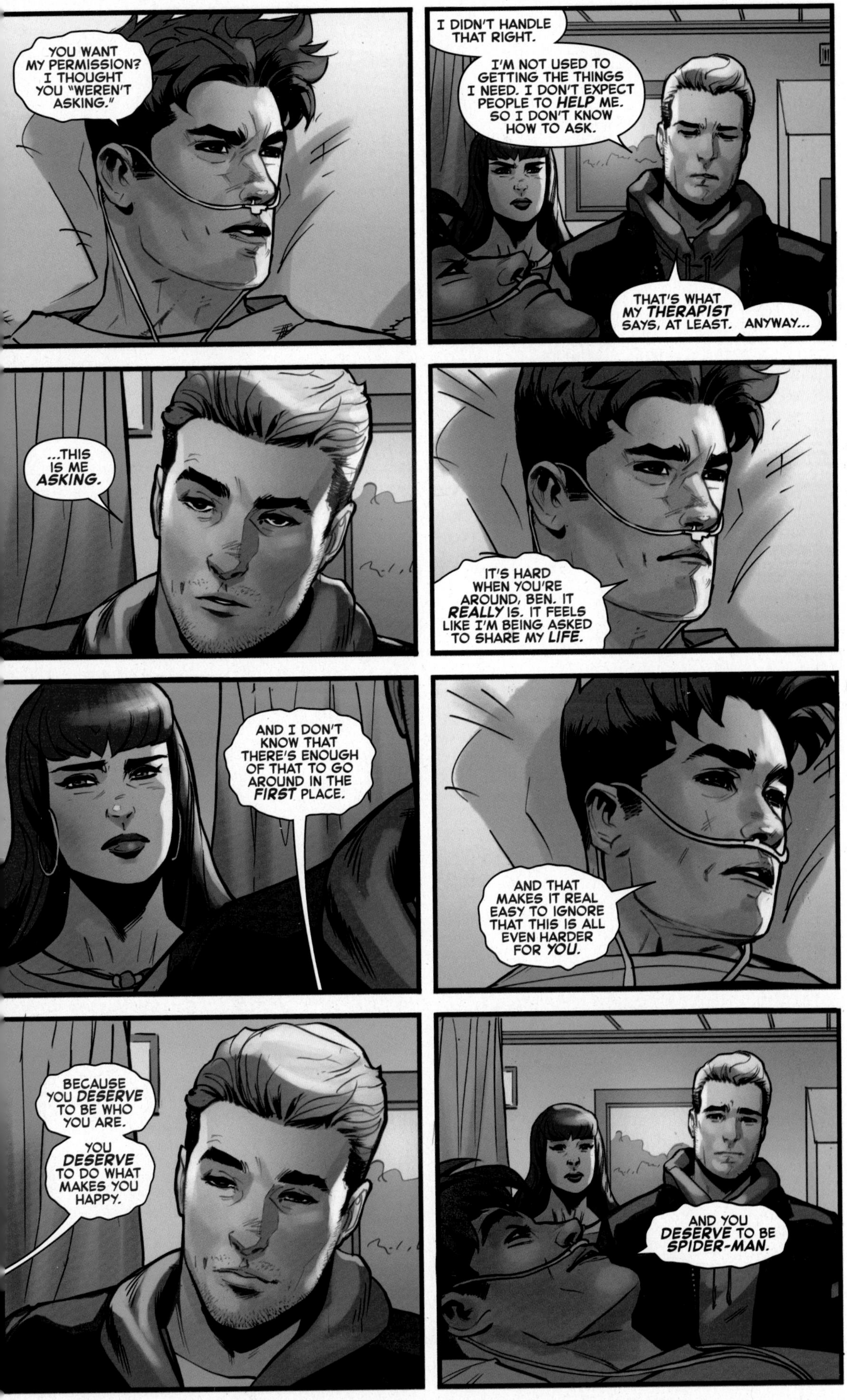
YOU WANT MY PERMISSION? I THOUGHT YOU "WEREN'T ASKING."
I DIDN'T HANDLE THAT RIGHT.
I'M NOT USED TO GETTING THE THINGS I NEED. I DON'T EXPECT PEOPLE TO HELP ME. SO I DON'T KNOW HOW TO ASK.
THAT'S WHAT MY THERAPIST SAYS, AT LEAST.
ANYWAY...
...THIS IS ME ASKING.
IT'S HARD WHEN YOU'RE AROUND, BEN. IT REALLY IS. IT FEELS LIKE I'M BEING ASKED TO SHARE MY LIFE.
AND I DON'T KNOW THAT THERE'S ENOUGH OF THAT TO GO AROUND IN THE FIRST PLACE.
AND THAT MAKES IT REAL EASY TO IGNORE THAT THIS IS ALL EVEN HARDER FOR YOU.
BECAUSE YOU DESERVE TO BE WHO YOU ARE.
YOU DESERVE TO DO WHAT MAKES YOU HAPPY.
AND YOU DESERVE TO BE SPIDER-MAN.

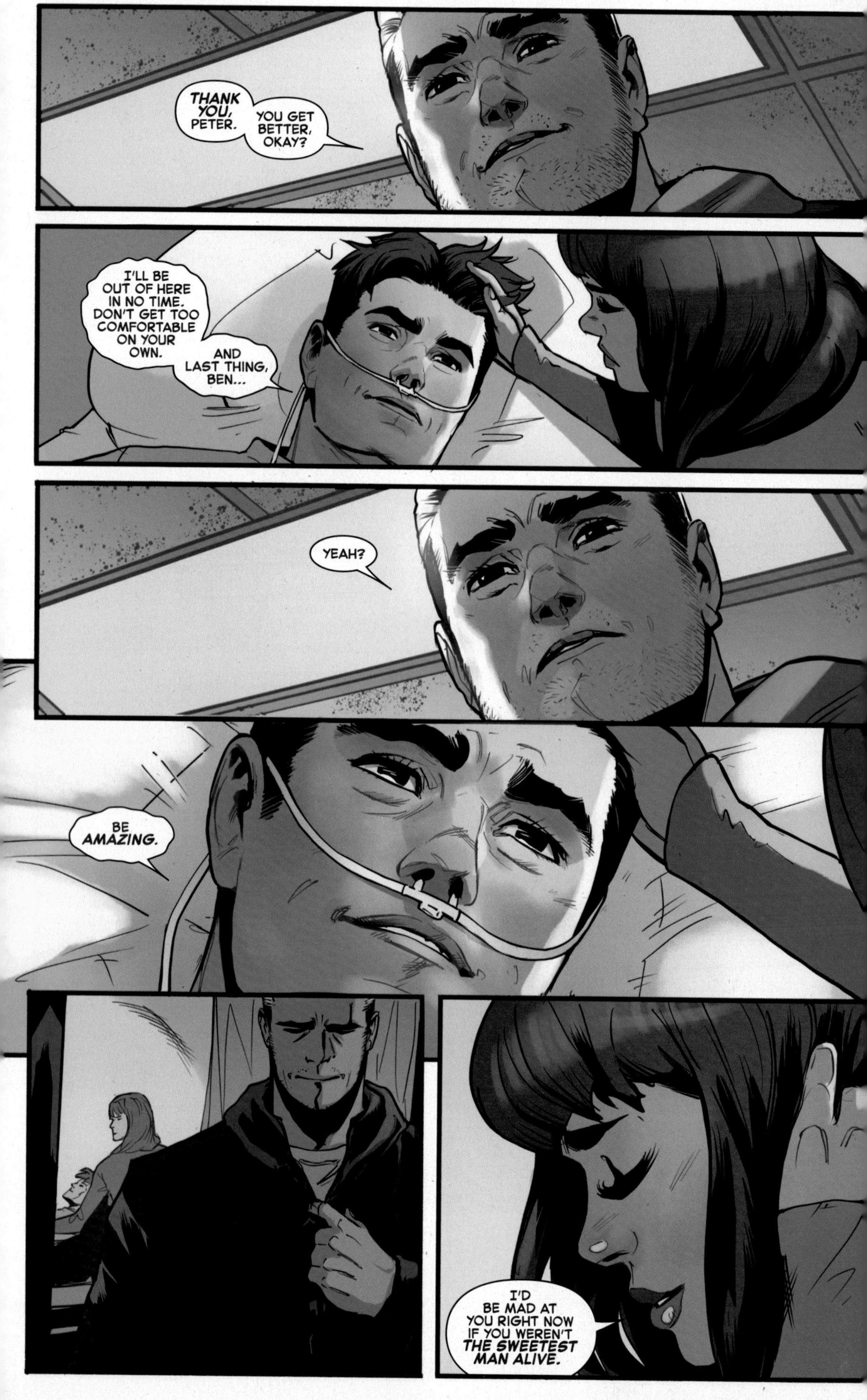
THANK YOU, PETER.
YOU GET BETTER, OKAY?
I'LL BE OUT OF HERE IN NO TIME. DON'T GET TOO COMFORTABLE ON YOUR OWN.
AND LAST THING, BEN...
YEAH?
BE AMAZING.
I'D BE MAD AT YOU RIGHT NOW IF YOU WEREN'T THE SWEETEST MAN ALIVE.

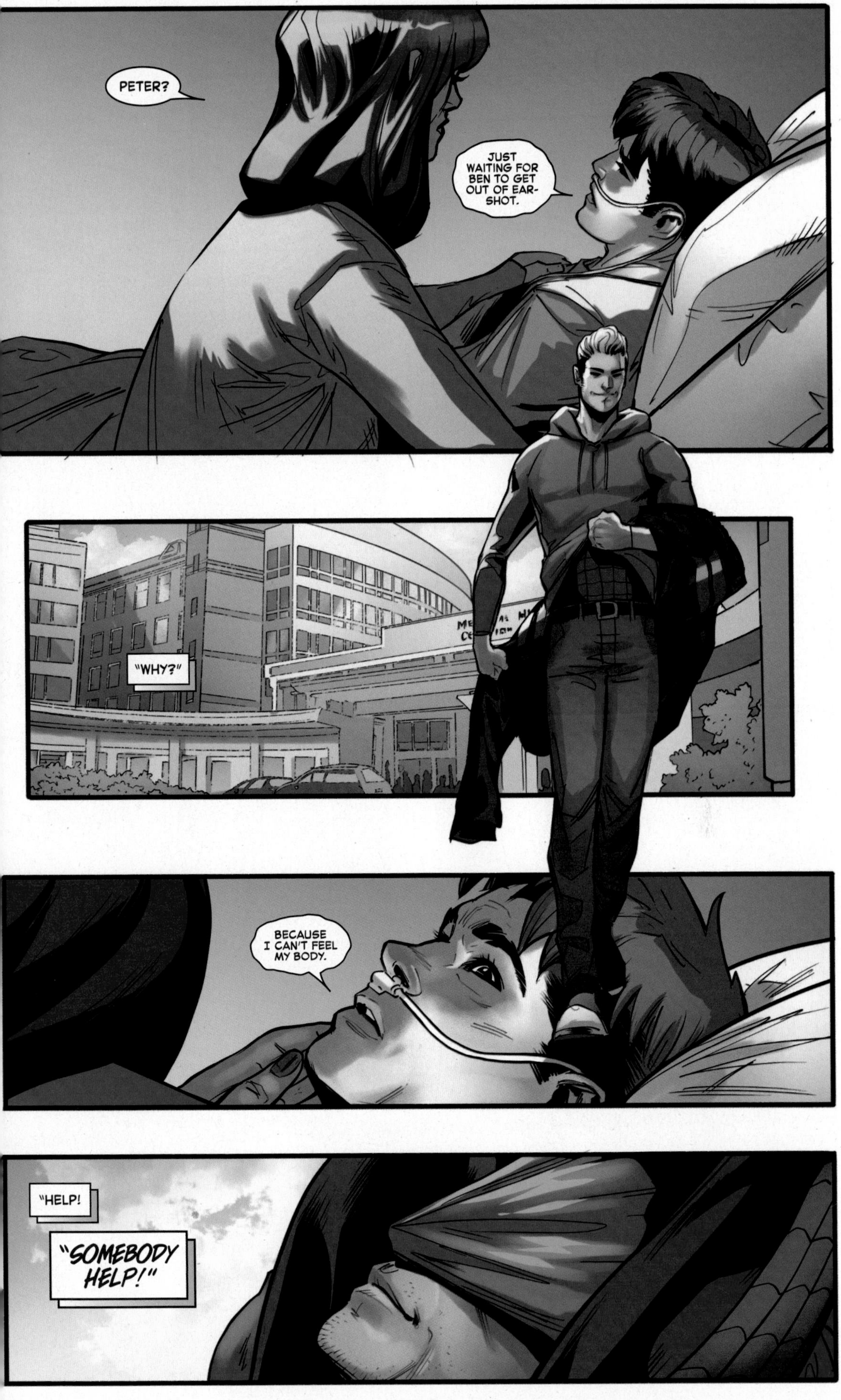
PETER?
JUST WAITING FOR BEN TO GET OUT OF EAR-SHOT.
"WHY?"
BECAUSE I CAN'T FEEL MY BODY.
"HELP!
"SOMEBODY HELP!"

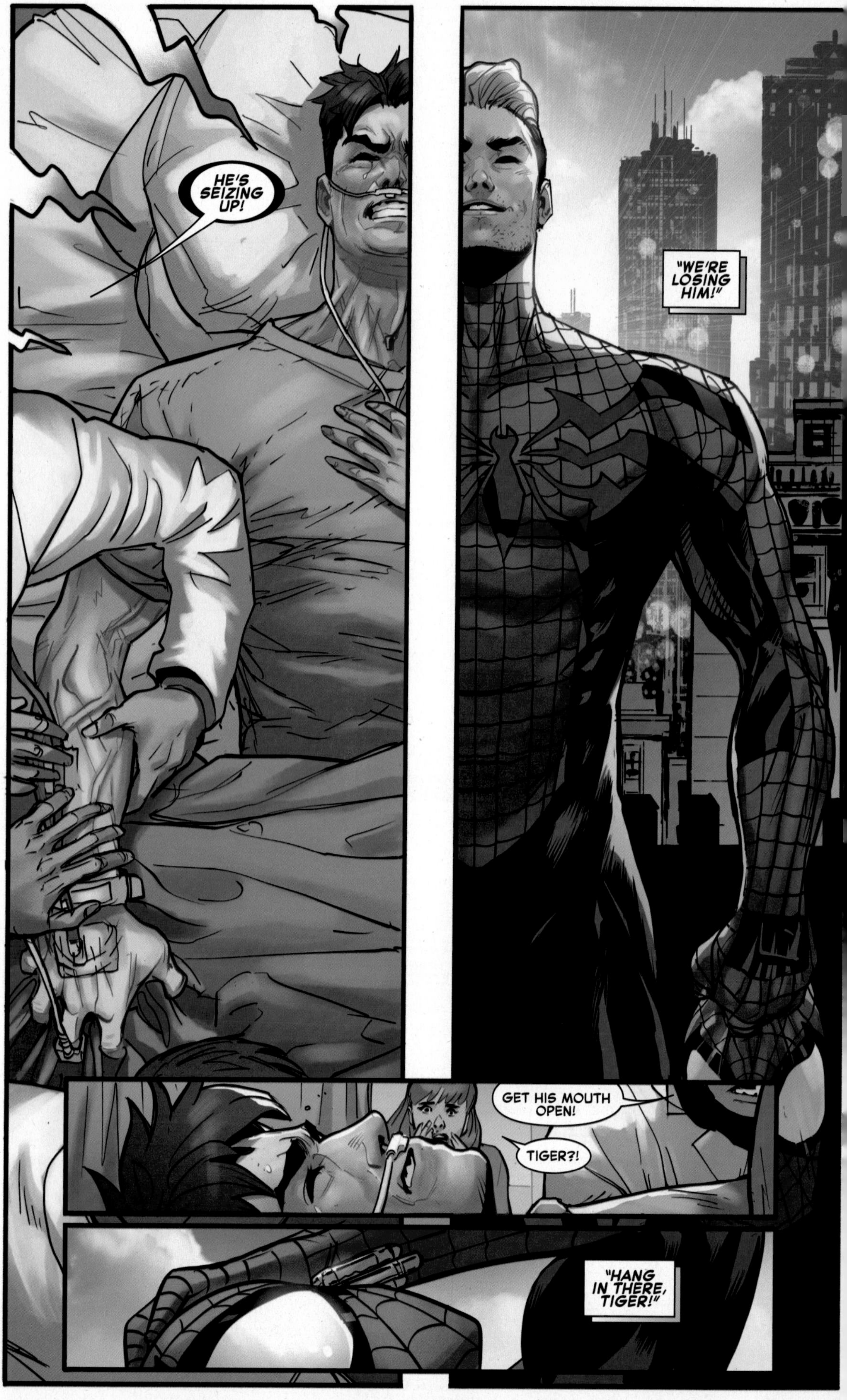
HE'S SEIZING UP!
"WE'RE LOSING HIM!"
GET HIS MOUTH OPEN!
TIGER?!
"HANG IN THERE, TIGER!"

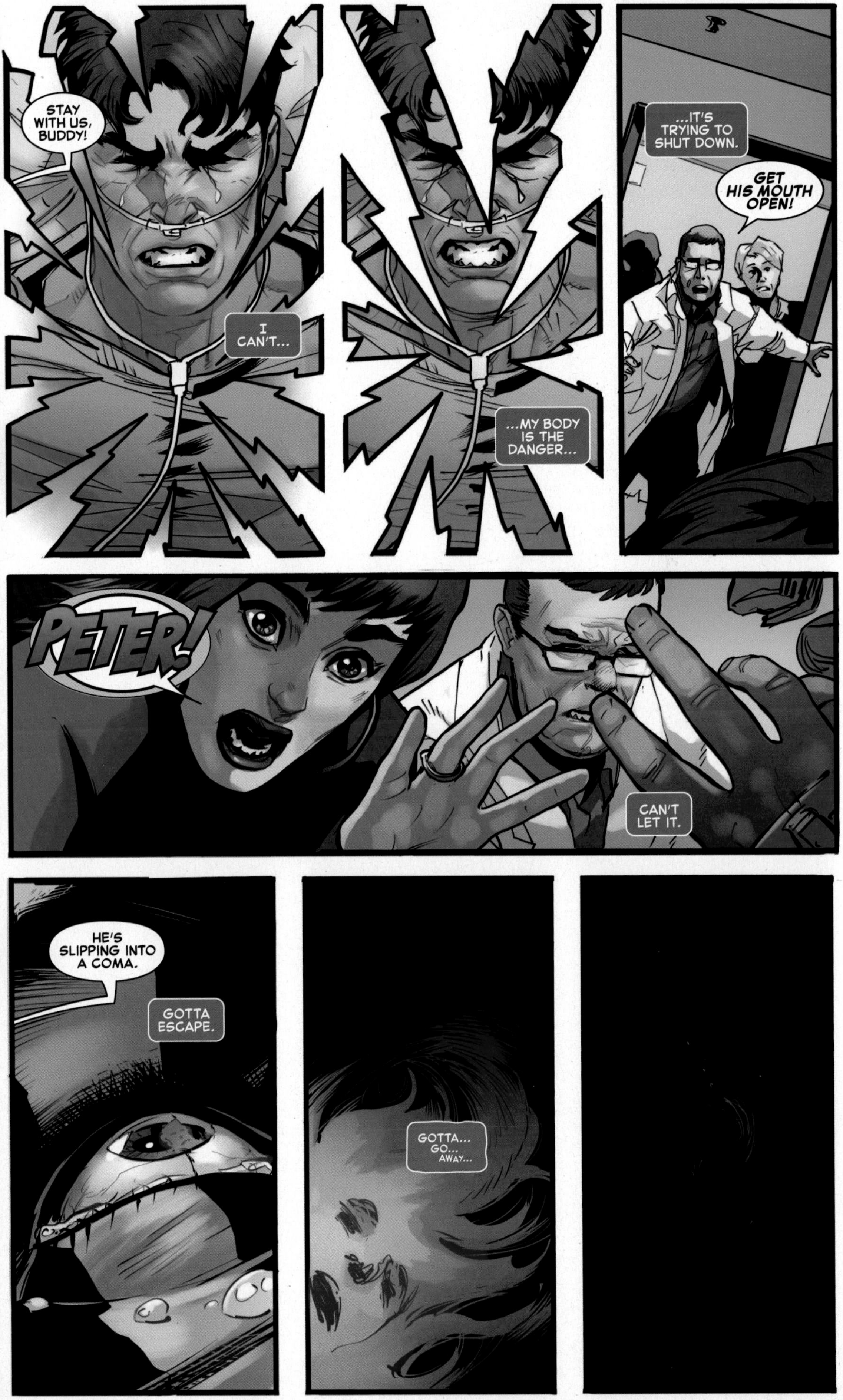
STAY WITH US, BUDDY!
I CAN'T...
...MY BODY IS THE DANGER...
...IT'S TRYING TO SHUT DOWN.
GET HIS MOUTH OPEN!
PETER!
CAN'T LET IT.
HE'S SLIPPING INTO A COMA.
GOTTA ESCAPE.
GOTTA... GO... AWAY...

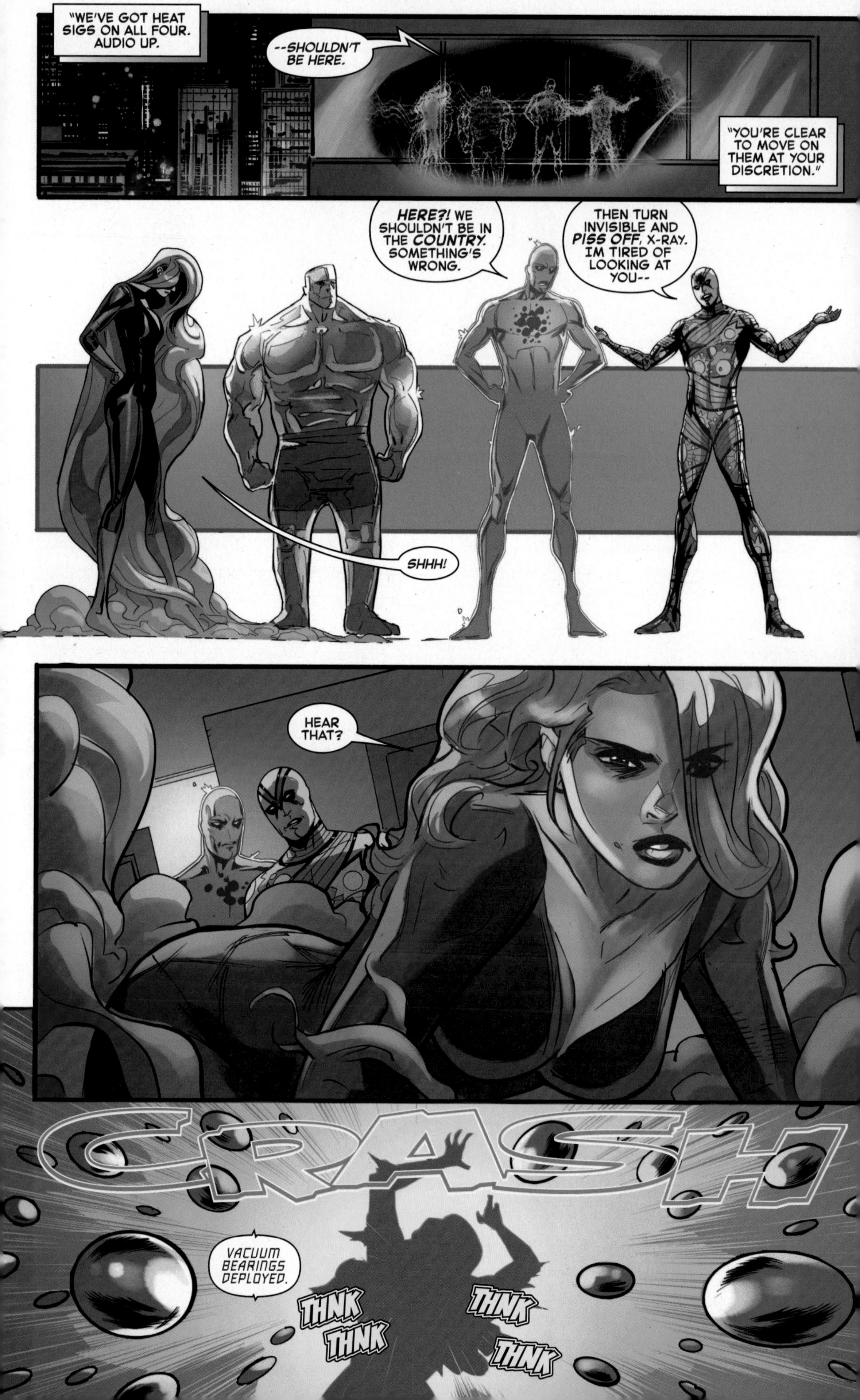
"WE'VE GOT HEAT SIGS ON ALL FOUR. AUDIO UP.
--SHOULDN'T BE HERE.
"YOU'RE CLEAR TO MOVE ON THEM AT YOUR DISCRETION."
HERE?! WE SHOULDN'T BE IN THE COUNTRY. SOMETHING'S WRONG.
THEN TURN INVISIBLE AND PISS OFF, X-RAY. IM TIRED OF LOOKING AT YOU--
SHHH!
HEAR THAT?
CRASH
VACUUM BEARINGS DEPLOYED.
THNK
THNK
THNK
THNK

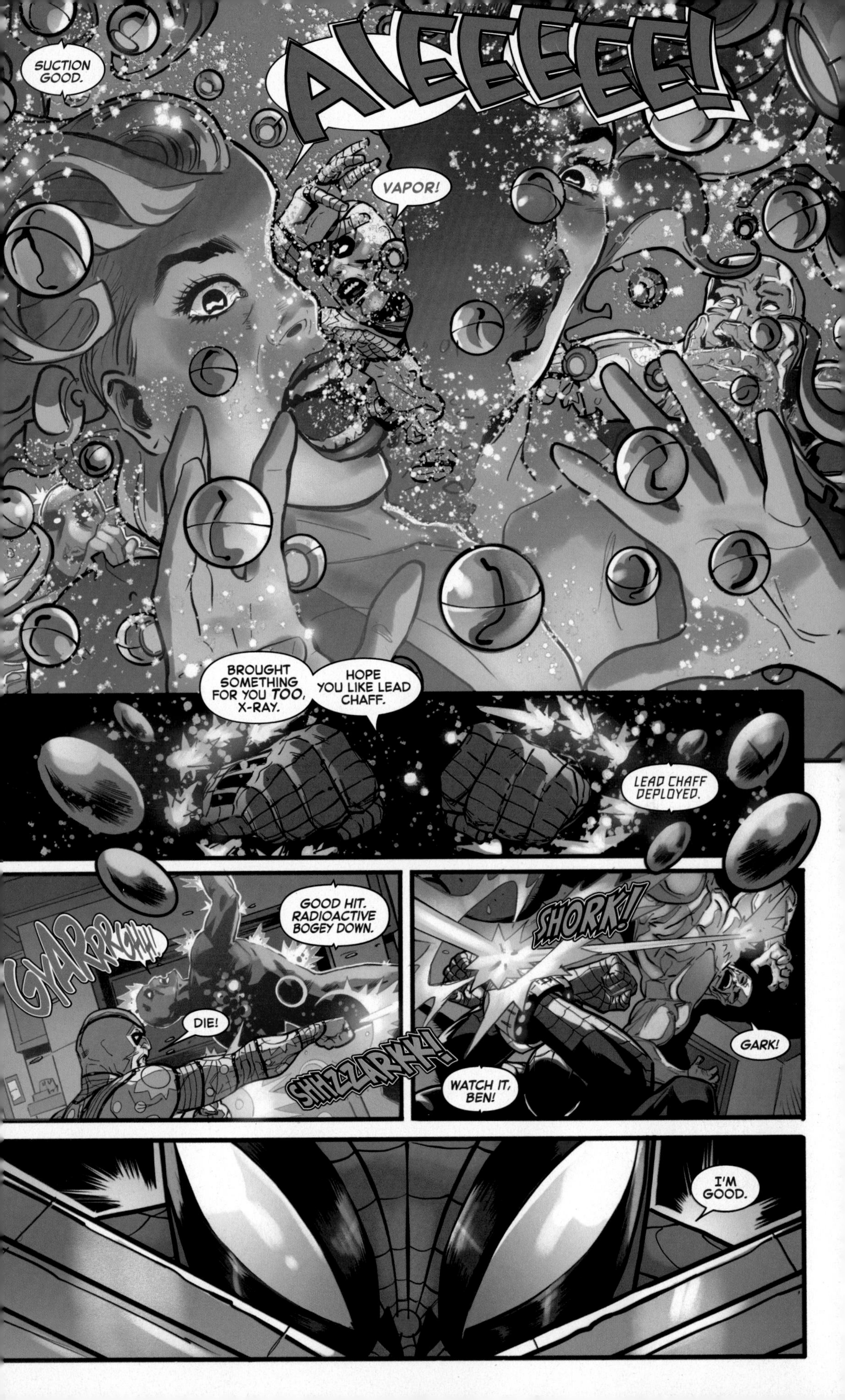

SUCTION GOOD.
AIEEEEE!
VAPOR!
BROUGHT SOMETHING FOR YOU TOO, X-RAY.
HOPE YOU LIKE LEAD CHAFF.
LEAD CHAFF DEPLOYED.
GOOD HIT. RADIOACTIVE BOGEY DOWN.
GYARRRGHH!
DIE!
SHZZARKK!
SHORK!
GARK!
WATCH IT, BEN!
I'M GOOD.

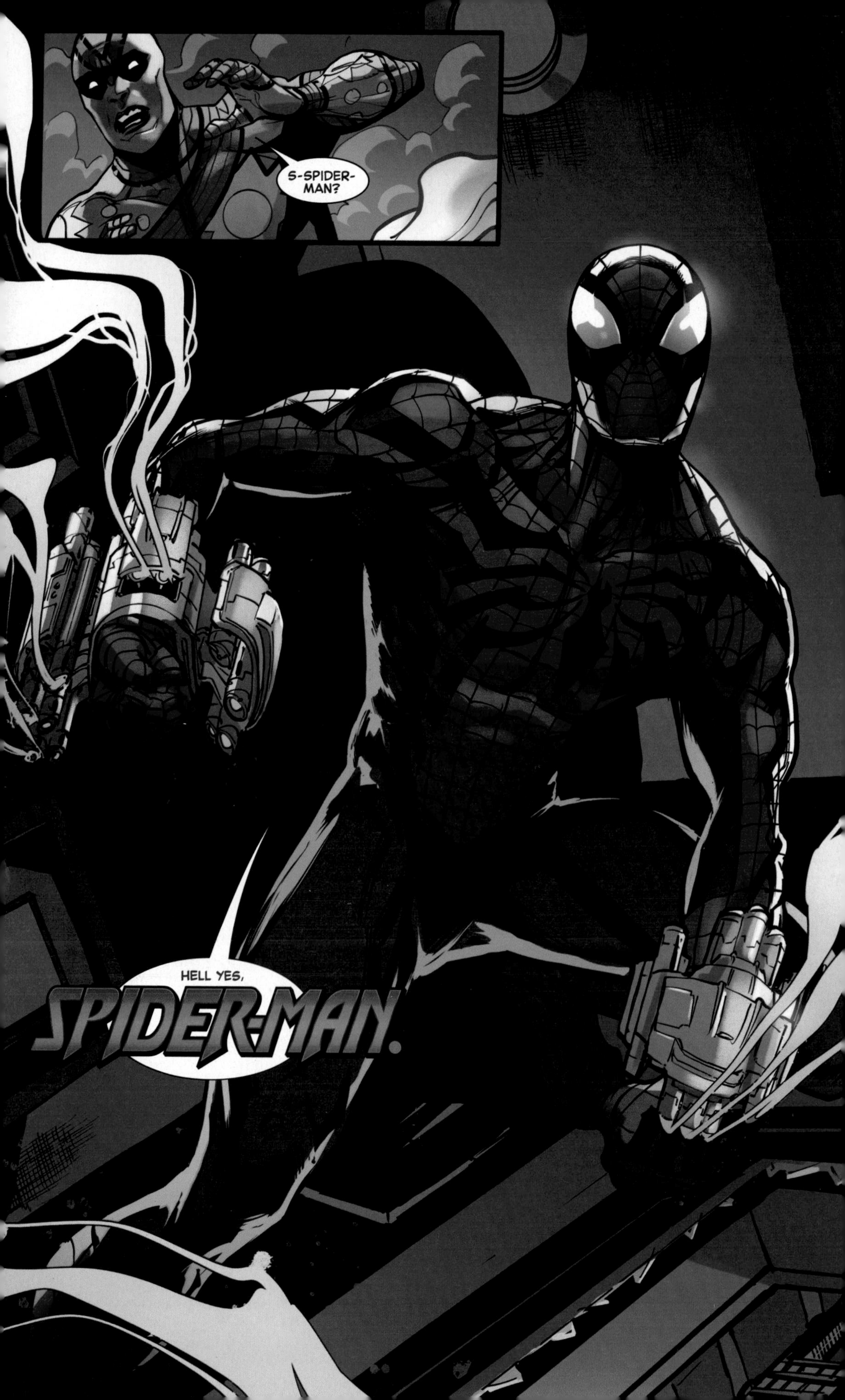
S-SPIDER-MAN?
HELL YES, SPIDER-MAN.

FREE COMIC BOOK DAY 2021:
SPIDER-MAN/VENOM

BEYOND
CORPORATION

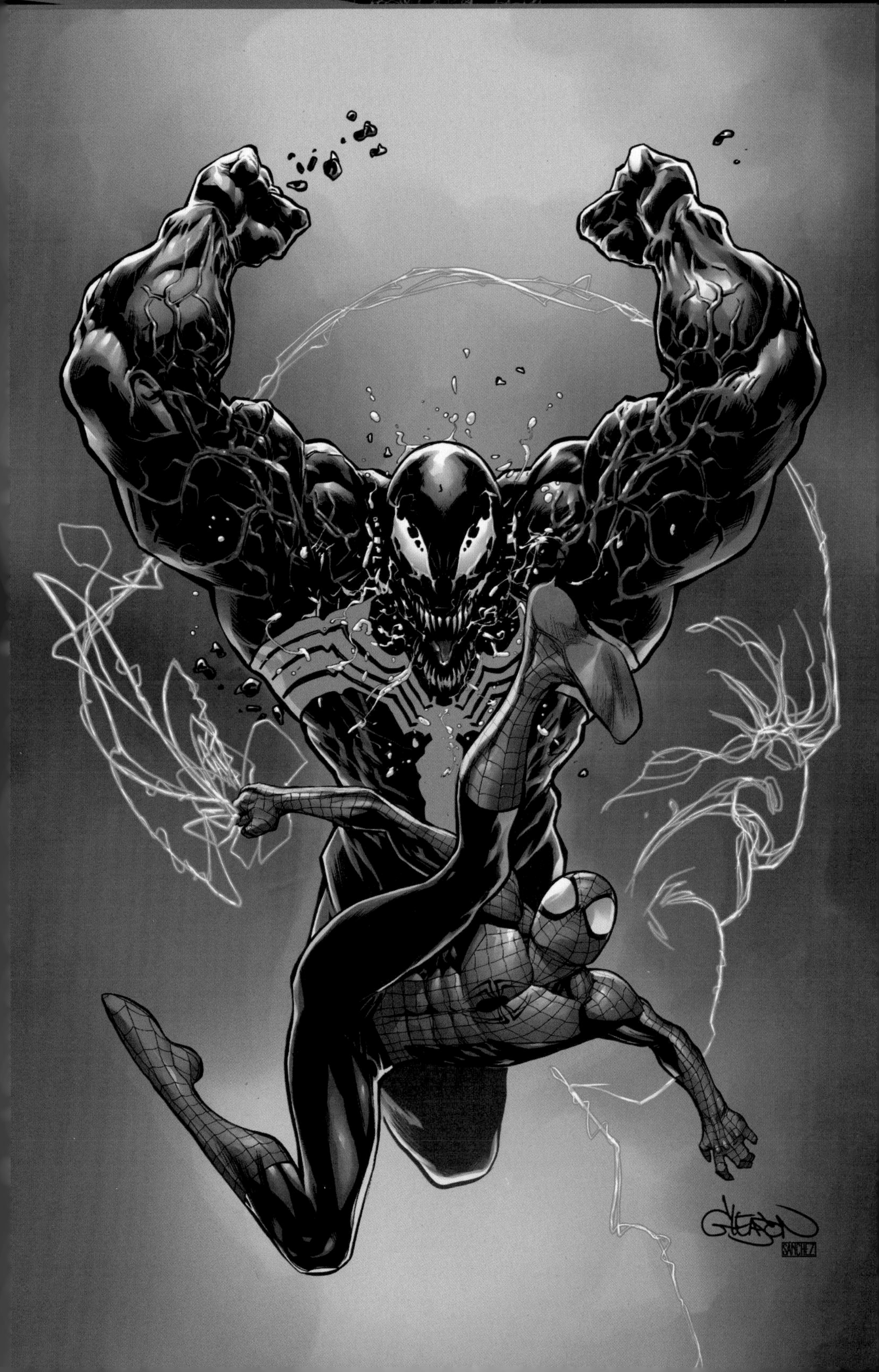
SANCHEZ

THREE
MONTHS
EARLIER

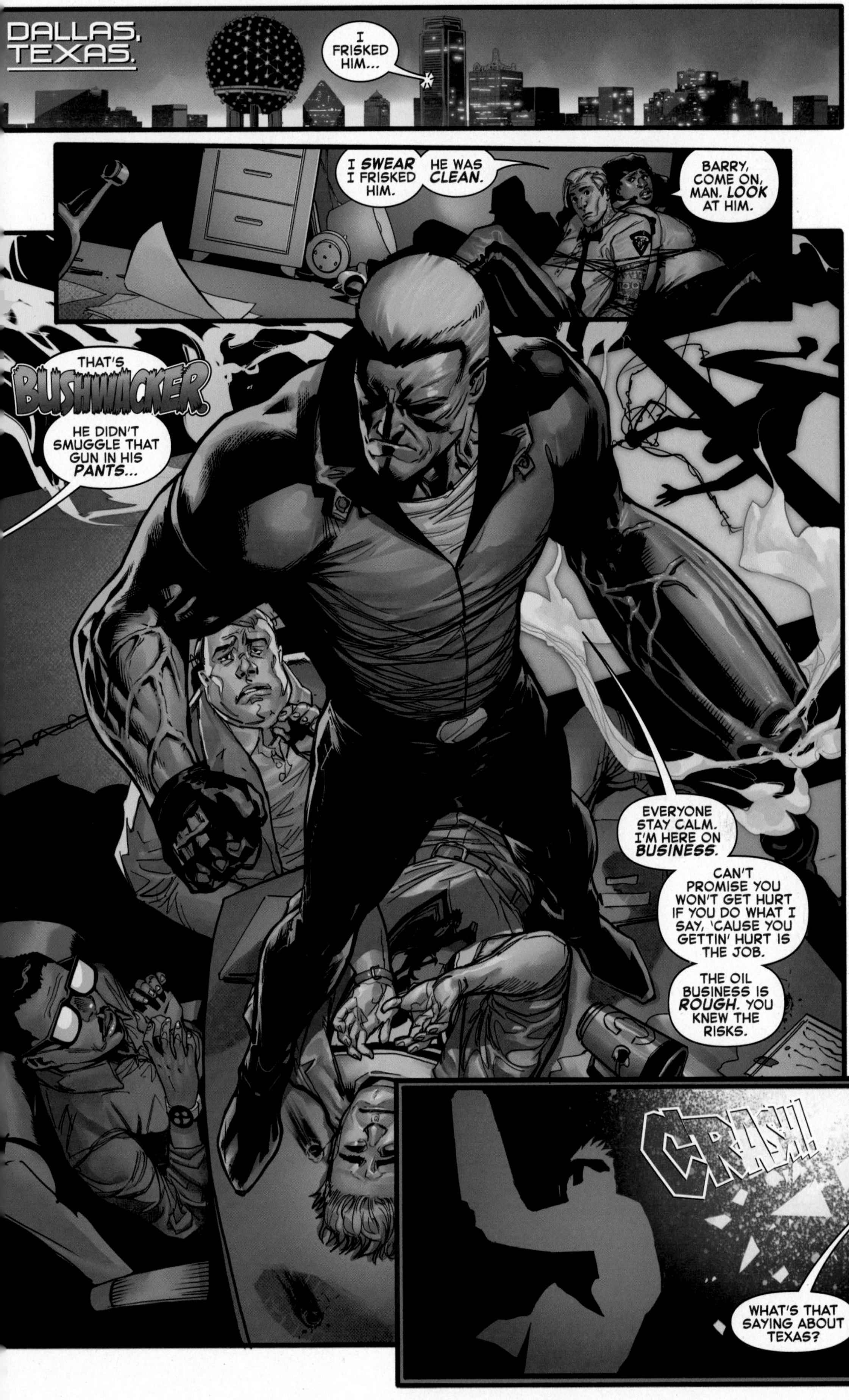

DALLAS, TEXAS.
I FRISKED HIM...
I SWEAR I FRISKED HIM.
HE WAS CLEAN.
BARRY, COME ON, MAN. LOOK AT HIM.
THAT'S BUSHWACKER.
HE DIDN'T SMUGGLE THAT GUN IN HIS PANTS...
EVERYONE STAY CALM. I'M HERE ON BUSINESS.
CAN'T PROMISE YOU WON'T GET HURT IF YOU DO WHAT I SAY, 'CAUSE YOU GETTIN' HURT IS THE JOB.
THE OIL BUSINESS IS ROUGH. YOU KNEW THE RISKS.
CRASH!
WHAT'S THAT SAYING ABOUT TEXAS?

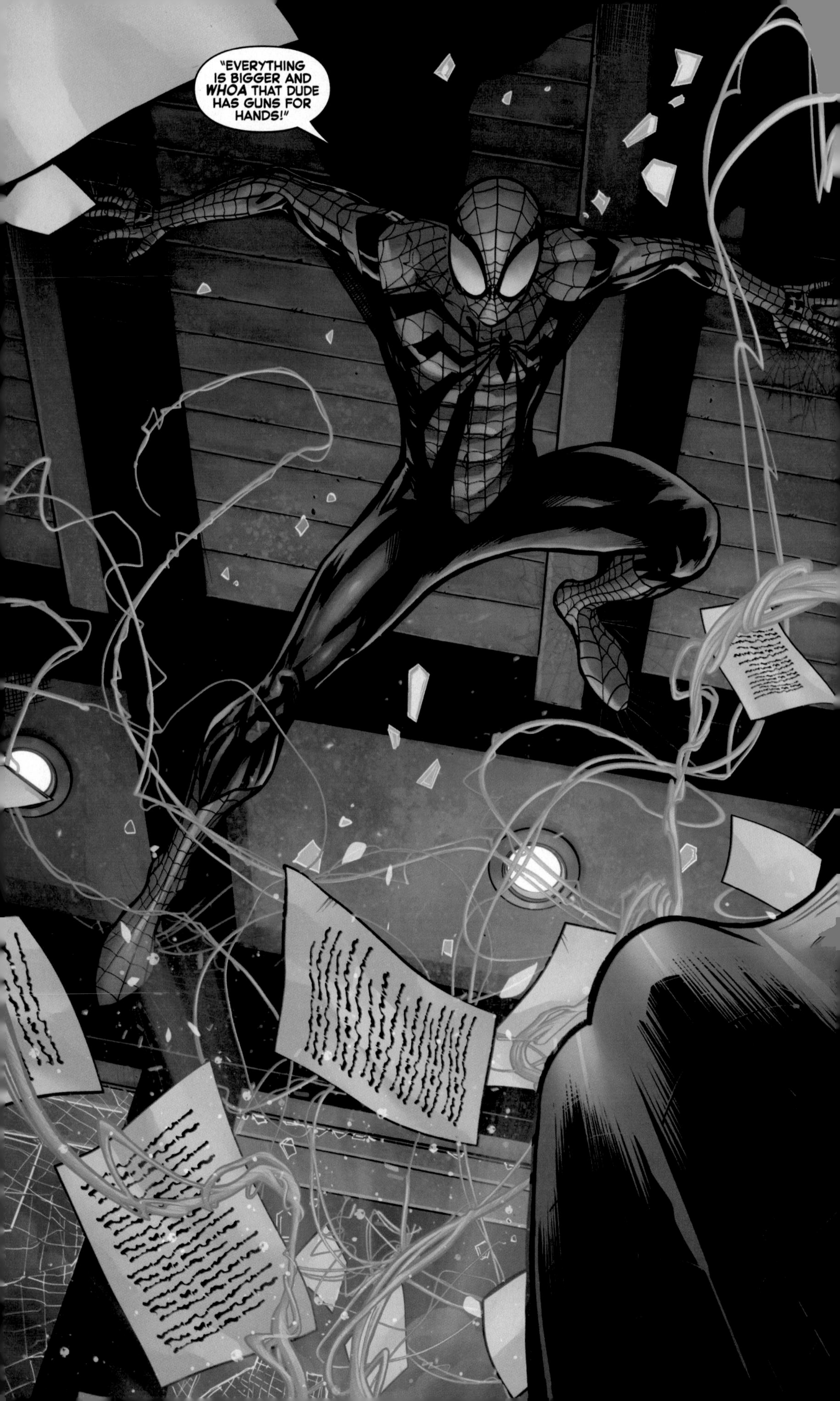
"EVERYTHING IS BIGGER AND *WHOA* THAT DUDE HAS GUNS FOR HANDS!"

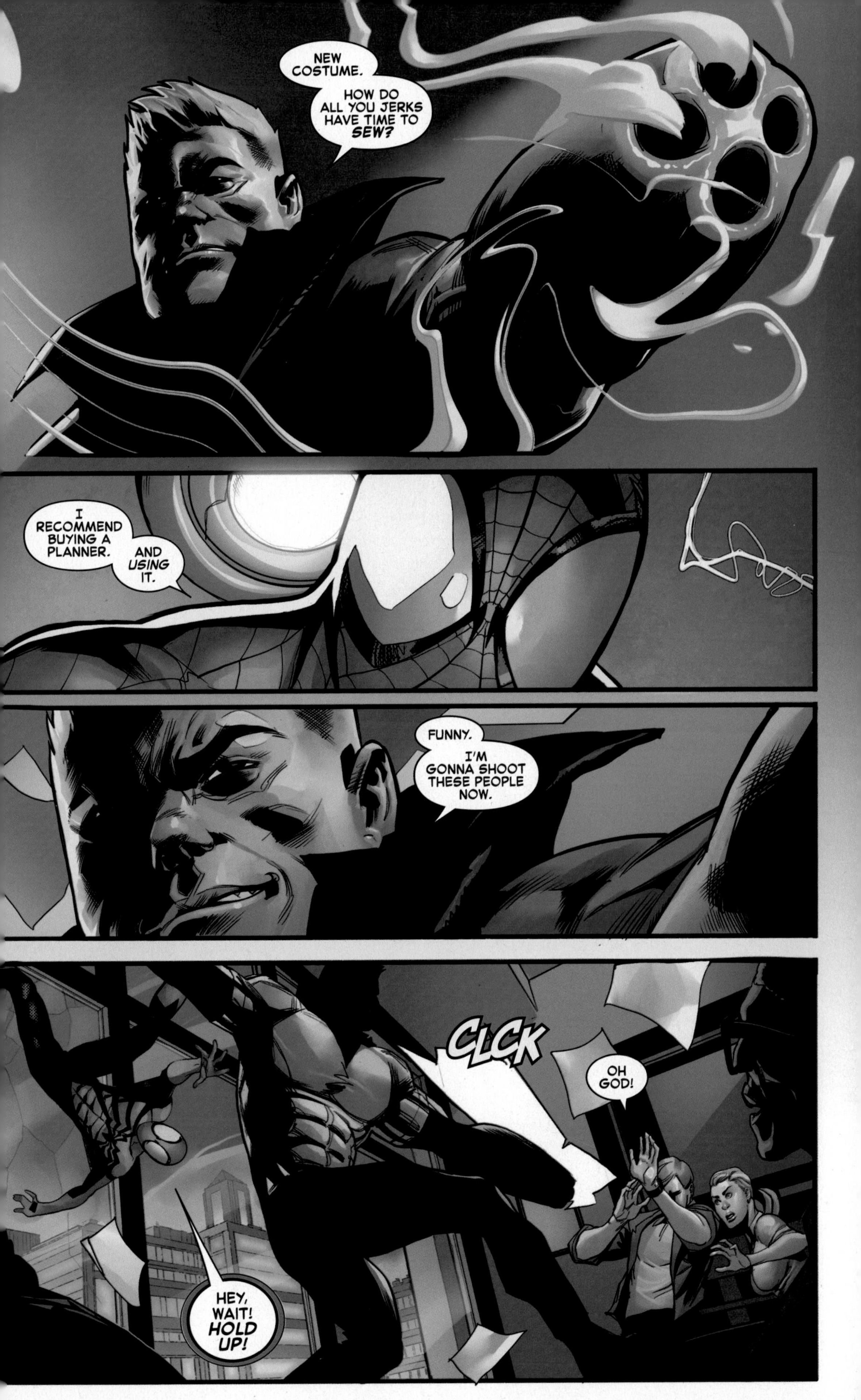
NEW COSTUME.
HOW DO ALL YOU JERKS HAVE TIME TO SEW?
I RECOMMEND BUYING A PLANNER.
AND USING IT.
FUNNY.
I'M GONNA SHOOT THESE PEOPLE NOW.
CLCK
OH GOD!
HEY, WAIT! HOLD UP!

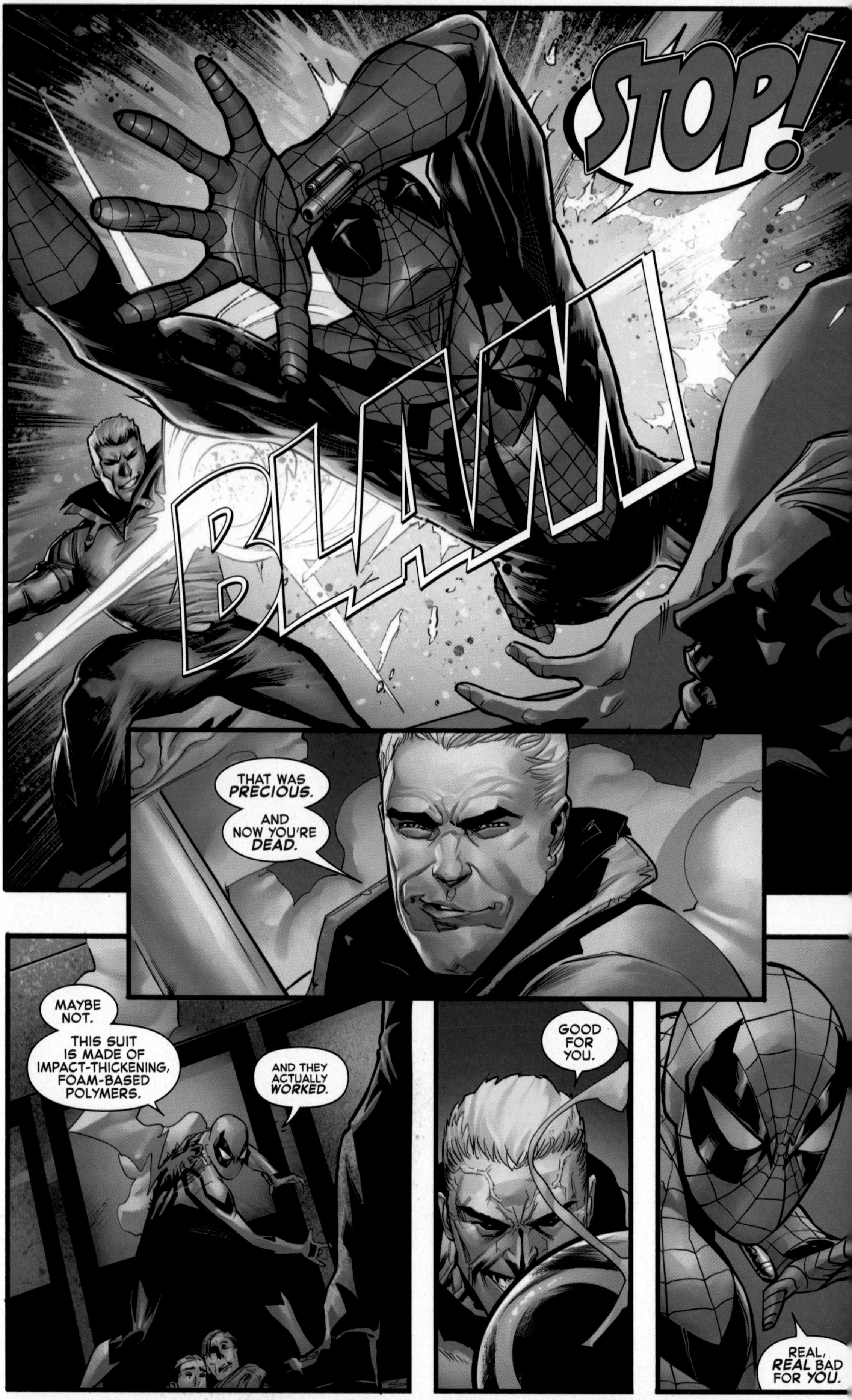
STOP!
BLAMM
THAT WAS PRECIOUS.
AND NOW YOU'RE DEAD.
MAYBE NOT.
THIS SUIT IS MADE OF IMPACT-THICKENING, FOAM-BASED POLYMERS.
AND THEY ACTUALLY WORKED.
GOOD FOR YOU.
REAL, REAL BAD FOR YOU.

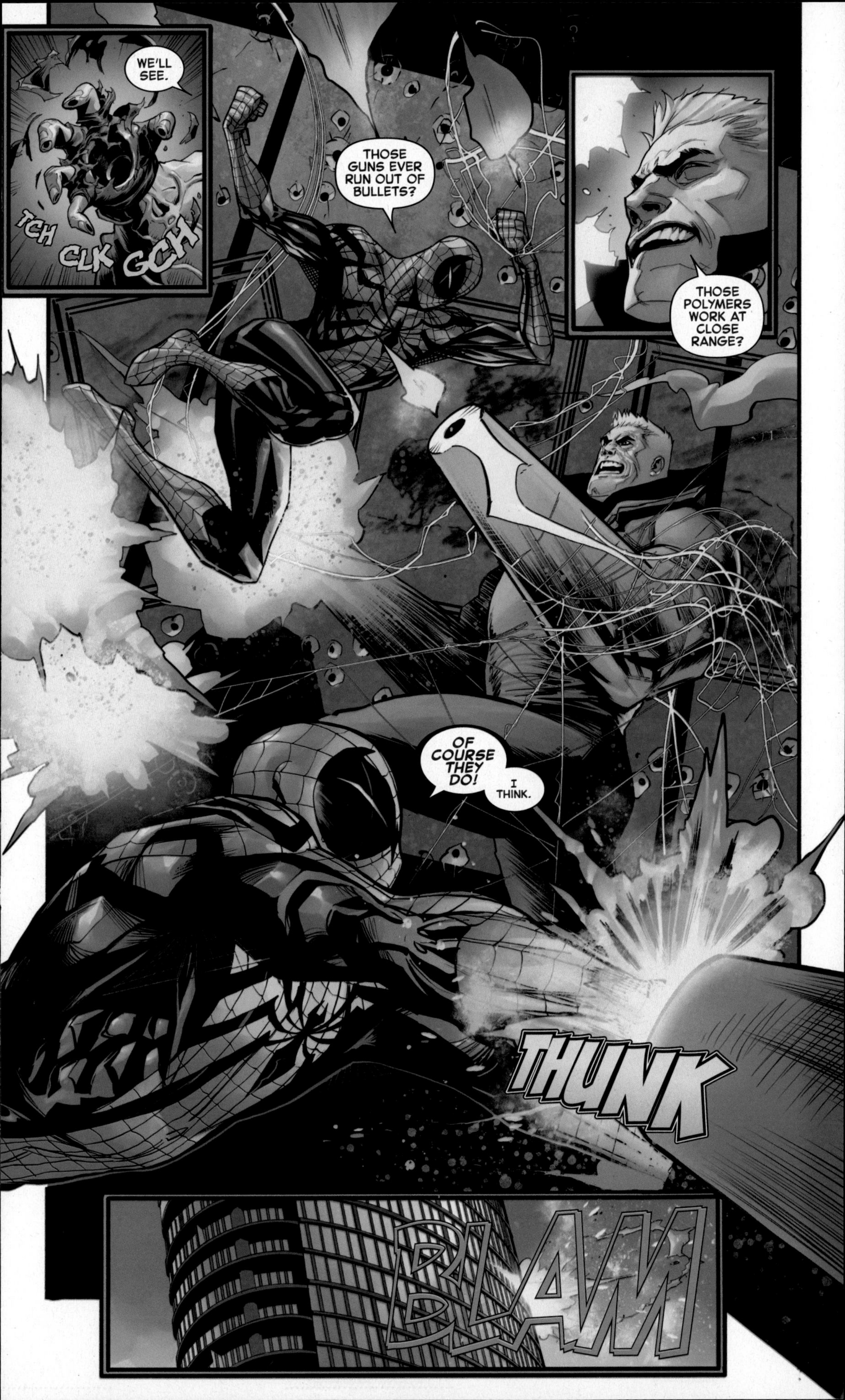

WE'LL SEE.
TCH CLK GCH
THOSE GUNS EVER RUN OUT OF BULLETS?
THOSE POLYMERS WORK AT CLOSE RANGE?
OF COURSE THEY DO!
I THINK.
THUNK
BLAM

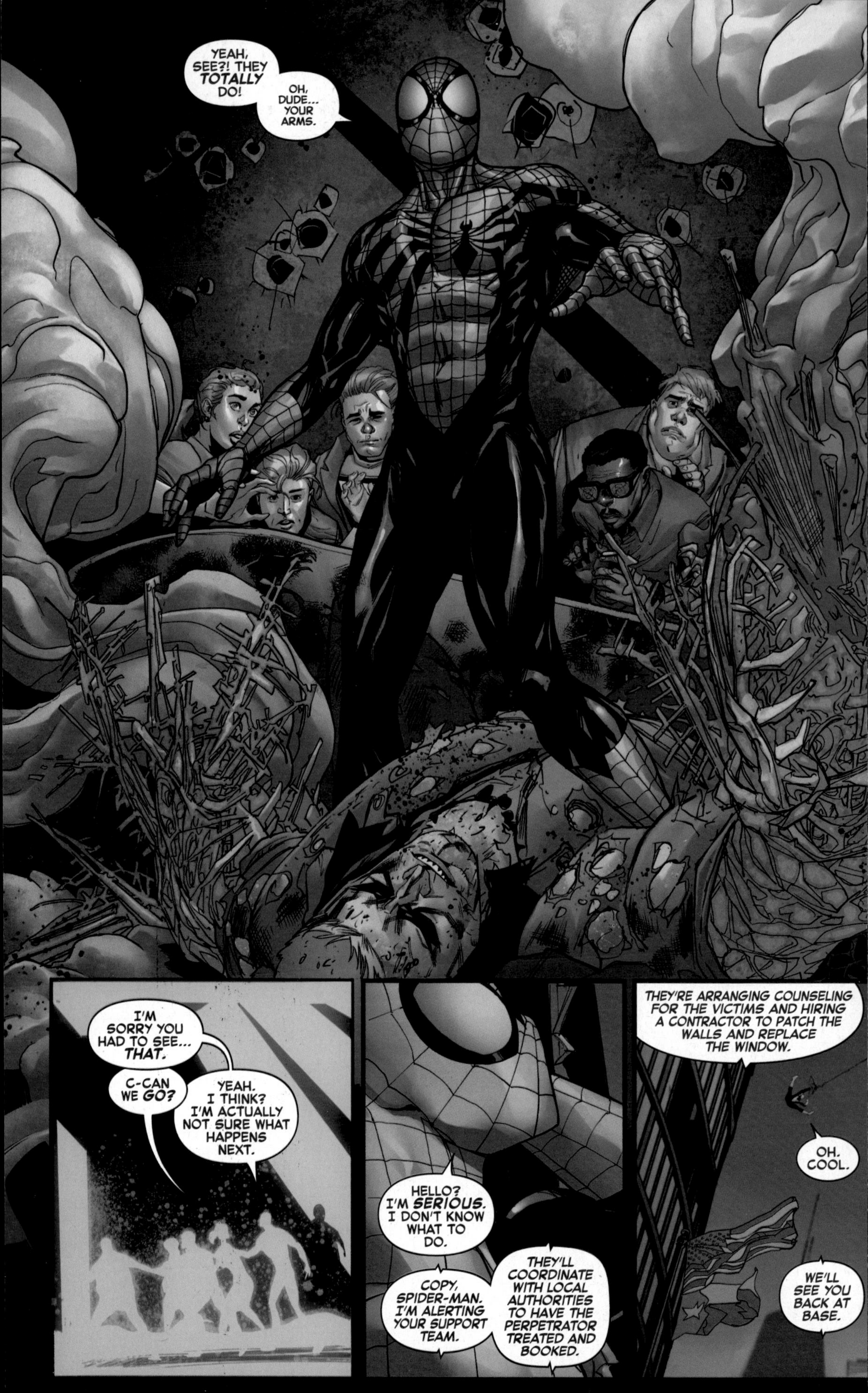
YEAH, SEE?! THEY TOTALLY DO!
OH, DUDE... YOUR ARMS.
I'M SORRY YOU HAD TO SEE... THAT.
C-CAN WE GO?
YEAH. I THINK? I'M ACTUALLY NOT SURE WHAT HAPPENS NEXT.
HELLO? I'M SERIOUS. I DON'T KNOW WHAT TO DO.
COPY, SPIDER-MAN. I'M ALERTING YOUR SUPPORT TEAM.
THEY'LL COORDINATE WITH LOCAL AUTHORITIES TO HAVE THE PERPETRATOR TREATED AND BOOKED.
THEY'RE ARRANGING COUNSELING FOR THE VICTIMS AND HIRING A CONTRACTOR TO PATCH THE WALLS AND REPLACE THE WINDOW.
OH. COOL.
WE'LL SEE YOU BACK AT BASE.

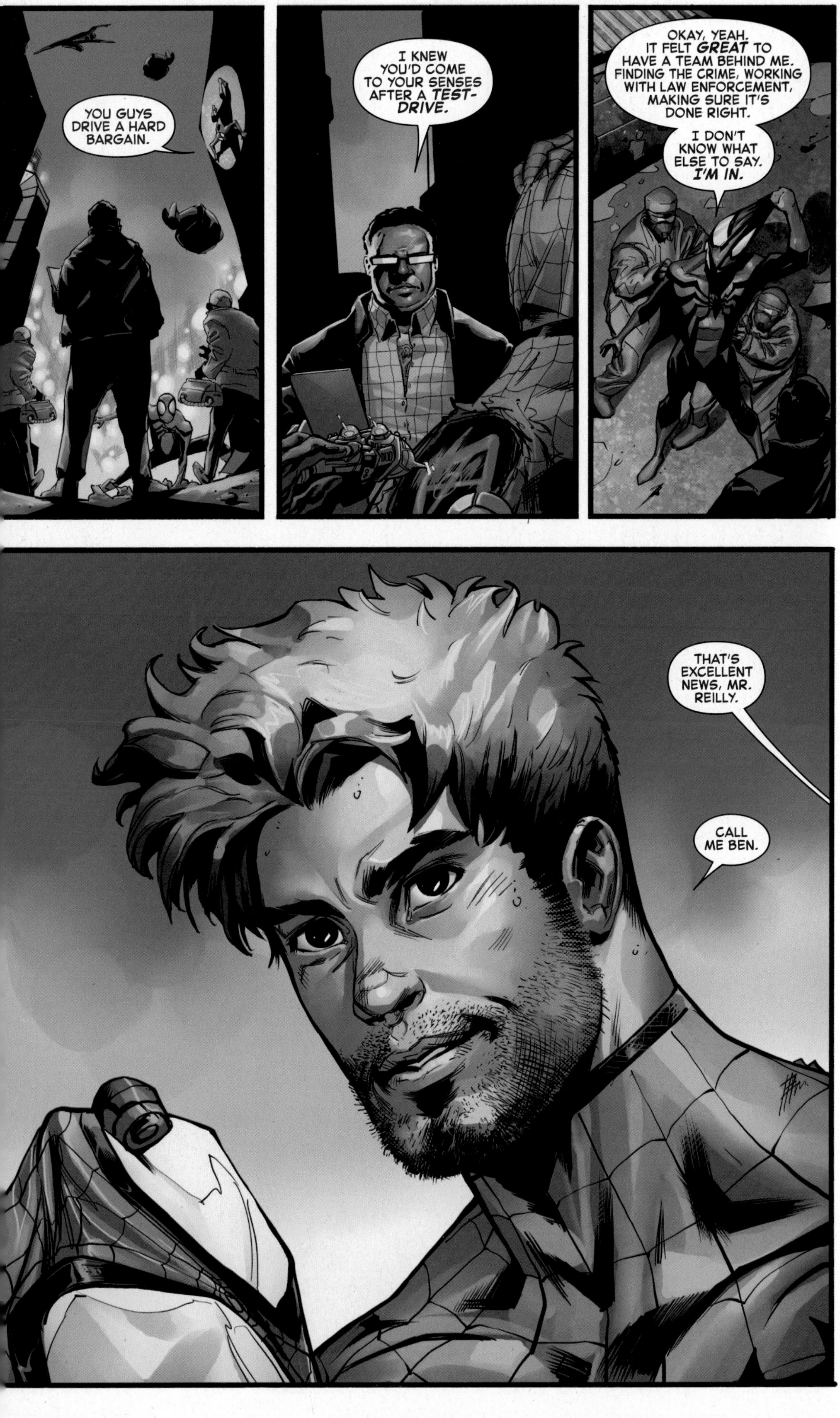
YOU GUYS DRIVE A HARD BARGAIN.
I KNEW YOU'D COME TO YOUR SENSES AFTER A TEST-DRIVE.
OKAY, YEAH. IT FELT GREAT TO HAVE A TEAM BEHIND ME. FINDING THE CRIME, WORKING WITH LAW ENFORCEMENT, MAKING SURE IT'S DONE RIGHT.
I DON'T KNOW WHAT ELSE TO SAY. I'M IN.
THAT'S EXCELLENT NEWS, MR. REILLY.
CALL ME BEN.

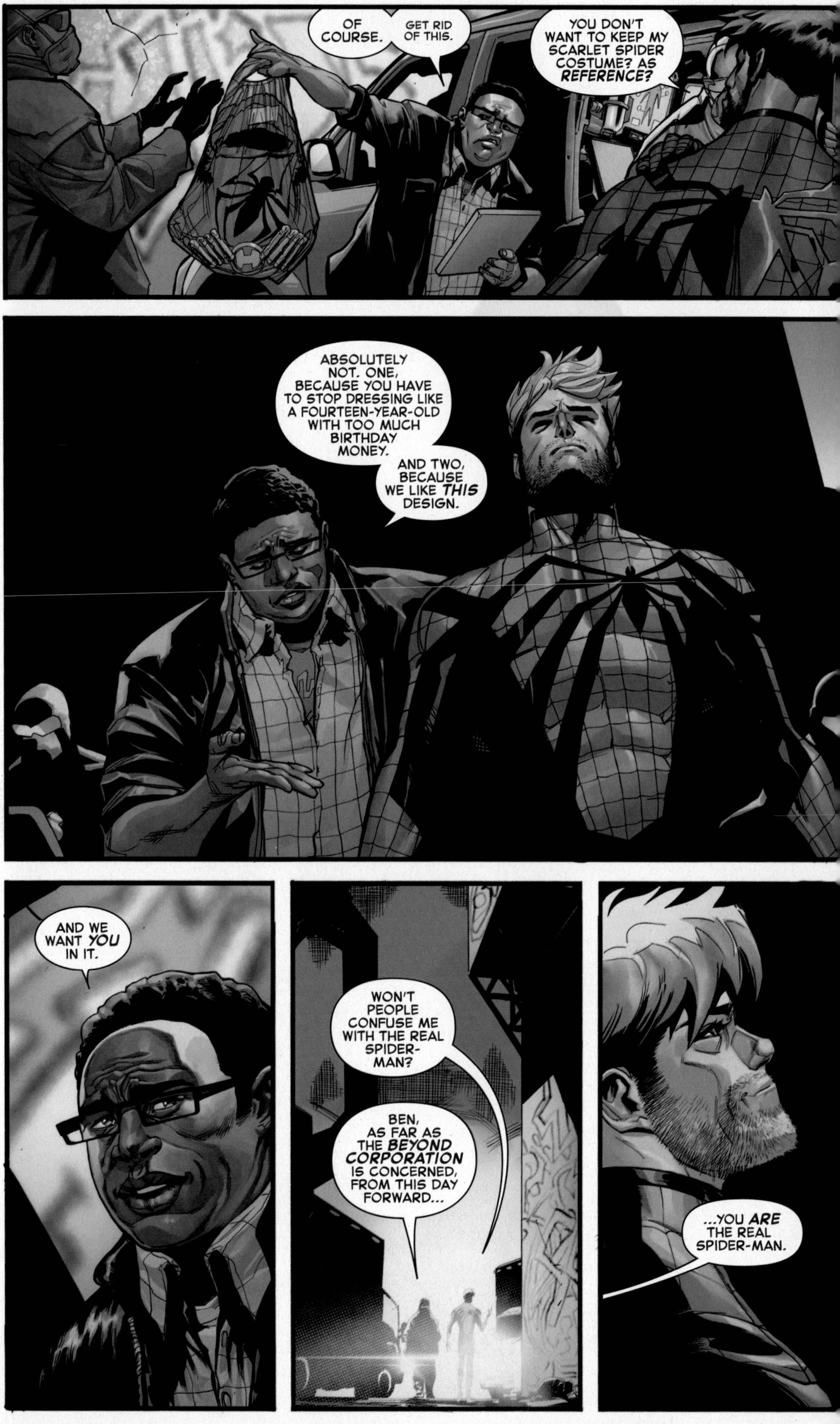
OF COURSE.
GET RID OF THIS.
YOU DON'T WANT TO KEEP MY SCARLET SPIDER COSTUME? AS *REFERENCE?*
ABSOLUTELY NOT. ONE, BECAUSE YOU HAVE TO STOP DRESSING LIKE A FOURTEEN-YEAR-OLD WITH TOO MUCH BIRTHDAY MONEY.
AND TWO, BECAUSE WE LIKE *THIS* DESIGN.
AND WE WANT *YOU* IN IT.
WON'T PEOPLE CONFUSE ME WITH THE REAL SPIDER-MAN?
BEN, AS FAR AS THE *BEYOND CORPORATION* IS CONCERNED, FROM THIS DAY FORWARD...
...YOU *ARE* THE REAL SPIDER-MAN.

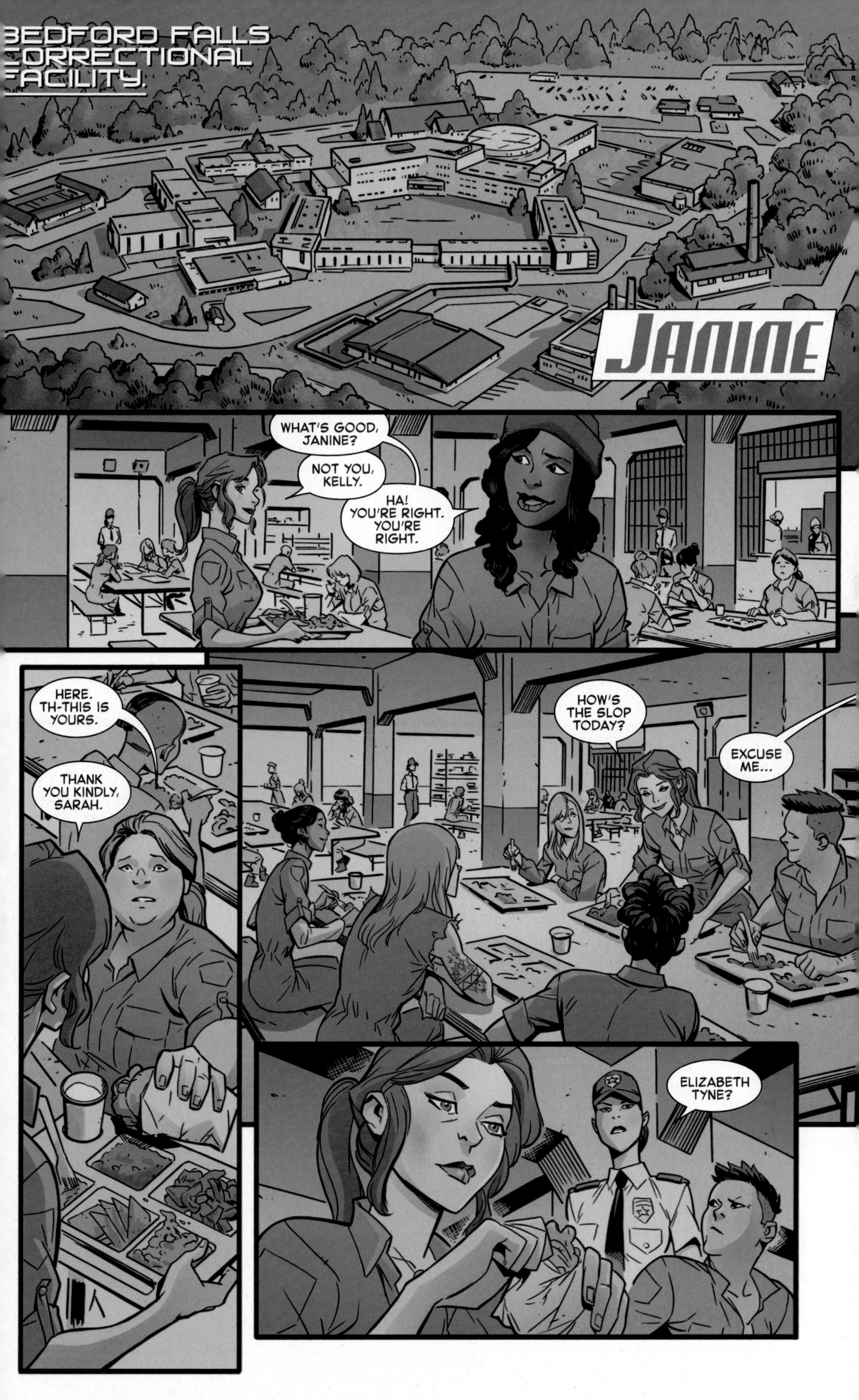
BEDFORD FALLS CORRECTIONAL FACILITY.
JANINE
WHAT'S GOOD, JANINE?
NOT YOU, KELLY.
HA! YOU'RE RIGHT. YOU'RE RIGHT.
HERE. TH-THIS IS YOURS.
THANK YOU KINDLY, SARAH.
HOW'S THE SLOP TODAY?
EXCUSE ME...
ELIZABETH TYNE?

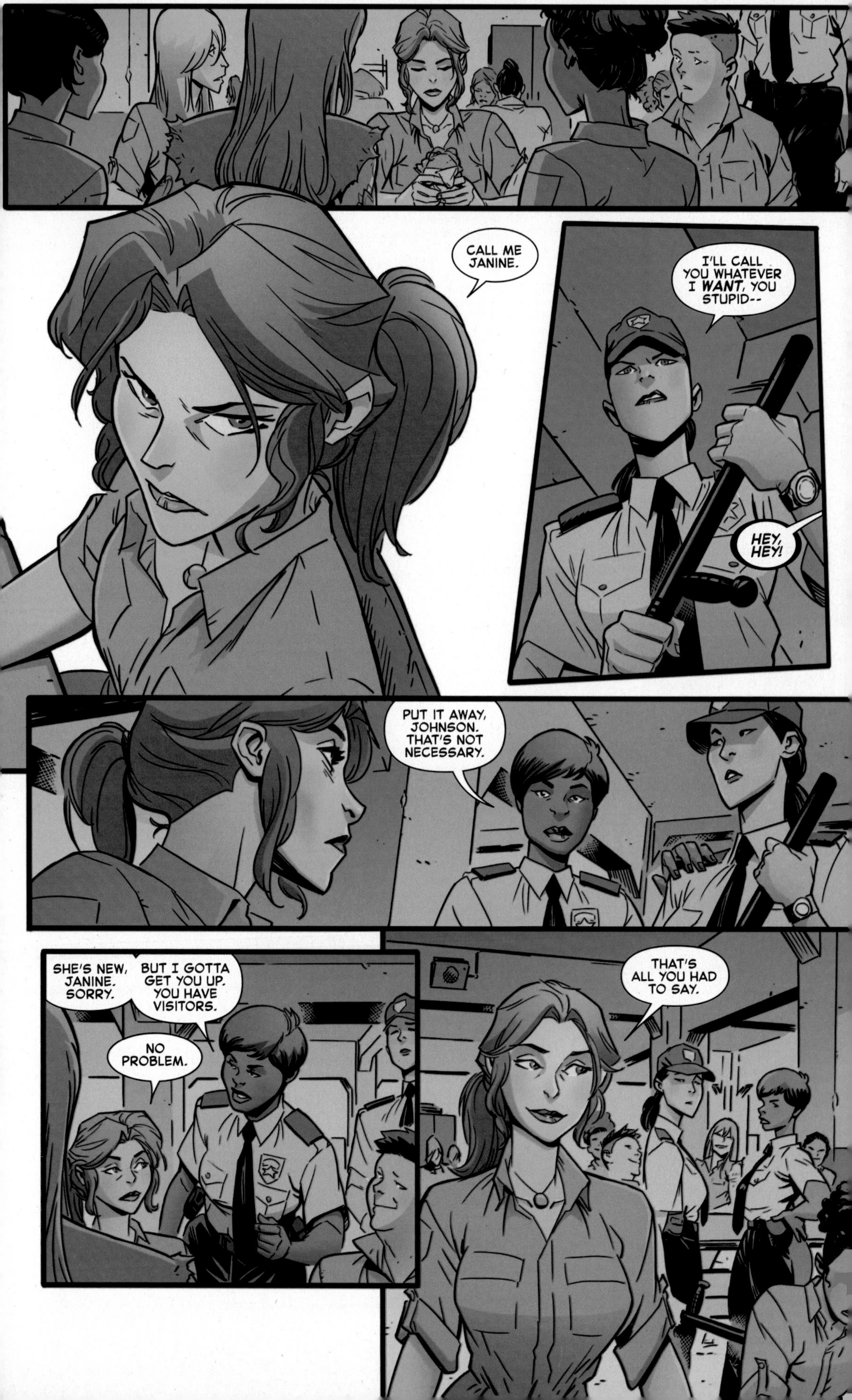
CALL ME JANINE.
I'LL CALL YOU WHATEVER I WANT, YOU STUPID--
HEY, HEY!
PUT IT AWAY, JOHNSON. THAT'S NOT NECESSARY.
SHE'S NEW, JANINE. SORRY.
BUT I GOTTA GET YOU UP. YOU HAVE VISITORS.
NO PROBLEM.
THAT'S ALL YOU HAD TO SAY.

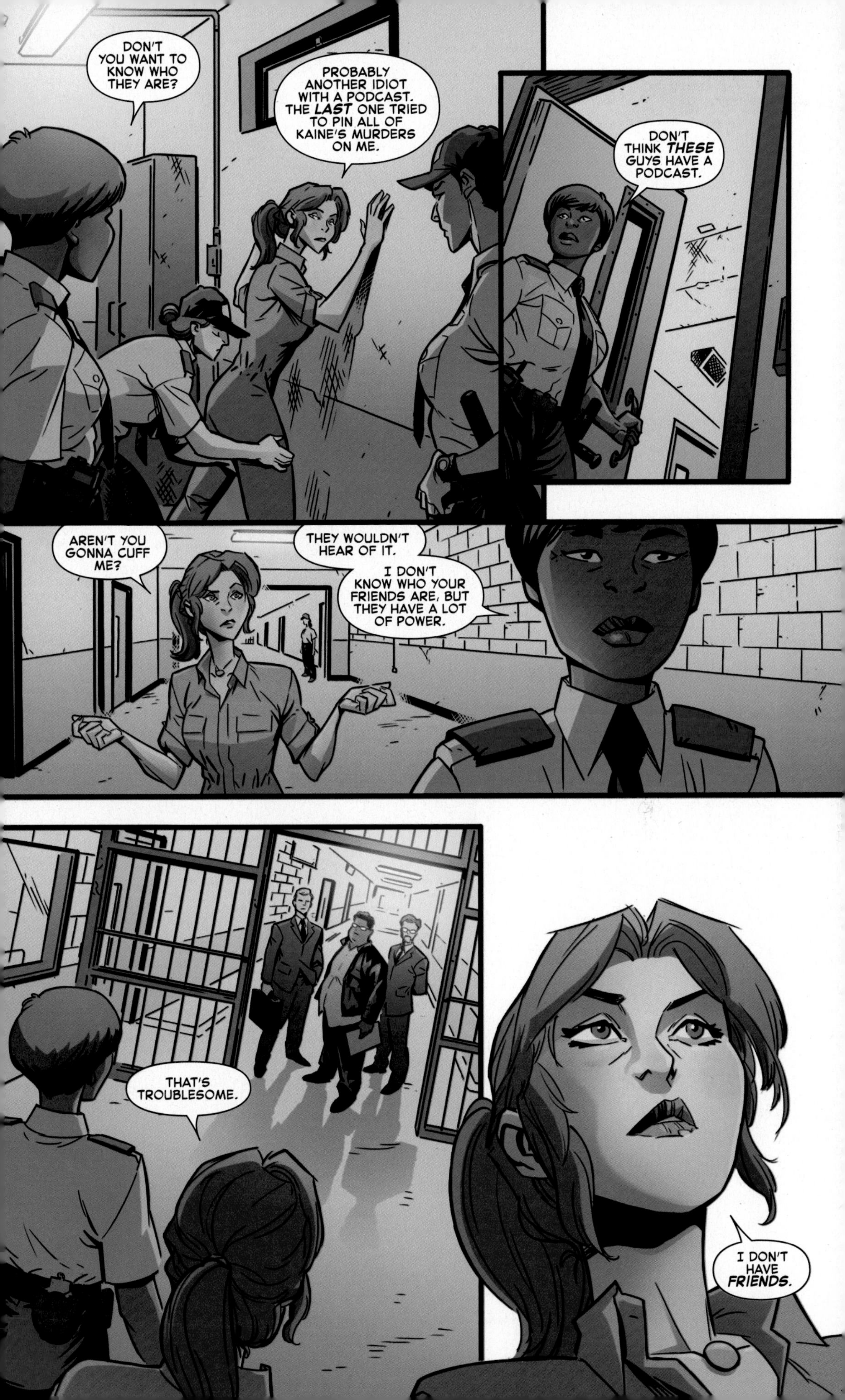
DON'T YOU WANT TO KNOW WHO THEY ARE?
PROBABLY ANOTHER IDIOT WITH A PODCAST. THE LAST ONE TRIED TO PIN ALL OF KAINE'S MURDERS ON ME.
DON'T THINK THESE GUYS HAVE A PODCAST.
AREN'T YOU GONNA CUFF ME?
THEY WOULDN'T HEAR OF IT.
I DON'T KNOW WHO YOUR FRIENDS ARE, BUT THEY HAVE A LOT OF POWER.
THAT'S TROUBLESOME.
I DON'T HAVE FRIENDS.

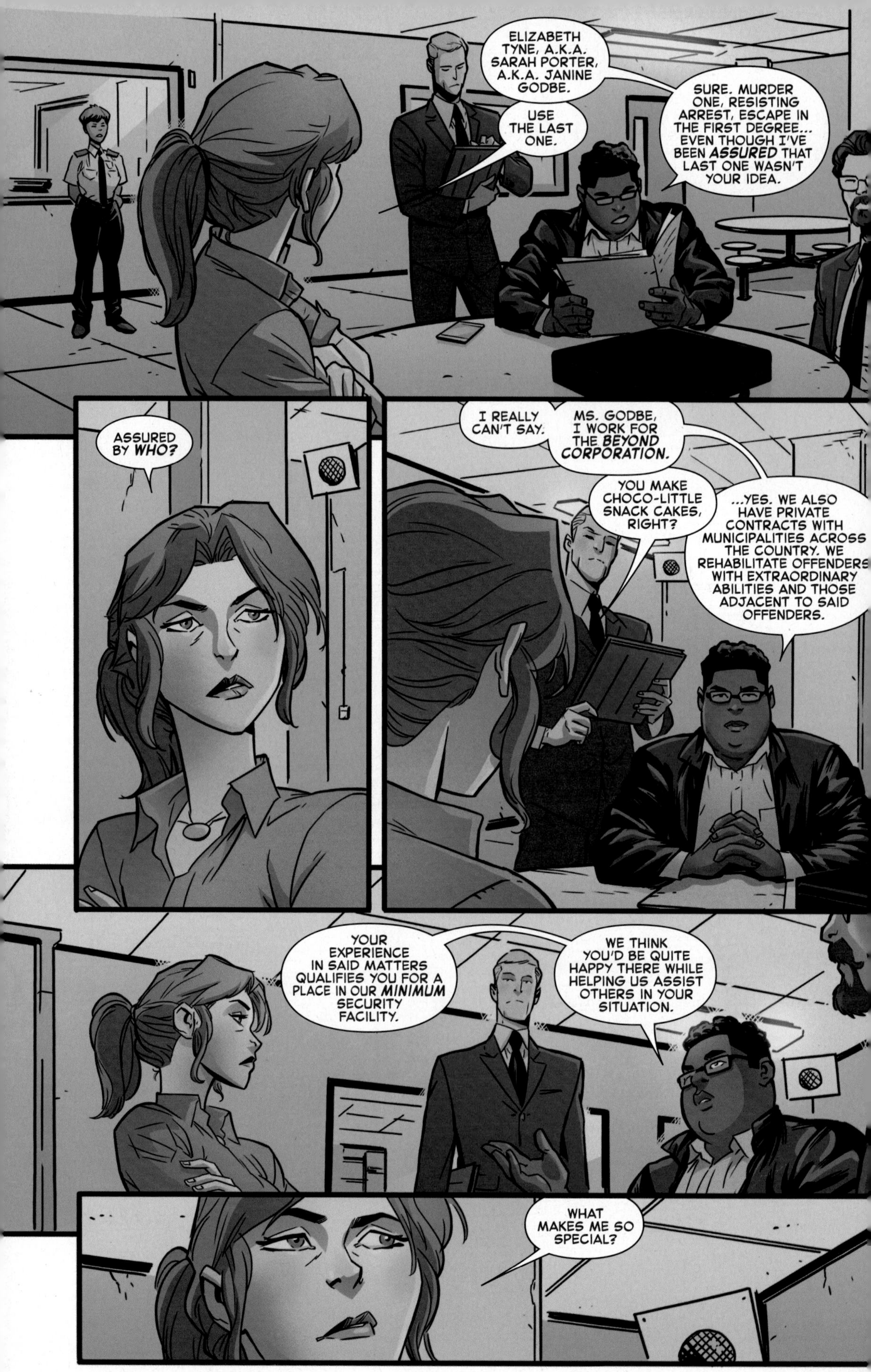
ELIZABETH TYNE, A.K.A. SARAH PORTER, A.K.A. JANINE GODBE.
USE THE LAST ONE.
SURE. MURDER ONE, RESISTING ARREST, ESCAPE IN THE FIRST DEGREE... EVEN THOUGH I'VE BEEN ASSURED THAT LAST ONE WASN'T YOUR IDEA.
ASSURED BY WHO?
I REALLY CAN'T SAY.
MS. GODBE, I WORK FOR THE BEYOND CORPORATION.
YOU MAKE CHOCO-LITTLE SNACK CAKES, RIGHT?
...YES. WE ALSO HAVE PRIVATE CONTRACTS WITH MUNICIPALITIES ACROSS THE COUNTRY. WE REHABILITATE OFFENDERS WITH EXTRAORDINARY ABILITIES AND THOSE ADJACENT TO SAID OFFENDERS.
YOUR EXPERIENCE IN SAID MATTERS QUALIFIES YOU FOR A PLACE IN OUR MINIMUM SECURITY FACILITY.
WE THINK YOU'D BE QUITE HAPPY THERE WHILE HELPING US ASSIST OTHERS IN YOUR SITUATION.
WHAT MAKES ME SO SPECIAL?

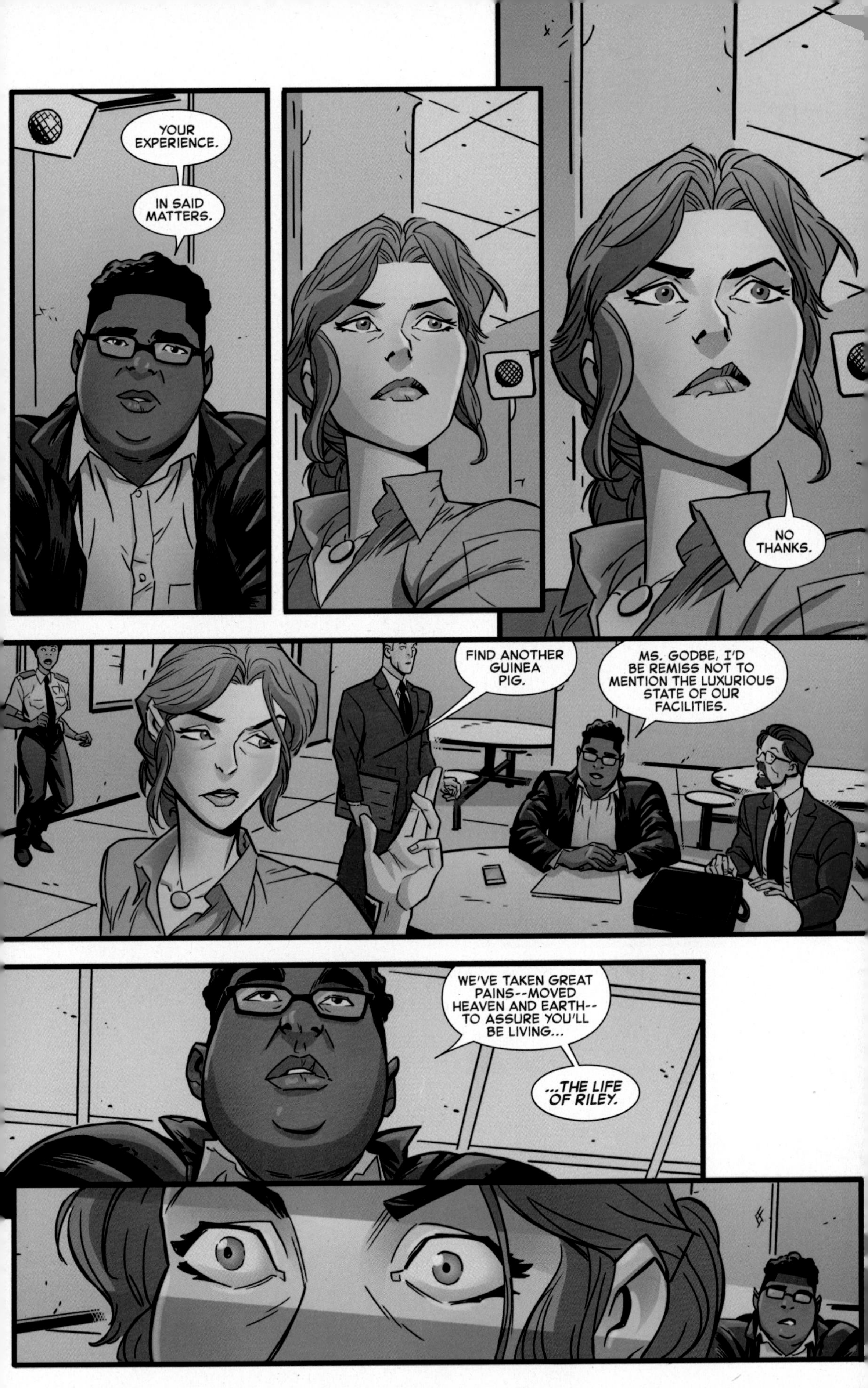
YOUR EXPERIENCE.
IN SAID MATTERS.
NO THANKS.
FIND ANOTHER GUINEA PIG.
MS. GODBE, I'D BE REMISS NOT TO MENTION THE LUXURIOUS STATE OF OUR FACILITIES.
WE'VE TAKEN GREAT PAINS--MOVED HEAVEN AND EARTH--TO ASSURE YOU'LL BE LIVING...
...THE LIFE OF RILEY.

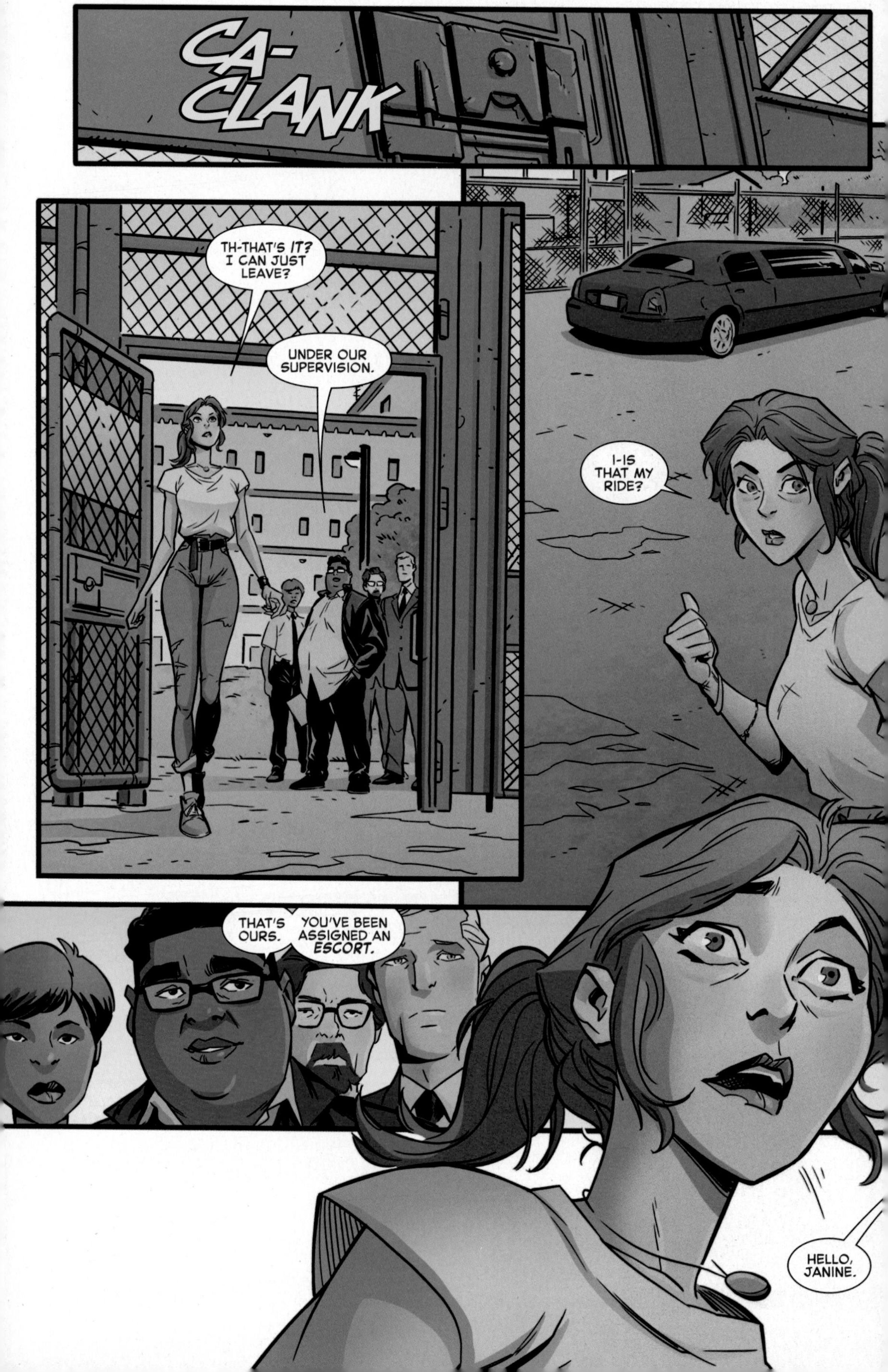
CA-CLANK
TH-THAT'S IT? I CAN JUST LEAVE?
UNDER OUR SUPERVISION.
I-IS THAT MY RIDE?
THAT'S OURS.
YOU'VE BEEN ASSIGNED AN ESCORT.
HELLO, JANINE.

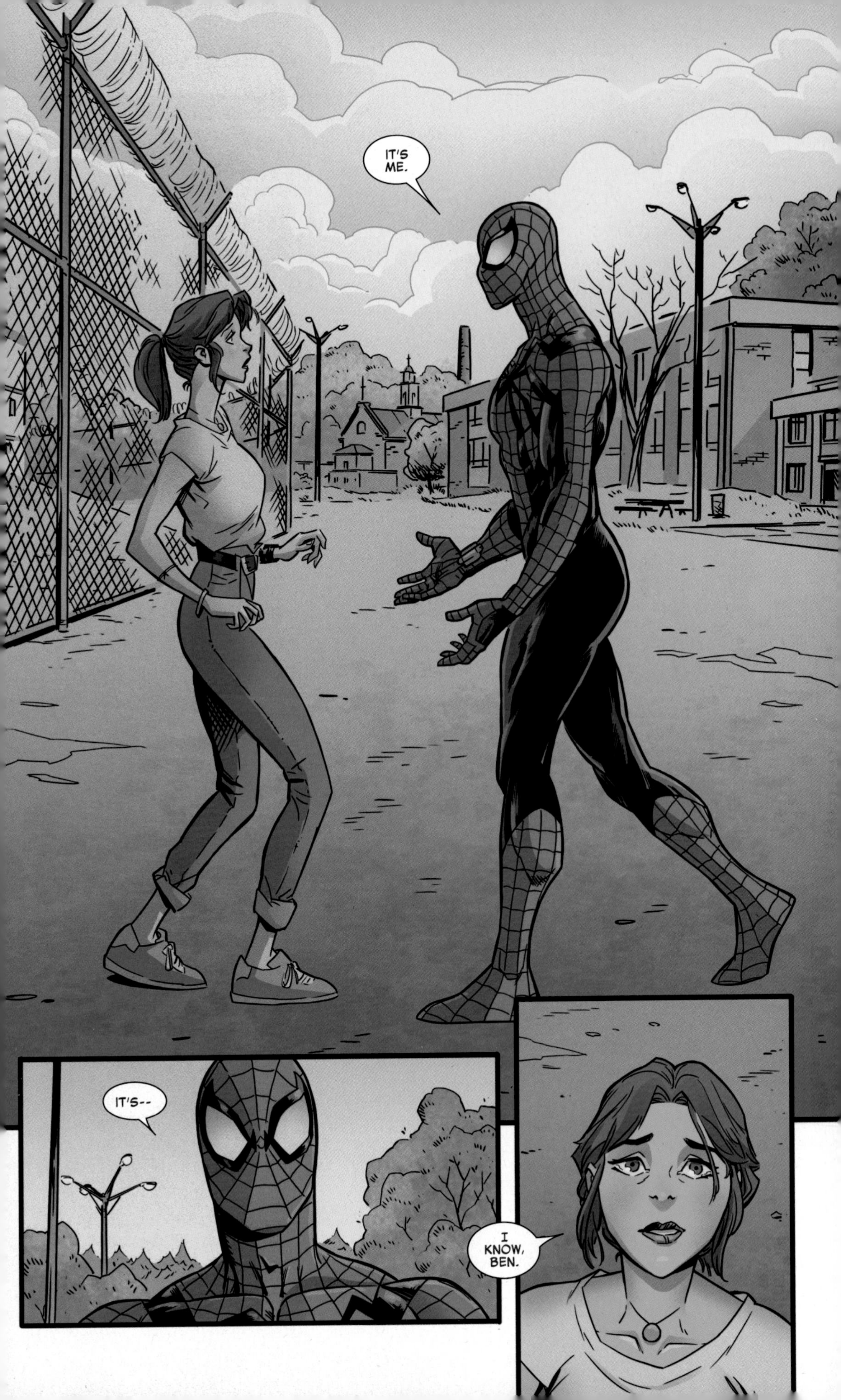

IT'S ME.
IT'S--
I KNOW, BEN.

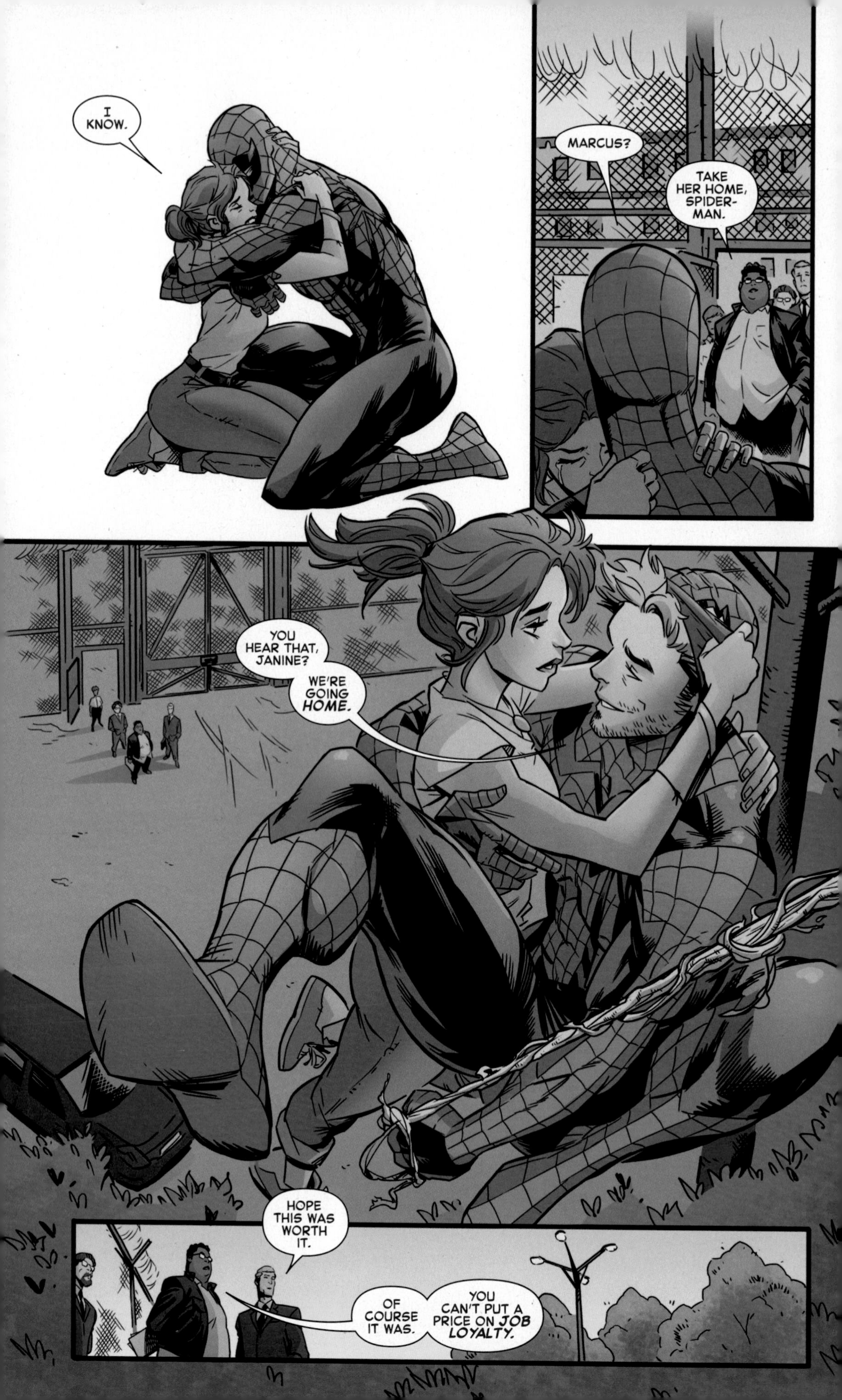

I KNOW.
MARCUS?
TAKE HER HOME, SPIDER-MAN.
YOU HEAR THAT, JANINE?
WE'RE GOING HOME.
HOPE THIS WAS WORTH IT.
OF COURSE IT WAS.
YOU CAN'T PUT A PRICE ON JOB LOYALTY.

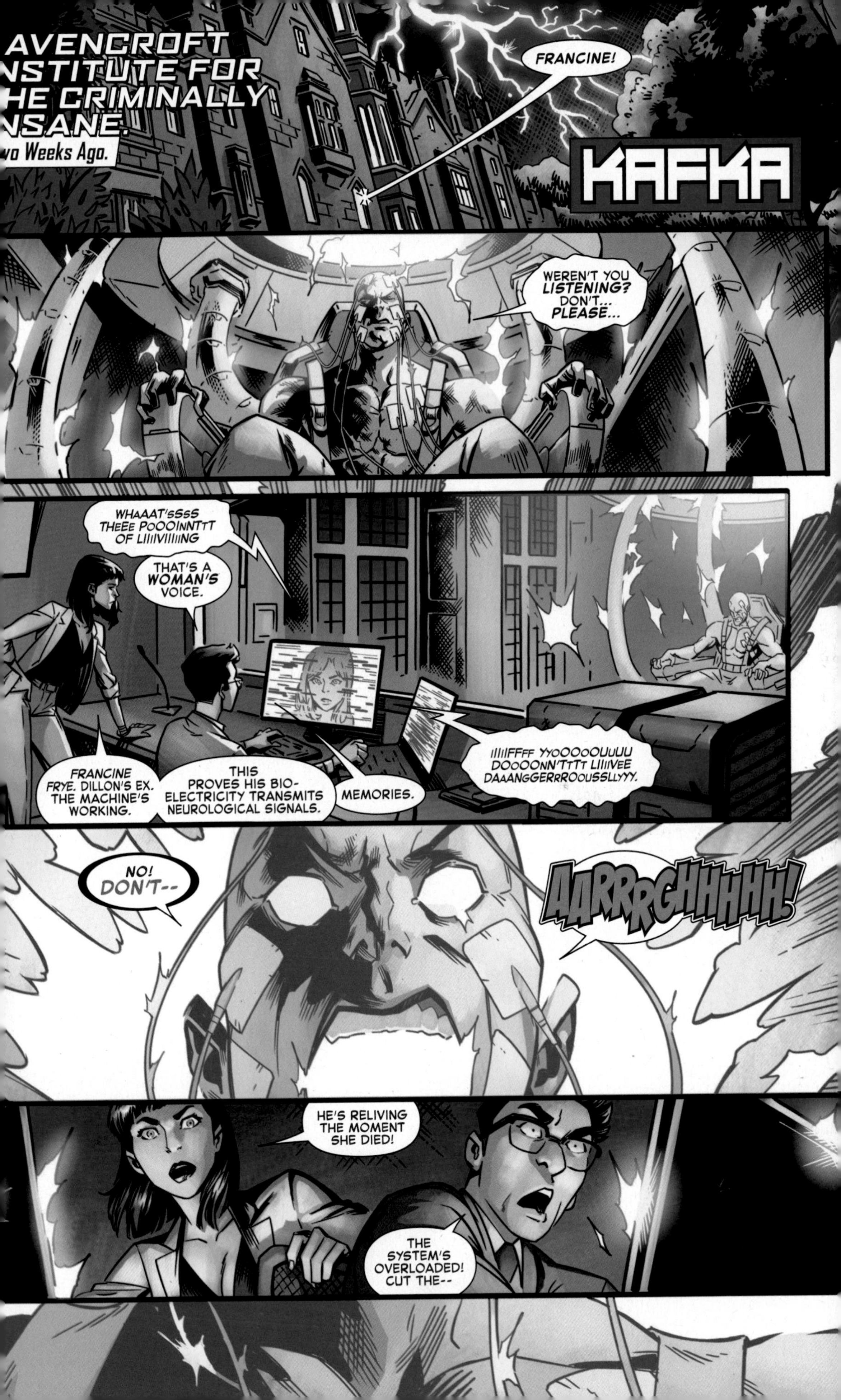
AVENCROFT NSTITUTE FOR HE CRIMINALLY NSANE.
vo Weeks Ago.
FRANCINE!
KAFKA
WEREN'T YOU LISTENING? DON'T... PLEASE...
WHAAAT'sSSS THEEE POOOINNTtT OF LIIIIVIIIIIING
THAT'S A WOMAN'S VOICE.
FRANCINE FRYE. DILLON'S EX. THE MACHINE'S WORKING.
THIS PROVES HIS BIO-ELECTRICITY TRANSMITS NEUROLOGICAL SIGNALS.
MEMORIES.
IIIIIFFFF YYOOOOOUUUU DOOOONN'TtTT LIIIIVEE DAAANGGERRROOUSSLLYYY.
NO! DON'T--
AARRRGHHHHH!
HE'S RELIVING THE MOMENT SHE DIED!
THE SYSTEM'S OVERLOADED! CUT THE--

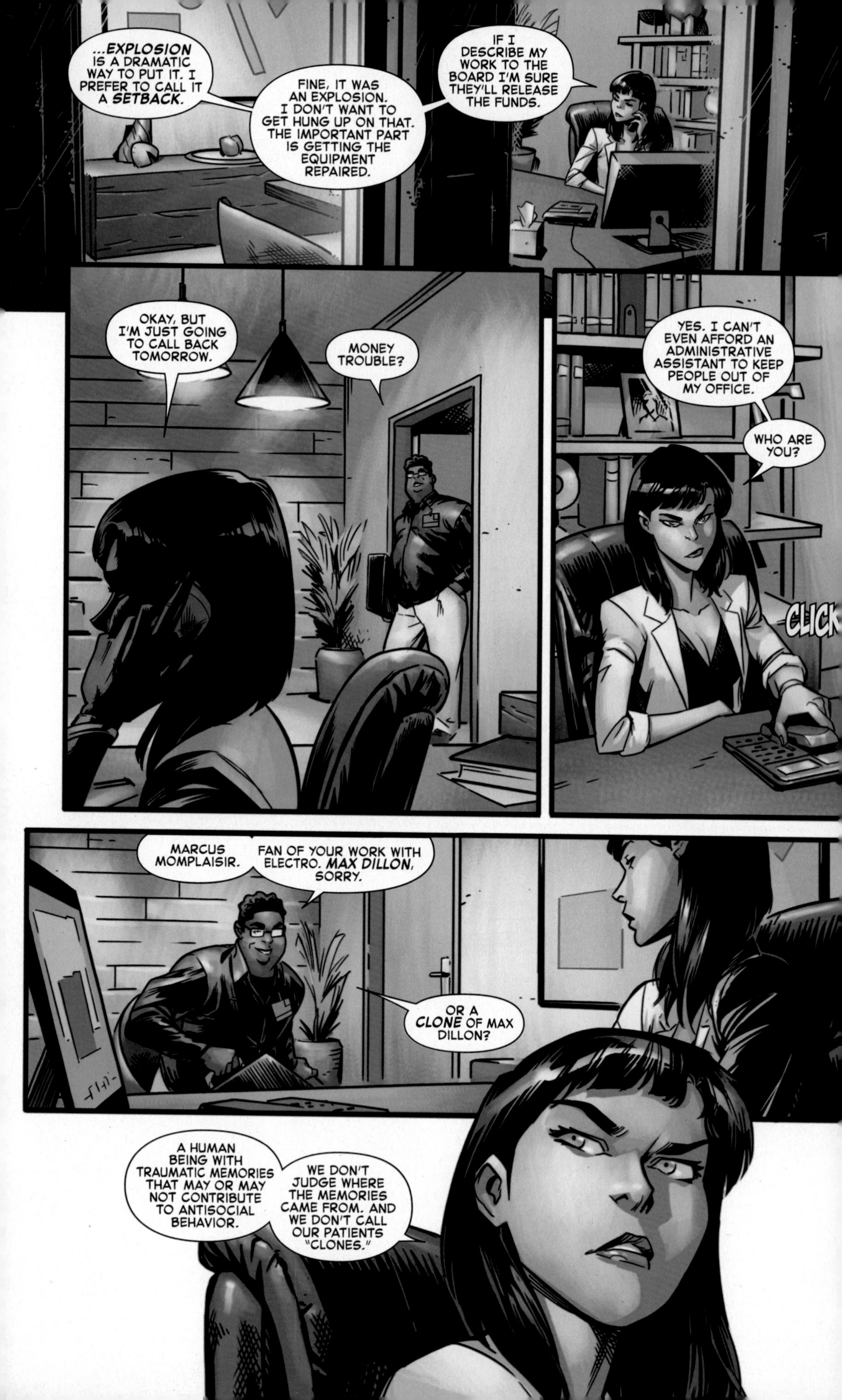
...EXPLOSION IS A DRAMATIC WAY TO PUT IT. I PREFER TO CALL IT A SETBACK.
FINE, IT WAS AN EXPLOSION. I DON'T WANT TO GET HUNG UP ON THAT. THE IMPORTANT PART IS GETTING THE EQUIPMENT REPAIRED.
IF I DESCRIBE MY WORK TO THE BOARD I'M SURE THEY'LL RELEASE THE FUNDS.
OKAY, BUT I'M JUST GOING TO CALL BACK TOMORROW.
MONEY TROUBLE?
YES. I CAN'T EVEN AFFORD AN ADMINISTRATIVE ASSISTANT TO KEEP PEOPLE OUT OF MY OFFICE.
WHO ARE YOU?
CLICK
MARCUS MOMPLAISIR.
FAN OF YOUR WORK WITH ELECTRO. MAX DILLON, SORRY.
OR A CLONE OF MAX DILLON?
A HUMAN BEING WITH TRAUMATIC MEMORIES THAT MAY OR MAY NOT CONTRIBUTE TO ANTISOCIAL BEHAVIOR.
WE DON'T JUDGE WHERE THE MEMORIES CAME FROM. AND WE DON'T CALL OUR PATIENTS "CLONES."

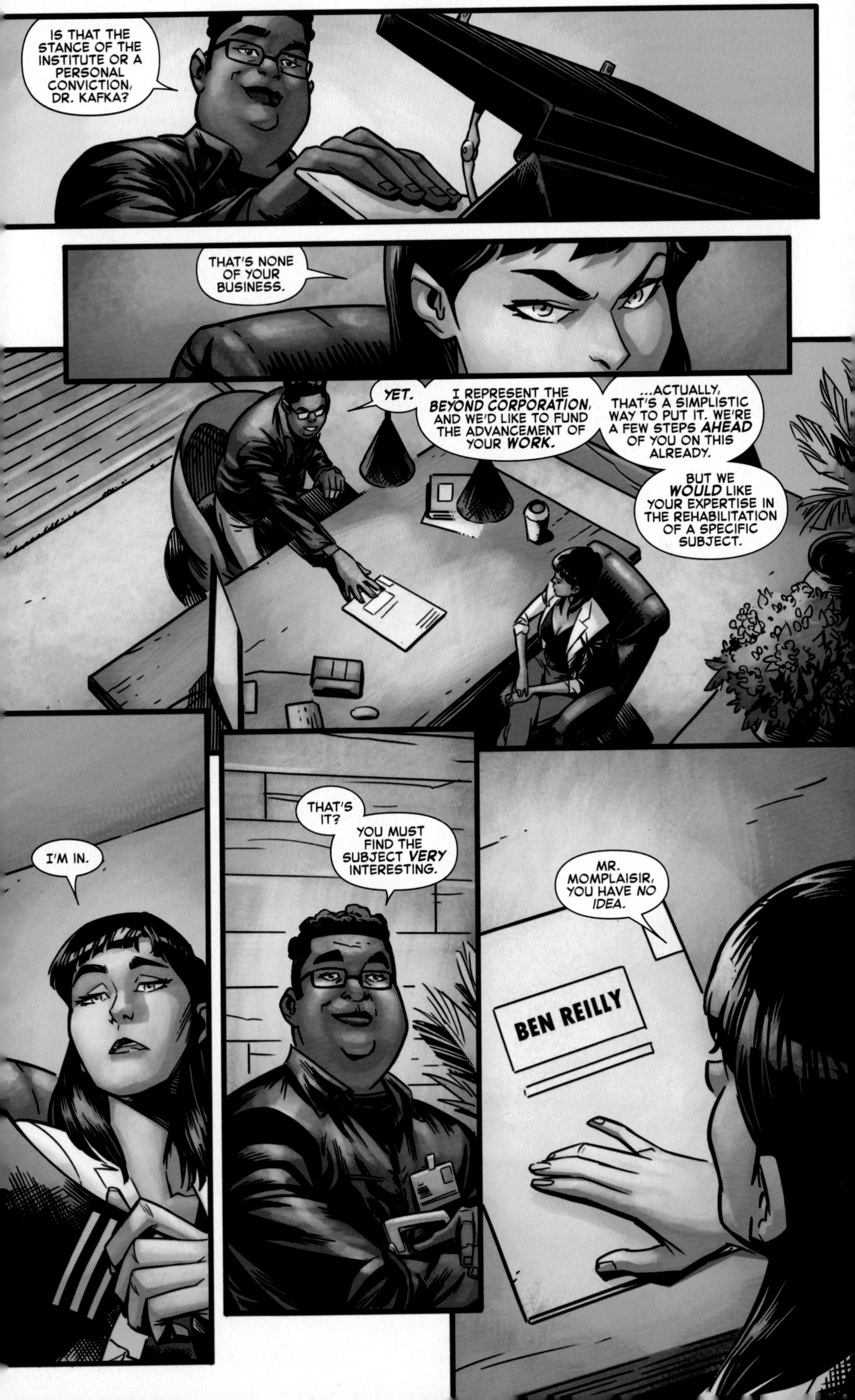

IS THAT THE STANCE OF THE INSTITUTE OR A PERSONAL CONVICTION, DR. KAFKA?
THAT'S NONE OF YOUR BUSINESS.
YET.
I REPRESENT THE BEYOND CORPORATION, AND WE'D LIKE TO FUND THE ADVANCEMENT OF YOUR WORK.
...ACTUALLY, THAT'S A SIMPLISTIC WAY TO PUT IT. WE'RE A FEW STEPS AHEAD OF YOU ON THIS ALREADY.
BUT WE WOULD LIKE YOUR EXPERTISE IN THE REHABILITATION OF A SPECIFIC SUBJECT.
I'M IN.
THAT'S IT?
YOU MUST FIND THE SUBJECT VERY INTERESTING.
MR. MOMPLAISIR, YOU HAVE NO IDEA.
BEN REILLY

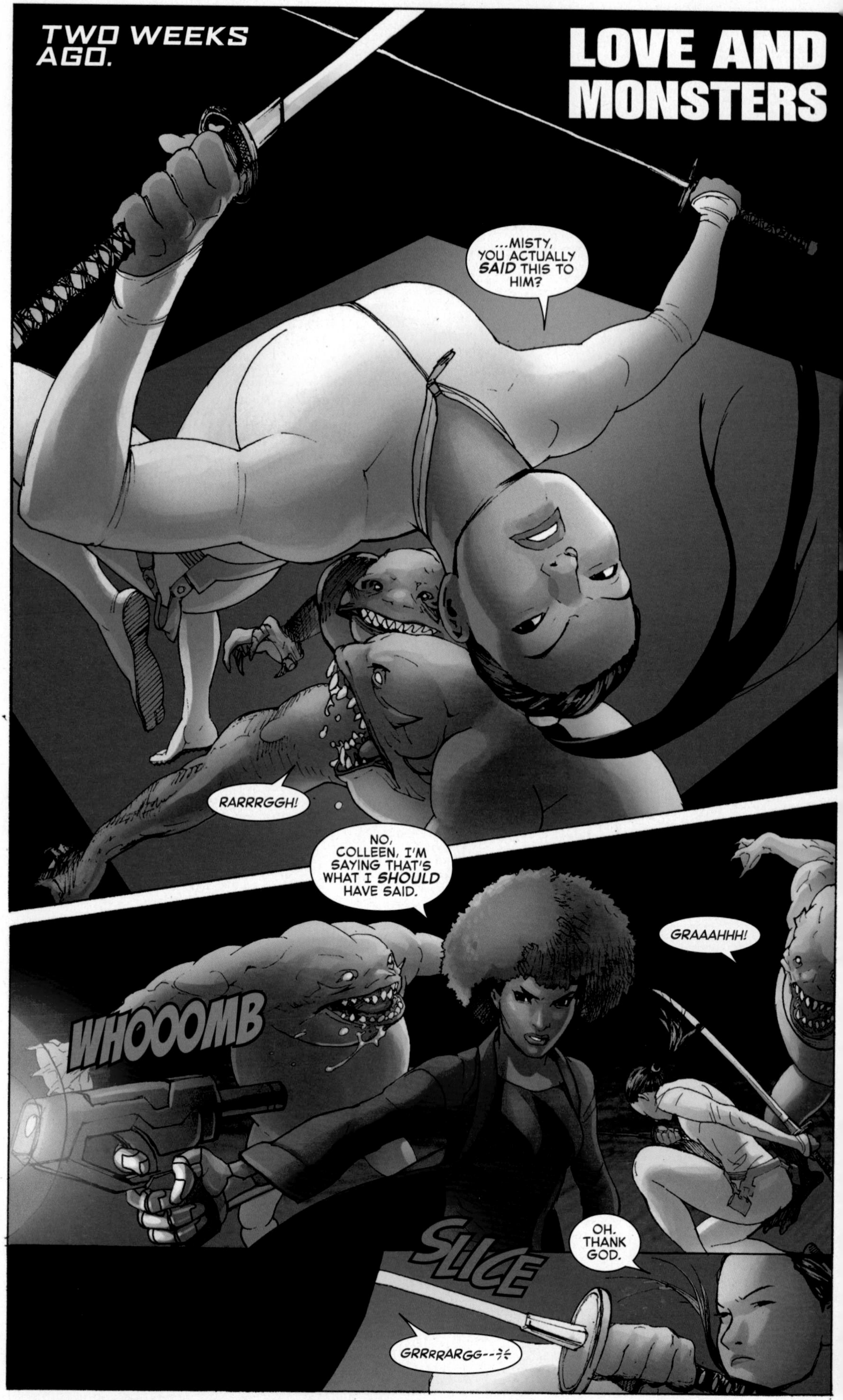

TWO WEEKS AGO.
LOVE AND MONSTERS
...MISTY, YOU ACTUALLY SAID THIS TO HIM?
RARRRGGH!
NO, COLLEEN, I'M SAYING THAT'S WHAT I SHOULD HAVE SAID.
GRAAAHHH!
WHOOOMB
SLICE
OH. THANK GOD.
GRRRRARGG--

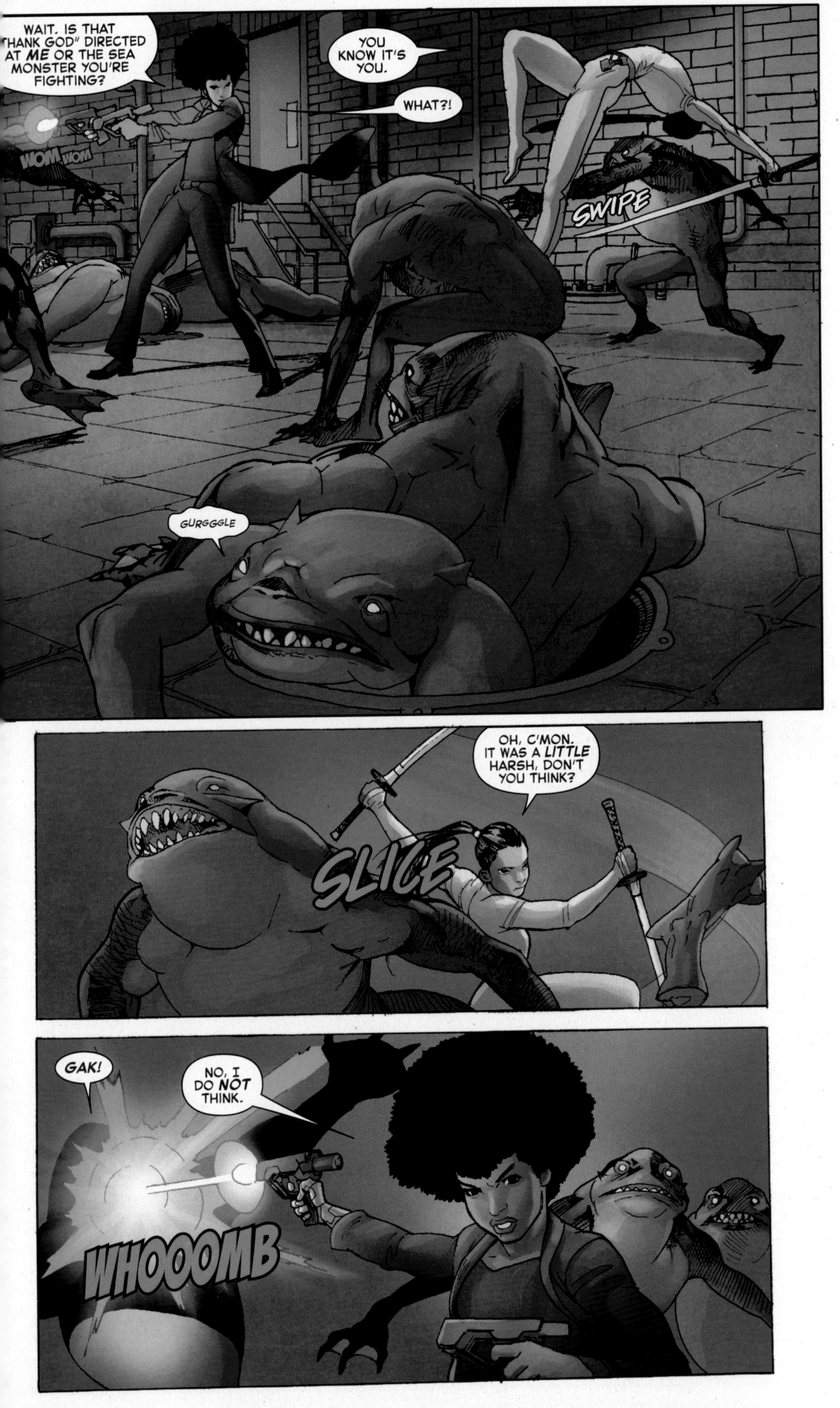

WAIT. IS THAT "THANK GOD" DIRECTED AT *ME* OR THE SEA MONSTER YOU'RE FIGHTING?
YOU KNOW IT'S YOU.
WHAT?!
WOM WOM
SWIPE
GURGGGLE
OH, C'MON. IT WAS A *LITTLE* HARSH, DON'T YOU THINK?
SLICE
GAK!
NO, I DO *NOT* THINK.
WHOOOMB

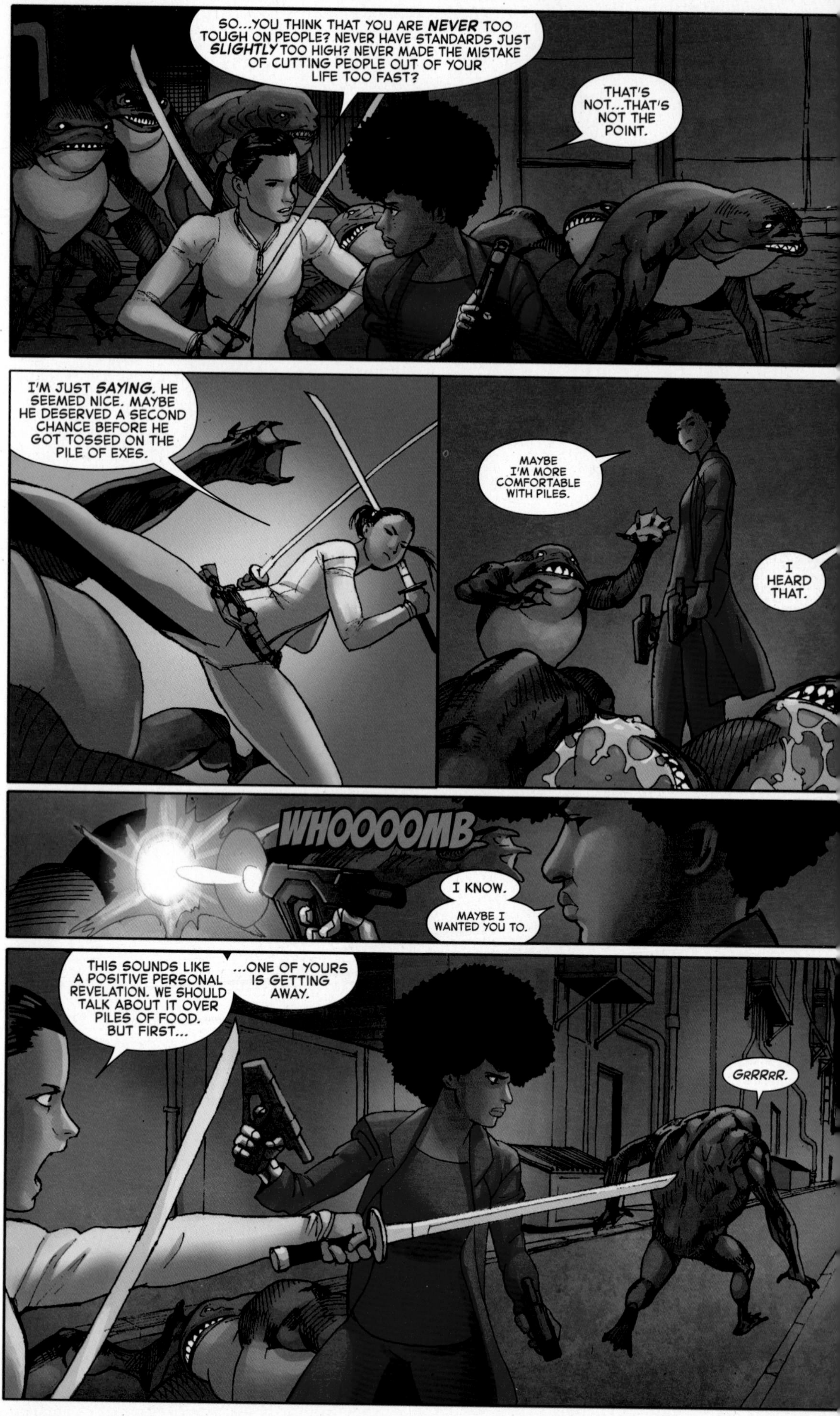
SO...YOU THINK THAT YOU ARE NEVER TOO TOUGH ON PEOPLE? NEVER HAVE STANDARDS JUST SLIGHTLY TOO HIGH? NEVER MADE THE MISTAKE OF CUTTING PEOPLE OUT OF YOUR LIFE TOO FAST?
THAT'S NOT...THAT'S NOT THE POINT.
I'M JUST SAYING. HE SEEMED NICE. MAYBE HE DESERVED A SECOND CHANCE BEFORE HE GOT TOSSED ON THE PILE OF EXES.
MAYBE I'M MORE COMFORTABLE WITH PILES.
I HEARD THAT.
WHOOOOMB
I KNOW.
MAYBE I WANTED YOU TO.
THIS SOUNDS LIKE A POSITIVE PERSONAL REVELATION. WE SHOULD TALK ABOUT IT OVER PILES OF FOOD. BUT FIRST...
...ONE OF YOURS IS GETTING AWAY.
GRRRRR.

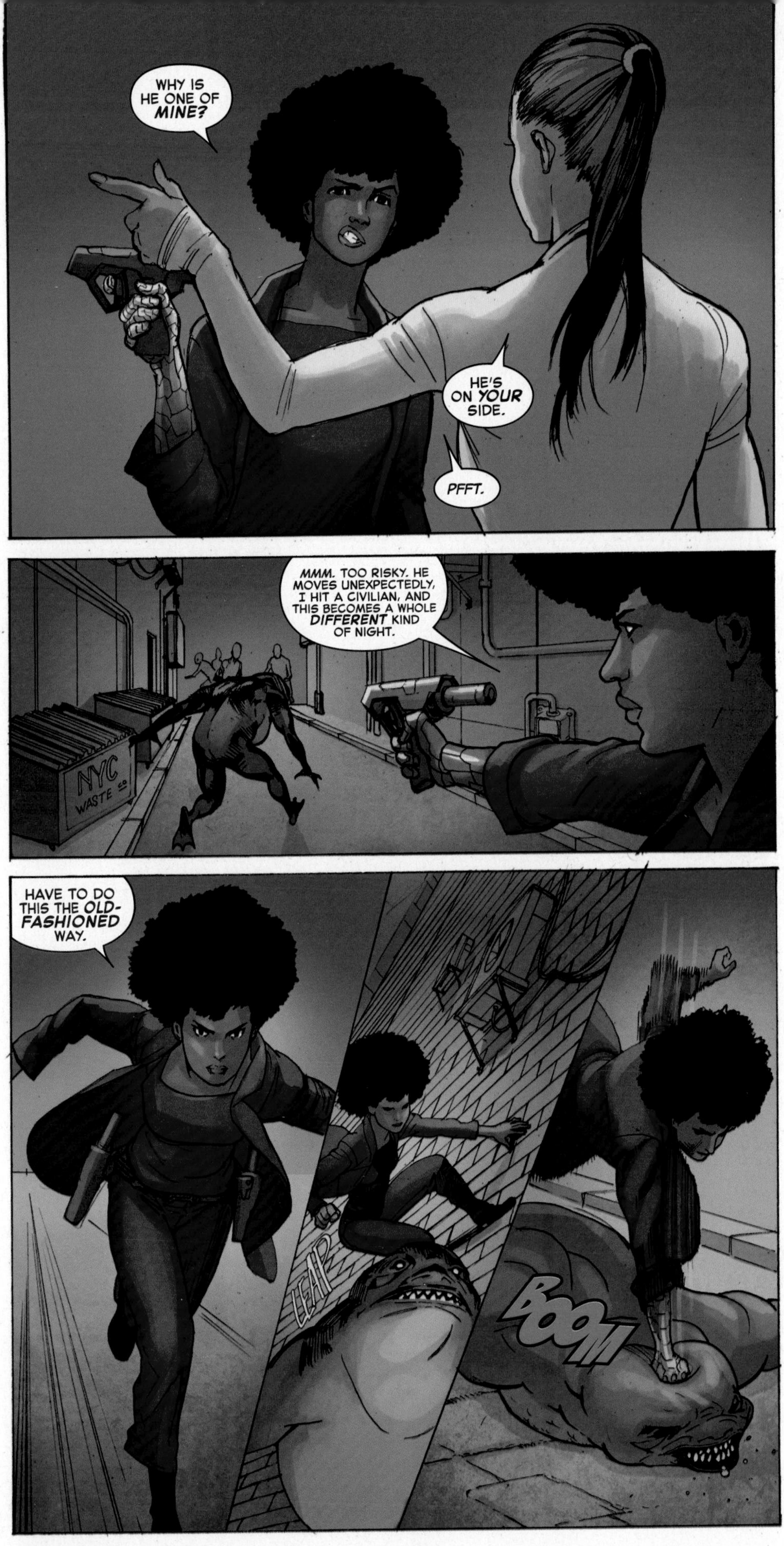
WHY IS HE ONE OF MINE?
HE'S ON YOUR SIDE.
PFFT.
MMM. TOO RISKY. HE MOVES UNEXPECTEDLY, I HIT A CIVILIAN, AND THIS BECOMES A WHOLE DIFFERENT KIND OF NIGHT.
NYC WASTE CO
HAVE TO DO THIS THE OLD-FASHIONED WAY.
LEAP
BOOM

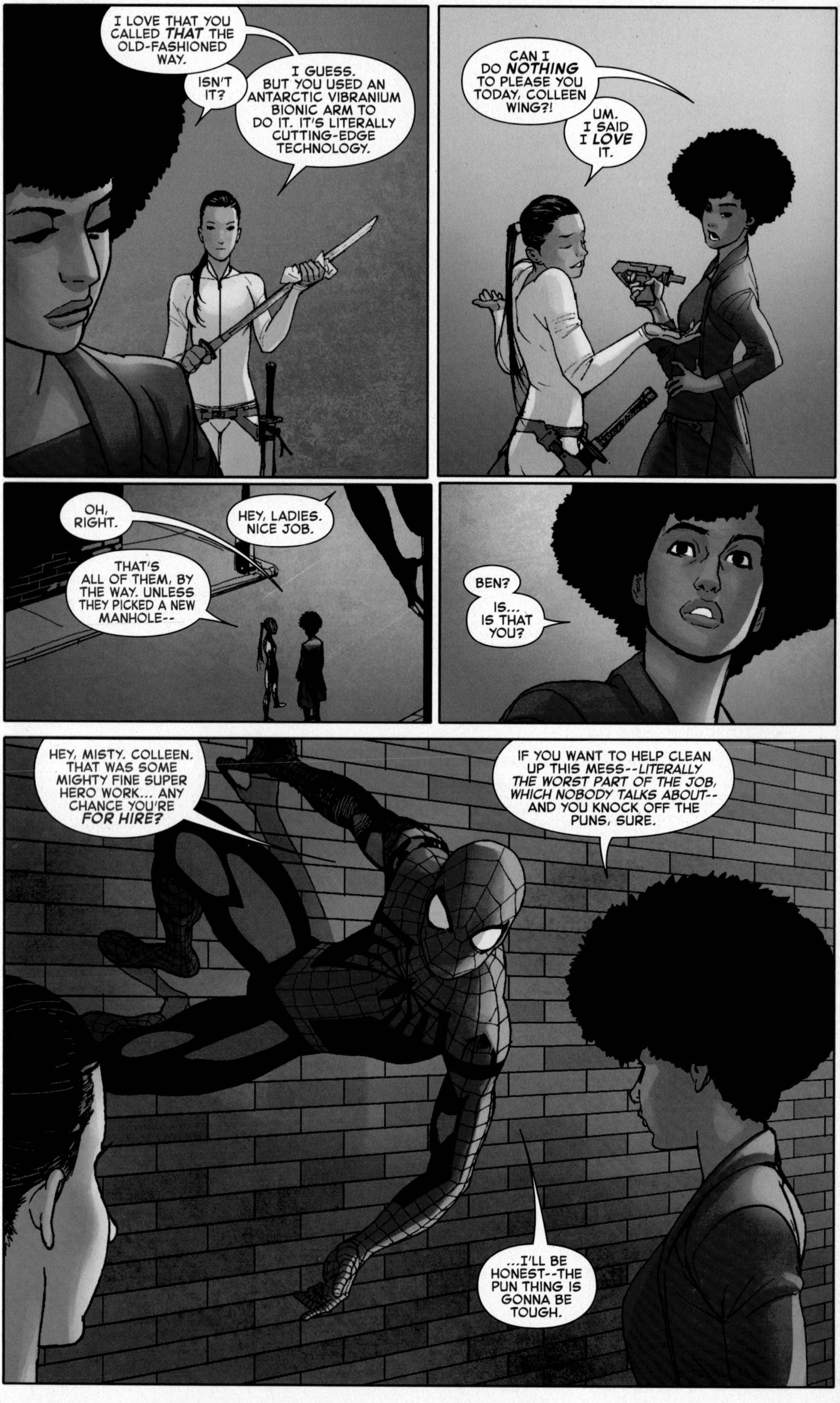
I LOVE THAT YOU CALLED THAT THE OLD-FASHIONED WAY.
ISN'T IT?
I GUESS. BUT YOU USED AN ANTARCTIC VIBRANIUM BIONIC ARM TO DO IT. IT'S LITERALLY CUTTING-EDGE TECHNOLOGY.
CAN I DO NOTHING TO PLEASE YOU TODAY, COLLEEN WING?!
UM. I SAID I LOVE IT.
OH, RIGHT.
HEY, LADIES. NICE JOB.
THAT'S ALL OF THEM, BY THE WAY. UNLESS THEY PICKED A NEW MANHOLE--
BEN?
IS... IS THAT YOU?
HEY, MISTY. COLLEEN. THAT WAS SOME MIGHTY FINE SUPER HERO WORK... ANY CHANCE YOU'RE FOR HIRE?
IF YOU WANT TO HELP CLEAN UP THIS MESS--LITERALLY THE WORST PART OF THE JOB, WHICH NOBODY TALKS ABOUT--AND YOU KNOCK OFF THE PUNS, SURE.
...I'LL BE HONEST--THE PUN THING IS GONNA BE TOUGH.

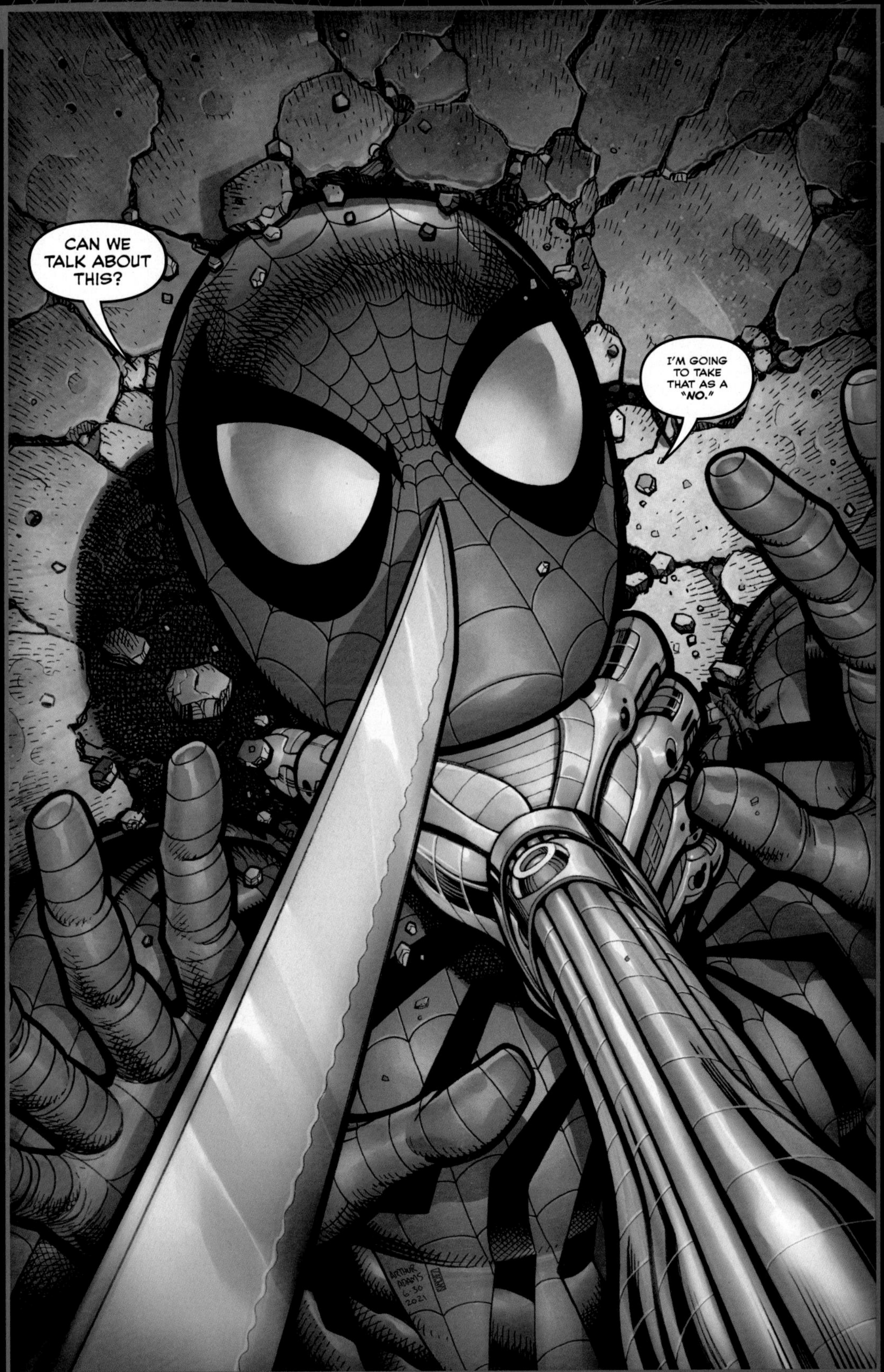
CAN WE TALK ABOUT THIS?
I'M GOING TO TAKE THAT AS A "NO."

NOW

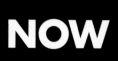

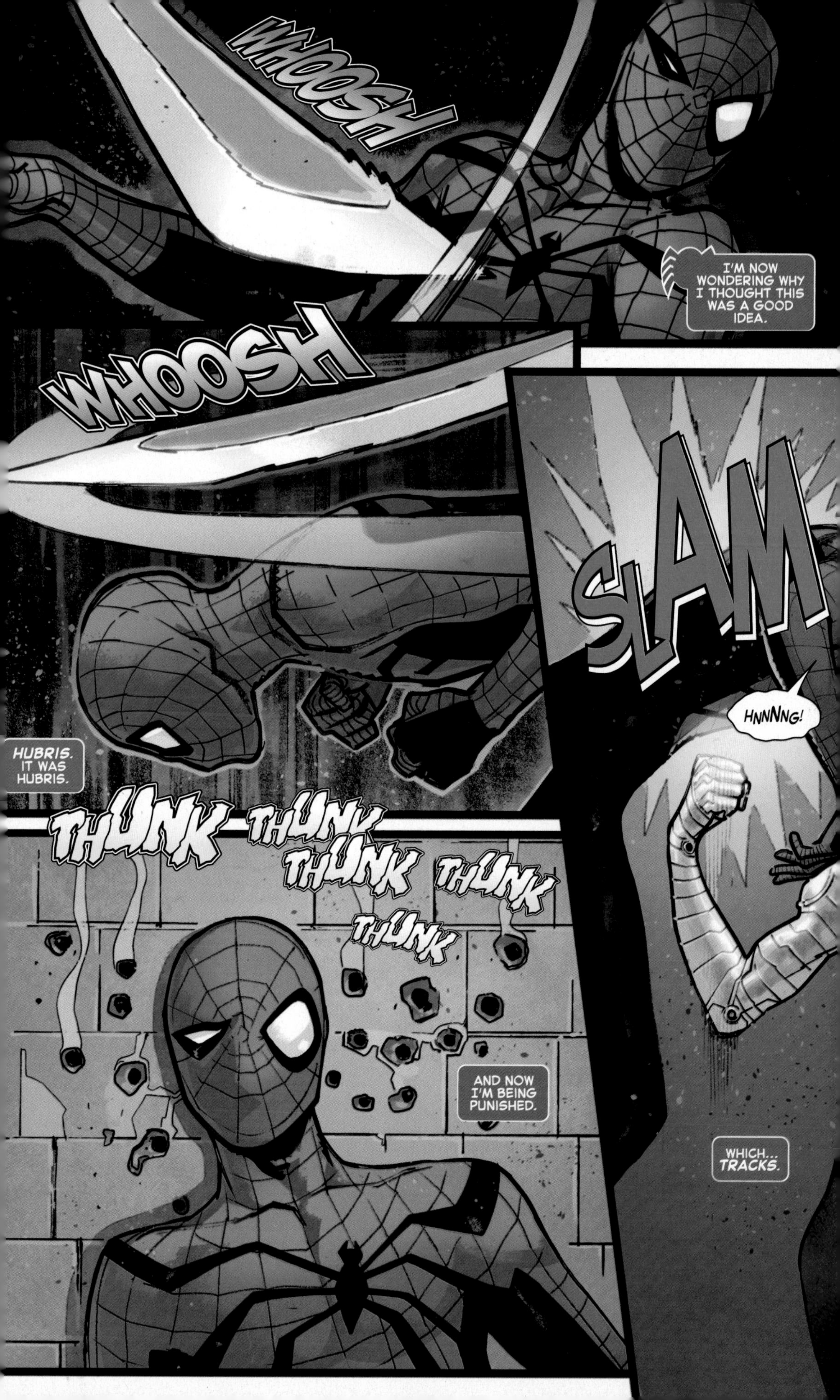
WHOOSH
I'M NOW WONDERING WHY I THOUGHT THIS WAS A GOOD IDEA.
WHOOSH
HUBRIS. IT WAS HUBRIS.
SLAM
HNNNNG!
THUNK THUNK THUNK THUNK THUNK
AND NOW I'M BEING PUNISHED.
WHICH... TRACKS.

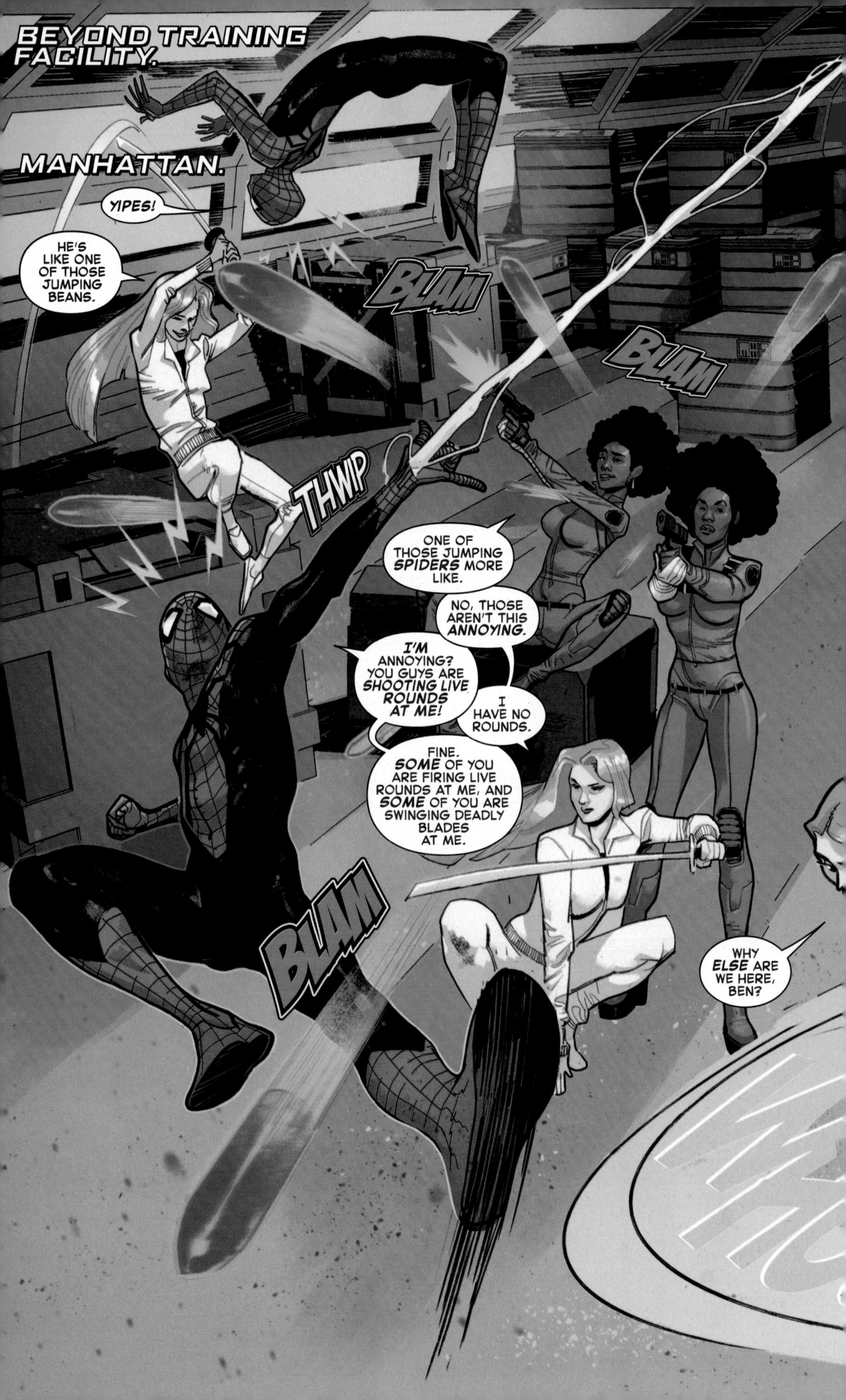
BEYOND TRAINING FACILITY.
MANHATTAN.
YIPES!
HE'S LIKE ONE OF THOSE JUMPING BEANS.
BLAM
BLAM
THWIP
ONE OF THOSE JUMPING SPIDERS MORE LIKE.
NO, THOSE AREN'T THIS ANNOYING.
I'M ANNOYING? YOU GUYS ARE SHOOTING LIVE ROUNDS AT ME!
I HAVE NO ROUNDS.
FINE. SOME OF YOU ARE FIRING LIVE ROUNDS AT ME, AND SOME OF YOU ARE SWINGING DEADLY BLADES AT ME.
BLAM
WHY ELSE ARE WE HERE, BEN?

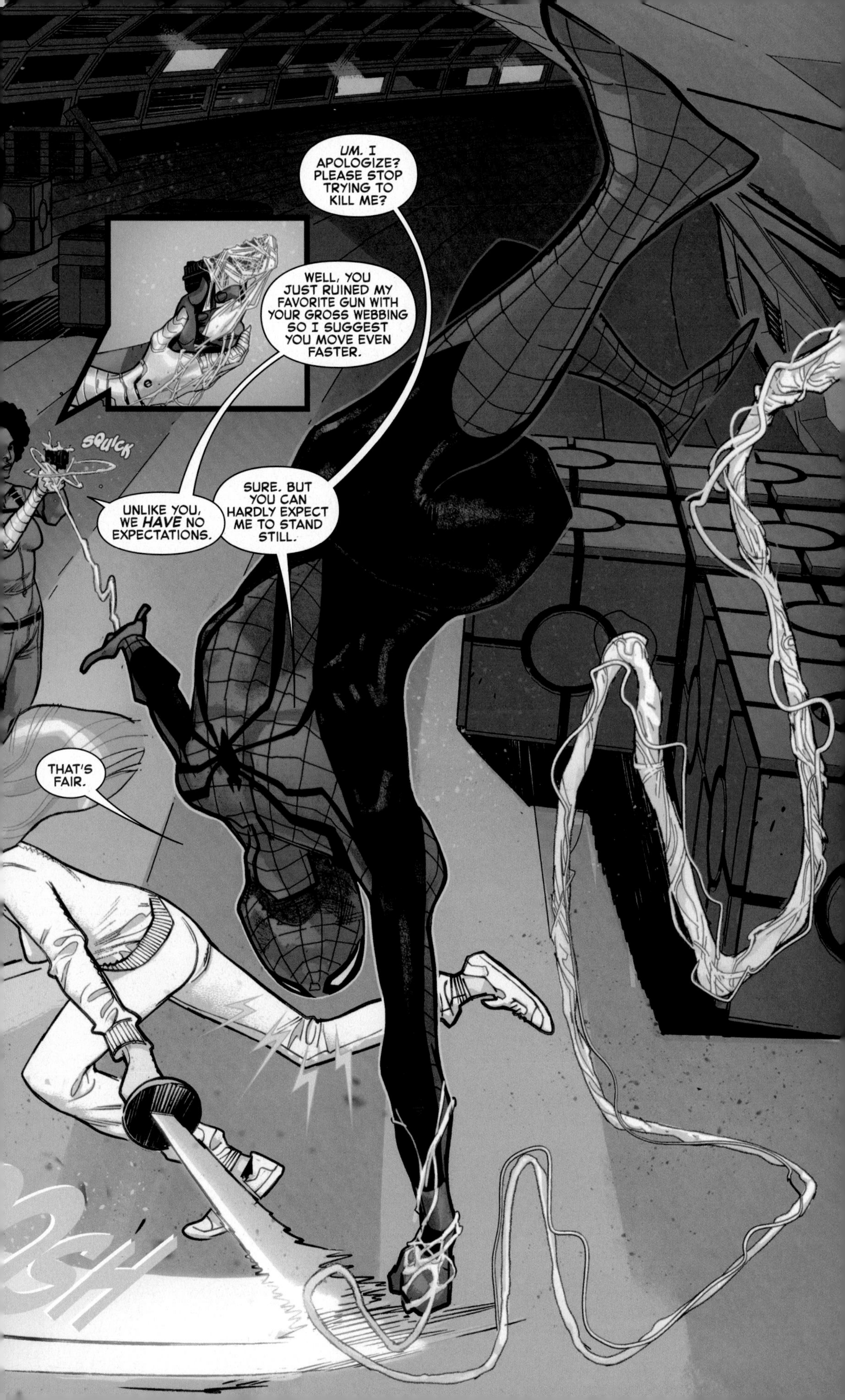

UM. I APOLOGIZE? PLEASE STOP TRYING TO KILL ME?
WELL, YOU JUST RUINED MY FAVORITE GUN WITH YOUR GROSS WEBBING SO I SUGGEST YOU MOVE EVEN FASTER.
SQUICK
SURE. BUT YOU CAN HARDLY EXPECT ME TO STAND STILL.
UNLIKE YOU, WE *HAVE* NO EXPECTATIONS.
THAT'S FAIR.

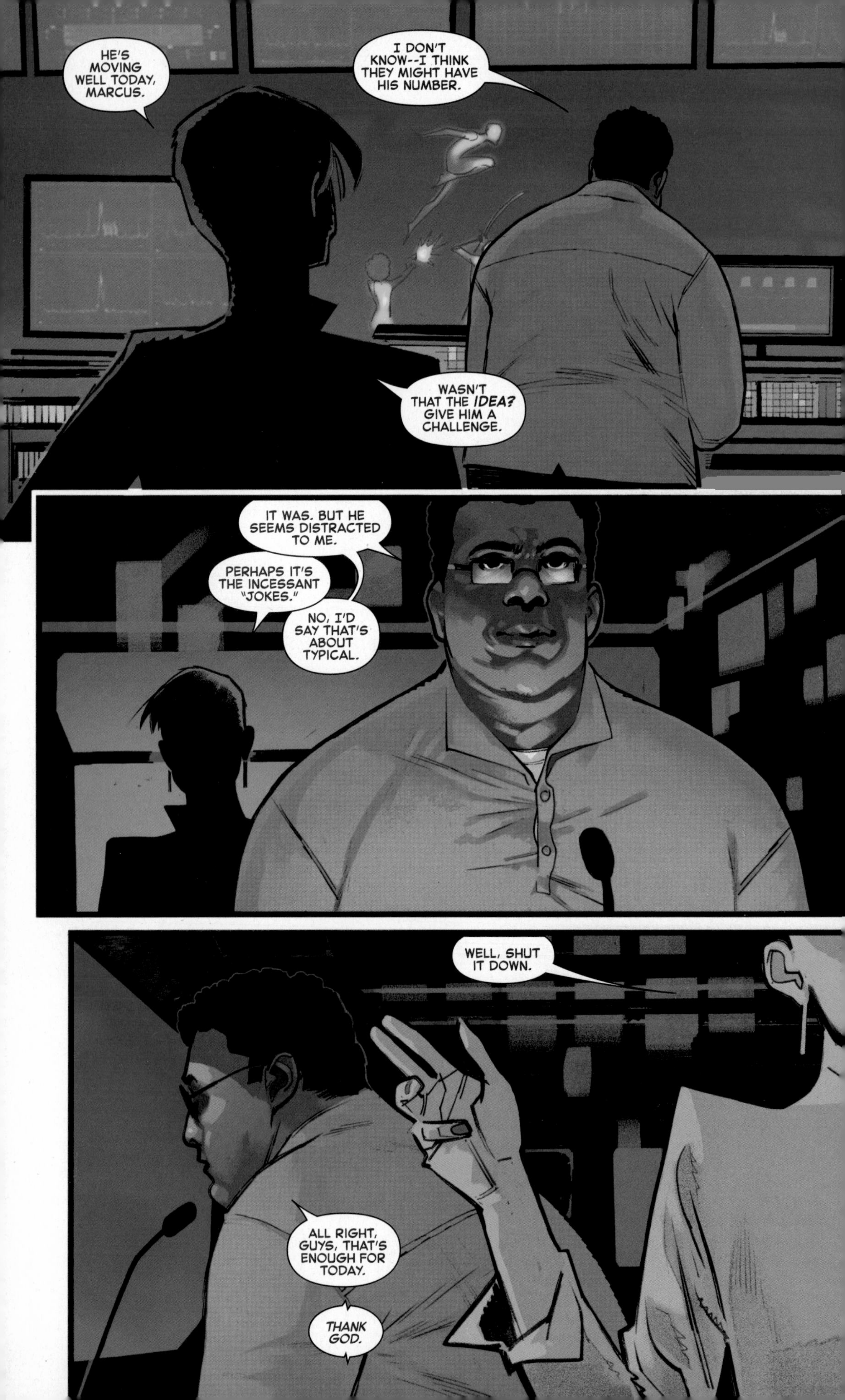
HE'S MOVING WELL TODAY, MARCUS.
I DON'T KNOW--I THINK THEY MIGHT HAVE HIS NUMBER.
WASN'T THAT THE *IDEA?* GIVE HIM A CHALLENGE.
IT WAS. BUT HE SEEMS DISTRACTED TO ME.
PERHAPS IT'S THE INCESSANT "JOKES."
NO, I'D SAY THAT'S ABOUT TYPICAL.
WELL, SHUT IT DOWN.
ALL RIGHT, GUYS, THAT'S ENOUGH FOR TODAY.
THANK GOD.

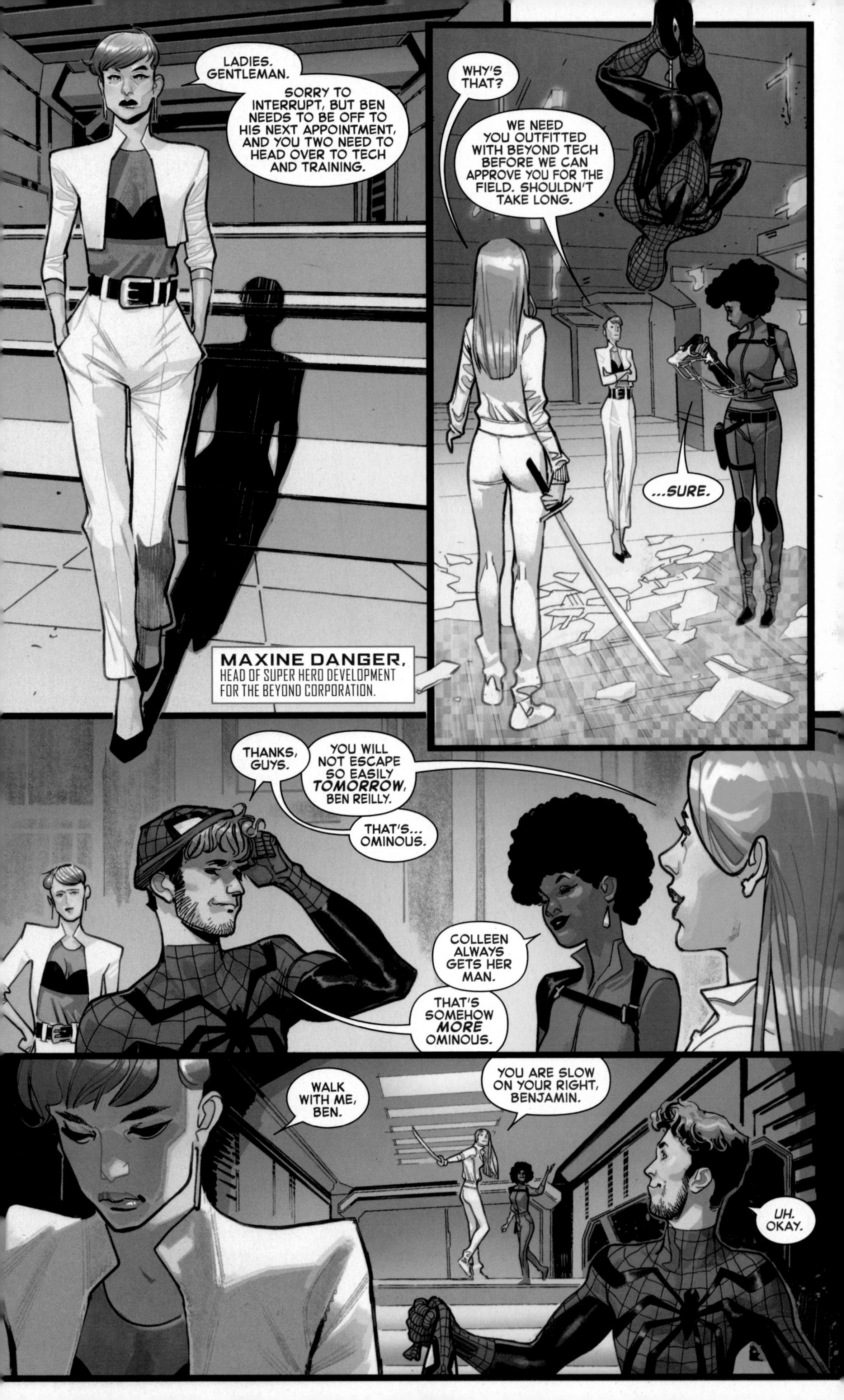
LADIES. GENTLEMAN.
SORRY TO INTERRUPT, BUT BEN NEEDS TO BE OFF TO HIS NEXT APPOINTMENT, AND YOU TWO NEED TO HEAD OVER TO TECH AND TRAINING.
MAXINE DANGER, HEAD OF SUPER HERO DEVELOPMENT FOR THE BEYOND CORPORATION.
WHY'S THAT?
WE NEED YOU OUTFITTED WITH BEYOND TECH BEFORE WE CAN APPROVE YOU FOR THE FIELD. SHOULDN'T TAKE LONG.
...SURE.
THANKS, GUYS.
YOU WILL NOT ESCAPE SO EASILY *TOMORROW*, BEN REILLY.
THAT'S... OMINOUS.
COLLEEN ALWAYS GETS HER MAN.
THAT'S SOMEHOW *MORE* OMINOUS.
WALK WITH ME, BEN.
YOU ARE SLOW ON YOUR RIGHT, BENJAMIN.
UH. OKAY.

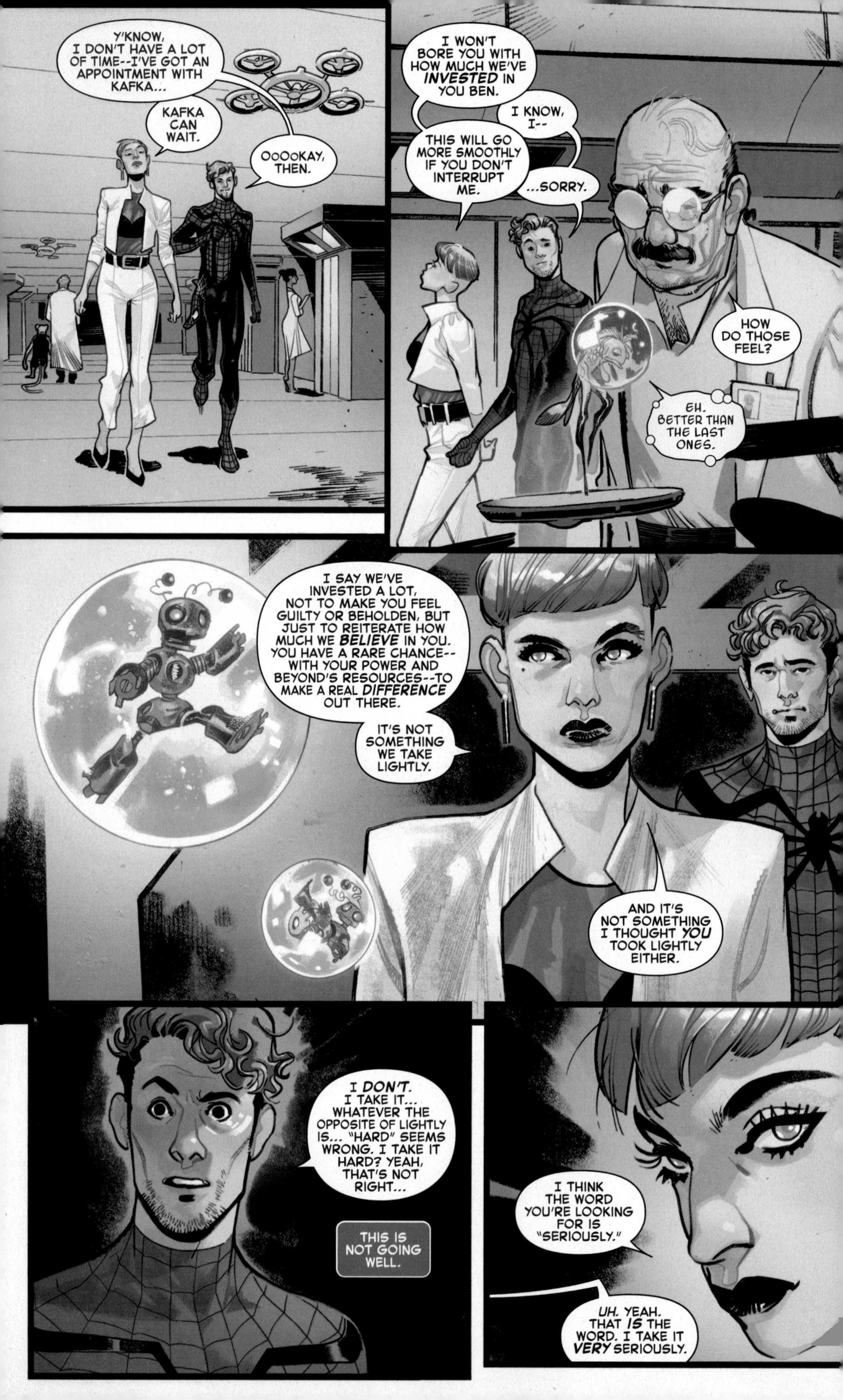
Y'KNOW, I DON'T HAVE A LOT OF TIME--I'VE GOT AN APPOINTMENT WITH KAFKA...
KAFKA CAN WAIT.
OoOoKAY, THEN.
I WON'T BORE YOU WITH HOW MUCH WE'VE INVESTED IN YOU BEN.
I KNOW, I--
THIS WILL GO MORE SMOOTHLY IF YOU DON'T INTERRUPT ME.
...SORRY.
HOW DO THOSE FEEL?
EH. BETTER THAN THE LAST ONES.
I SAY WE'VE INVESTED A LOT, NOT TO MAKE YOU FEEL GUILTY OR BEHOLDEN, BUT JUST TO REITERATE HOW MUCH WE BELIEVE IN YOU. YOU HAVE A RARE CHANCE-- WITH YOUR POWER AND BEYOND'S RESOURCES--TO MAKE A REAL DIFFERENCE OUT THERE.
IT'S NOT SOMETHING WE TAKE LIGHTLY.
AND IT'S NOT SOMETHING I THOUGHT YOU TOOK LIGHTLY EITHER.
I DON'T. I TAKE IT... WHATEVER THE OPPOSITE OF LIGHTLY IS... "HARD" SEEMS WRONG. I TAKE IT HARD? YEAH, THAT'S NOT RIGHT...
THIS IS NOT GOING WELL.
I THINK THE WORD YOU'RE LOOKING FOR IS "SERIOUSLY."
UH. YEAH. THAT IS THE WORD. I TAKE IT VERY SERIOUSLY.

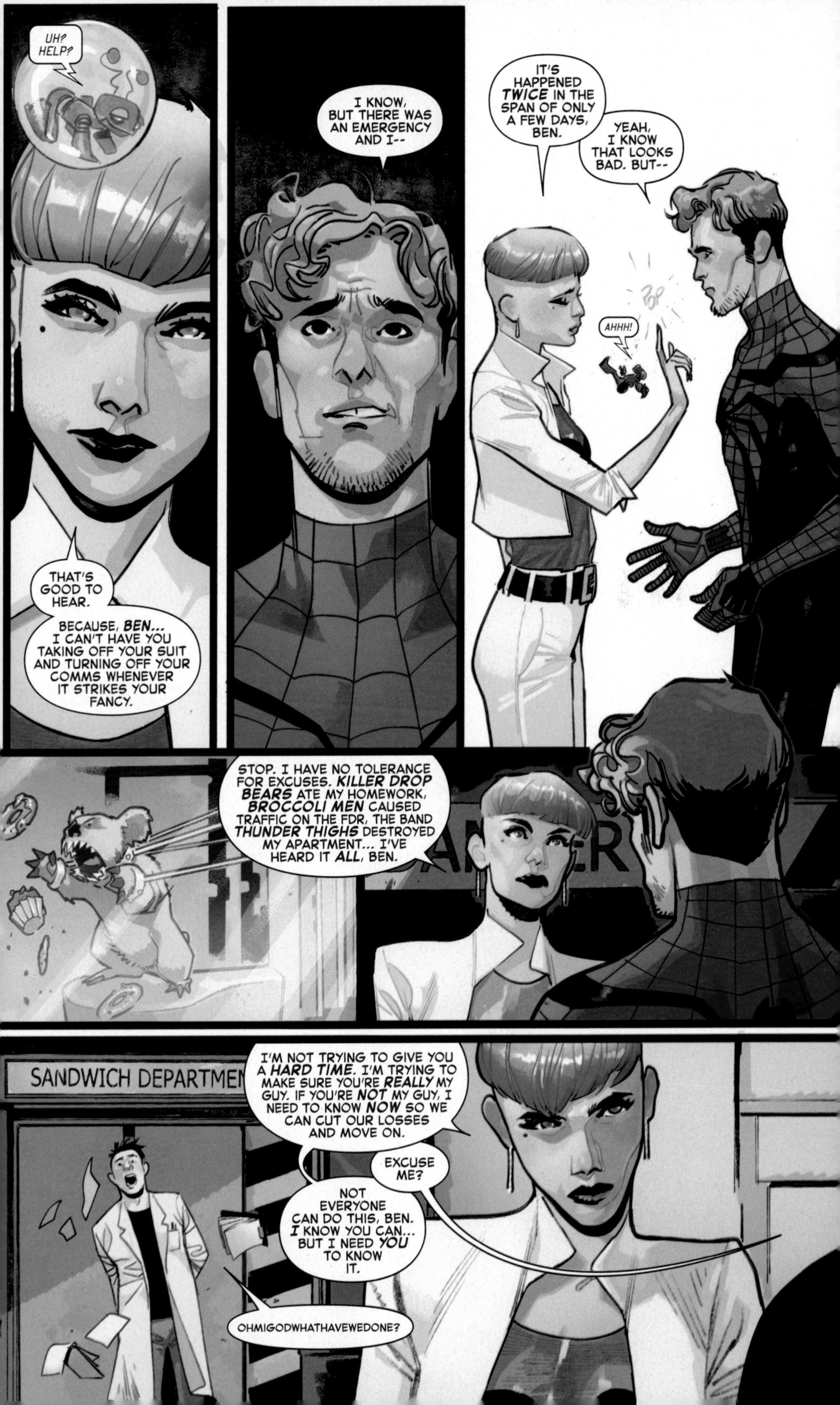
UH? HELP?
THAT'S GOOD TO HEAR.
BECAUSE, BEN... I CAN'T HAVE YOU TAKING OFF YOUR SUIT AND TURNING OFF YOUR COMMS WHENEVER IT STRIKES YOUR FANCY.
I KNOW, BUT THERE WAS AN EMERGENCY AND I--
IT'S HAPPENED TWICE IN THE SPAN OF ONLY A FEW DAYS, BEN.
YEAH, I KNOW THAT LOOKS BAD. BUT--
AHHH!
STOP. I HAVE NO TOLERANCE FOR EXCUSES. KILLER DROP BEARS ATE MY HOMEWORK, BROCCOLI MEN CAUSED TRAFFIC ON THE FDR, THE BAND THUNDER THIGHS DESTROYED MY APARTMENT... I'VE HEARD IT ALL, BEN.
SANDWICH DEPARTMEN
I'M NOT TRYING TO GIVE YOU A HARD TIME. I'M TRYING TO MAKE SURE YOU'RE REALLY MY GUY. IF YOU'RE NOT MY GUY, I NEED TO KNOW NOW SO WE CAN CUT OUR LOSSES AND MOVE ON.
EXCUSE ME?
NOT EVERYONE CAN DO THIS, BEN. I KNOW YOU CAN... BUT I NEED YOU TO KNOW IT.
OHMIGODWHATHAVEWEDONE?

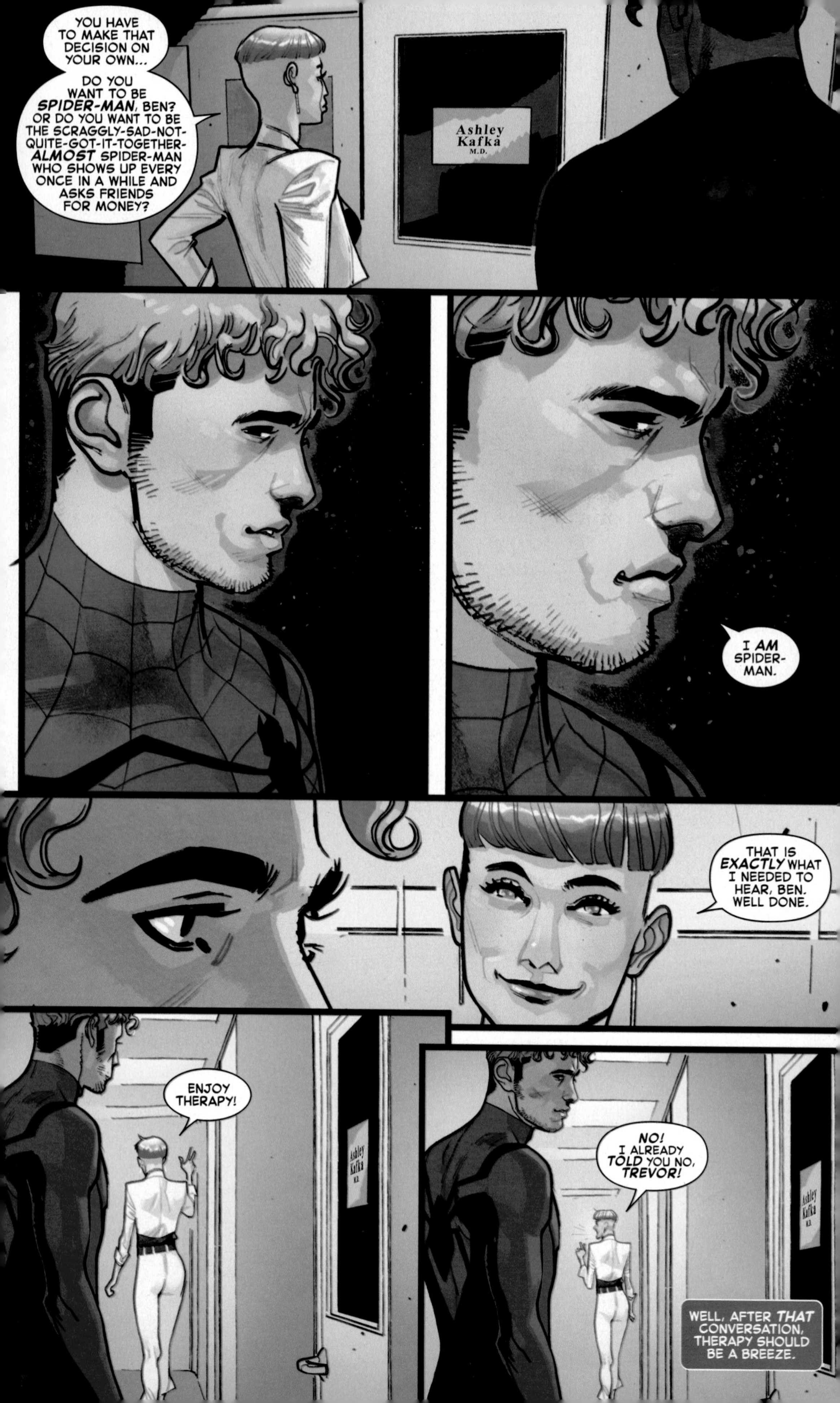

YOU HAVE TO MAKE THAT DECISION ON YOUR OWN...
DO YOU WANT TO BE SPIDER-MAN, BEN? OR DO YOU WANT TO BE THE SCRAGGLY-SAD-NOT-QUITE-GOT-IT-TOGETHER-ALMOST SPIDER-MAN WHO SHOWS UP EVERY ONCE IN A WHILE AND ASKS FRIENDS FOR MONEY?
Ashley Kafka M.D.
I AM SPIDER-MAN.
THAT IS EXACTLY WHAT I NEEDED TO HEAR, BEN. WELL DONE.
ENJOY THERAPY!
NO! I ALREADY TOLD YOU NO, TREVOR!
WELL, AFTER THAT CONVERSATION, THERAPY SHOULD BE A BREEZE.

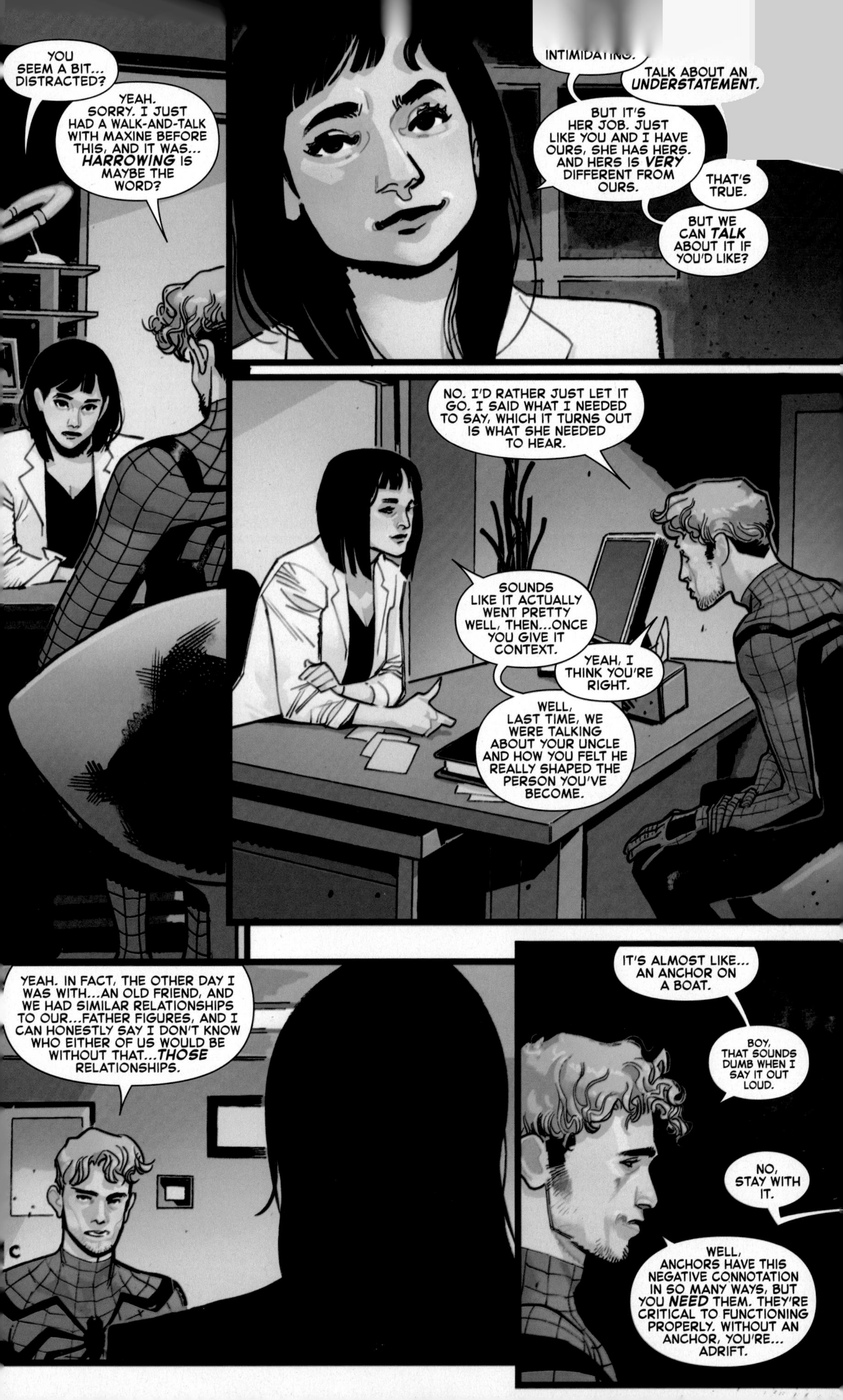
YOU SEEM A BIT... DISTRACTED?
YEAH. SORRY. I JUST HAD A WALK-AND-TALK WITH MAXINE BEFORE THIS, AND IT WAS... HARROWING IS MAYBE THE WORD?
INTIMIDATING.
TALK ABOUT AN UNDERSTATEMENT.
BUT IT'S HER JOB. JUST LIKE YOU AND I HAVE OURS, SHE HAS HERS. AND HERS IS VERY DIFFERENT FROM OURS.
THAT'S TRUE.
BUT WE CAN TALK ABOUT IT IF YOU'D LIKE?
NO. I'D RATHER JUST LET IT GO. I SAID WHAT I NEEDED TO SAY, WHICH IT TURNS OUT IS WHAT SHE NEEDED TO HEAR.
SOUNDS LIKE IT ACTUALLY WENT PRETTY WELL, THEN...ONCE YOU GIVE IT CONTEXT.
YEAH, I THINK YOU'RE RIGHT.
WELL, LAST TIME, WE WERE TALKING ABOUT YOUR UNCLE AND HOW YOU FELT HE REALLY SHAPED THE PERSON YOU'VE BECOME.
YEAH. IN FACT, THE OTHER DAY I WAS WITH...AN OLD FRIEND, AND WE HAD SIMILAR RELATIONSHIPS TO OUR...FATHER FIGURES, AND I CAN HONESTLY SAY I DON'T KNOW WHO EITHER OF US WOULD BE WITHOUT THAT...THOSE RELATIONSHIPS.
IT'S ALMOST LIKE... AN ANCHOR ON A BOAT.
BOY, THAT SOUNDS DUMB WHEN I SAY IT OUT LOUD.
NO, STAY WITH IT.
WELL, ANCHORS HAVE THIS NEGATIVE CONNOTATION IN SO MANY WAYS, BUT YOU NEED THEM. THEY'RE CRITICAL TO FUNCTIONING PROPERLY. WITHOUT AN ANCHOR, YOU'RE... ADRIFT.

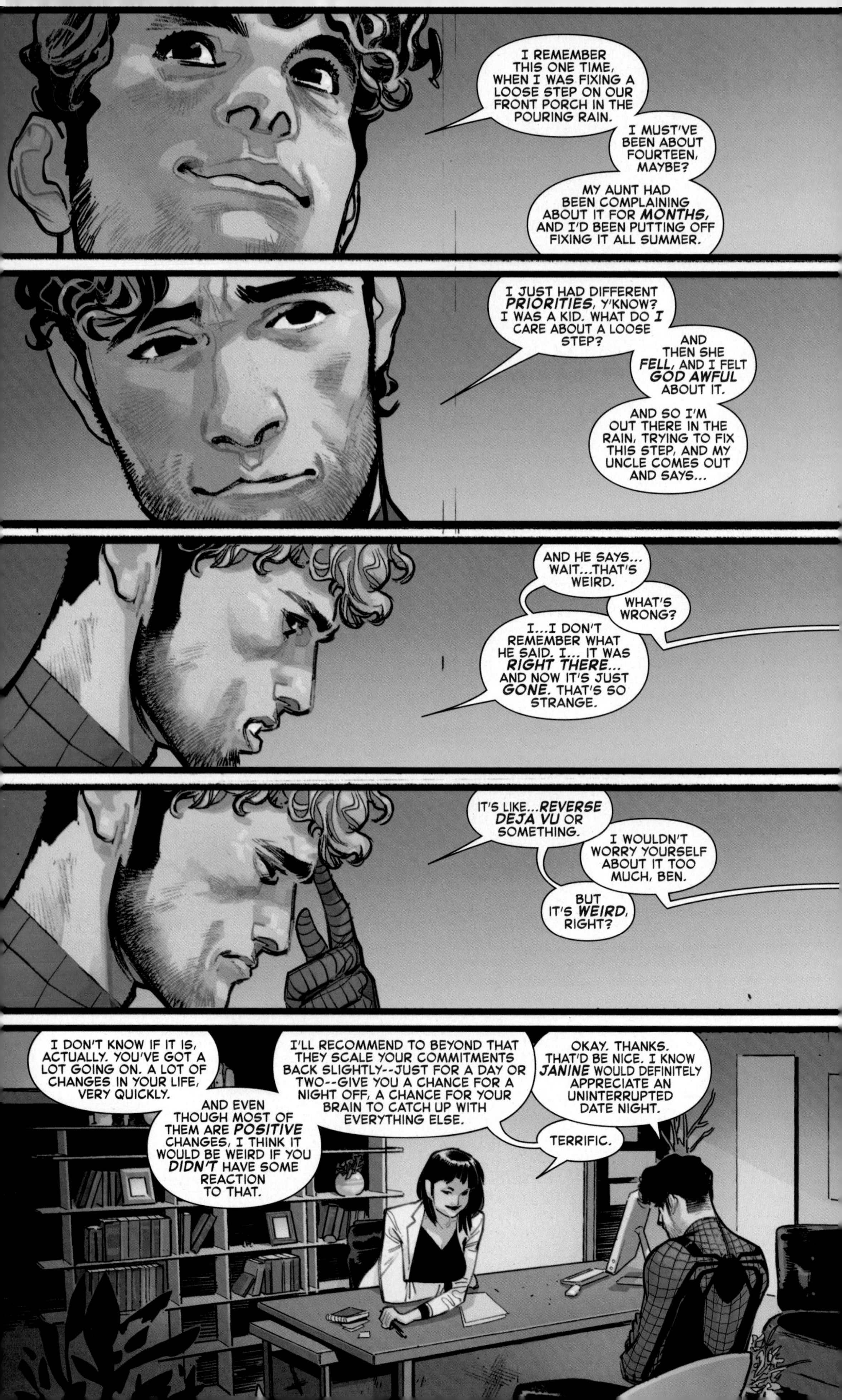
I REMEMBER THIS ONE TIME, WHEN I WAS FIXING A LOOSE STEP ON OUR FRONT PORCH IN THE POURING RAIN.
I MUST'VE BEEN ABOUT FOURTEEN, MAYBE?
MY AUNT HAD BEEN COMPLAINING ABOUT IT FOR *MONTHS,* AND I'D BEEN PUTTING OFF FIXING IT ALL SUMMER.
I JUST HAD DIFFERENT *PRIORITIES,* Y'KNOW? I WAS A KID. WHAT DO *I* CARE ABOUT A LOOSE STEP?
AND THEN SHE *FELL,* AND I FELT *GOD AWFUL* ABOUT IT.
AND SO I'M OUT THERE IN THE RAIN, TRYING TO FIX THIS STEP, AND MY UNCLE COMES OUT AND SAYS...
AND HE SAYS... WAIT...THAT'S WEIRD.
WHAT'S WRONG?
I...I DON'T REMEMBER WHAT HE SAID. I... IT WAS *RIGHT THERE...* AND NOW IT'S JUST *GONE.* THAT'S SO STRANGE.
IT'S LIKE...*REVERSE DEJA VU* OR SOMETHING.
I WOULDN'T WORRY YOURSELF ABOUT IT TOO MUCH, BEN.
BUT IT'S *WEIRD,* RIGHT?
I DON'T KNOW IF IT IS, ACTUALLY. YOU'VE GOT A LOT GOING ON. A LOT OF CHANGES IN YOUR LIFE, VERY QUICKLY.
AND EVEN THOUGH MOST OF THEM ARE *POSITIVE* CHANGES, I THINK IT WOULD BE WEIRD IF YOU *DIDN'T* HAVE SOME REACTION TO THAT.
I'LL RECOMMEND TO BEYOND THAT THEY SCALE YOUR COMMITMENTS BACK SLIGHTLY--JUST FOR A DAY OR TWO--GIVE YOU A CHANCE FOR A NIGHT OFF, A CHANCE FOR YOUR BRAIN TO CATCH UP WITH EVERYTHING ELSE.
OKAY. THANKS. THAT'D BE NICE. I KNOW *JANINE* WOULD DEFINITELY APPRECIATE AN UNINTERRUPTED DATE NIGHT.
TERRIFIC.

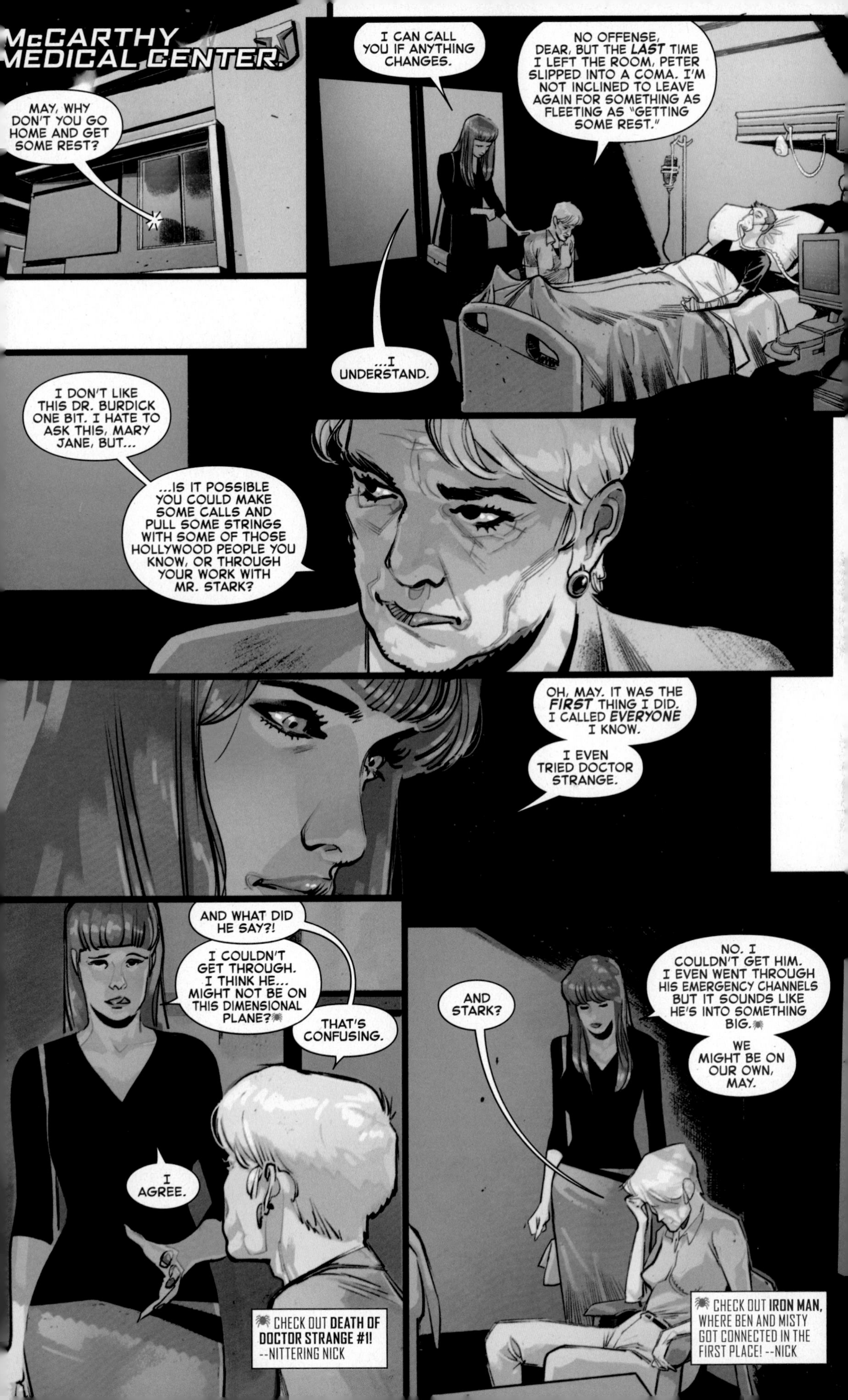
McCARTHY MEDICAL CENTER.
MAY, WHY DON'T YOU GO HOME AND GET SOME REST?
I CAN CALL YOU IF ANYTHING CHANGES.
NO OFFENSE, DEAR, BUT THE LAST TIME I LEFT THE ROOM, PETER SLIPPED INTO A COMA. I'M NOT INCLINED TO LEAVE AGAIN FOR SOMETHING AS FLEETING AS "GETTING SOME REST."
...I UNDERSTAND.
I DON'T LIKE THIS DR. BURDICK ONE BIT. I HATE TO ASK THIS, MARY JANE, BUT...
...IS IT POSSIBLE YOU COULD MAKE SOME CALLS AND PULL SOME STRINGS WITH SOME OF THOSE HOLLYWOOD PEOPLE YOU KNOW, OR THROUGH YOUR WORK WITH MR. STARK?
OH, MAY. IT WAS THE FIRST THING I DID. I CALLED EVERYONE I KNOW.
I EVEN TRIED DOCTOR STRANGE.
AND WHAT DID HE SAY?!
I COULDN'T GET THROUGH. I THINK HE... MIGHT NOT BE ON THIS DIMENSIONAL PLANE?
THAT'S CONFUSING.
I AGREE.
CHECK OUT DEATH OF DOCTOR STRANGE #1! --NITTERING NICK
AND STARK?
NO. I COULDN'T GET HIM. I EVEN WENT THROUGH HIS EMERGENCY CHANNELS BUT IT SOUNDS LIKE HE'S INTO SOMETHING BIG.
WE MIGHT BE ON OUR OWN, MAY.
CHECK OUT IRON MAN, WHERE BEN AND MISTY GOT CONNECTED IN THE FIRST PLACE! --NICK

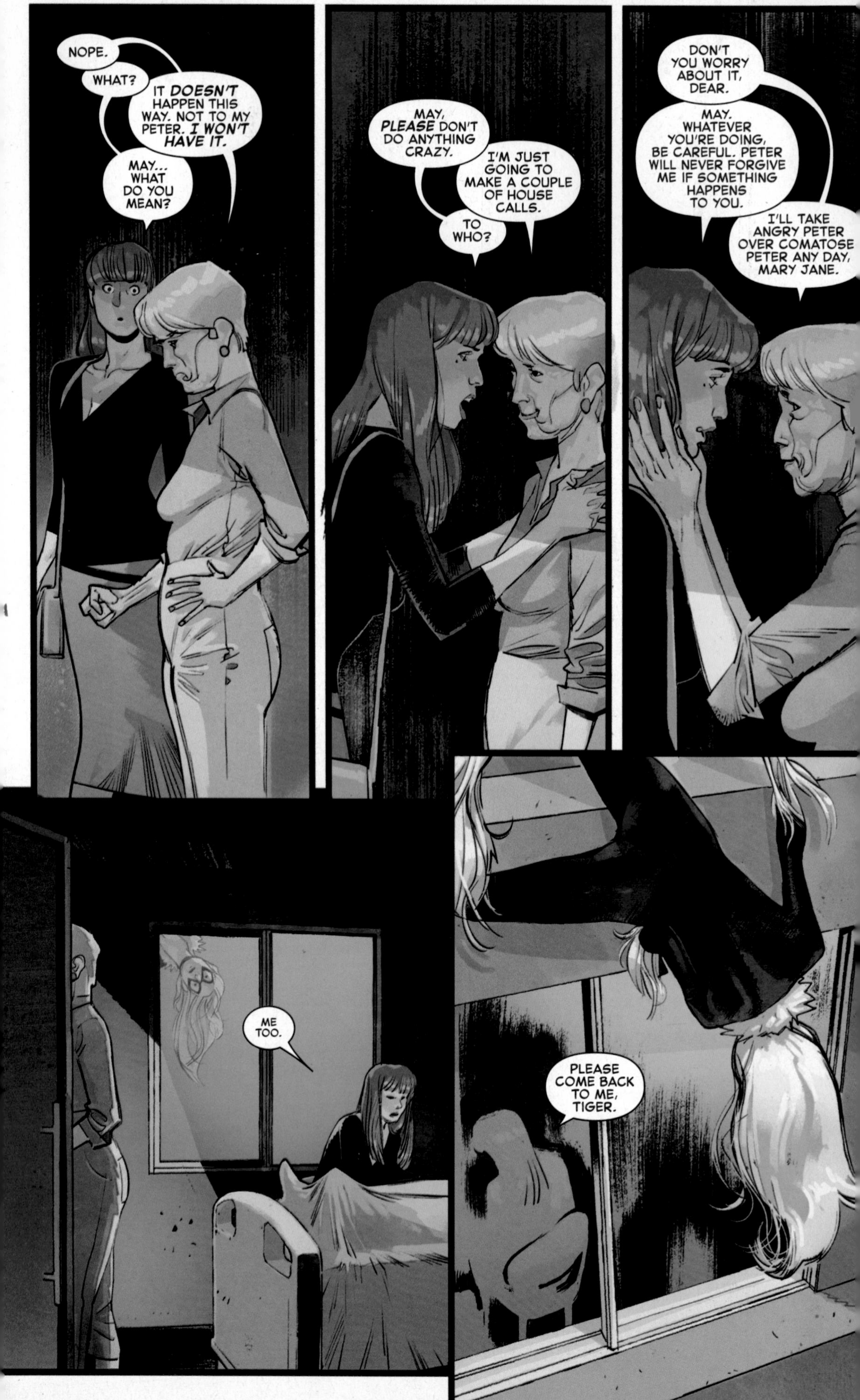
NOPE.
WHAT?
IT DOESN'T HAPPEN THIS WAY. NOT TO MY PETER. I WON'T HAVE IT.
MAY... WHAT DO YOU MEAN?
MAY, PLEASE DON'T DO ANYTHING CRAZY.
I'M JUST GOING TO MAKE A COUPLE OF HOUSE CALLS.
TO WHO?
DON'T YOU WORRY ABOUT IT, DEAR.
MAY. WHATEVER YOU'RE DOING, BE CAREFUL. PETER WILL NEVER FORGIVE ME IF SOMETHING HAPPENS TO YOU.
I'LL TAKE ANGRY PETER OVER COMATOSE PETER ANY DAY, MARY JANE.
ME TOO.
PLEASE COME BACK TO ME, TIGER.

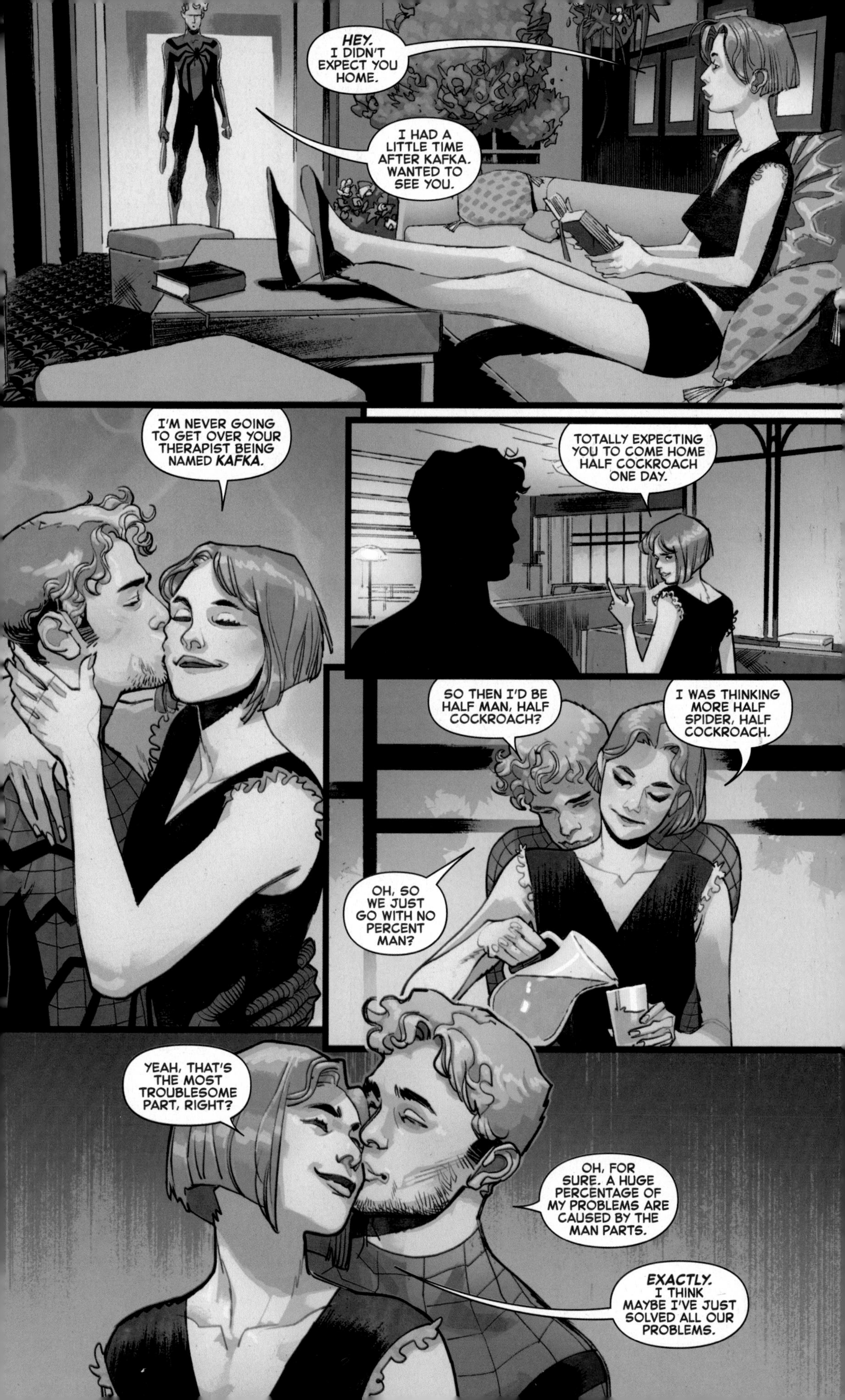
HEY. I DIDN'T EXPECT YOU HOME.
I HAD A LITTLE TIME AFTER KAFKA. WANTED TO SEE YOU.
I'M NEVER GOING TO GET OVER YOUR THERAPIST BEING NAMED KAFKA.
TOTALLY EXPECTING YOU TO COME HOME HALF COCKROACH ONE DAY.
SO THEN I'D BE HALF MAN, HALF COCKROACH?
I WAS THINKING MORE HALF SPIDER, HALF COCKROACH.
OH, SO WE JUST GO WITH NO PERCENT MAN?
YEAH, THAT'S THE MOST TROUBLESOME PART, RIGHT?
OH, FOR SURE. A HUGE PERCENTAGE OF MY PROBLEMS ARE CAUSED BY THE MAN PARTS.
EXACTLY. I THINK MAYBE I'VE JUST SOLVED ALL OUR PROBLEMS.

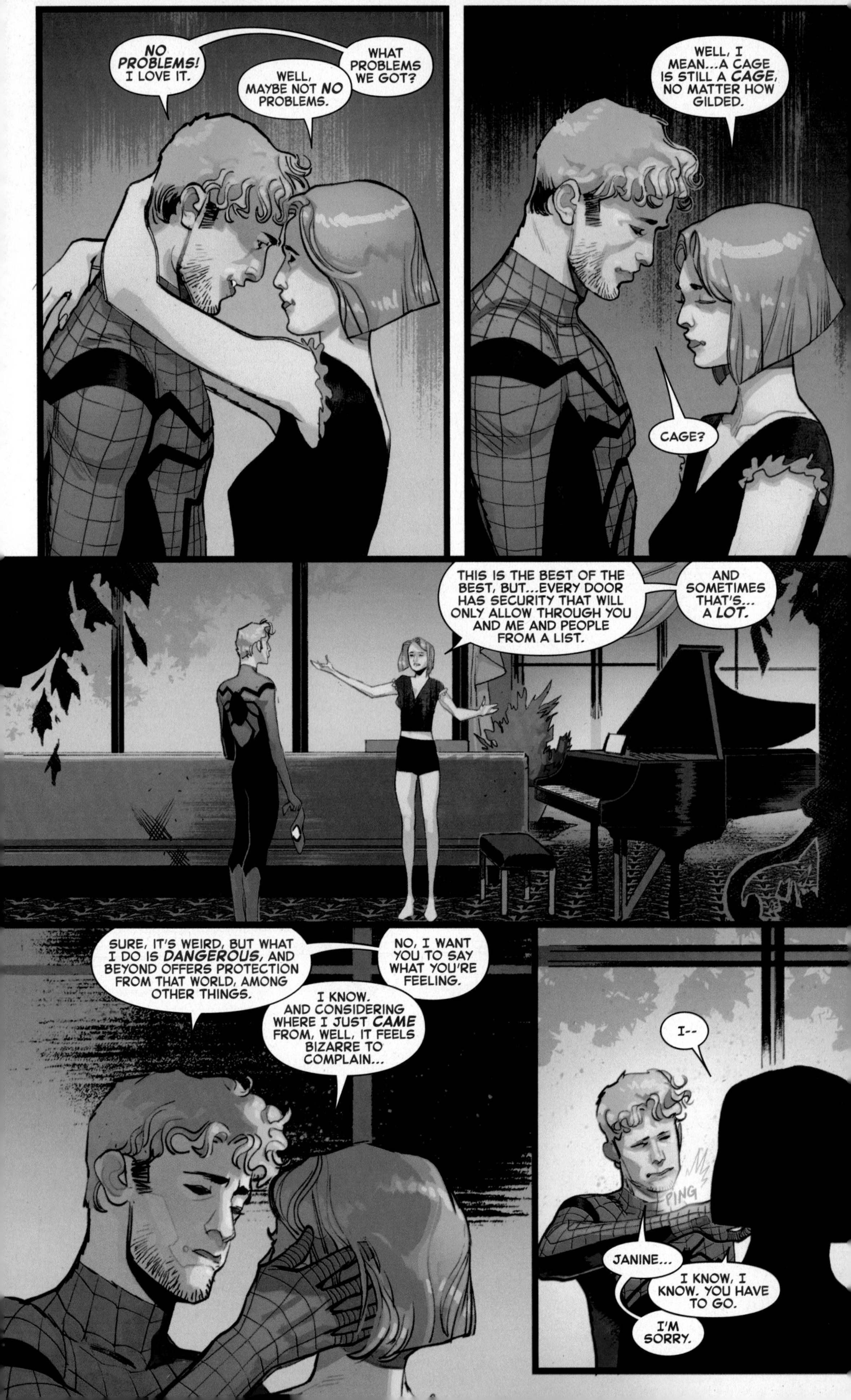
WHAT PROBLEMS WE GOT?
NO PROBLEMS! I LOVE IT.
WELL, MAYBE NOT NO PROBLEMS.
WELL, I MEAN...A CAGE IS STILL A CAGE, NO MATTER HOW GILDED.
CAGE?
THIS IS THE BEST OF THE BEST, BUT...EVERY DOOR HAS SECURITY THAT WILL ONLY ALLOW THROUGH YOU AND ME AND PEOPLE FROM A LIST.
AND SOMETIMES THAT'S... A LOT.
SURE, IT'S WEIRD, BUT WHAT I DO IS DANGEROUS, AND BEYOND OFFERS PROTECTION FROM THAT WORLD, AMONG OTHER THINGS.
NO, I WANT YOU TO SAY WHAT YOU'RE FEELING.
I KNOW. AND CONSIDERING WHERE I JUST CAME FROM, WELL, IT FEELS BIZARRE TO COMPLAIN...
I--
PING
JANINE...
I KNOW, I KNOW. YOU HAVE TO GO.
I'M SORRY.

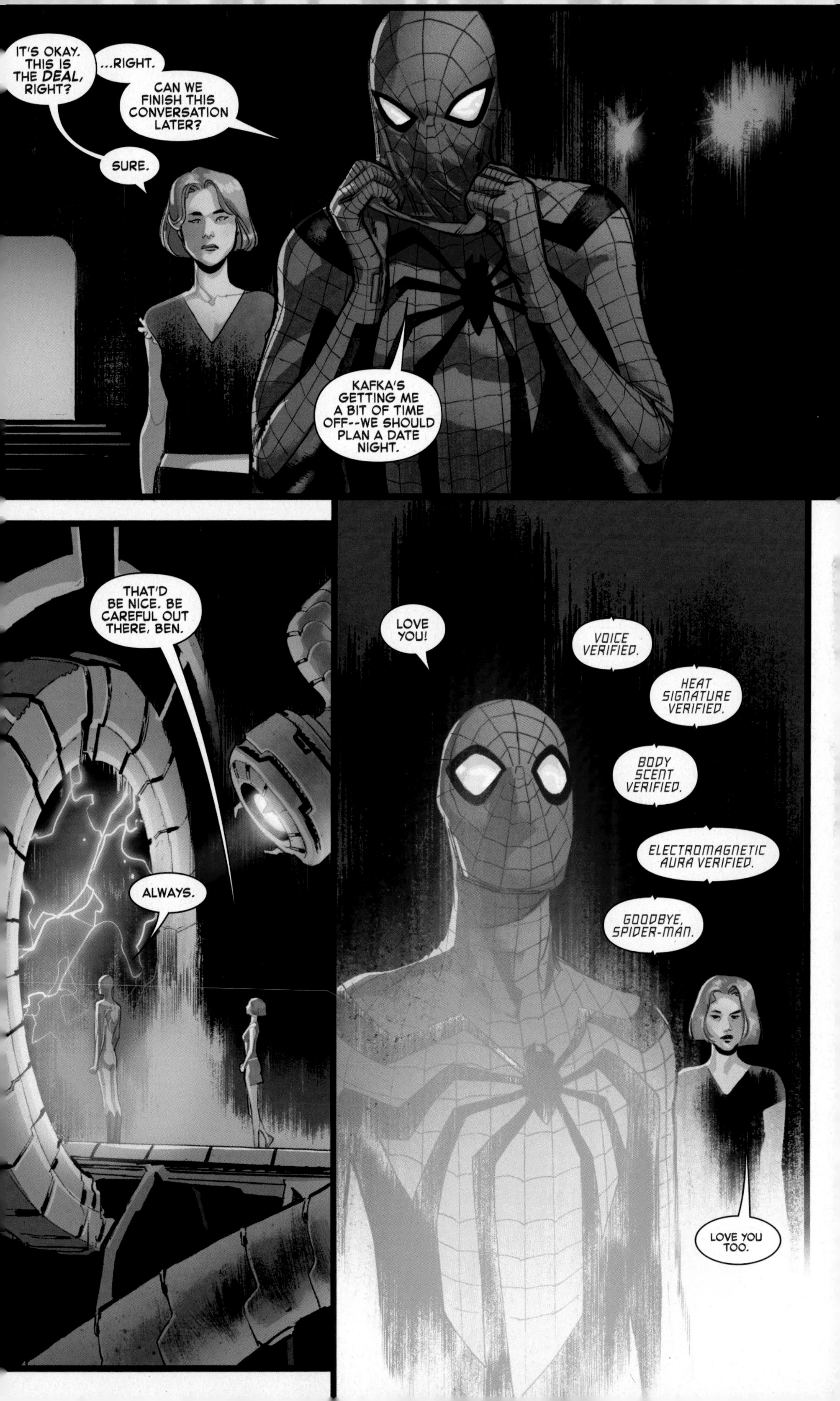
IT'S OKAY. THIS IS THE DEAL, RIGHT?
...RIGHT.
CAN WE FINISH THIS CONVERSATION LATER?
SURE.
KAFKA'S GETTING ME A BIT OF TIME OFF--WE SHOULD PLAN A DATE NIGHT.
THAT'D BE NICE. BE CAREFUL OUT THERE, BEN.
ALWAYS.
LOVE YOU!
VOICE VERIFIED.
HEAT SIGNATURE VERIFIED.
BODY SCENT VERIFIED.
ELECTROMAGNETIC AURA VERIFIED.
GOODBYE, SPIDER-MAN.
LOVE YOU TOO.

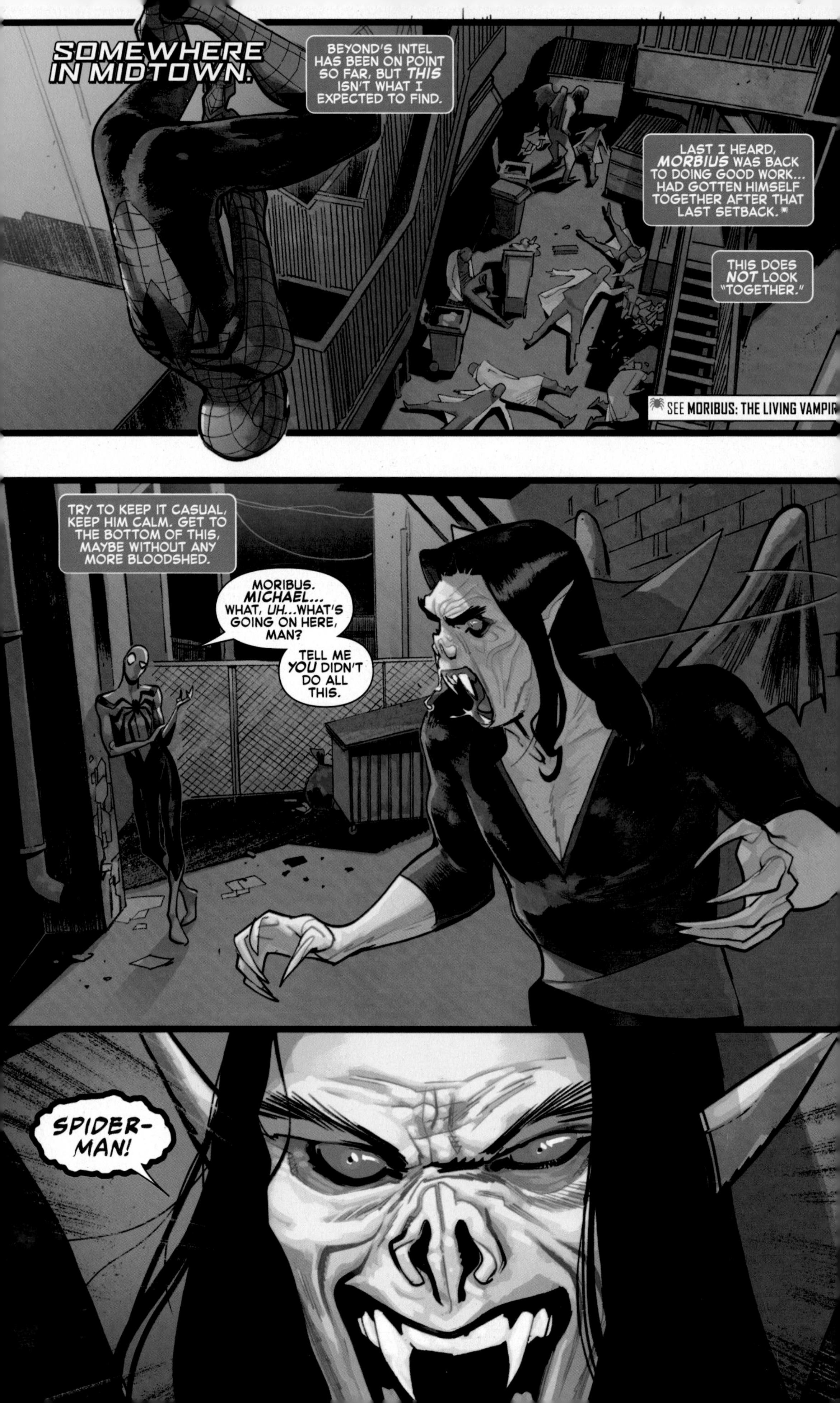

SOMEWHERE IN MIDTOWN.
BEYOND'S INTEL HAS BEEN ON POINT SO FAR, BUT THIS ISN'T WHAT I EXPECTED TO FIND.
LAST I HEARD, MORBIUS WAS BACK TO DOING GOOD WORK... HAD GOTTEN HIMSELF TOGETHER AFTER THAT LAST SETBACK.*
THIS DOES NOT LOOK "TOGETHER."
*SEE MORIBUS: THE LIVING VAMPIR
TRY TO KEEP IT CASUAL, KEEP HIM CALM. GET TO THE BOTTOM OF THIS, MAYBE WITHOUT ANY MORE BLOODSHED.
MORIBUS. MICHAEL... WHAT, UH...WHAT'S GOING ON HERE, MAN?
TELL ME YOU DIDN'T DO ALL THIS.
SPIDER-MAN!

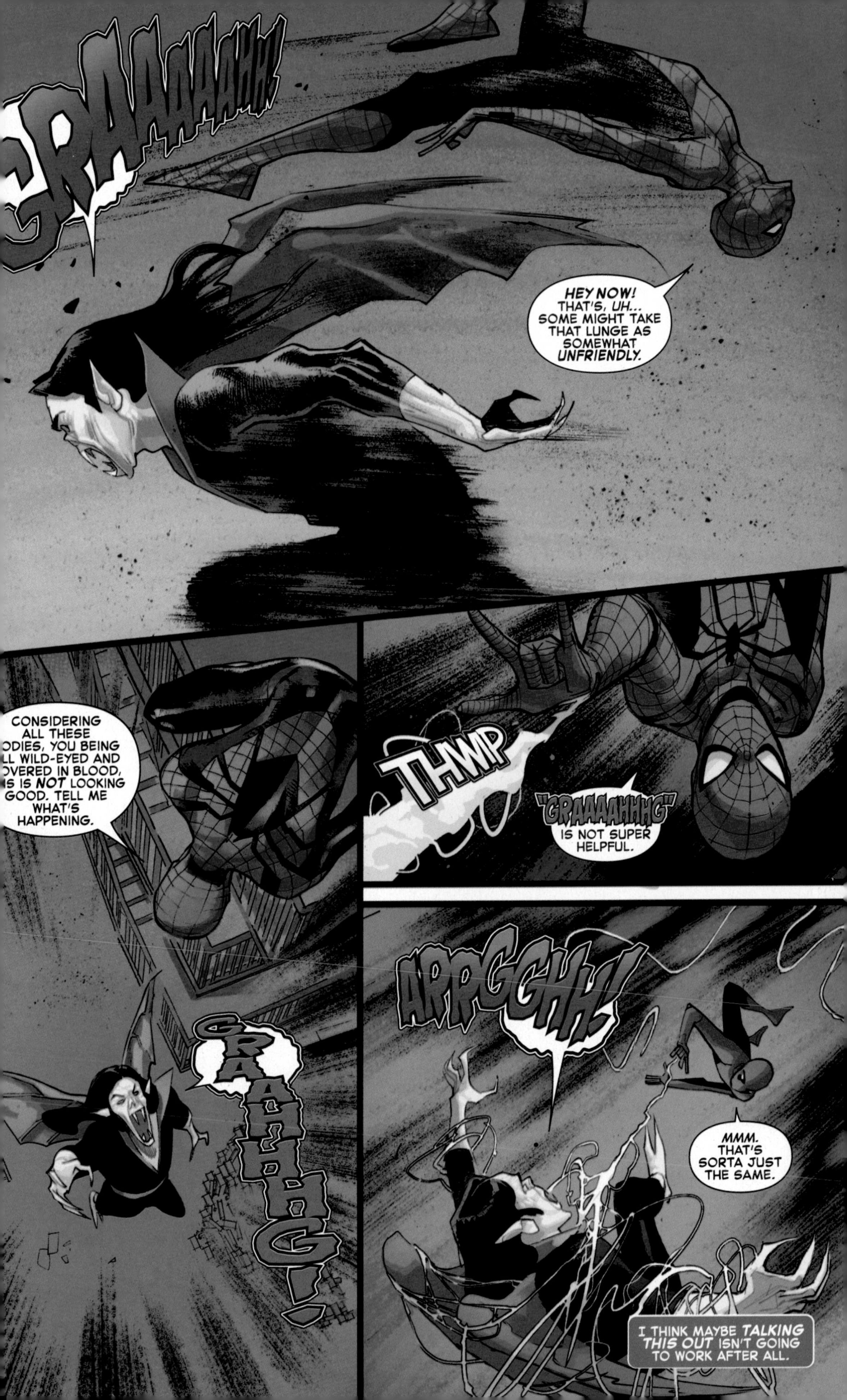

GRAAAAAHH!
HEY NOW! THAT'S, UH... SOME MIGHT TAKE THAT LUNGE AS SOMEWHAT UNFRIENDLY.
CONSIDERING ALL THESE ODIES, YOU BEING LL WILD-EYED AND OVERED IN BLOOD, IS IS NOT LOOKING GOOD. TELL ME WHAT'S HAPPENING.
THWIP
"GRAAAAHHHG" IS NOT SUPER HELPFUL.
GRAAHHHG!
ARRGGHH!
MMM. THAT'S SORTA JUST THE SAME.
I THINK MAYBE TALKING THIS OUT ISN'T GOING TO WORK AFTER ALL.

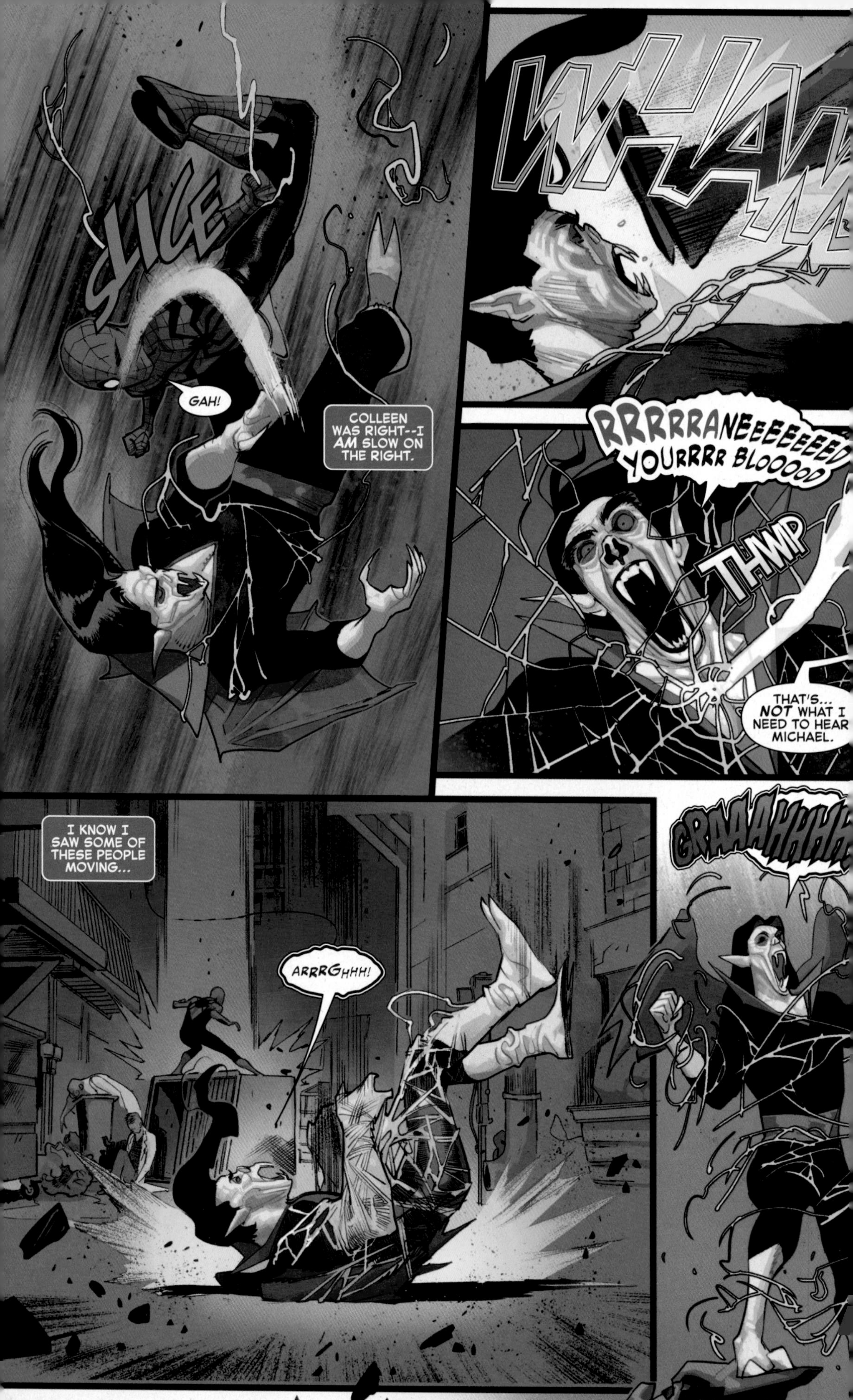
SLICE
GAH!
COLLEEN WAS RIGHT--I AM SLOW ON THE RIGHT.
WHAM
RRRRRANEEEEEEED YOURRRR BLOOOOD
THWIP
THAT'S... NOT WHAT I NEED TO HEAR MICHAEL.
I KNOW I SAW SOME OF THESE PEOPLE MOVING...
ARRRGHHH!
GRAAAHHHH

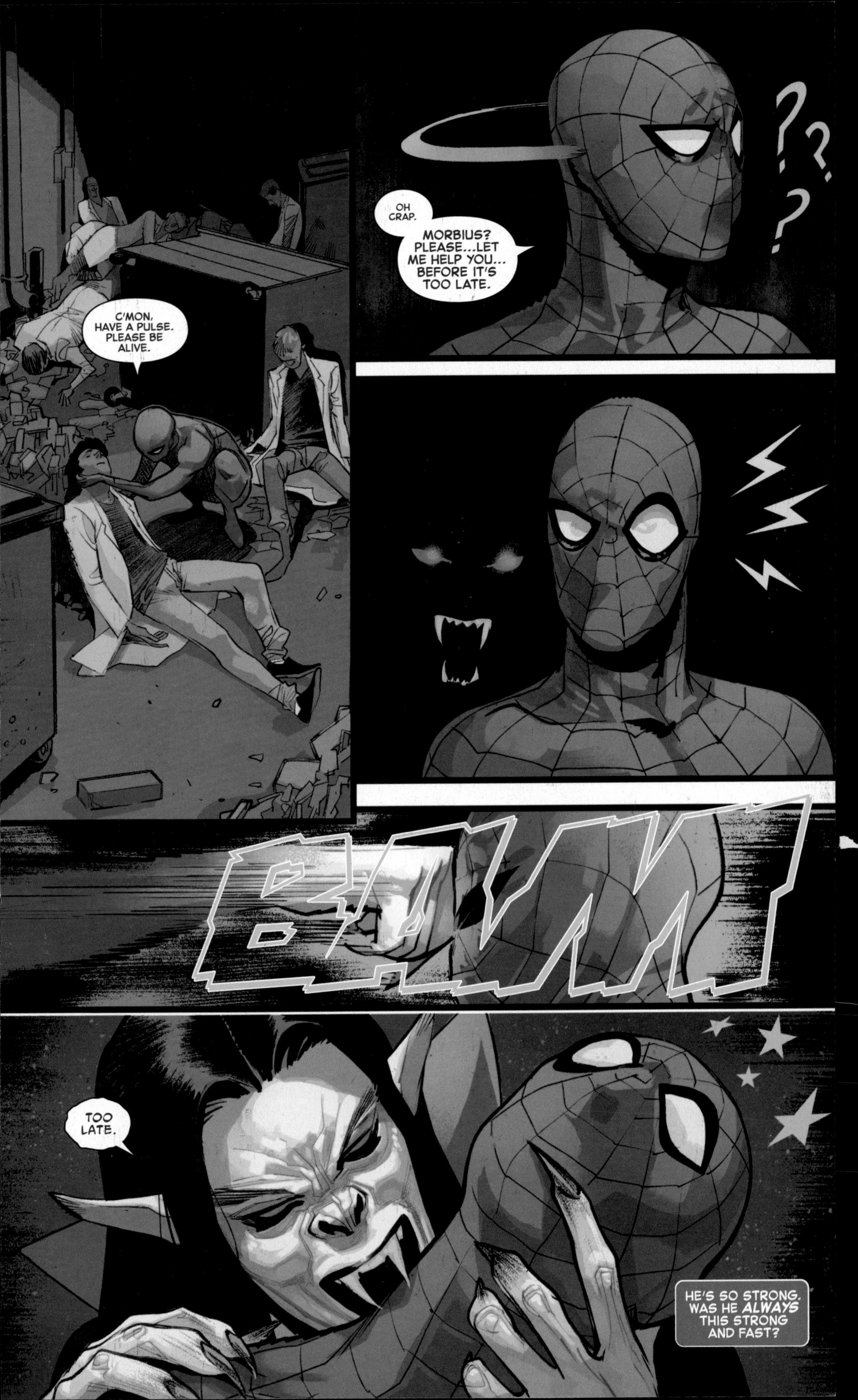
C'MON, HAVE A PULSE. PLEASE BE ALIVE.
OH CRAP.
MORBIUS? PLEASE...LET ME HELP YOU... BEFORE IT'S TOO LATE.
BAM
TOO LATE.
HE'S SO STRONG. WAS HE *ALWAYS* THIS STRONG AND FAST?

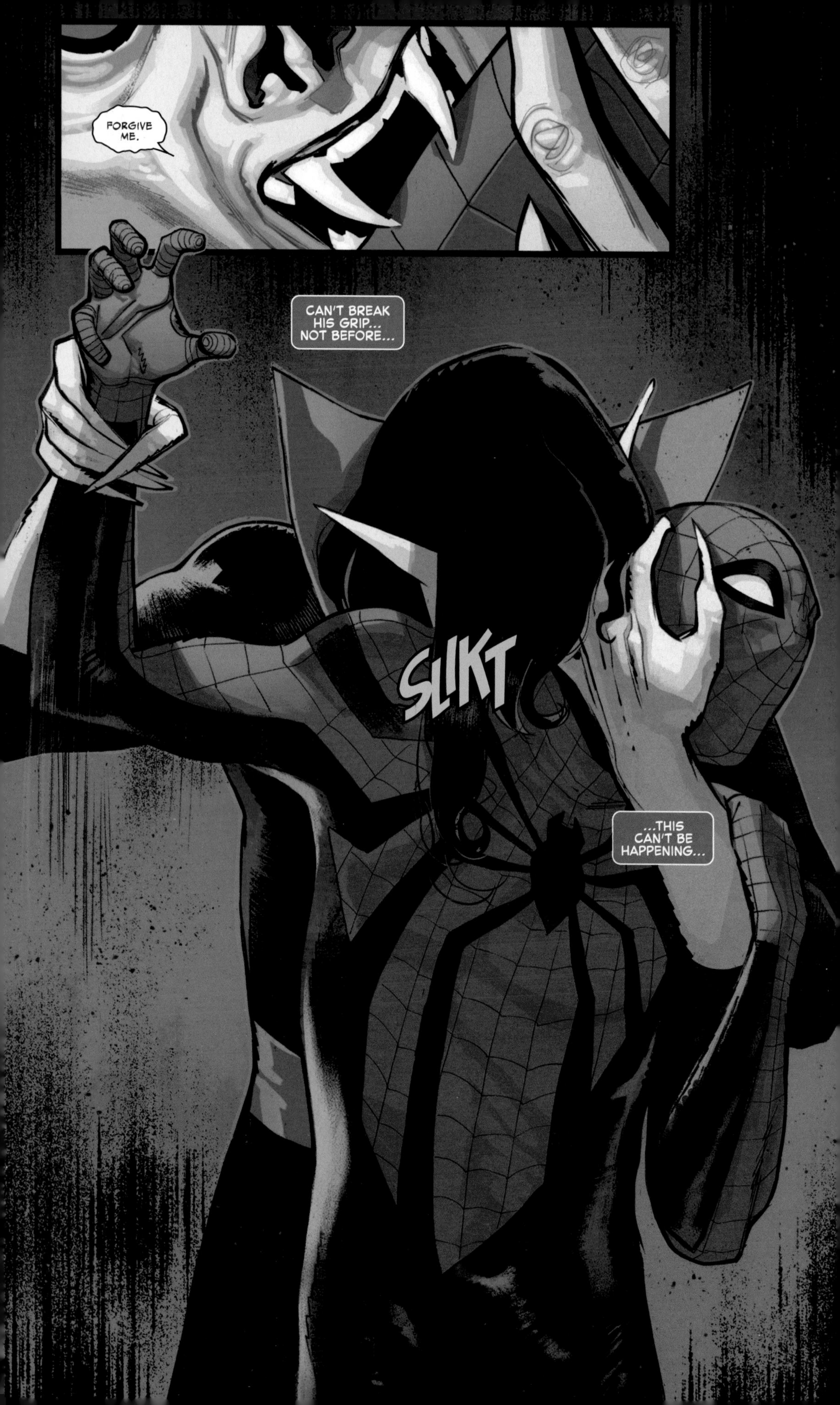
FORGIVE ME.
CAN'T BREAK HIS GRIP... NOT BEFORE...
SLIKT
...THIS CAN'T BE HAPPENING...

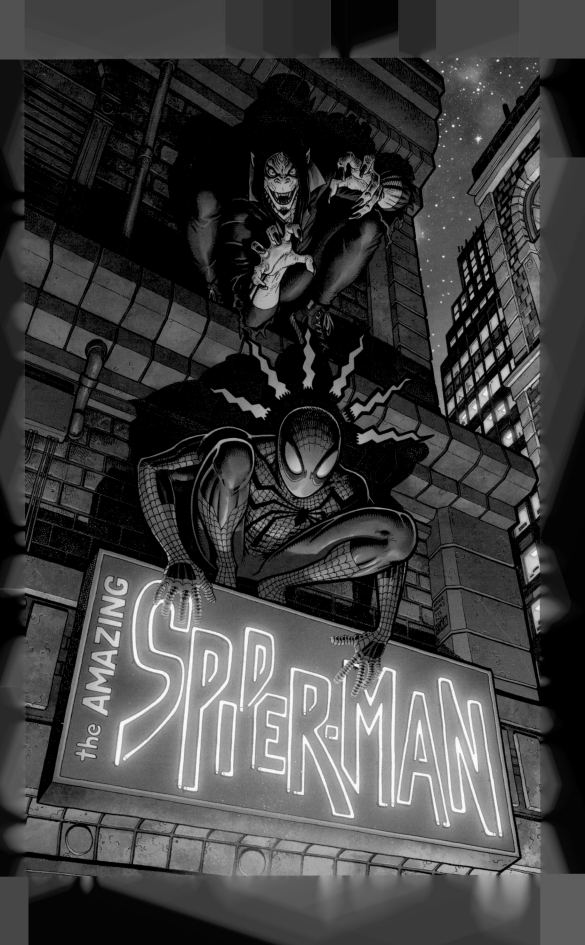

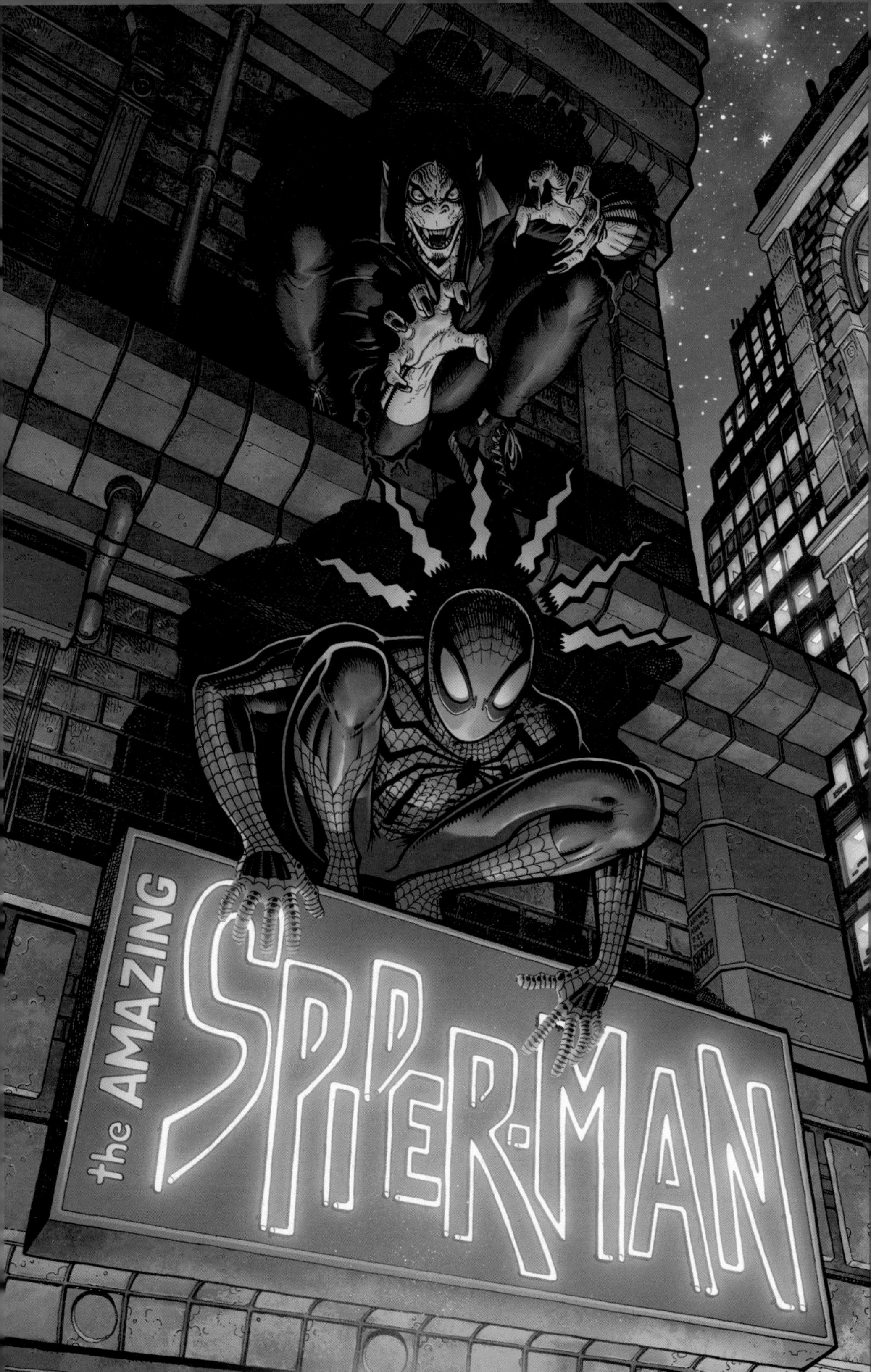
the AMAZING
SPIDER-MAN

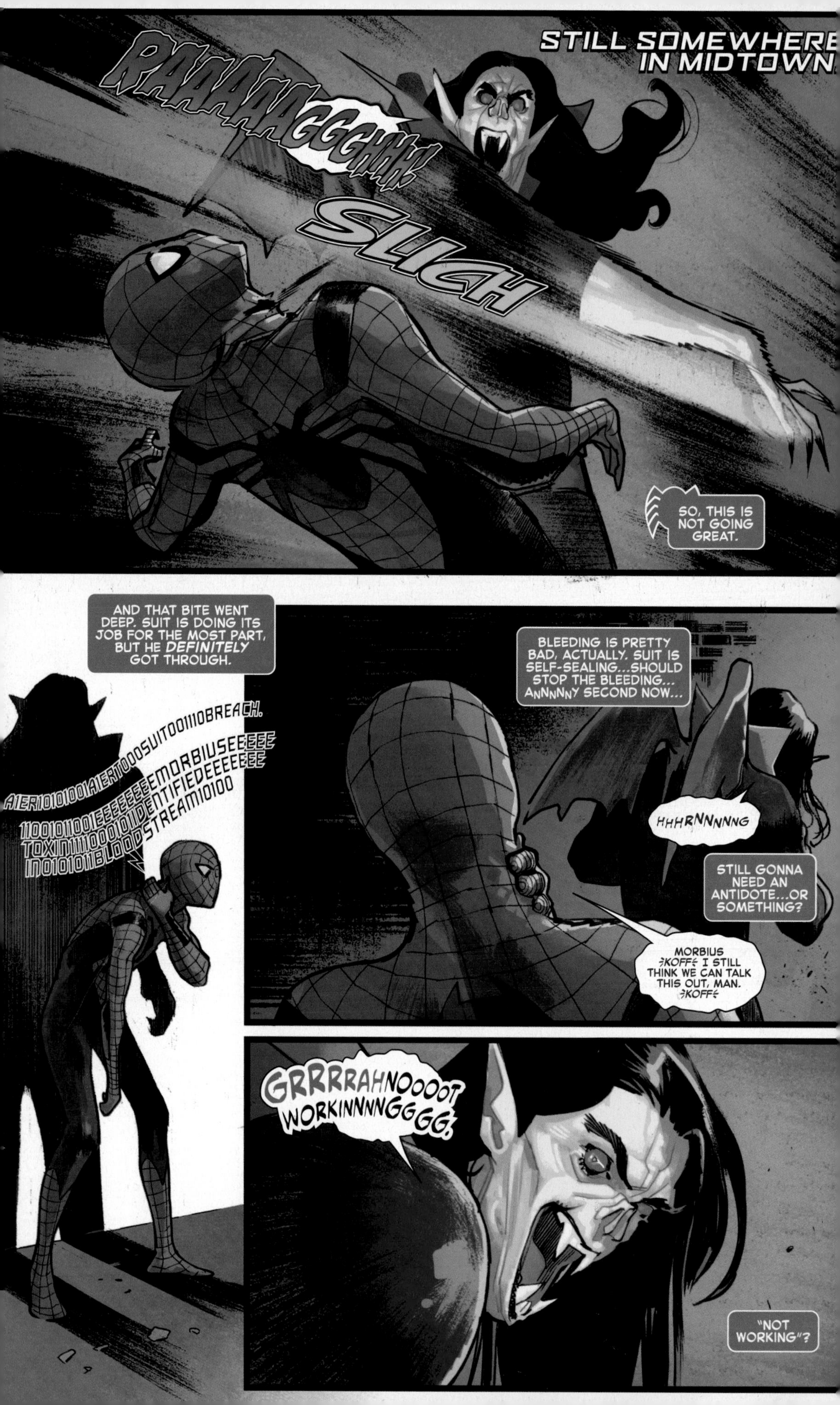
STILL SOMEWHERE IN MIDTOWN.
RAAAAAAGGGHHH!
SLICH
SO, THIS IS NOT GOING GREAT.
AND THAT BITE WENT DEEP. SUIT IS DOING ITS JOB FOR THE MOST PART, BUT HE DEFINITELY GOT THROUGH.
A1ER1010100A1ERT000SUIT001110BREACH.
1100101100EEEEEEEEEEMORBIUSEEEEEE
TOXIN11110000101IDENTIFIEDEEEEEEEE
IN0101011BLOODSTREAM10100
BLEEDING IS PRETTY BAD, ACTUALLY. SUIT IS SELF-SEALING...SHOULD STOP THE BLEEDING... ANNNNNY SECOND NOW...
HHHRNNNNNG
STILL GONNA NEED AN ANTIDOTE...OR SOMETHING?
MORBIUS ⸗KOFF⸗ I STILL THINK WE CAN TALK THIS OUT, MAN. ⸗KOFF⸗
GRRRRAHNOOOOT WORKINNNNGGGG.
"NOT WORKING"?

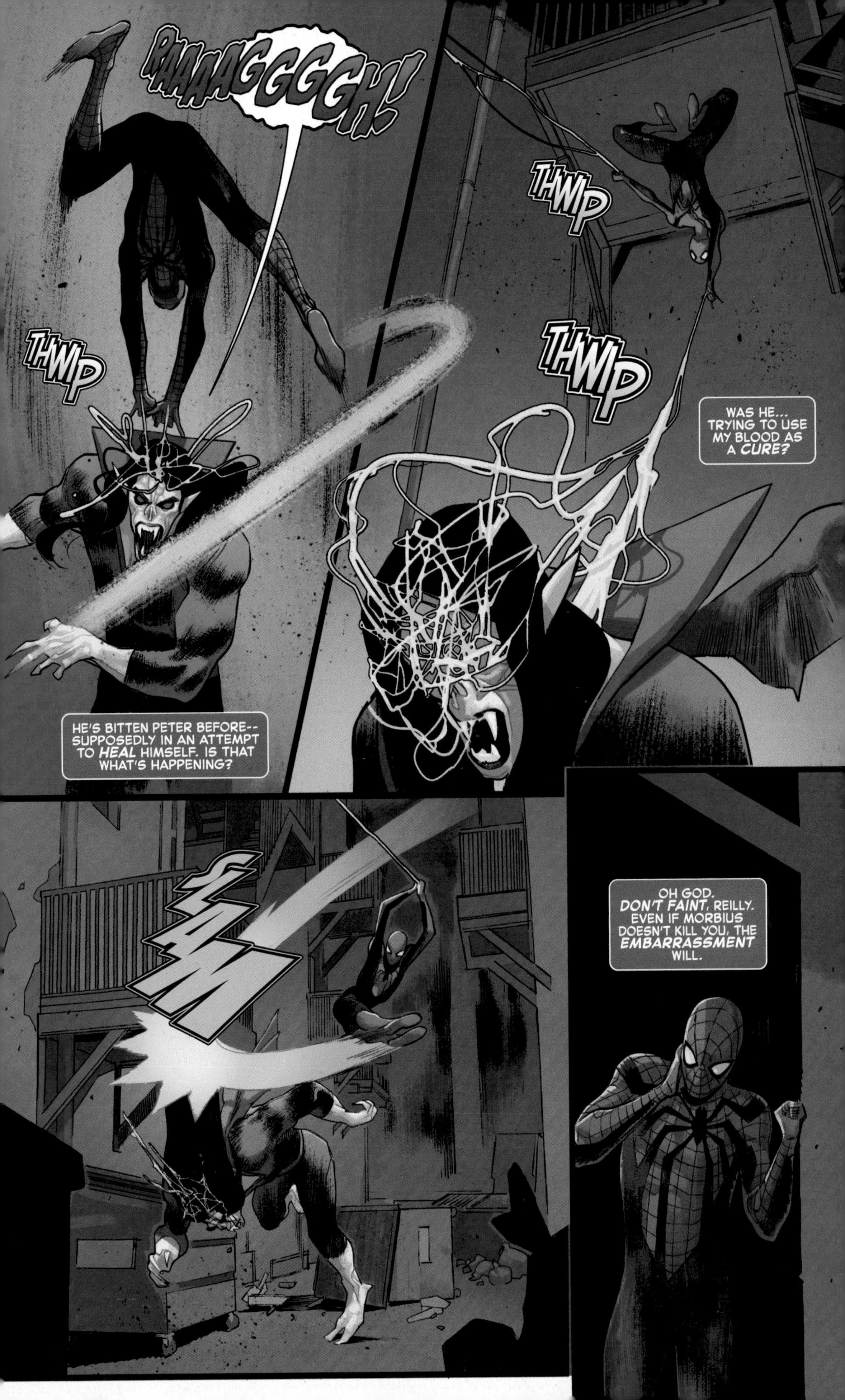
RAAAAGGGGH!
THWIP
HE'S BITTEN PETER BEFORE--SUPPOSEDLY IN AN ATTEMPT TO HEAL HIMSELF. IS THAT WHAT'S HAPPENING?
THWIP
THWIP
WAS HE... TRYING TO USE MY BLOOD AS A CURE?
SLAM
OH GOD. DON'T FAINT, REILLY. EVEN IF MORBIUS DOESN'T KILL YOU, THE EMBARRASSMENT WILL.

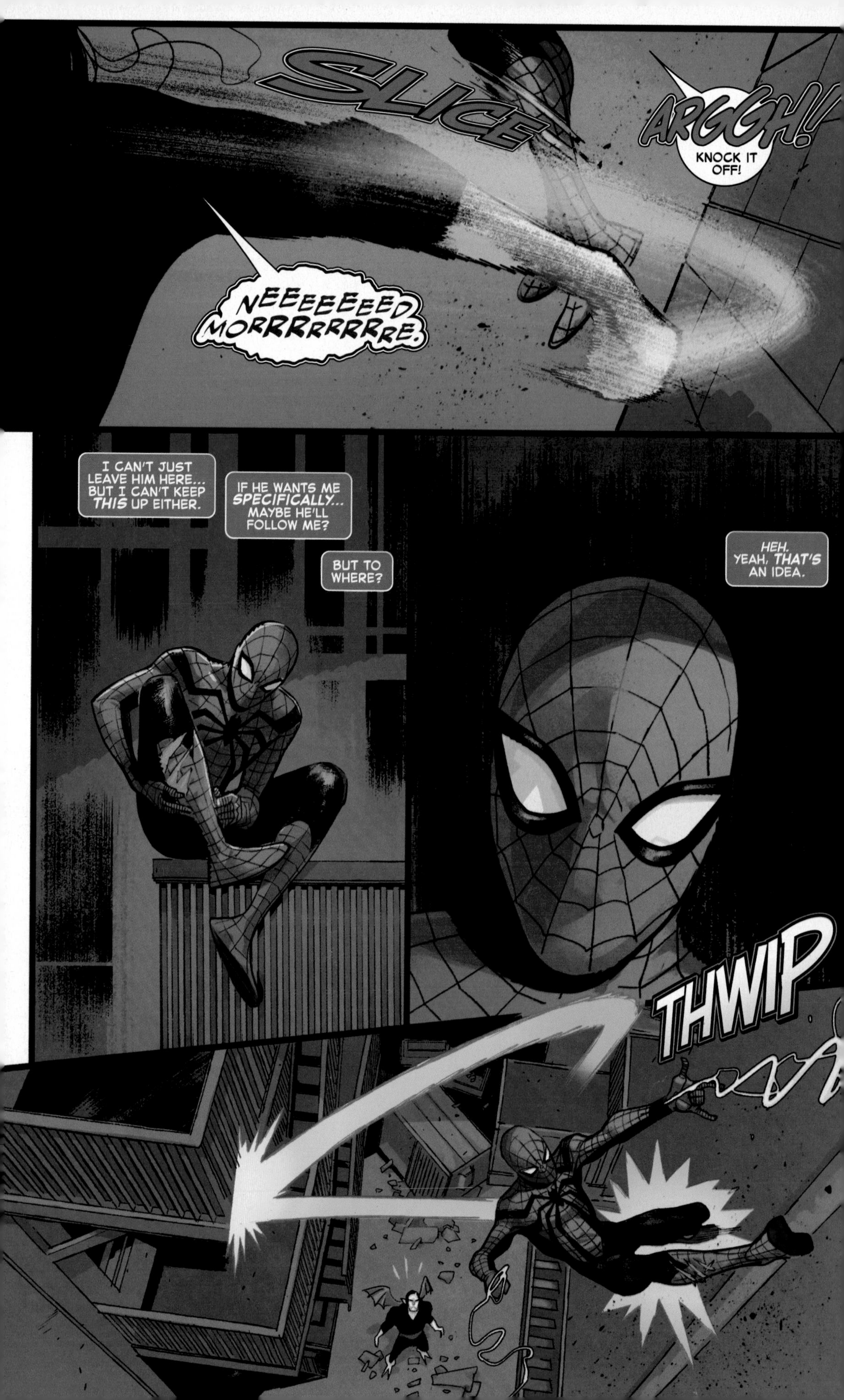
SLICE
ARGGH!
KNOCK IT OFF!
NEEEEEEEED MORRRRRRRRE.
I CAN'T JUST LEAVE HIM HERE... BUT I CAN'T KEEP THIS UP EITHER.
IF HE WANTS ME SPECIFICALLY... MAYBE HE'LL FOLLOW ME?
BUT TO WHERE?
HEH. YEAH, THAT'S AN IDEA.
THWIP

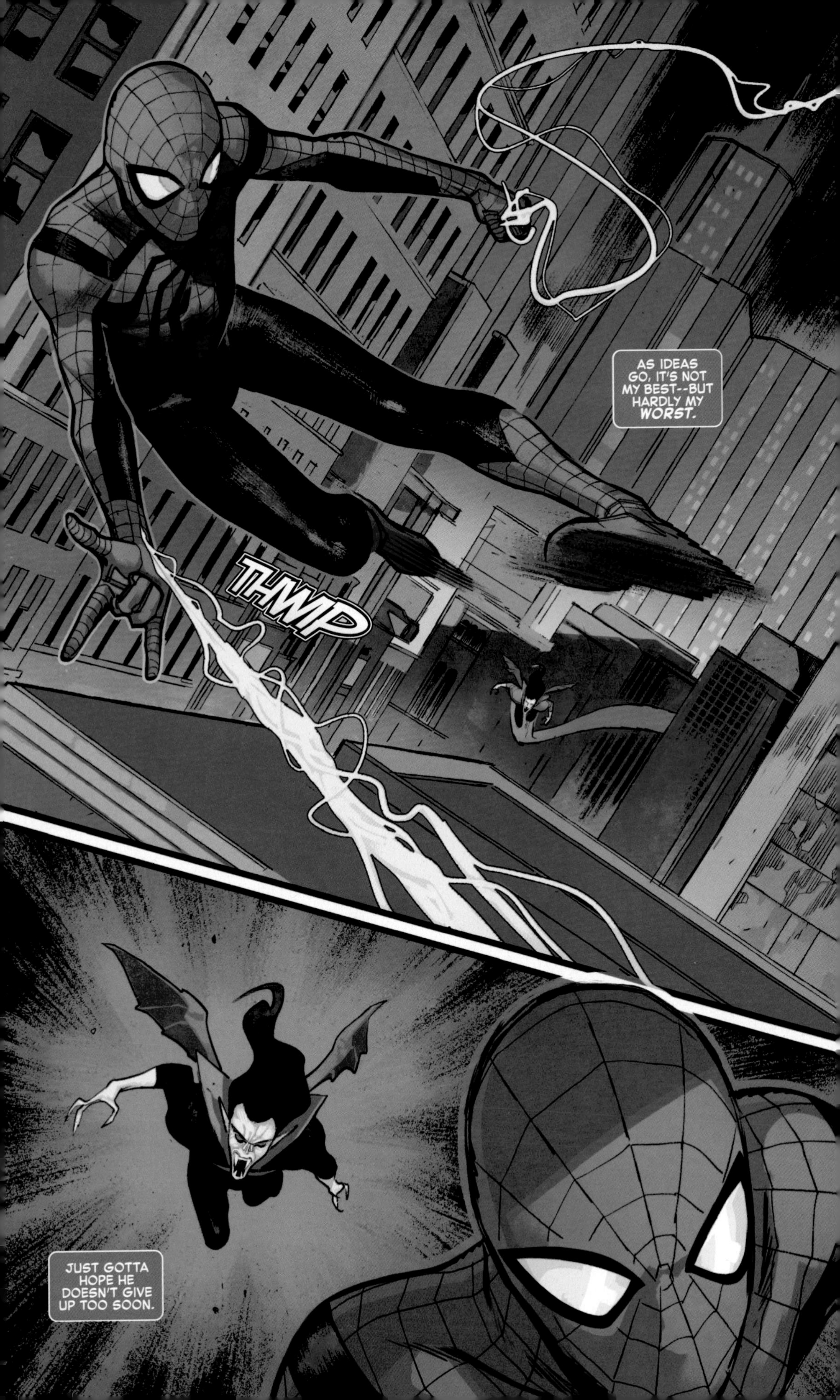

AS IDEAS GO, IT'S NOT MY BEST--BUT HARDLY MY WORST.
THWIP
JUST GOTTA HOPE HE DOESN'T GIVE UP TOO SOON.

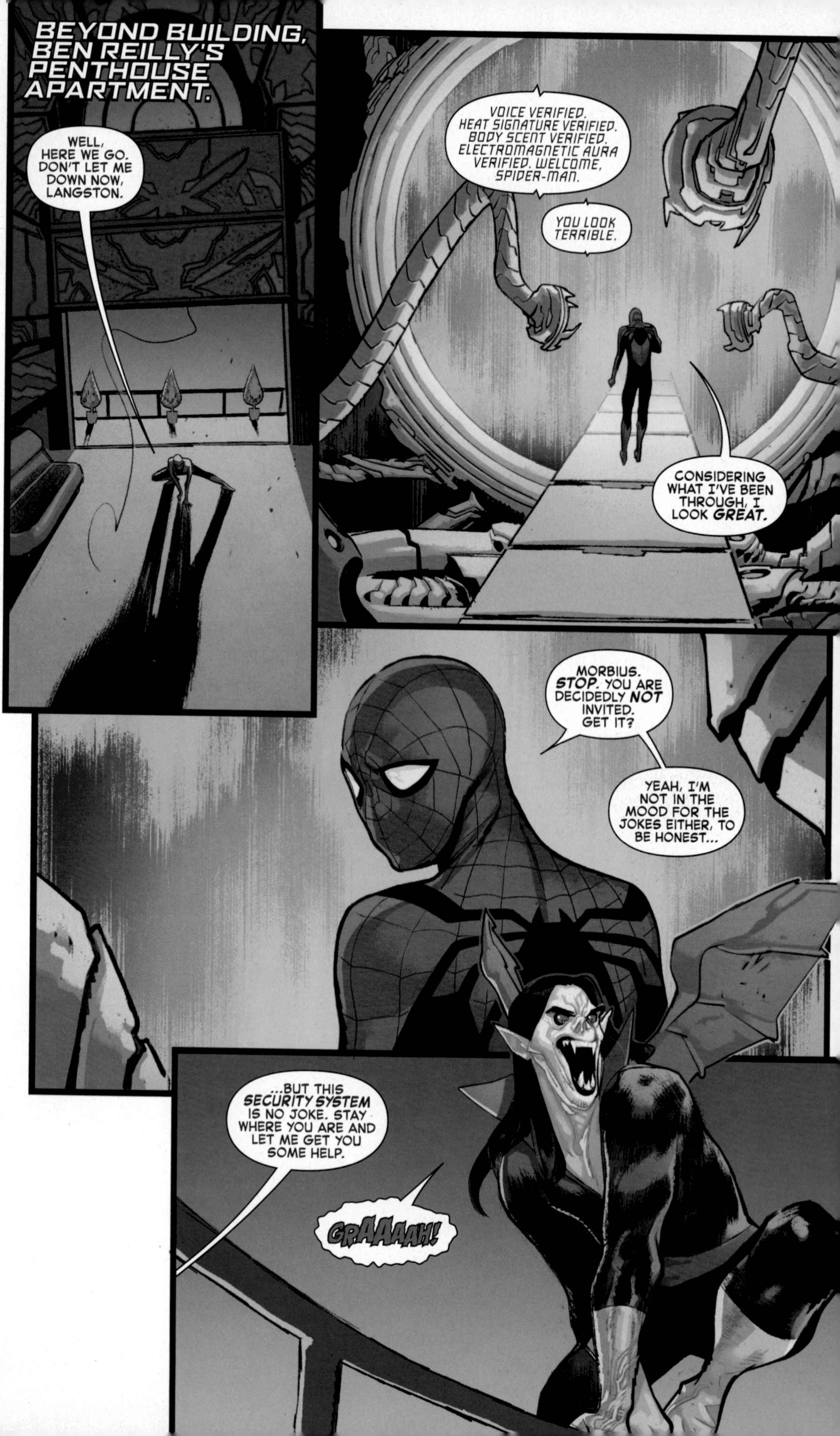

BEYOND BUILDING, BEN REILLY'S PENTHOUSE APARTMENT.
WELL, HERE WE GO. DON'T LET ME DOWN NOW, LANGSTON.
VOICE VERIFIED. HEAT SIGNATURE VERIFIED. BODY SCENT VERIFIED. ELECTROMAGNETIC AURA VERIFIED. WELCOME, SPIDER-MAN.
YOU LOOK TERRIBLE.
CONSIDERING WHAT I'VE BEEN THROUGH, I LOOK GREAT.
MORBIUS. STOP. YOU ARE DECIDEDLY NOT INVITED. GET IT?
YEAH, I'M NOT IN THE MOOD FOR THE JOKES EITHER, TO BE HONEST...
...BUT THIS SECURITY SYSTEM IS NO JOKE. STAY WHERE YOU ARE AND LET ME GET YOU SOME HELP.
GRAAAAAH!

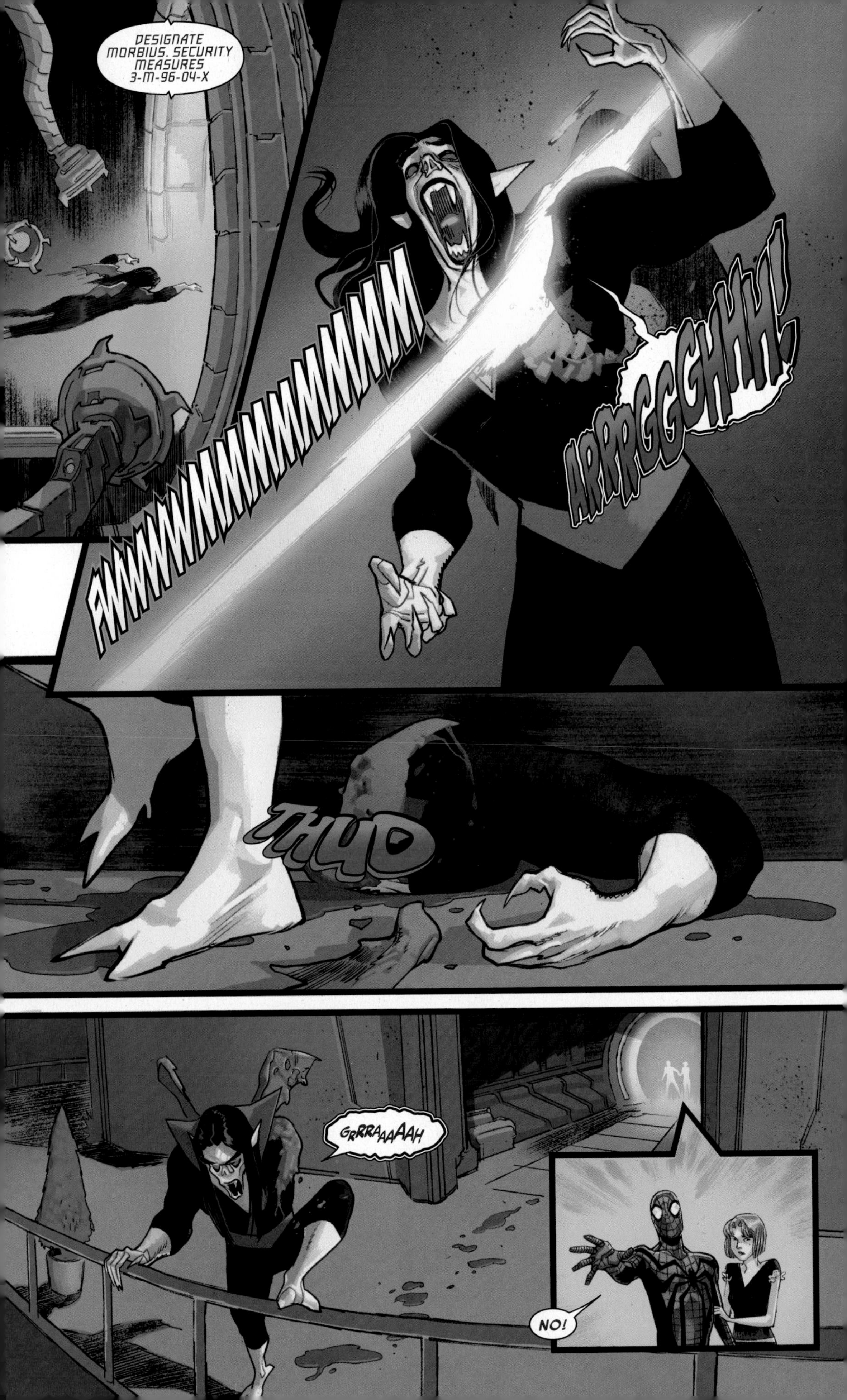
DESIGNATE MORBIUS. SECURITY MEASURES 3-M-96-04-X
AWWWWMMMMMMMMMMM
ARRRGGGHHH!
THUD
GRRRAAAAAH
NO!

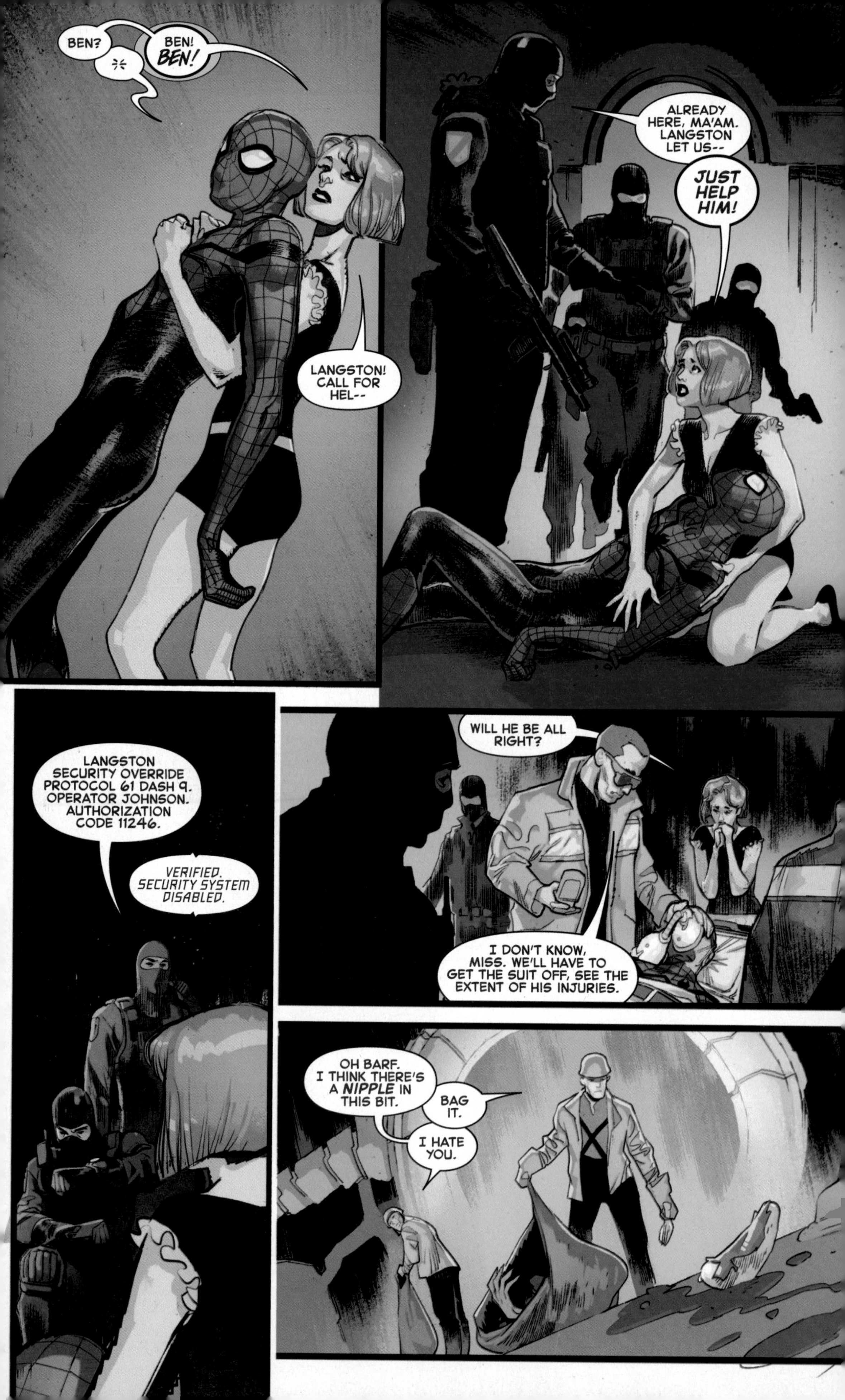
BEN?
BEN! BEN!
LANGSTON! CALL FOR HEL--
ALREADY HERE, MA'AM. LANGSTON LET US--
JUST HELP HIM!
LANGSTON SECURITY OVERRIDE PROTOCOL 61 DASH 9. OPERATOR JOHNSON. AUTHORIZATION CODE 11246.
VERIFIED. SECURITY SYSTEM DISABLED.
WILL HE BE ALL RIGHT?
I DON'T KNOW, MISS. WE'LL HAVE TO GET THE SUIT OFF, SEE THE EXTENT OF HIS INJURIES.
OH BARF. I THINK THERE'S A NIPPLE IN THIS BIT.
BAG IT.
I HATE YOU.

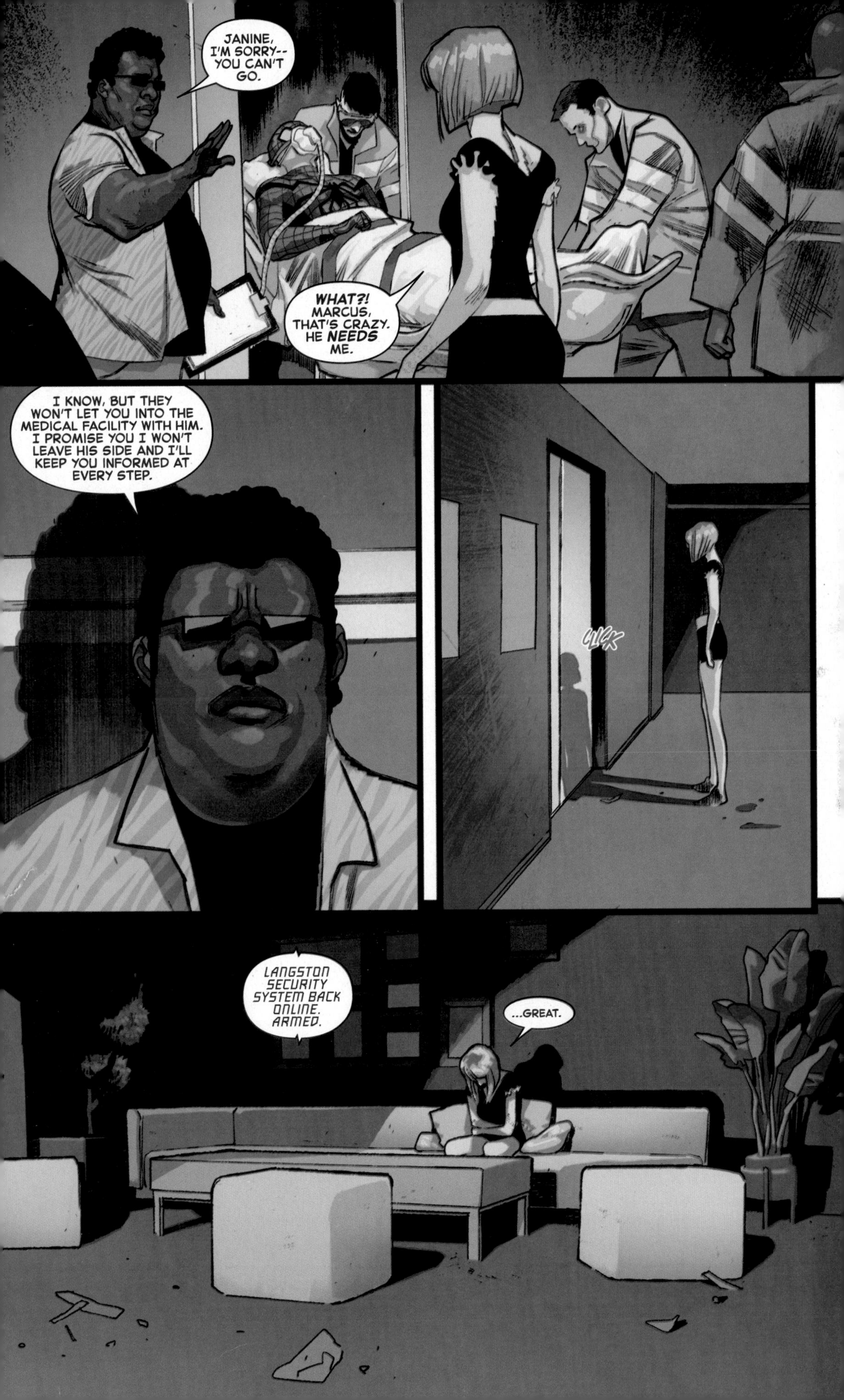
JANINE, I'M SORRY-- YOU CAN'T GO.
WHAT?! MARCUS, THAT'S CRAZY. HE NEEDS ME.
I KNOW, BUT THEY WON'T LET YOU INTO THE MEDICAL FACILITY WITH HIM. I PROMISE YOU I WON'T LEAVE HIS SIDE AND I'LL KEEP YOU INFORMED AT EVERY STEP.
CLICK
LANGSTON SECURITY SYSTEM BACK ONLINE. ARMED.
...GREAT.

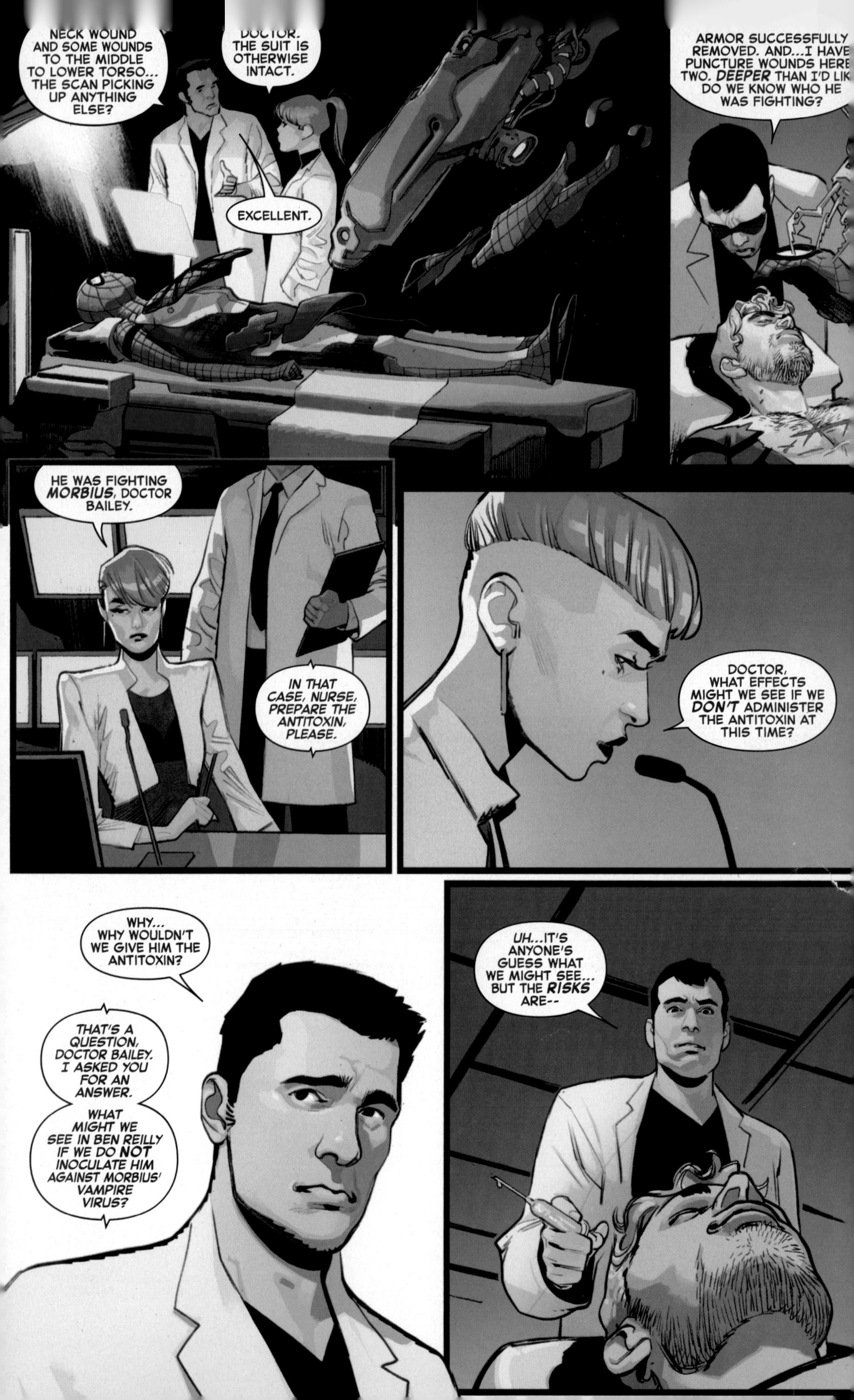
NECK WOUND AND SOME WOUNDS TO THE MIDDLE TO LOWER TORSO... THE SCAN PICKING UP ANYTHING ELSE?
DOCTOR. THE SUIT IS OTHERWISE INTACT.
EXCELLENT.
ARMOR SUCCESSFULLY REMOVED. AND...I HAVE PUNCTURE WOUNDS HERE TWO. DEEPER THAN I'D LIK DO WE KNOW WHO HE WAS FIGHTING?
HE WAS FIGHTING MORBIUS, DOCTOR BAILEY.
IN THAT CASE, NURSE, PREPARE THE ANTITOXIN, PLEASE.
DOCTOR, WHAT EFFECTS MIGHT WE SEE IF WE DON'T ADMINISTER THE ANTITOXIN AT THIS TIME?
WHY... WHY WOULDN'T WE GIVE HIM THE ANTITOXIN?
THAT'S A QUESTION, DOCTOR BAILEY. I ASKED YOU FOR AN ANSWER.
WHAT MIGHT WE SEE IN BEN REILLY IF WE DO NOT INOCULATE HIM AGAINST MORBIUS' VAMPIRE VIRUS?
UH...IT'S ANYONE'S GUESS WHAT WE MIGHT SEE... BUT THE RISKS ARE--

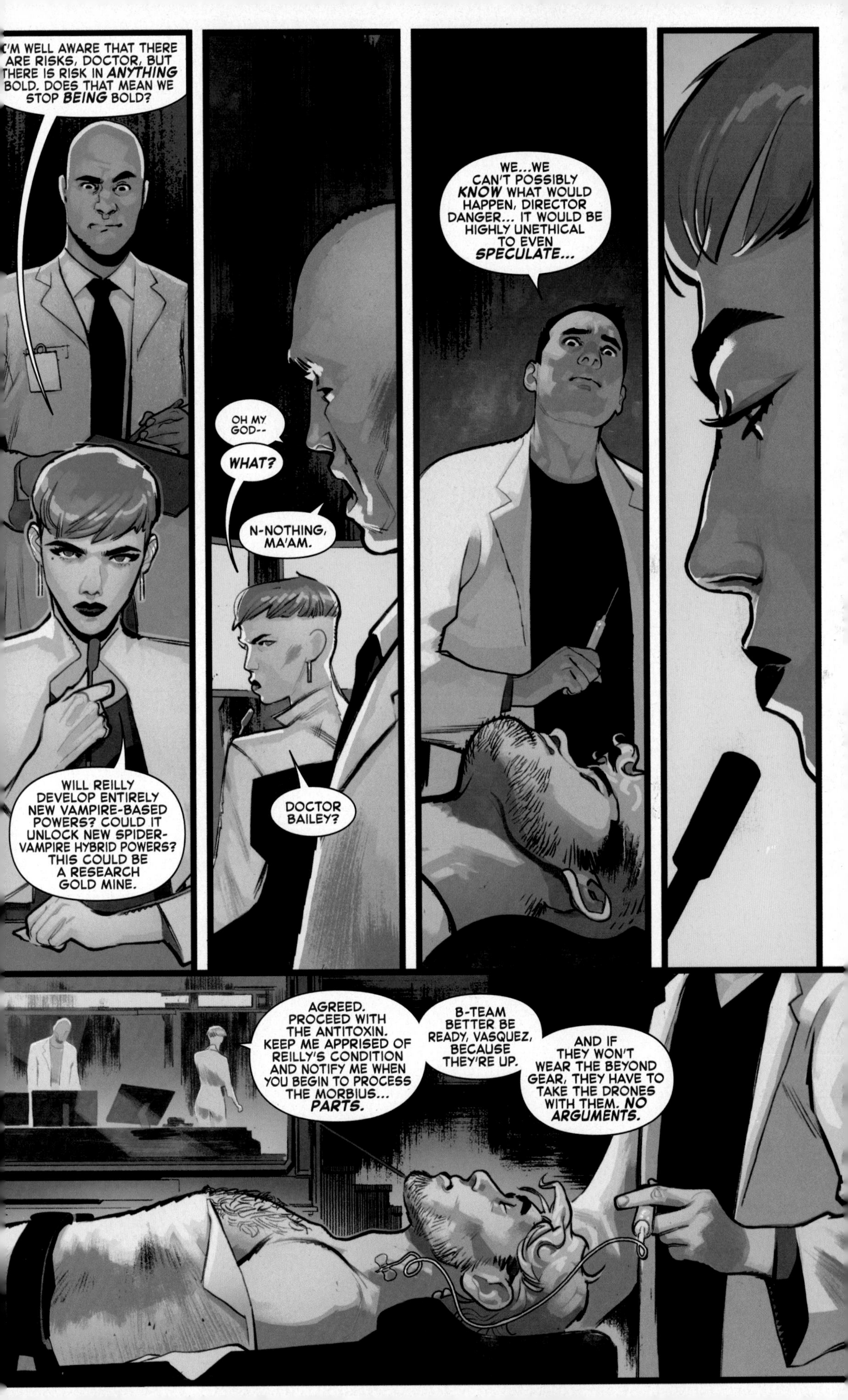
I'M WELL AWARE THAT THERE ARE RISKS, DOCTOR, BUT THERE IS RISK IN *ANYTHING* BOLD. DOES THAT MEAN WE STOP *BEING* BOLD?
WILL REILLY DEVELOP ENTIRELY NEW VAMPIRE-BASED POWERS? COULD IT UNLOCK NEW SPIDER-VAMPIRE HYBRID POWERS? THIS COULD BE A RESEARCH GOLD MINE.
OH MY GOD--
WHAT?
N-NOTHING, MA'AM.
DOCTOR BAILEY?
WE...WE CAN'T POSSIBLY *KNOW* WHAT WOULD HAPPEN, DIRECTOR DANGER... IT WOULD BE HIGHLY UNETHICAL TO EVEN *SPECULATE...*
AGREED. PROCEED WITH THE ANTITOXIN. KEEP ME APPRISED OF REILLY'S CONDITION AND NOTIFY ME WHEN YOU BEGIN TO PROCESS THE MORBIUS... *PARTS.*
B-TEAM BETTER BE READY, VASQUEZ, BECAUSE THEY'RE UP.
AND IF THEY WON'T WEAR THE BEYOND GEAR, THEY HAVE TO TAKE THE DRONES WITH THEM. *NO ARGUMENTS.*

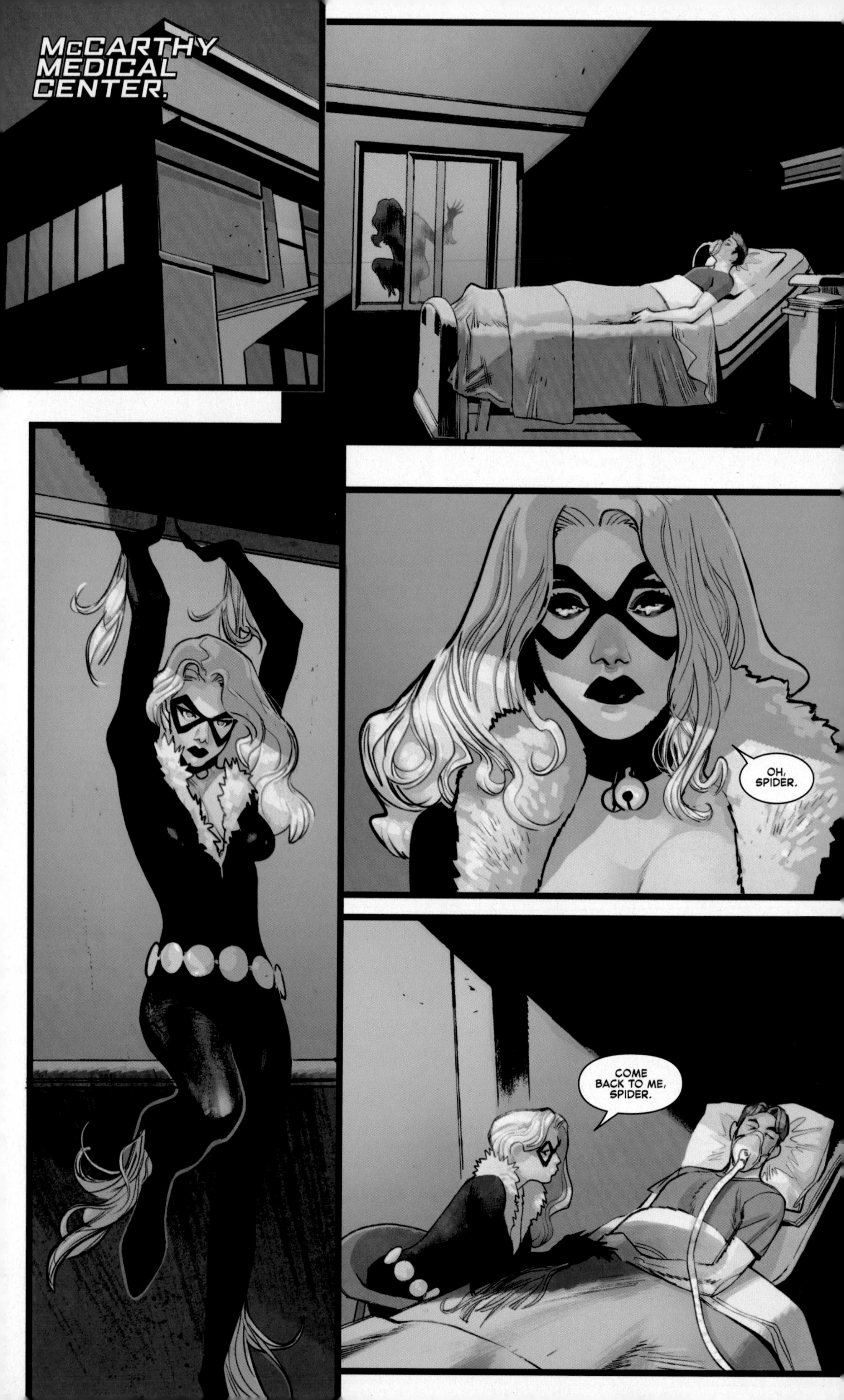
McCARTHY MEDICAL CENTER.
OH, SPIDER.
COME BACK TO ME, SPIDER.

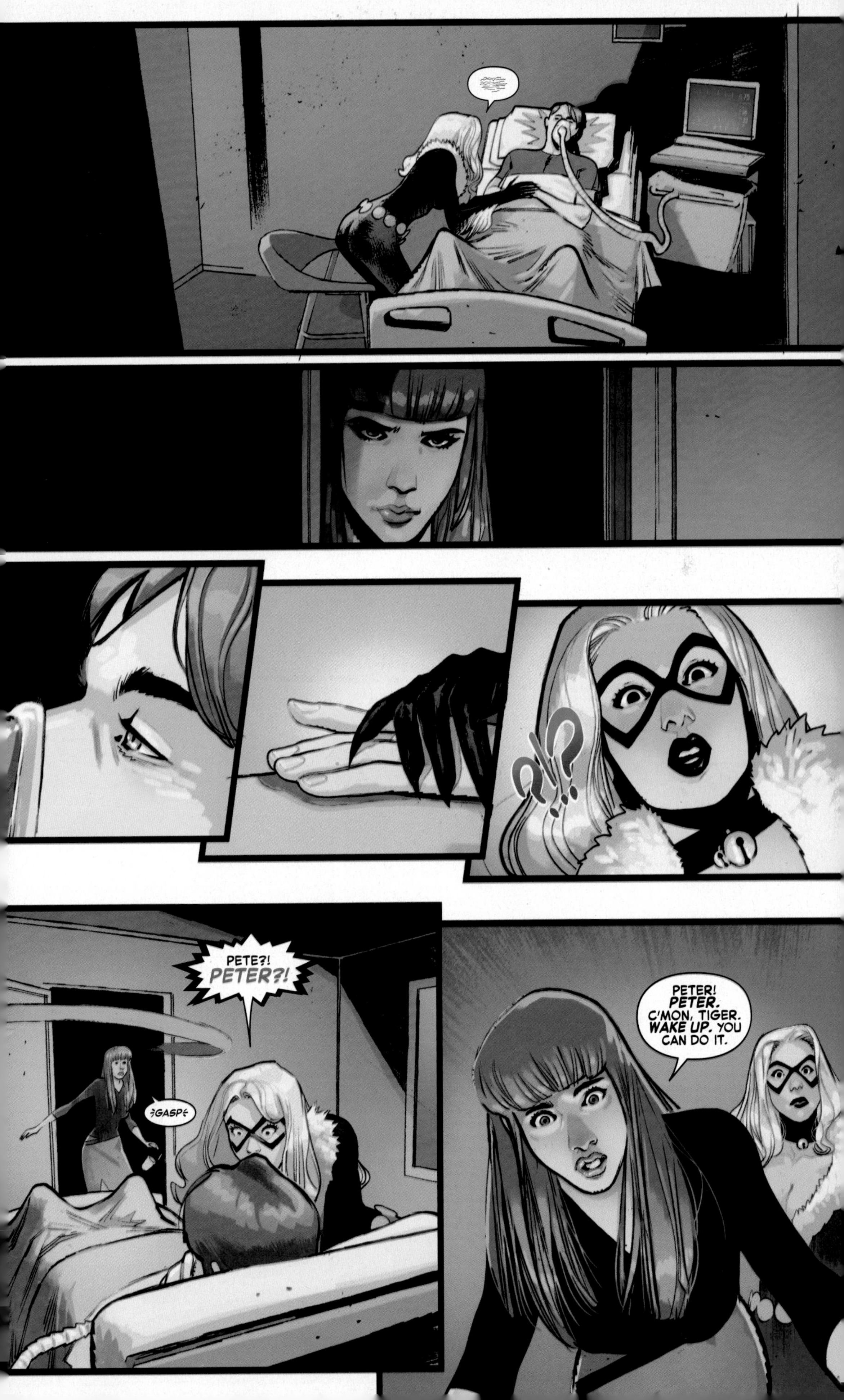

?!?
PETE?! PETER?!
GASP
PETER! PETER. C'MON, TIGER. WAKE UP. YOU CAN DO IT.

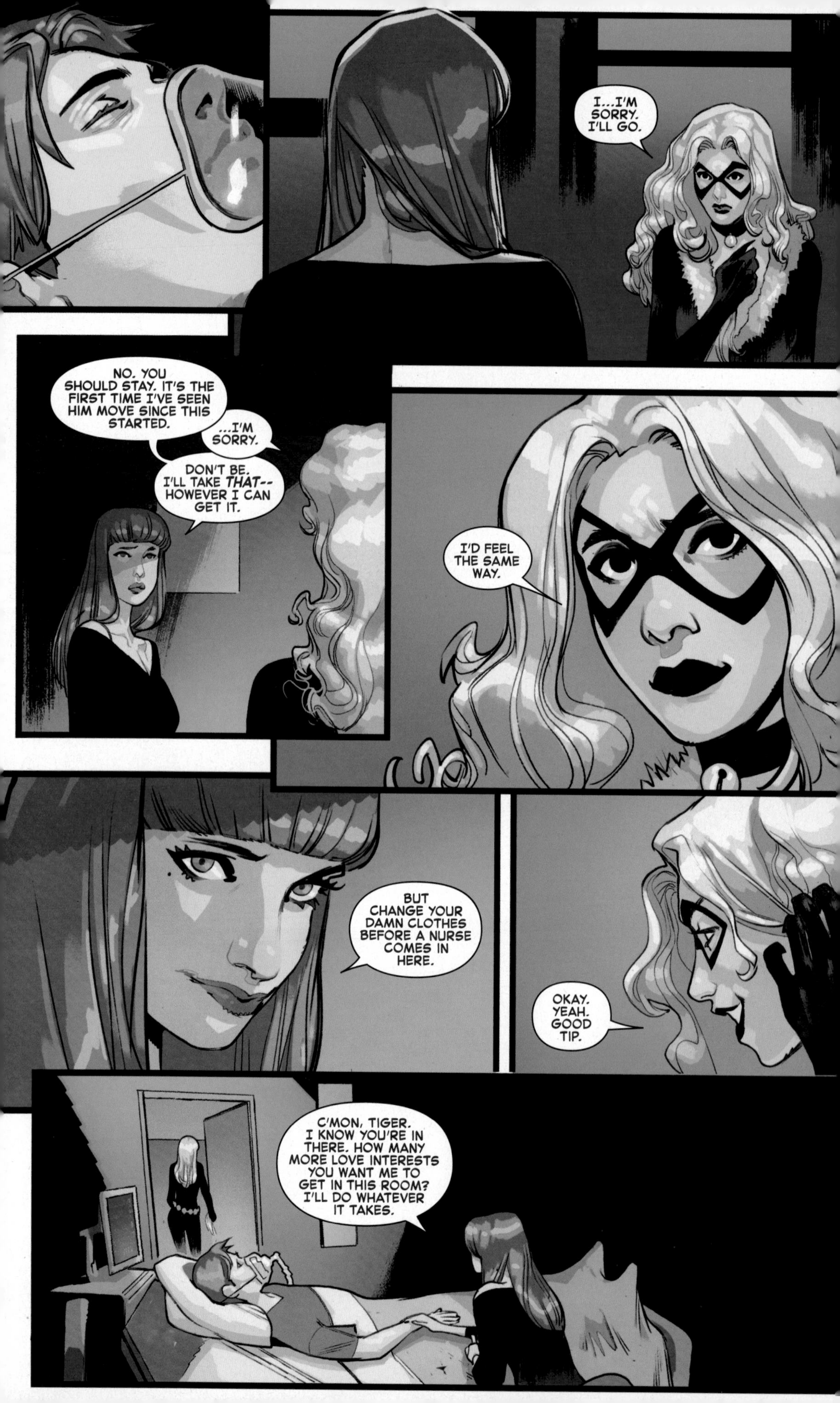
I...I'M SORRY. I'LL GO.
NO. YOU SHOULD STAY. IT'S THE FIRST TIME I'VE SEEN HIM MOVE SINCE THIS STARTED.
...I'M SORRY.
DON'T BE. I'LL TAKE *THAT*-- HOWEVER I CAN GET IT.
I'D FEEL THE SAME WAY.
BUT CHANGE YOUR DAMN CLOTHES BEFORE A NURSE COMES IN HERE.
OKAY. YEAH. GOOD TIP.
C'MON, TIGER. I KNOW YOU'RE IN THERE. HOW MANY MORE LOVE INTERESTS YOU WANT ME TO GET IN THIS ROOM? I'LL DO WHATEVER IT TAKES.

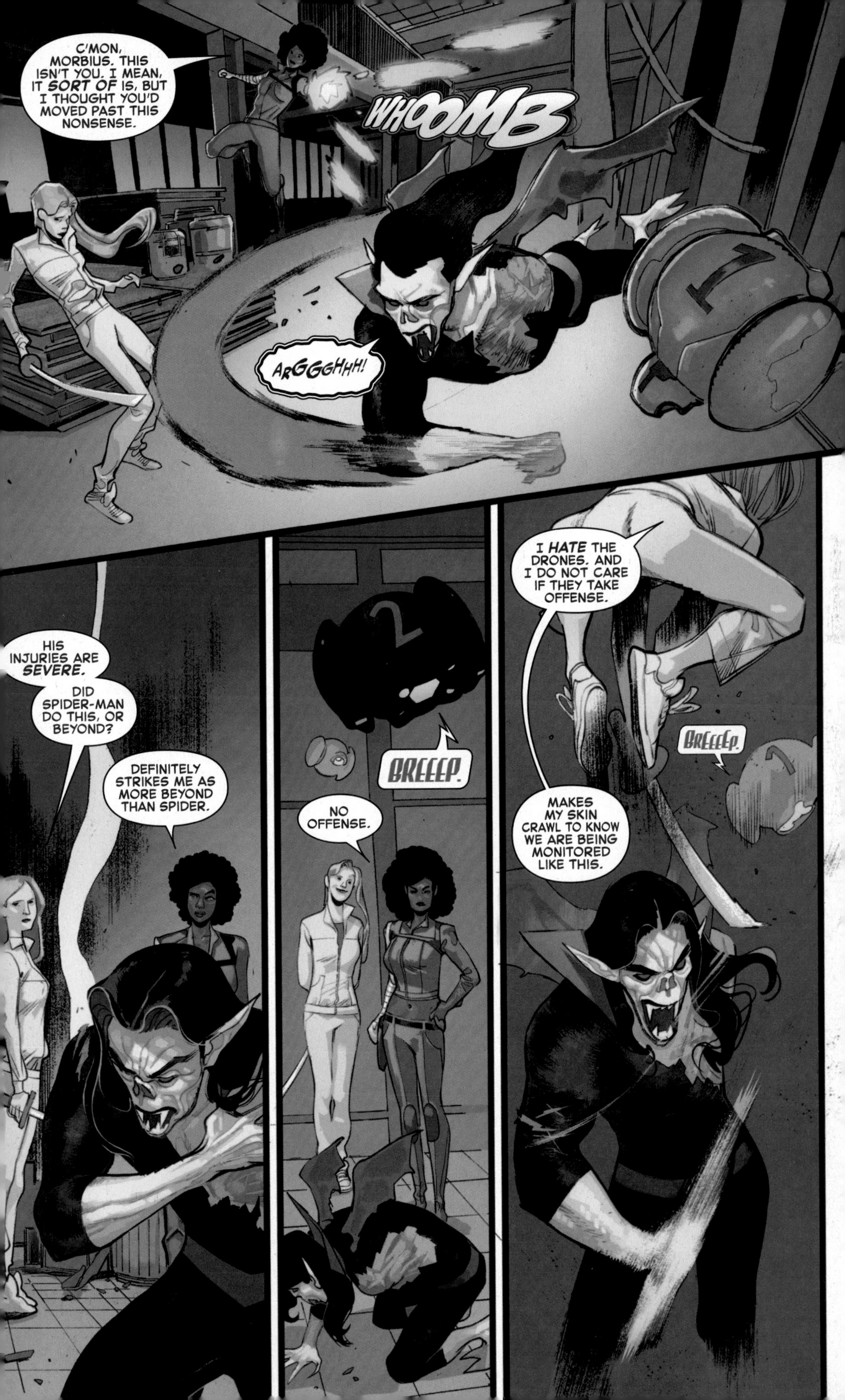

C'MON, MORBIUS. THIS ISN'T YOU. I MEAN, IT SORT OF IS, BUT I THOUGHT YOU'D MOVED PAST THIS NONSENSE.
WHOOMB
ARGGGHHH!
HIS INJURIES ARE SEVERE.
DID SPIDER-MAN DO THIS, OR BEYOND?
DEFINITELY STRIKES ME AS MORE BEYOND THAN SPIDER.
BREEEP.
NO OFFENSE.
I HATE THE DRONES. AND I DO NOT CARE IF THEY TAKE OFFENSE.
BREEEEP.
MAKES MY SKIN CRAWL TO KNOW WE ARE BEING MONITORED LIKE THIS.

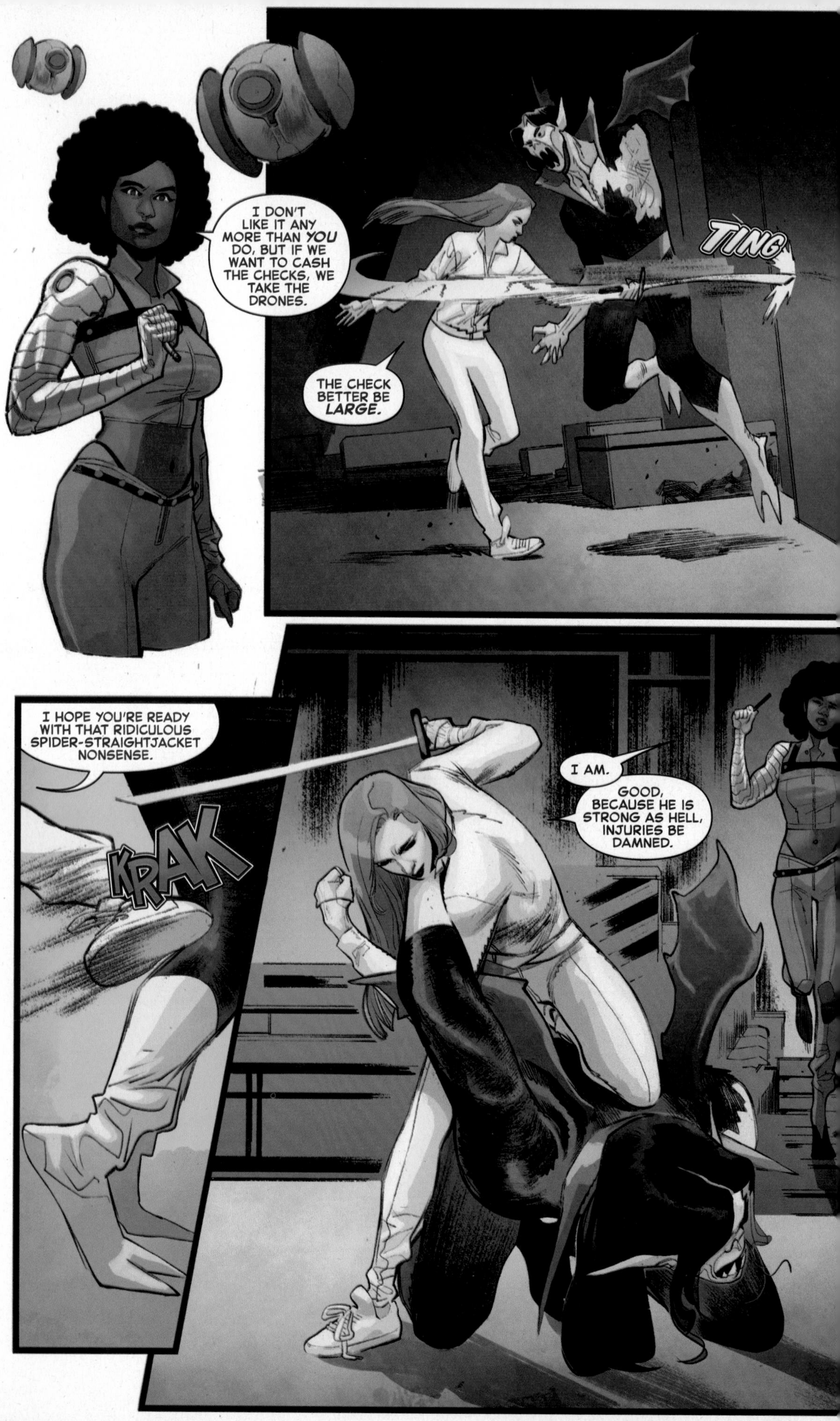
I DON'T LIKE IT ANY MORE THAN *YOU* DO, BUT IF WE WANT TO CASH THE CHECKS, WE TAKE THE DRONES.
TING
THE CHECK BETTER BE *LARGE.*
I HOPE YOU'RE READY WITH THAT RIDICULOUS SPIDER-STRAIGHTJACKET NONSENSE.
KRAK
I AM.
GOOD, BECAUSE HE IS STRONG AS HELL, INJURIES BE DAMNED.

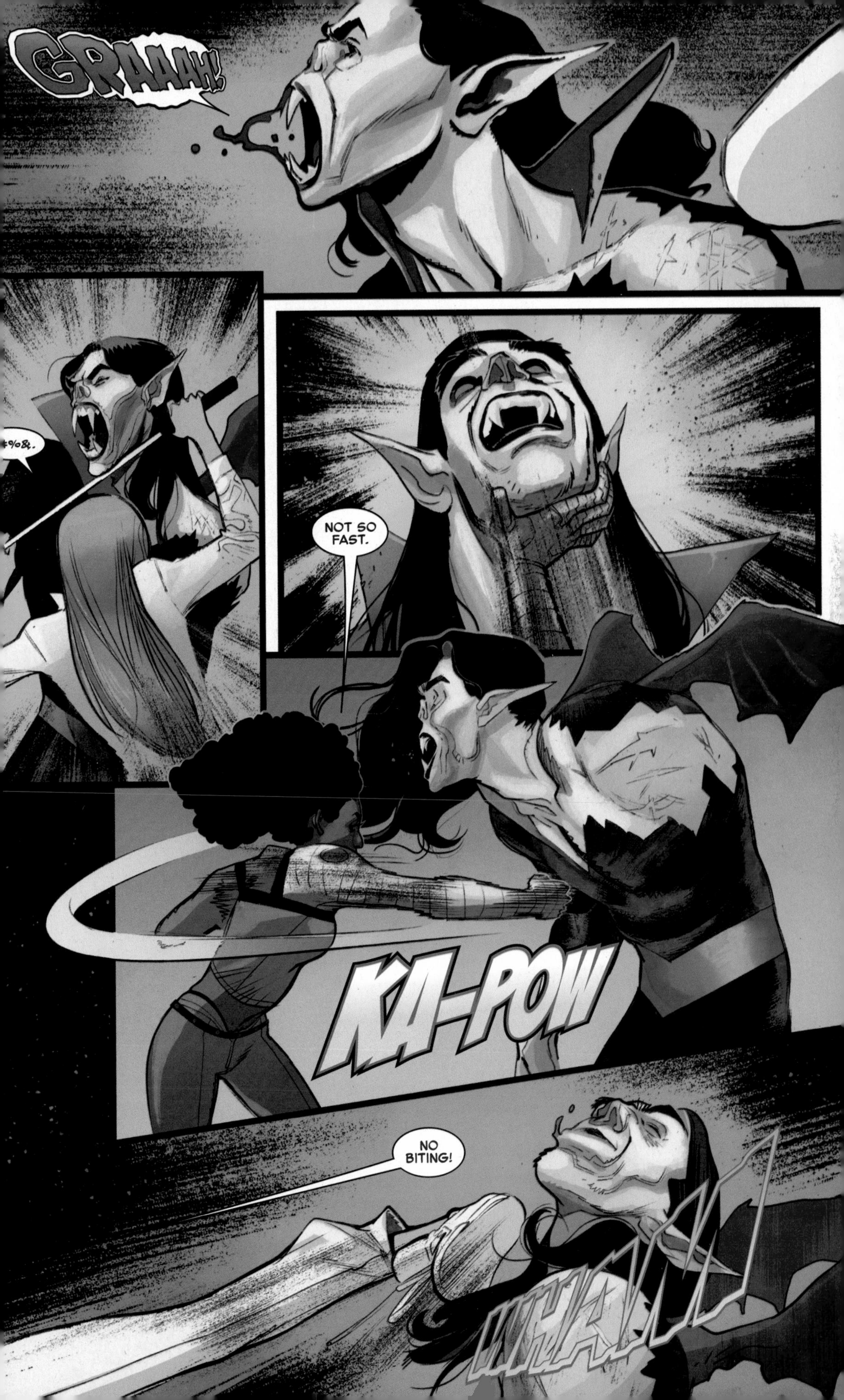
GRAAAH!
NOT SO FAST.
KA-POW
NO BITING!

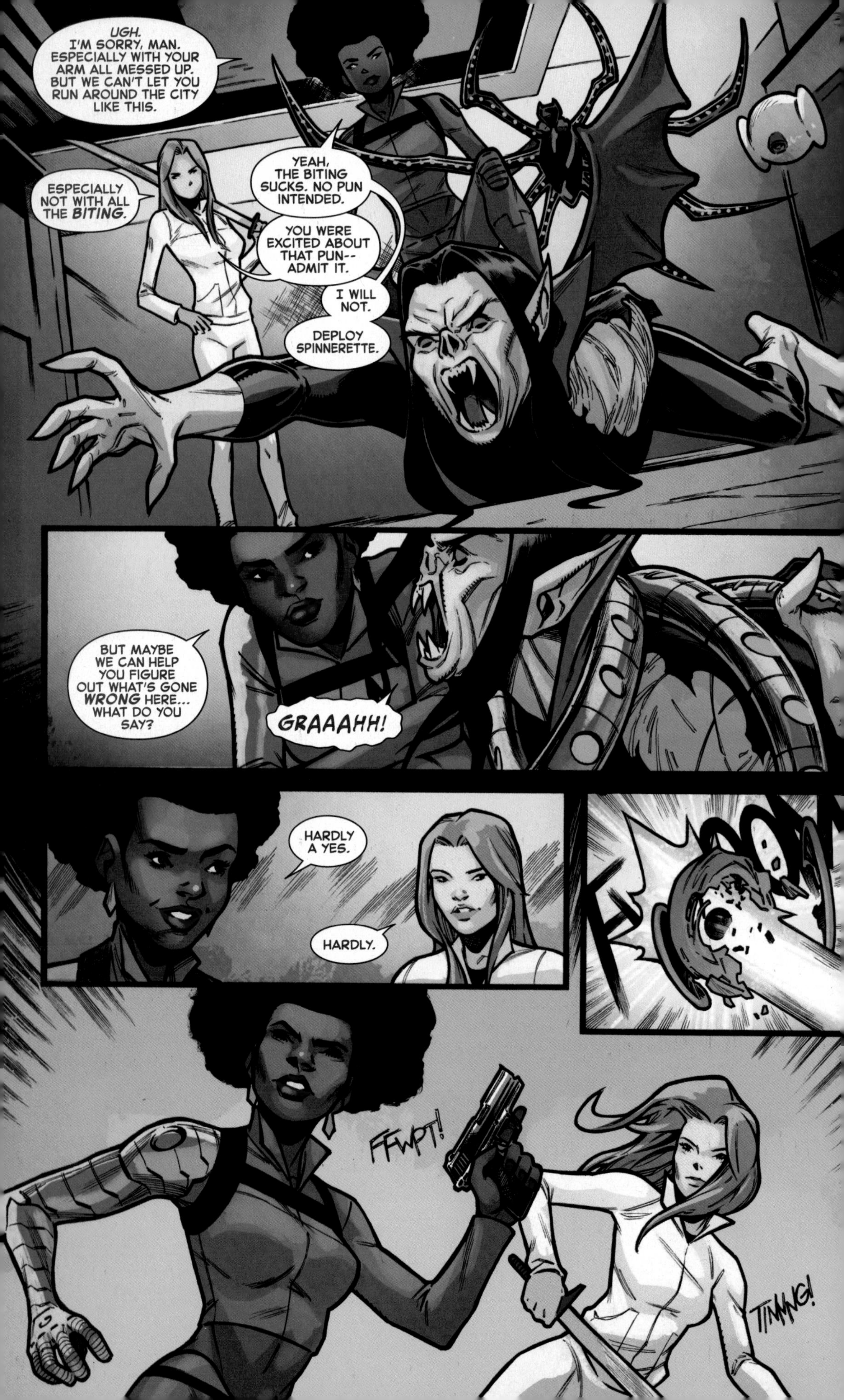

UGH. I'M SORRY, MAN. ESPECIALLY WITH YOUR ARM ALL MESSED UP. BUT WE CAN'T LET YOU RUN AROUND THE CITY LIKE THIS.
ESPECIALLY NOT WITH ALL THE *BITING*.
YEAH, THE BITING SUCKS. NO PUN INTENDED.
YOU WERE EXCITED ABOUT THAT PUN-- ADMIT IT.
I WILL NOT.
DEPLOY SPINNERETTE.
BUT MAYBE WE CAN HELP YOU FIGURE OUT WHAT'S GONE *WRONG* HERE... WHAT DO YOU SAY?
GRAAAHH!
HARDLY A YES.
HARDLY.
FFWPT!
TINNNG!

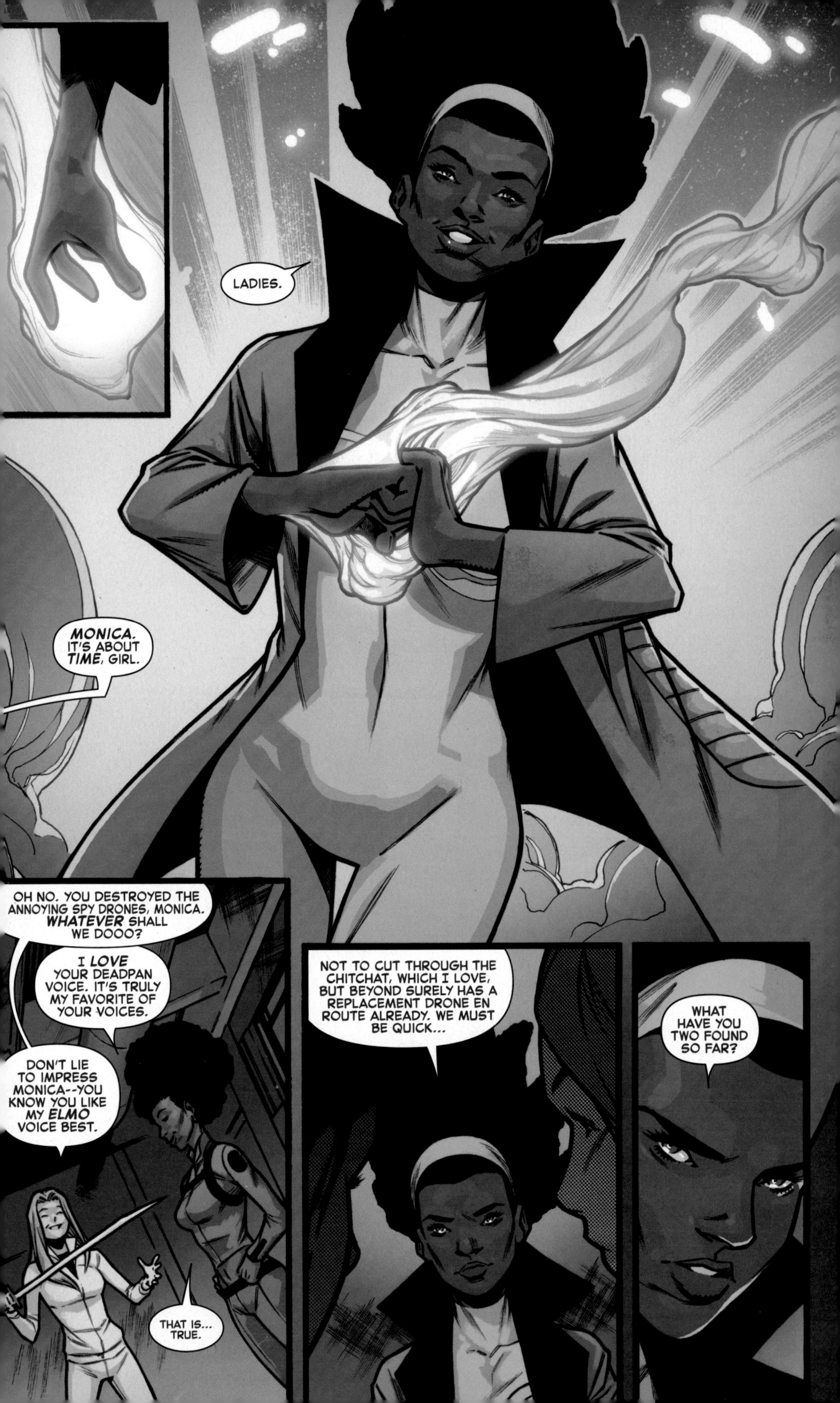

LADIES.
MONICA. IT'S ABOUT TIME, GIRL.
OH NO. YOU DESTROYED THE ANNOYING SPY DRONES, MONICA. WHATEVER SHALL WE DOOO?
I LOVE YOUR DEADPAN VOICE. IT'S TRULY MY FAVORITE OF YOUR VOICES.
DON'T LIE TO IMPRESS MONICA--YOU KNOW YOU LIKE MY ELMO VOICE BEST.
THAT IS... TRUE.
NOT TO CUT THROUGH THE CHITCHAT, WHICH I LOVE, BUT BEYOND SURELY HAS A REPLACEMENT DRONE EN ROUTE ALREADY. WE MUST BE QUICK...
WHAT HAVE YOU TWO FOUND SO FAR?

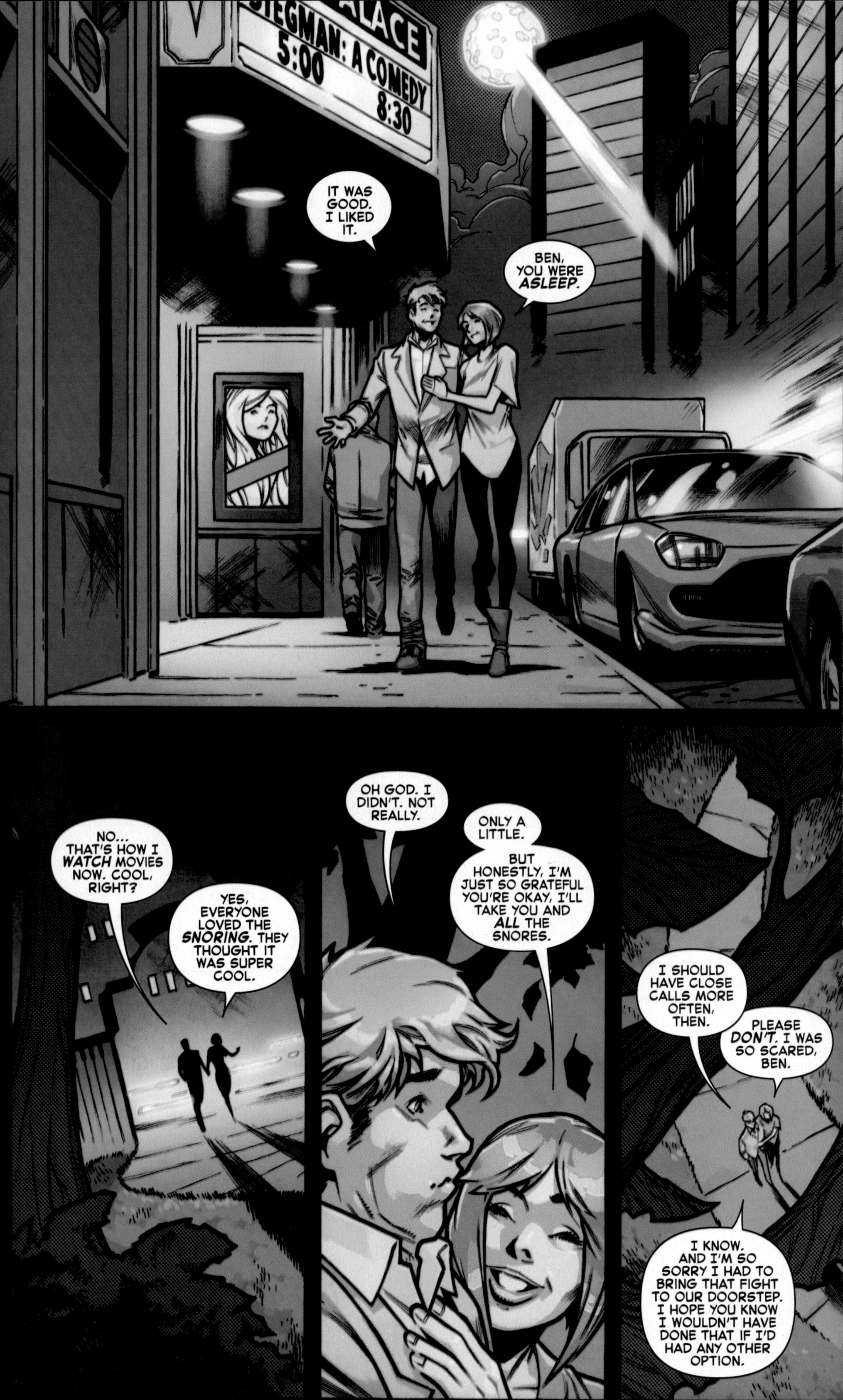
PALACE
SIEGMAN: A COMEDY
5:00
8:30
IT WAS GOOD. I LIKED IT.
BEN, YOU WERE *ASLEEP.*
NO... THAT'S HOW I *WATCH* MOVIES NOW. COOL, RIGHT?
YES, EVERYONE LOVED THE *SNORING.* THEY THOUGHT IT WAS SUPER COOL.
OH GOD. I DIDN'T. NOT REALLY.
ONLY A LITTLE.
BUT HONESTLY, I'M JUST SO GRATEFUL YOU'RE OKAY, I'LL TAKE YOU AND *ALL* THE SNORES.
I SHOULD HAVE CLOSE CALLS MORE OFTEN, THEN.
PLEASE *DON'T.* I WAS SO SCARED, BEN.
I KNOW. AND I'M SO SORRY I HAD TO BRING THAT FIGHT TO OUR DOORSTEP. I HOPE YOU KNOW I WOULDN'T HAVE DONE THAT IF I'D HAD ANY OTHER OPTION.

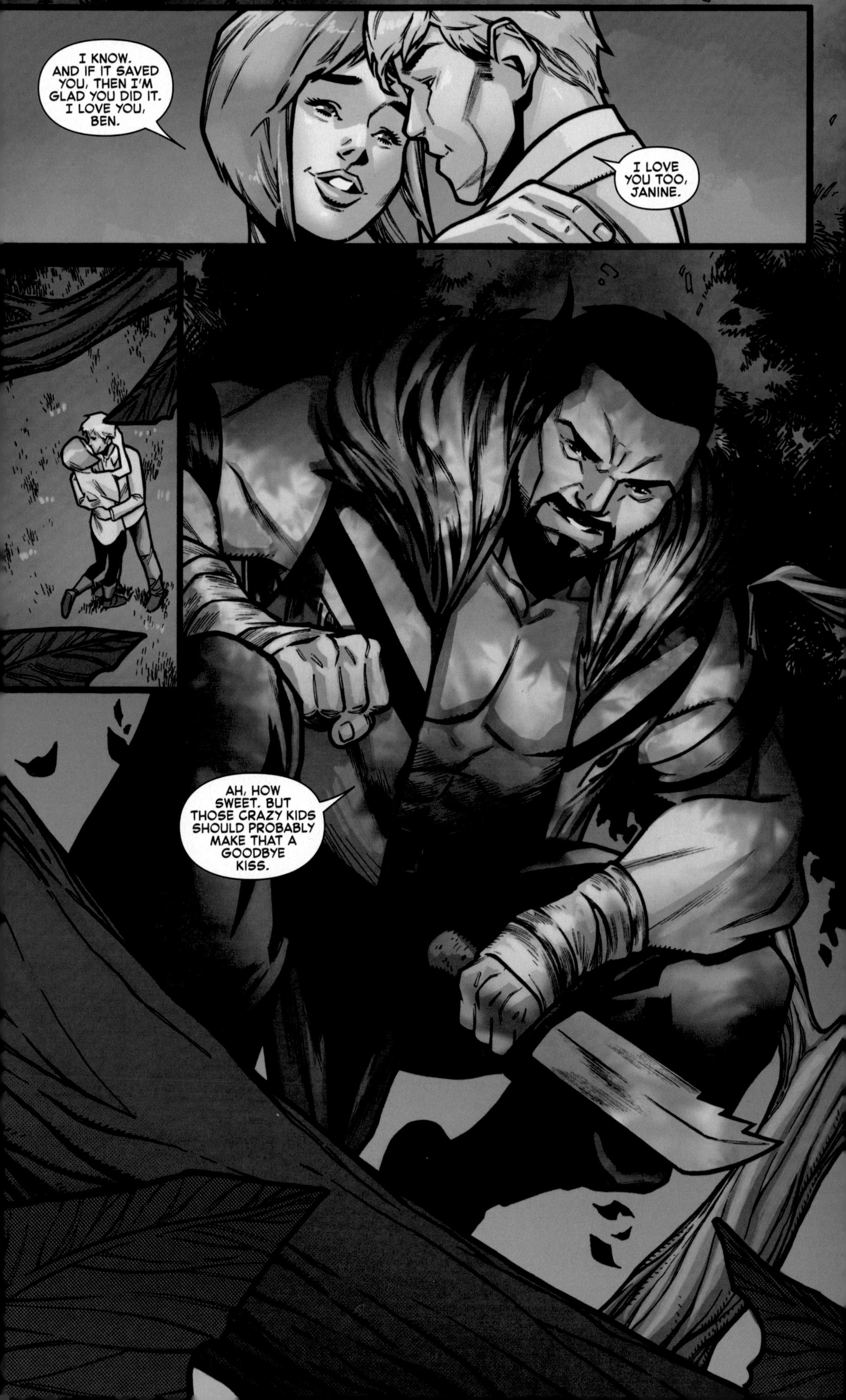
I KNOW. AND IF IT SAVED YOU, THEN I'M GLAD YOU DID IT. I LOVE YOU, BEN.
I LOVE YOU TOO, JANINE.
AH, HOW SWEET. BUT THOSE CRAZY KIDS SHOULD PROBABLY MAKE THAT A GOODBYE KISS.

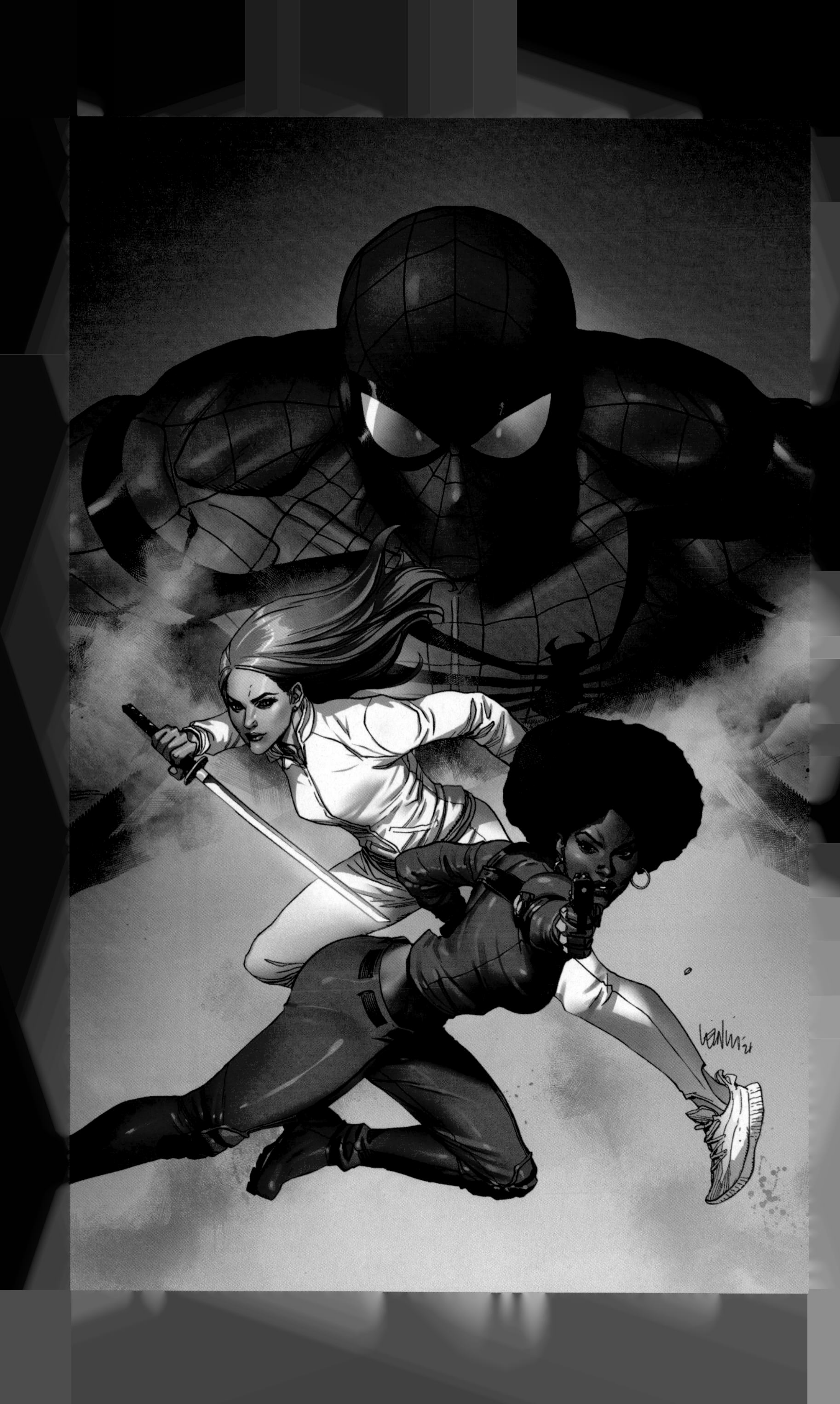

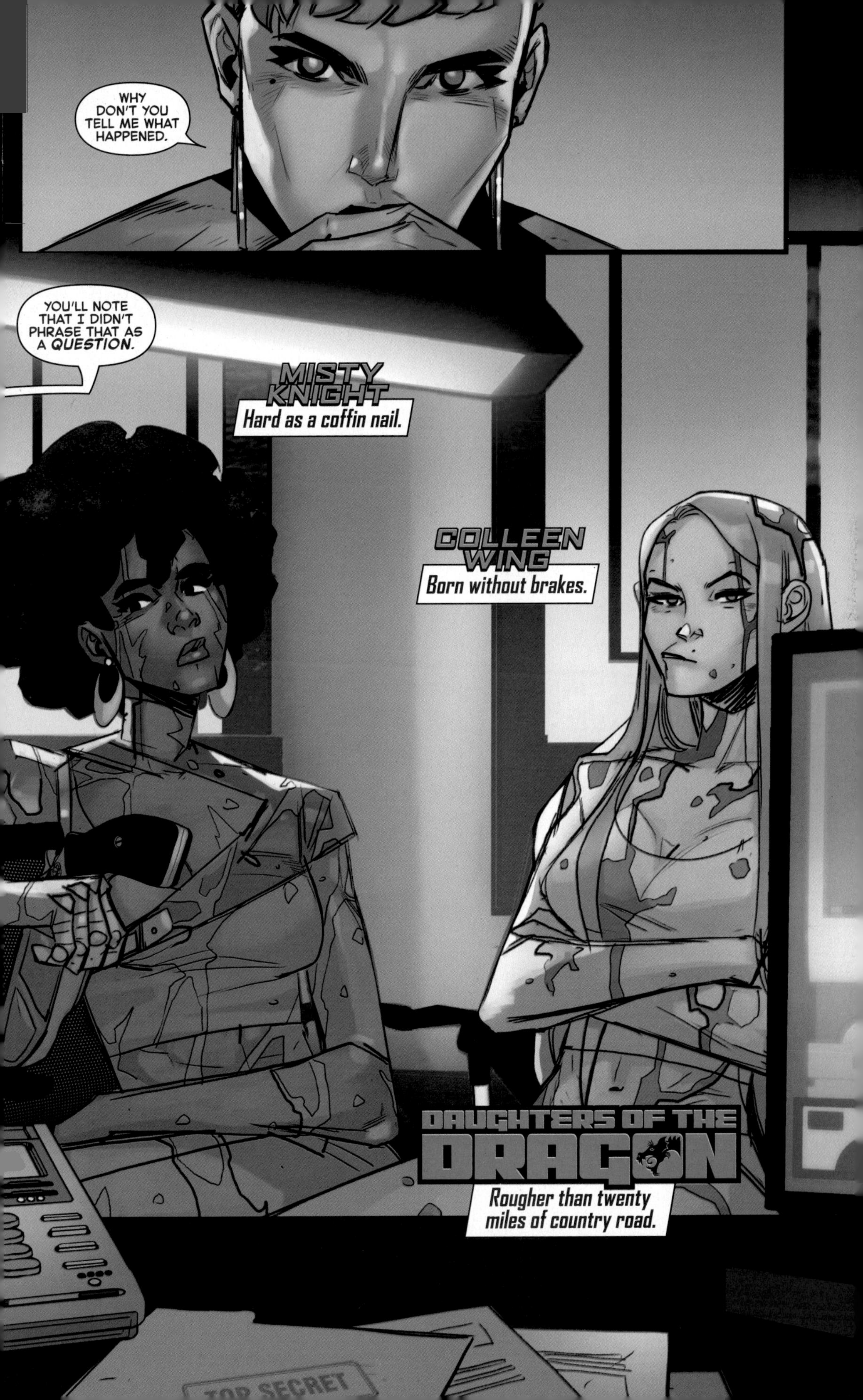
WHY DON'T YOU TELL ME WHAT HAPPENED.
YOU'LL NOTE THAT I DIDN'T PHRASE THAT AS A *QUESTION*.
MISTY KNIGHT
Hard as a coffin nail.
COLLEEN WING
Born without brakes.
DAUGHTERS OF THE DRAGON
Rougher than twenty miles of country road.
TOP SECRET

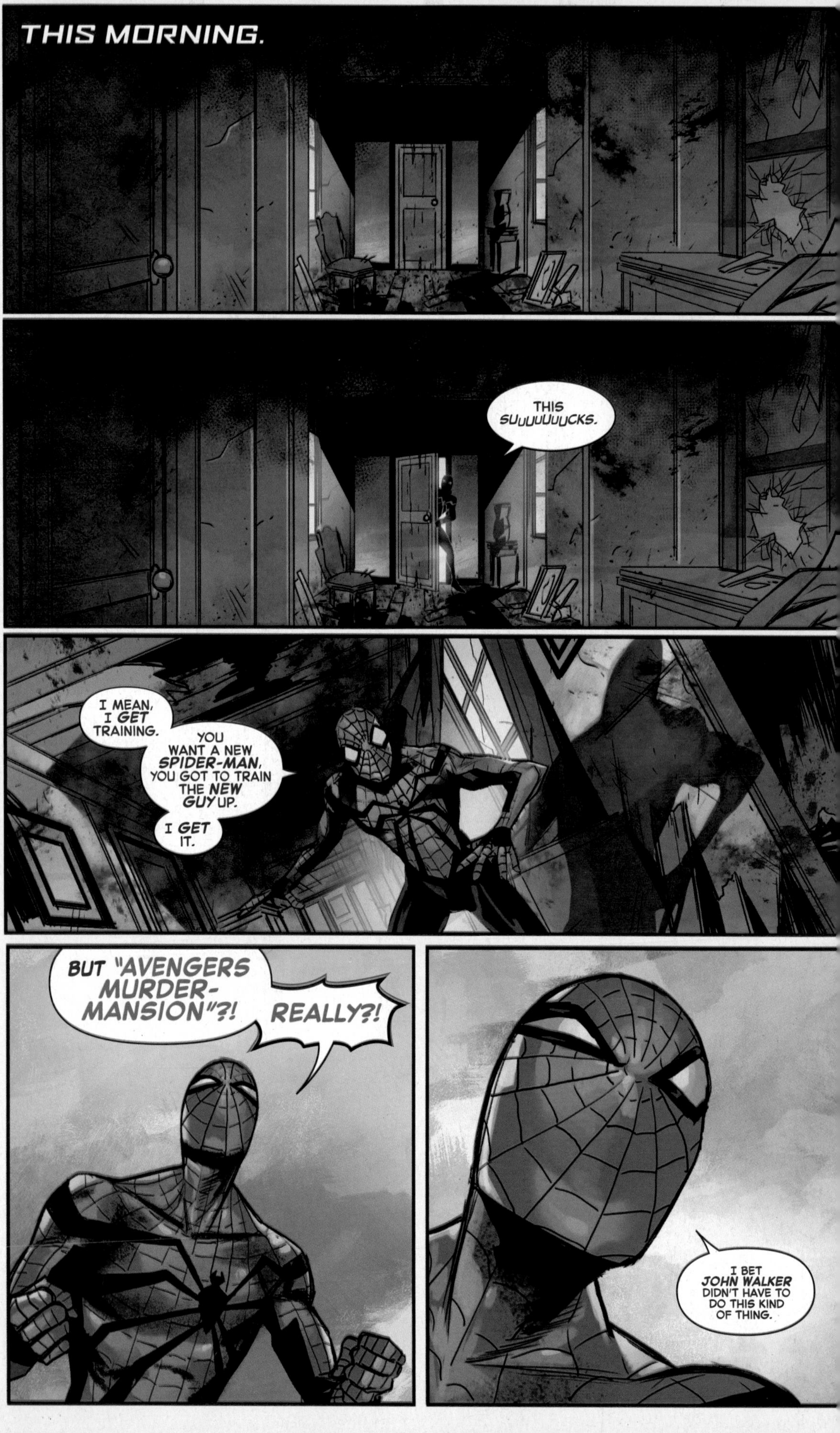
THIS MORNING.
THIS SUUUUUUUCKS.
I MEAN, I GET TRAINING.
YOU WANT A NEW SPIDER-MAN, YOU GOT TO TRAIN THE NEW GUY UP.
I GET IT.
BUT "AVENGERS MURDER-MANSION"?!
REALLY?!
I BET JOHN WALKER DIDN'T HAVE TO DO THIS KIND OF THING.

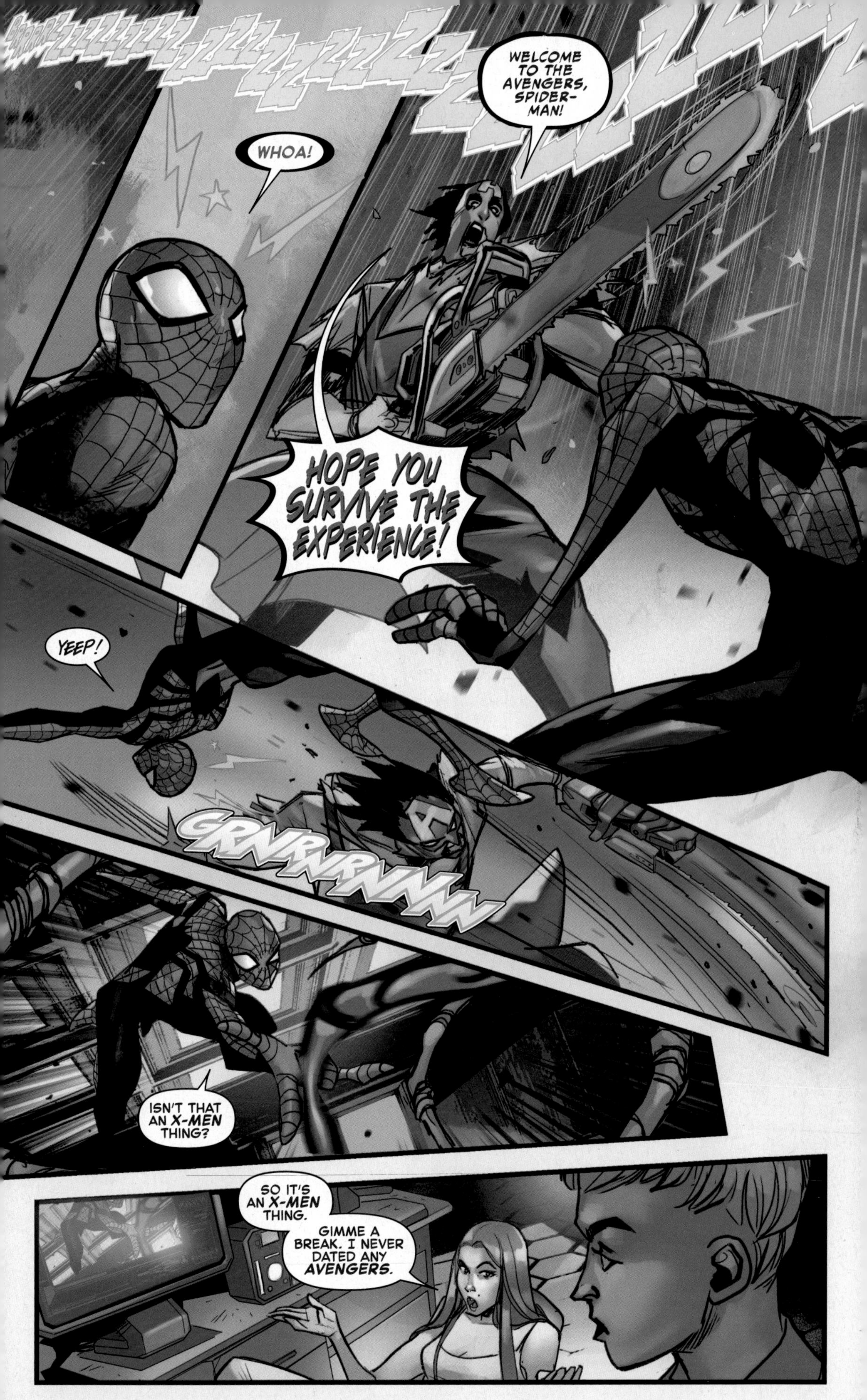
WHOA!
WELCOME TO THE AVENGERS, SPIDER-MAN!
HOPE YOU SURVIVE THE EXPERIENCE!
YEEP!
ISN'T THAT AN *X-MEN* THING?
SO IT'S AN *X-MEN* THING.
GIMME A BREAK. I NEVER DATED ANY *AVENGERS.*

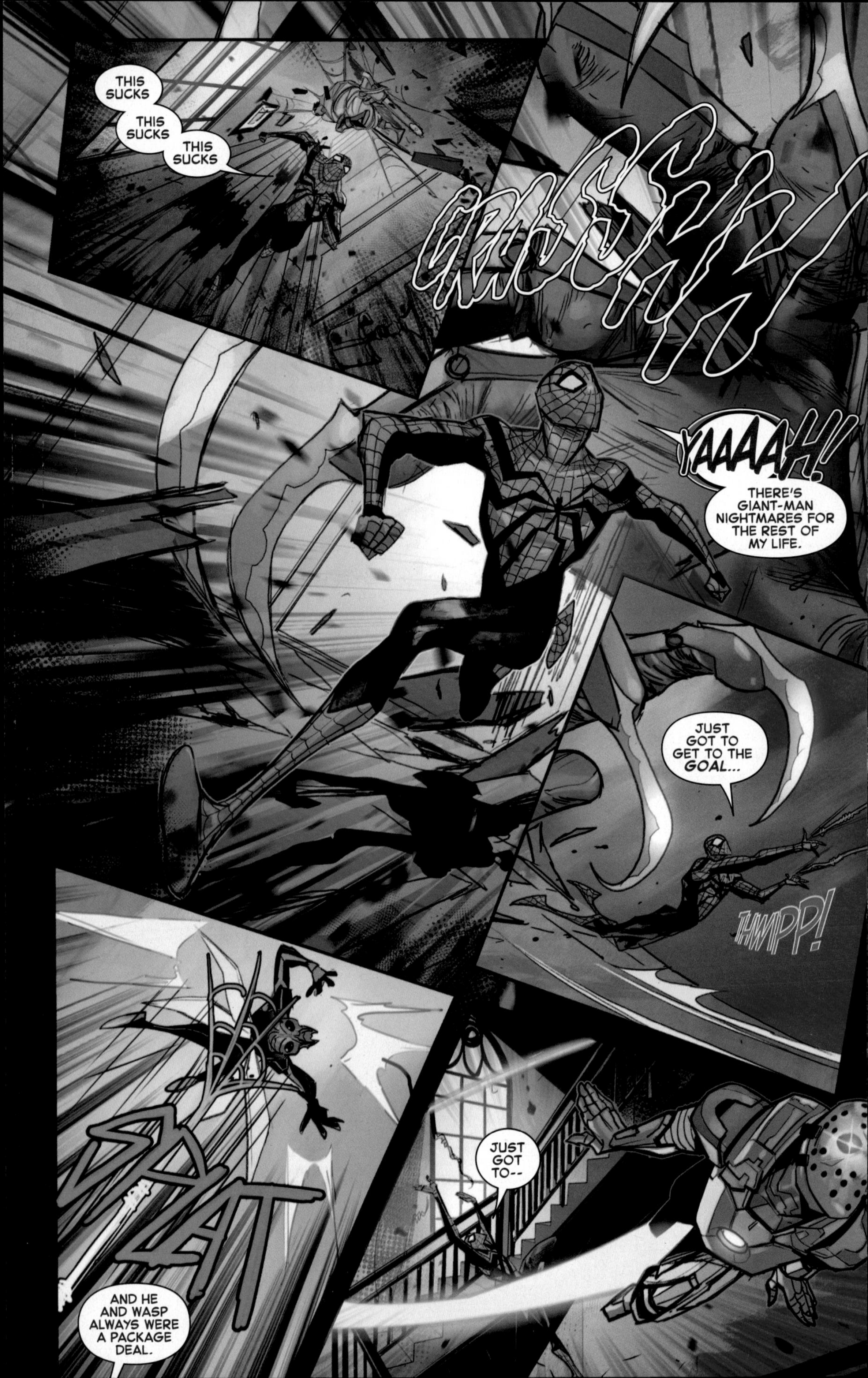
THIS SUCKS
THIS SUCKS
THIS SUCKS
YAAAAH!!
THERE'S GIANT-MAN NIGHTMARES FOR THE REST OF MY LIFE.
JUST GOT TO GET TO THE GOAL...
THWIPP!
AND HE AND WASP ALWAYS WERE A PACKAGE DEAL.
JUST GOT TO--

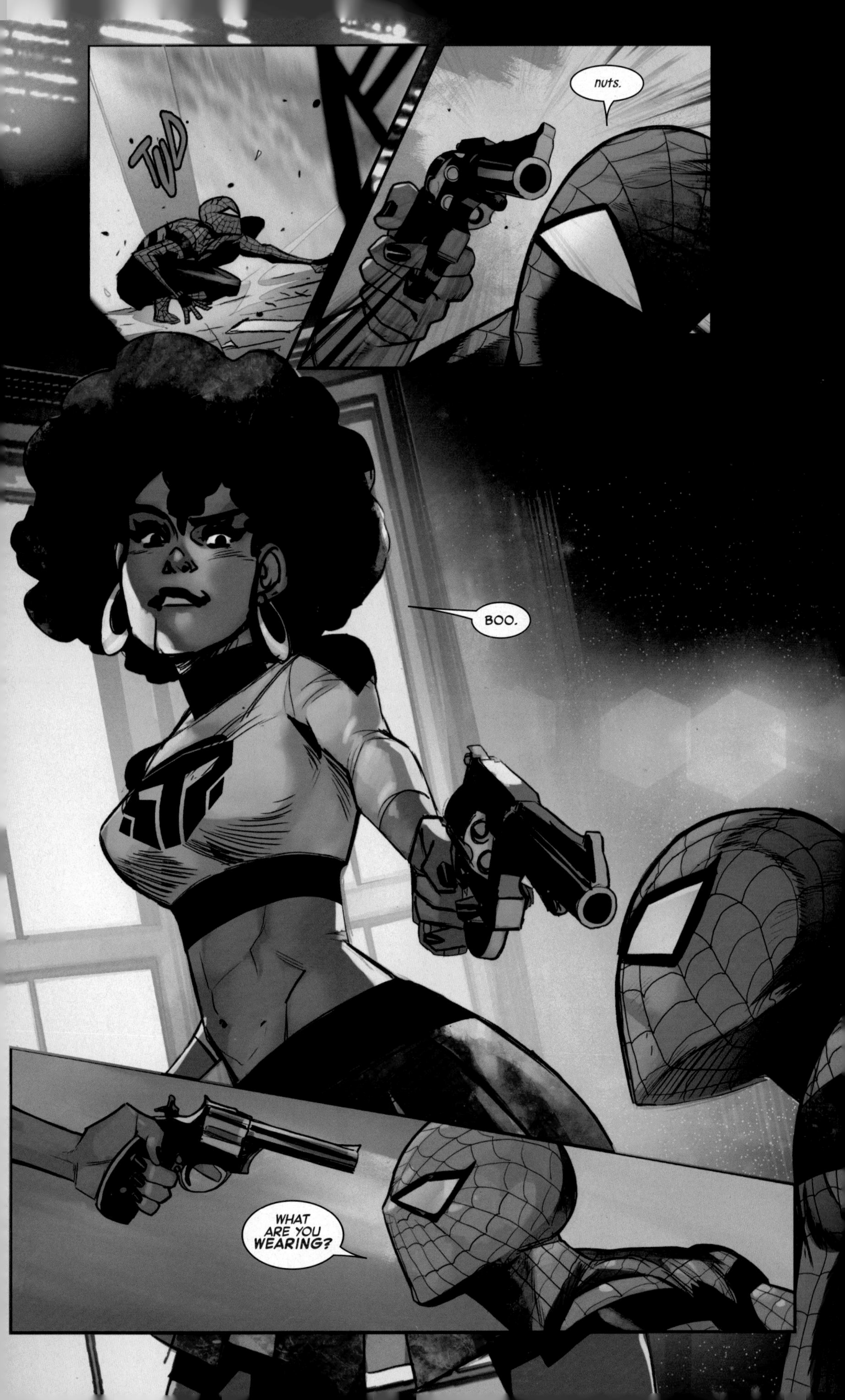
TUD
nuts.
BOO.
WHAT ARE YOU WEARING?

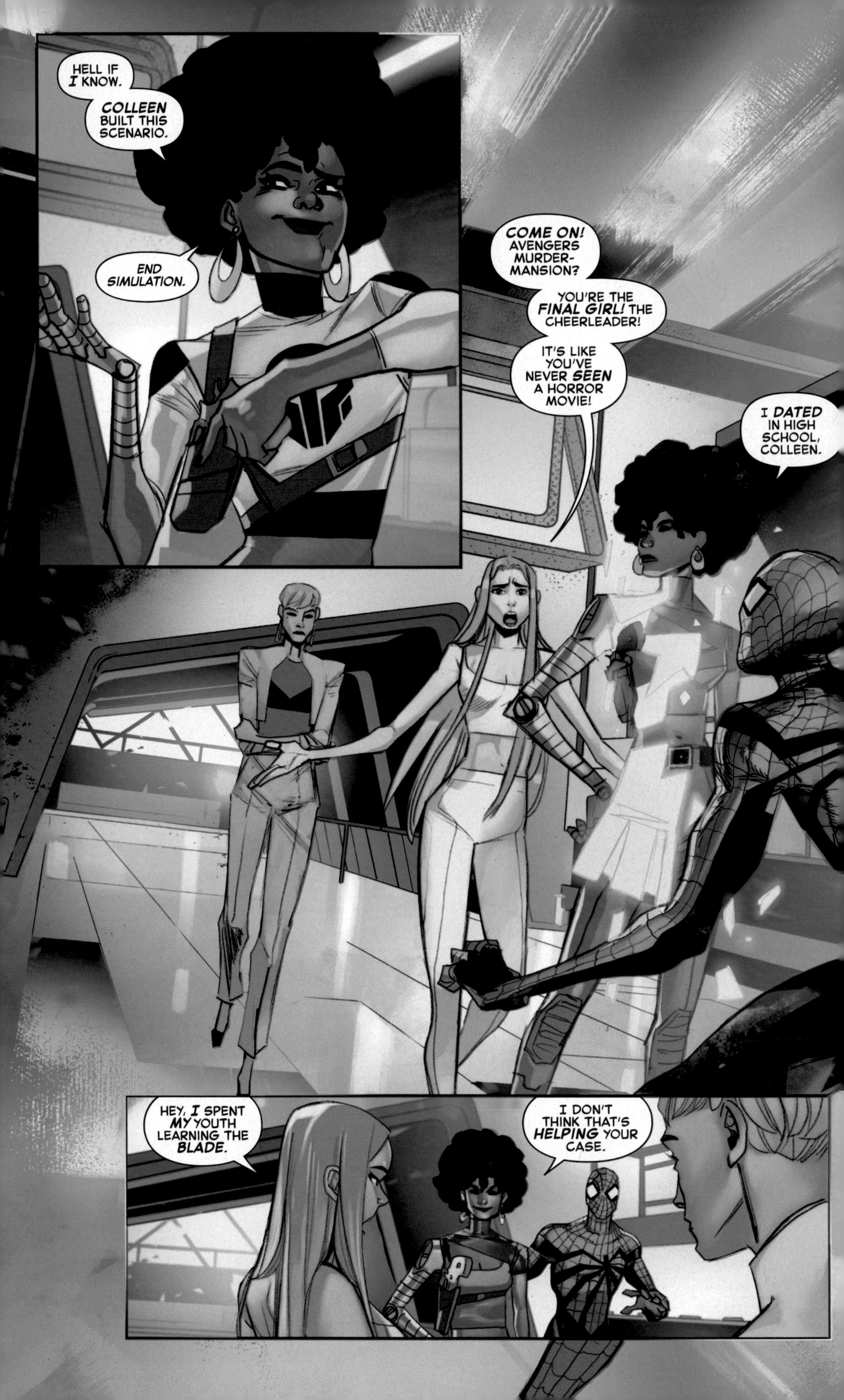
HELL IF I KNOW.
COLLEEN BUILT THIS SCENARIO.
END SIMULATION.
COME ON! AVENGERS MURDER-MANSION?
YOU'RE THE FINAL GIRL! THE CHEERLEADER!
IT'S LIKE YOU'VE NEVER SEEN A HORROR MOVIE!
I DATED IN HIGH SCHOOL, COLLEEN.
HEY, I SPENT MY YOUTH LEARNING THE BLADE.
I DON'T THINK THAT'S HELPING YOUR CASE.

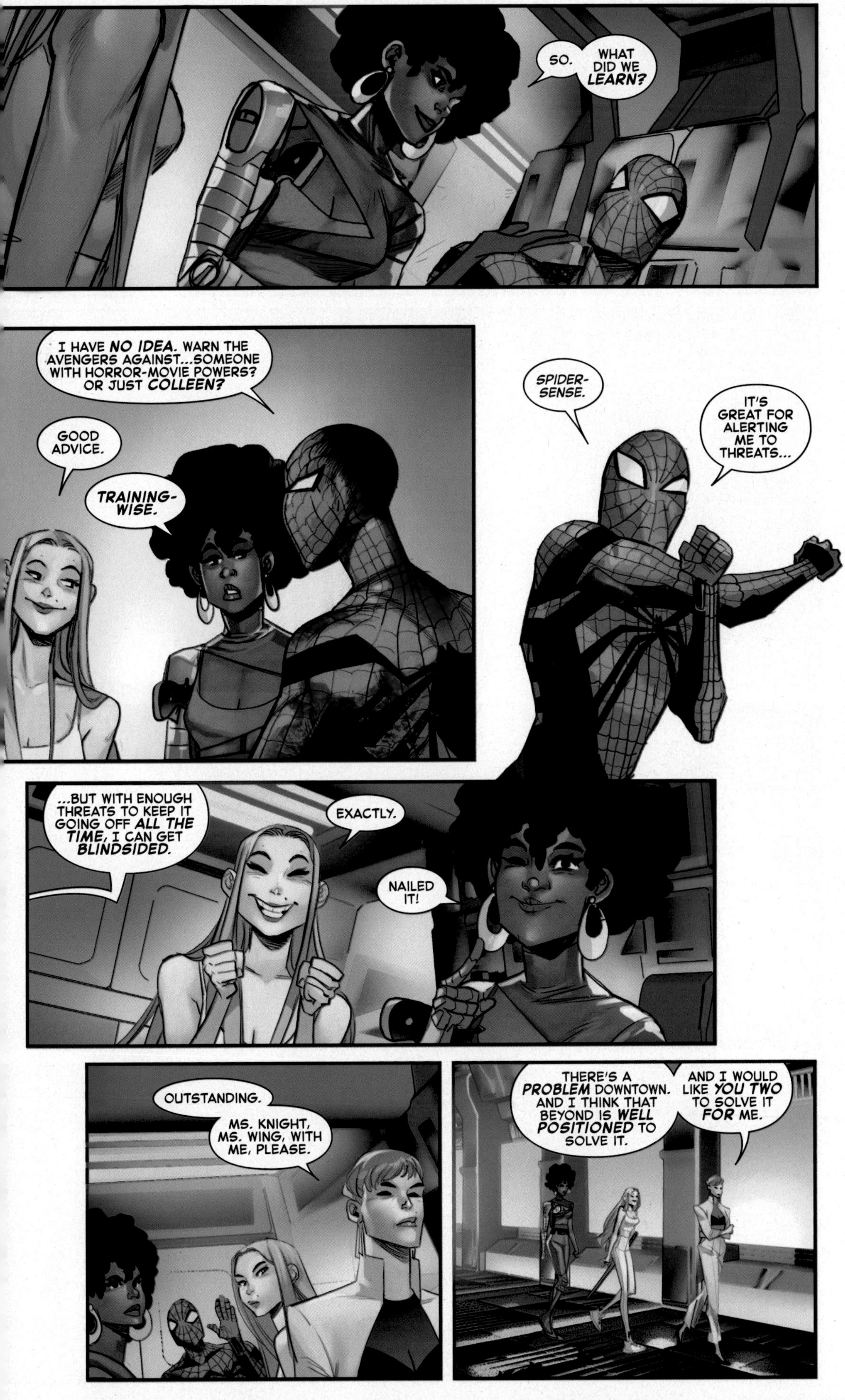
SO.
WHAT DID WE LEARN?
I HAVE NO IDEA. WARN THE AVENGERS AGAINST...SOMEONE WITH HORROR-MOVIE POWERS? OR JUST COLLEEN?
GOOD ADVICE.
TRAINING-WISE.
SPIDER-SENSE.
IT'S GREAT FOR ALERTING ME TO THREATS...
...BUT WITH ENOUGH THREATS TO KEEP IT GOING OFF ALL THE TIME, I CAN GET BLINDSIDED.
EXACTLY.
NAILED IT!
OUTSTANDING.
MS. KNIGHT, MS. WING, WITH ME, PLEASE.
THERE'S A PROBLEM DOWNTOWN. AND I THINK THAT BEYOND IS WELL POSITIONED TO SOLVE IT.
AND I WOULD LIKE YOU TWO TO SOLVE IT FOR ME.

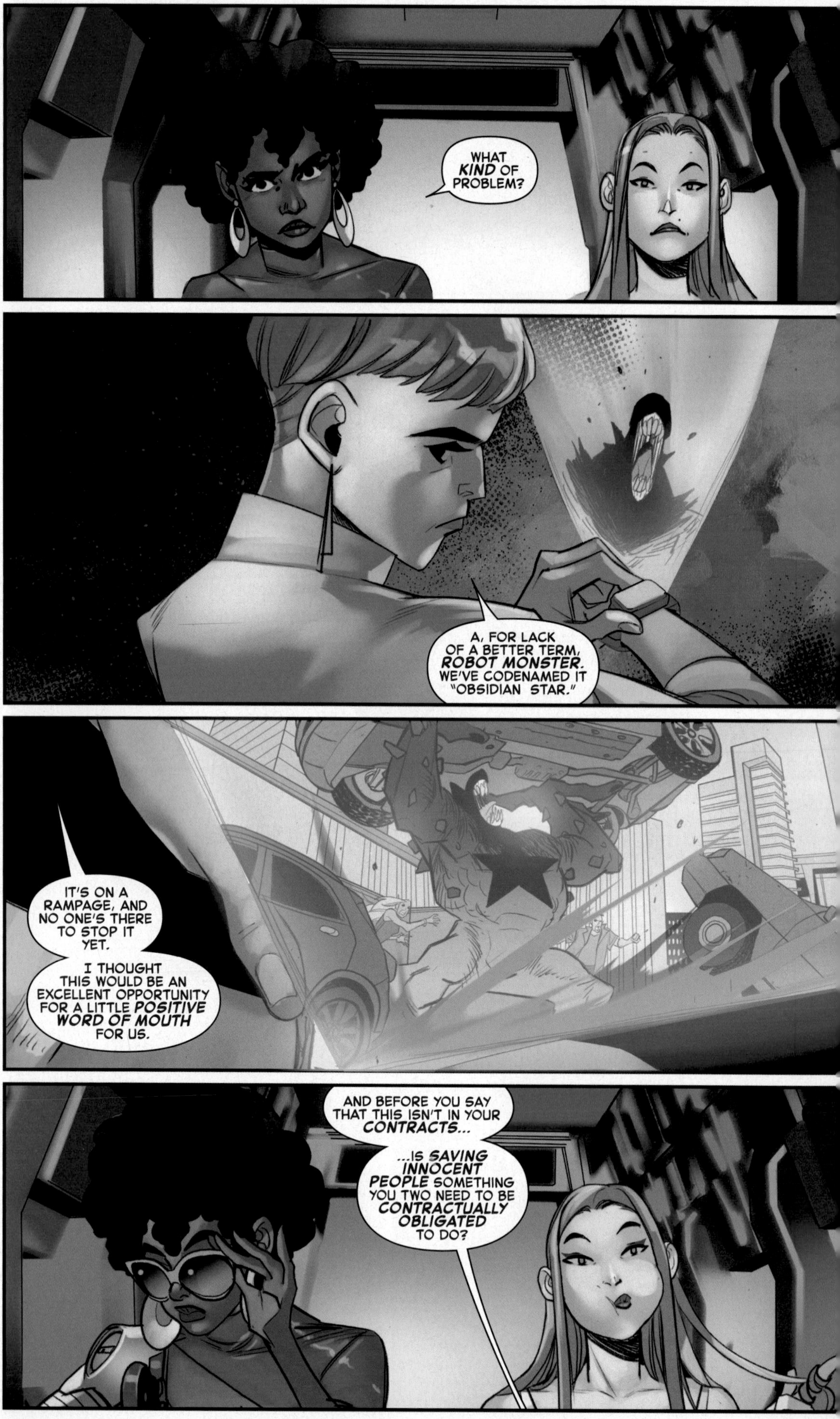

WHAT KIND OF PROBLEM?
A, FOR LACK OF A BETTER TERM, ROBOT MONSTER. WE'VE CODENAMED IT "OBSIDIAN STAR."
IT'S ON A RAMPAGE, AND NO ONE'S THERE TO STOP IT YET.
I THOUGHT THIS WOULD BE AN EXCELLENT OPPORTUNITY FOR A LITTLE POSITIVE WORD OF MOUTH FOR US.
AND BEFORE YOU SAY THAT THIS ISN'T IN YOUR CONTRACTS...
...IS SAVING INNOCENT PEOPLE SOMETHING YOU TWO NEED TO BE CONTRACTUALLY OBLIGATED TO DO?

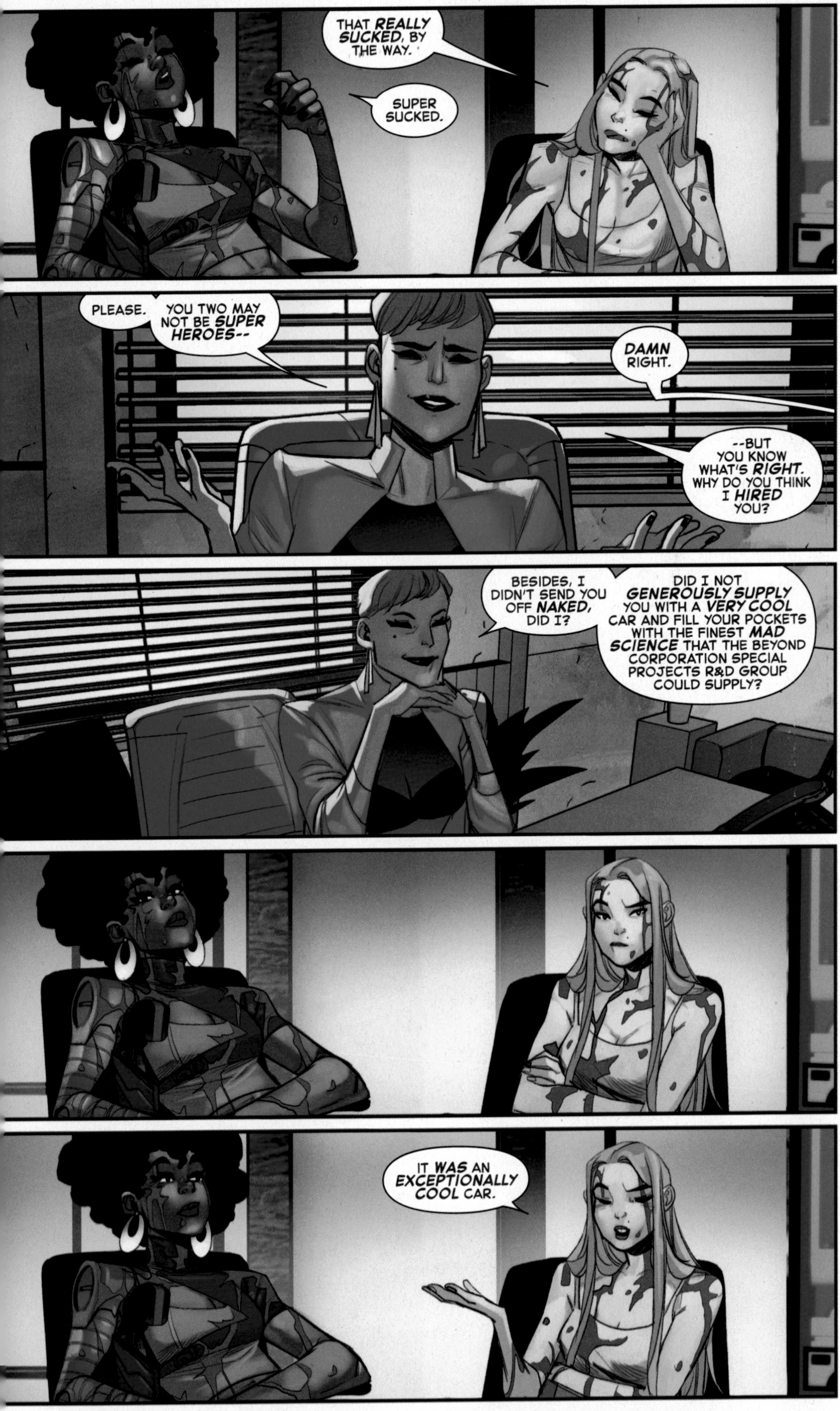

THAT REALLY SUCKED, BY THE WAY.
SUPER SUCKED.
PLEASE.
YOU TWO MAY NOT BE SUPER HEROES--
DAMN RIGHT.
--BUT YOU KNOW WHAT'S RIGHT. WHY DO YOU THINK I HIRED YOU?
BESIDES, I DIDN'T SEND YOU OFF NAKED, DID I?
DID I NOT GENEROUSLY SUPPLY YOU WITH A VERY COOL CAR AND FILL YOUR POCKETS WITH THE FINEST MAD SCIENCE THAT THE BEYOND CORPORATION SPECIAL PROJECTS R&D GROUP COULD SUPPLY?
IT WAS AN EXCEPTIONALLY COOL CAR.

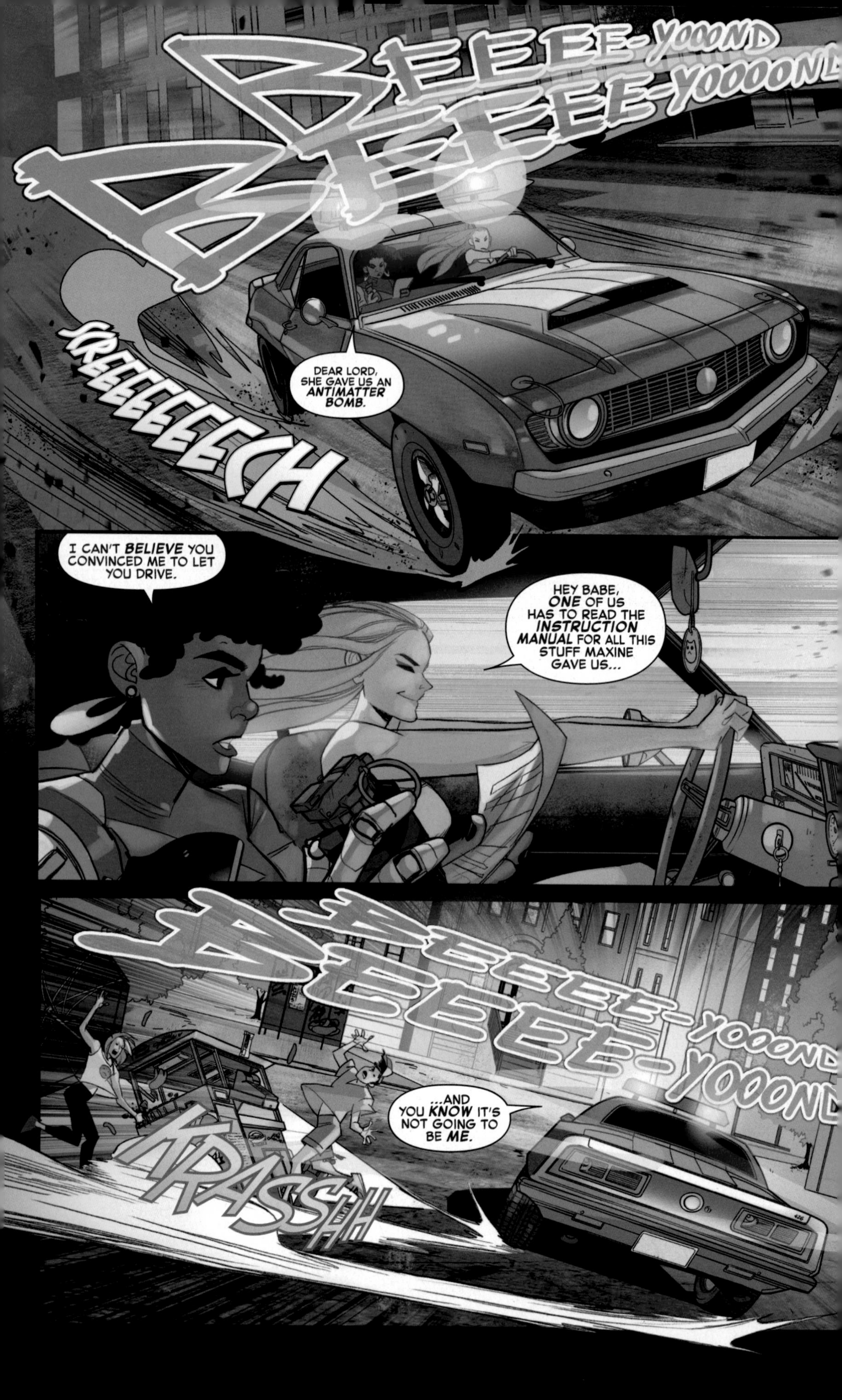
BEEEEE-YOOOND
BEEEEE-YOOOOND
SCREEEEEEEECH
DEAR LORD, SHE GAVE US AN ANTIMATTER BOMB.
I CAN'T BELIEVE YOU CONVINCED ME TO LET YOU DRIVE.
HEY BABE, ONE OF US HAS TO READ THE INSTRUCTION MANUAL FOR ALL THIS STUFF MAXINE GAVE US...
BEEEEE-YOOOND
BEEEEE-YOOOND
...AND YOU KNOW IT'S NOT GOING TO BE ME.
KRASSHH

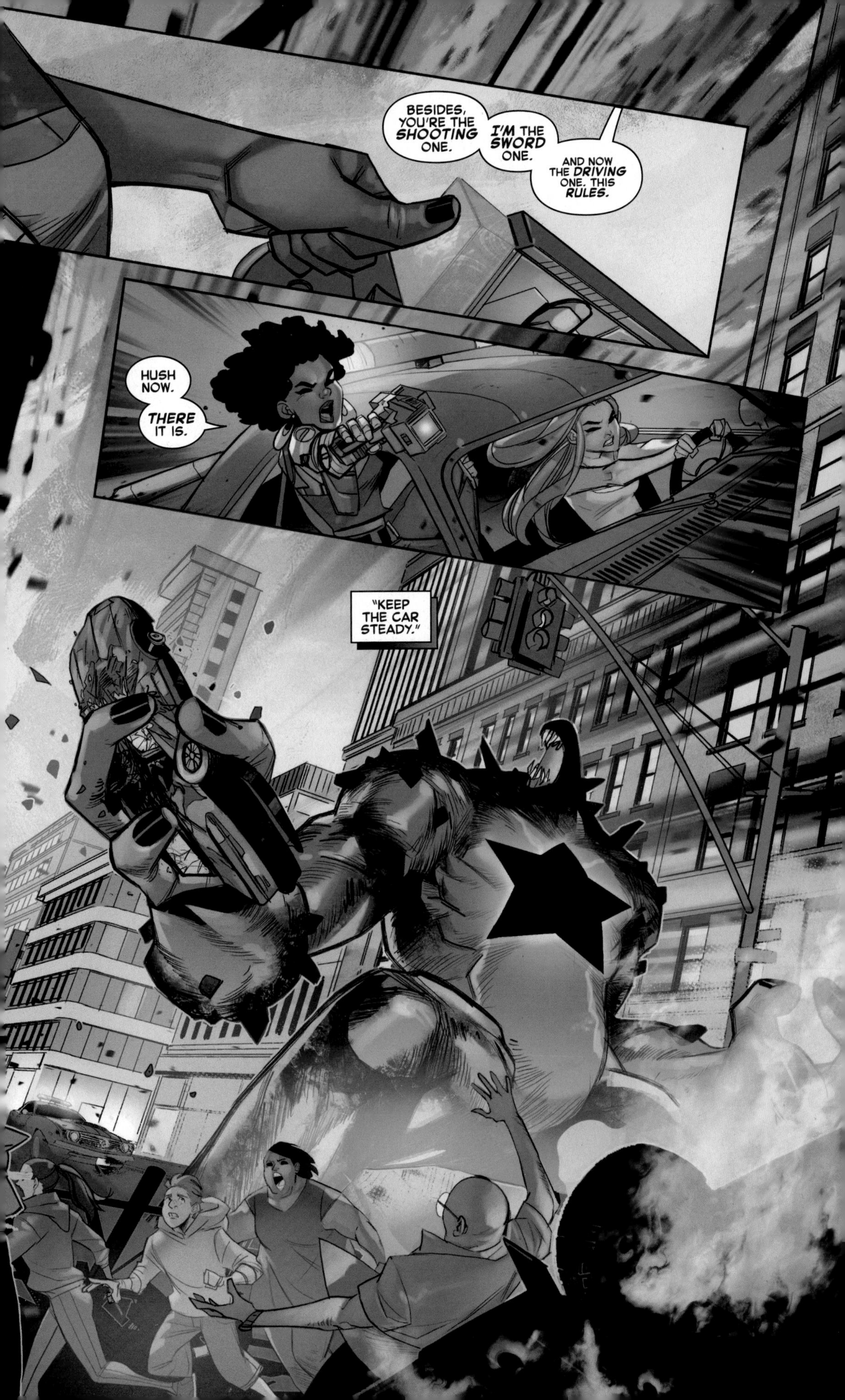
BESIDES, YOU'RE THE SHOOTING ONE.
I'M THE SWORD ONE.
AND NOW THE DRIVING ONE. THIS RULES.
HUSH NOW.
THERE IT IS.
"KEEP THE CAR STEADY."

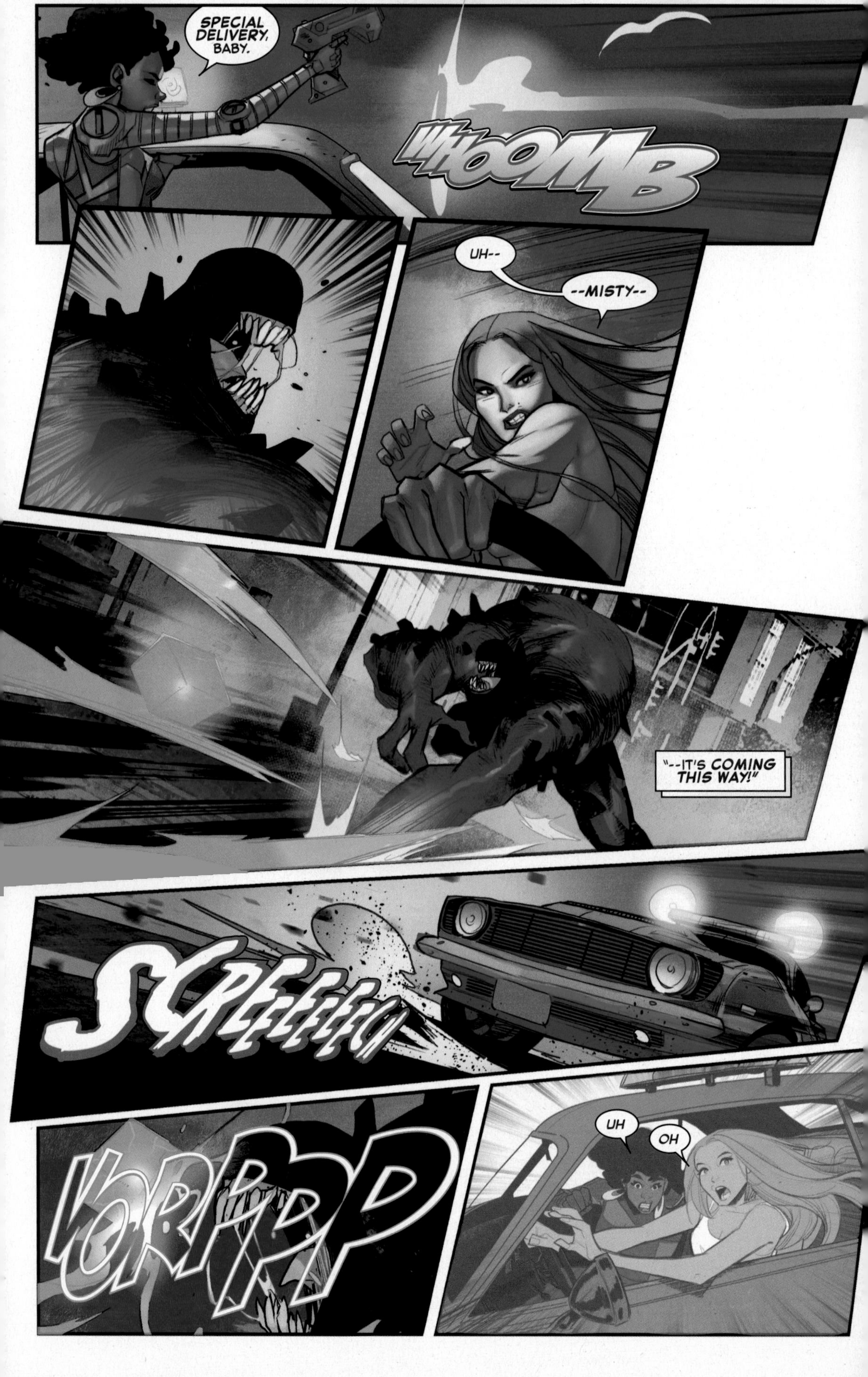
SPECIAL DELIVERY, BABY.
WHOOMB
UH--
--MISTY--
"--IT'S COMING THIS WAY!"
SCREEEEECH
VORPPP
UH
OH

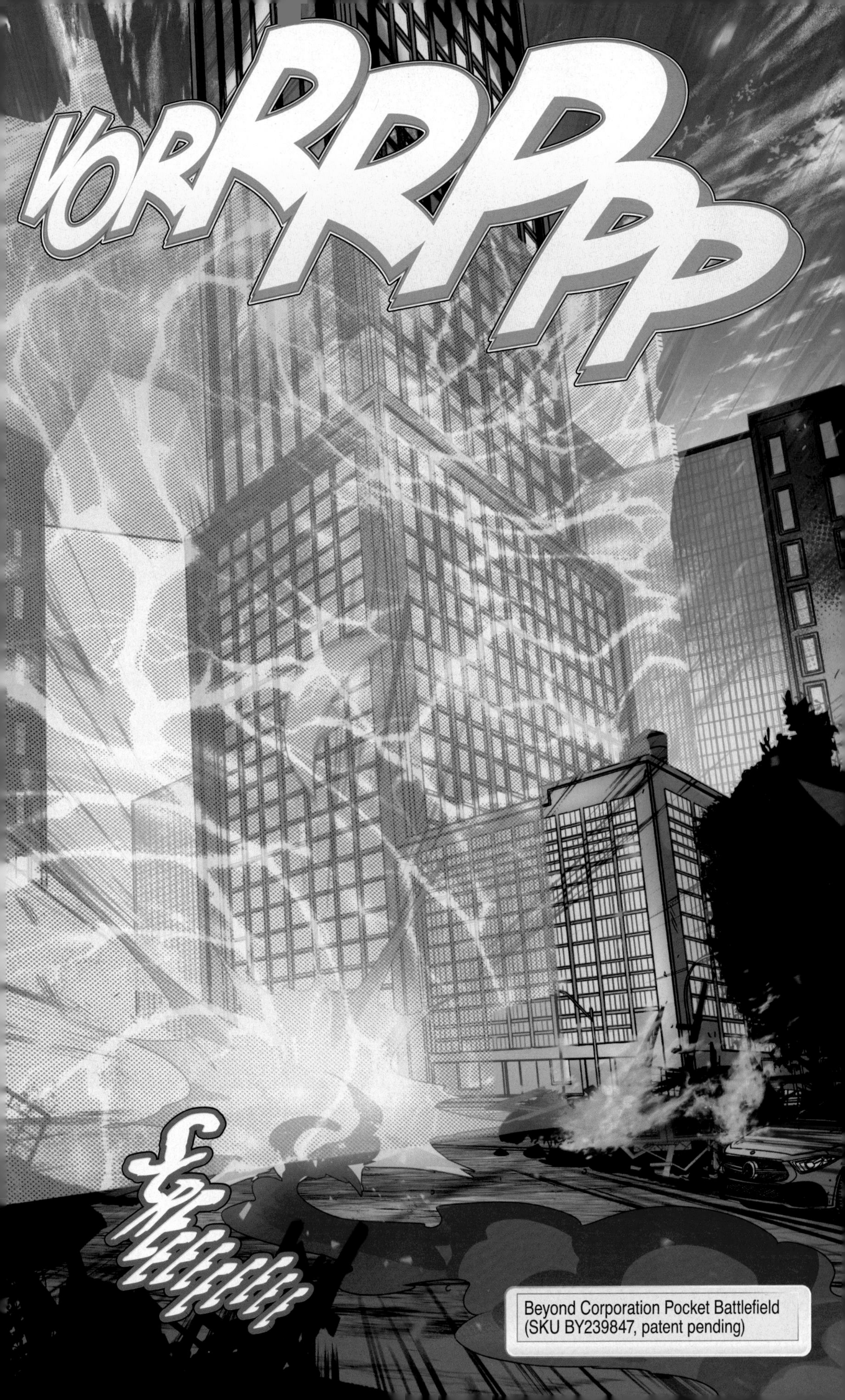
VORRRPPP
SKREEEEEEEE
Beyond Corporation Pocket Battlefield
(SKU BY239847, patent pending)

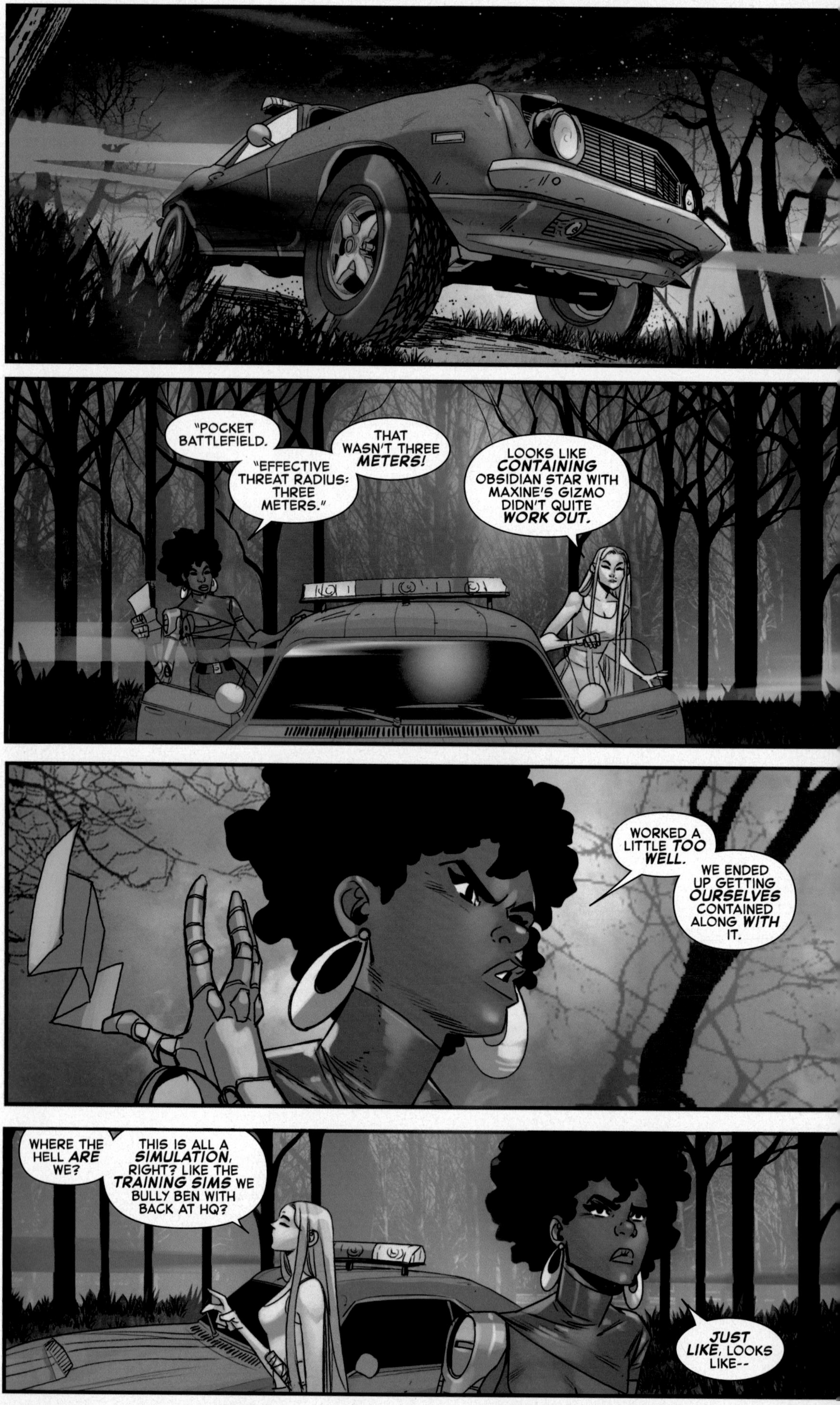
"POCKET BATTLEFIELD.
"EFFECTIVE THREAT RADIUS: THREE METERS."
THAT WASN'T THREE METERS!
LOOKS LIKE CONTAINING OBSIDIAN STAR WITH MAXINE'S GIZMO DIDN'T QUITE WORK OUT.
WORKED A LITTLE TOO WELL.
WE ENDED UP GETTING OURSELVES CONTAINED ALONG WITH IT.
WHERE THE HELL ARE WE?
THIS IS ALL A SIMULATION, RIGHT? LIKE THE TRAINING SIMS WE BULLY BEN WITH BACK AT HQ?
JUST LIKE, LOOKS LIKE--

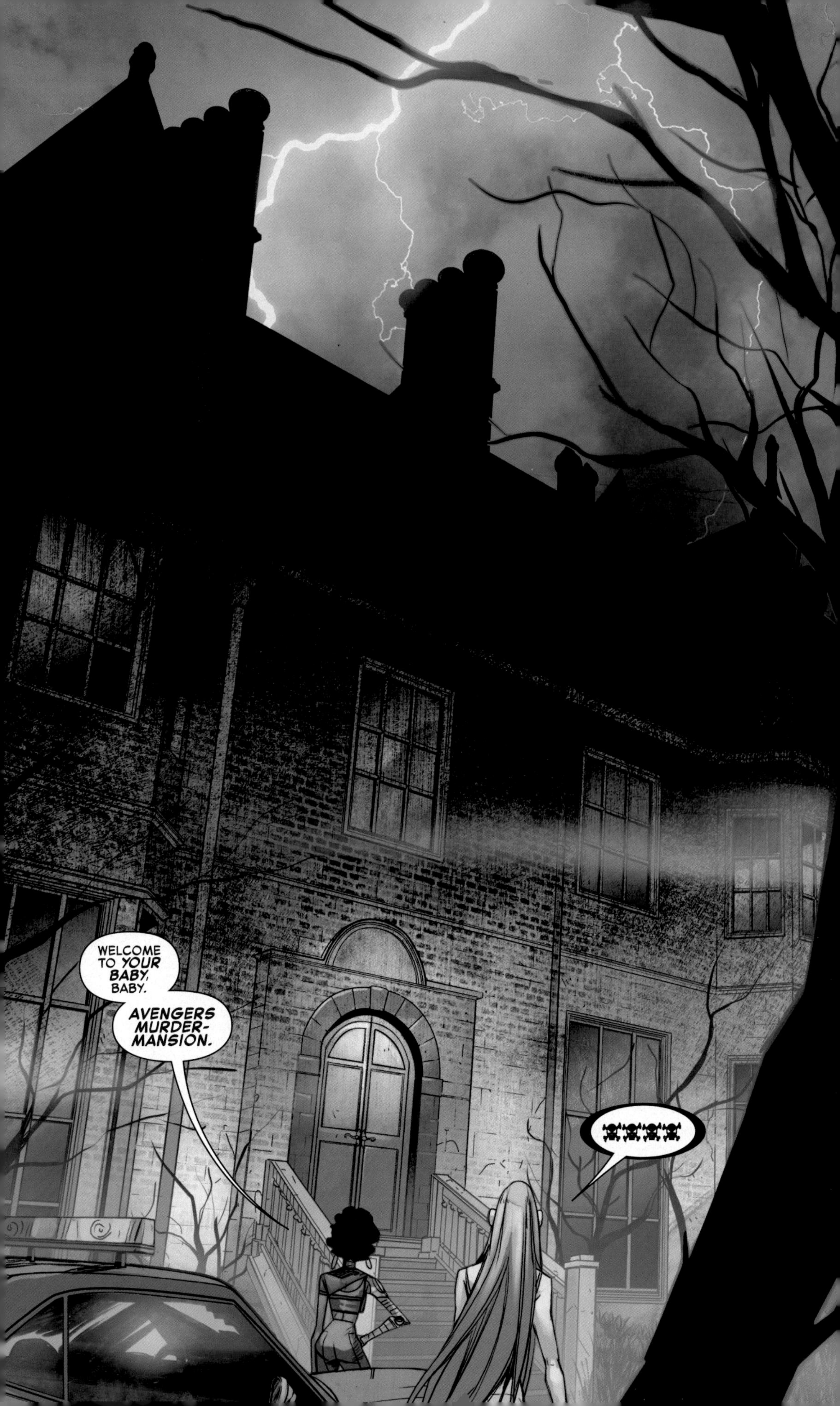
WELCOME TO YOUR BABY, BABY.
AVENGERS MURDER-MANSION.

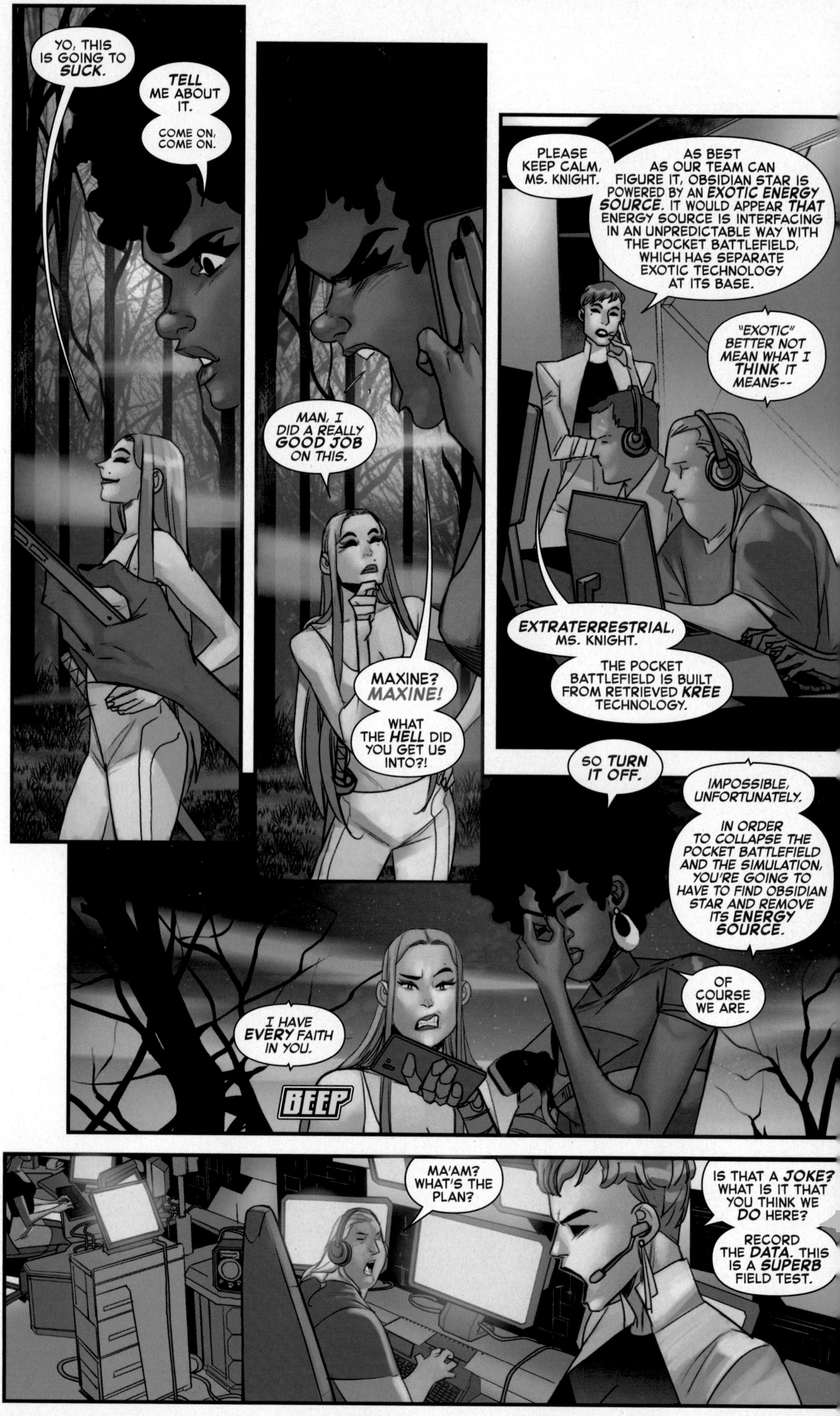

YO, THIS IS GOING TO SUCK.
TELL ME ABOUT IT.
COME ON, COME ON.
MAN, I DID A REALLY GOOD JOB ON THIS.
MAXINE? MAXINE!
WHAT THE HELL DID YOU GET US INTO?!
PLEASE KEEP CALM, MS. KNIGHT.
AS BEST AS OUR TEAM CAN FIGURE IT, OBSIDIAN STAR IS POWERED BY AN EXOTIC ENERGY SOURCE. IT WOULD APPEAR THAT ENERGY SOURCE IS INTERFACING IN AN UNPREDICTABLE WAY WITH THE POCKET BATTLEFIELD, WHICH HAS SEPARATE EXOTIC TECHNOLOGY AT ITS BASE.
"EXOTIC" BETTER NOT MEAN WHAT I THINK IT MEANS--
EXTRATERRESTRIAL, MS. KNIGHT.
THE POCKET BATTLEFIELD IS BUILT FROM RETRIEVED KREE TECHNOLOGY.
SO TURN IT OFF.
IMPOSSIBLE, UNFORTUNATELY.
IN ORDER TO COLLAPSE THE POCKET BATTLEFIELD AND THE SIMULATION, YOU'RE GOING TO HAVE TO FIND OBSIDIAN STAR AND REMOVE ITS ENERGY SOURCE.
OF COURSE WE ARE.
I HAVE EVERY FAITH IN YOU.
BEEP
MA'AM? WHAT'S THE PLAN?
IS THAT A JOKE? WHAT IS IT THAT YOU THINK WE DO HERE?
RECORD THE DATA. THIS IS A SUPERB FIELD TEST.

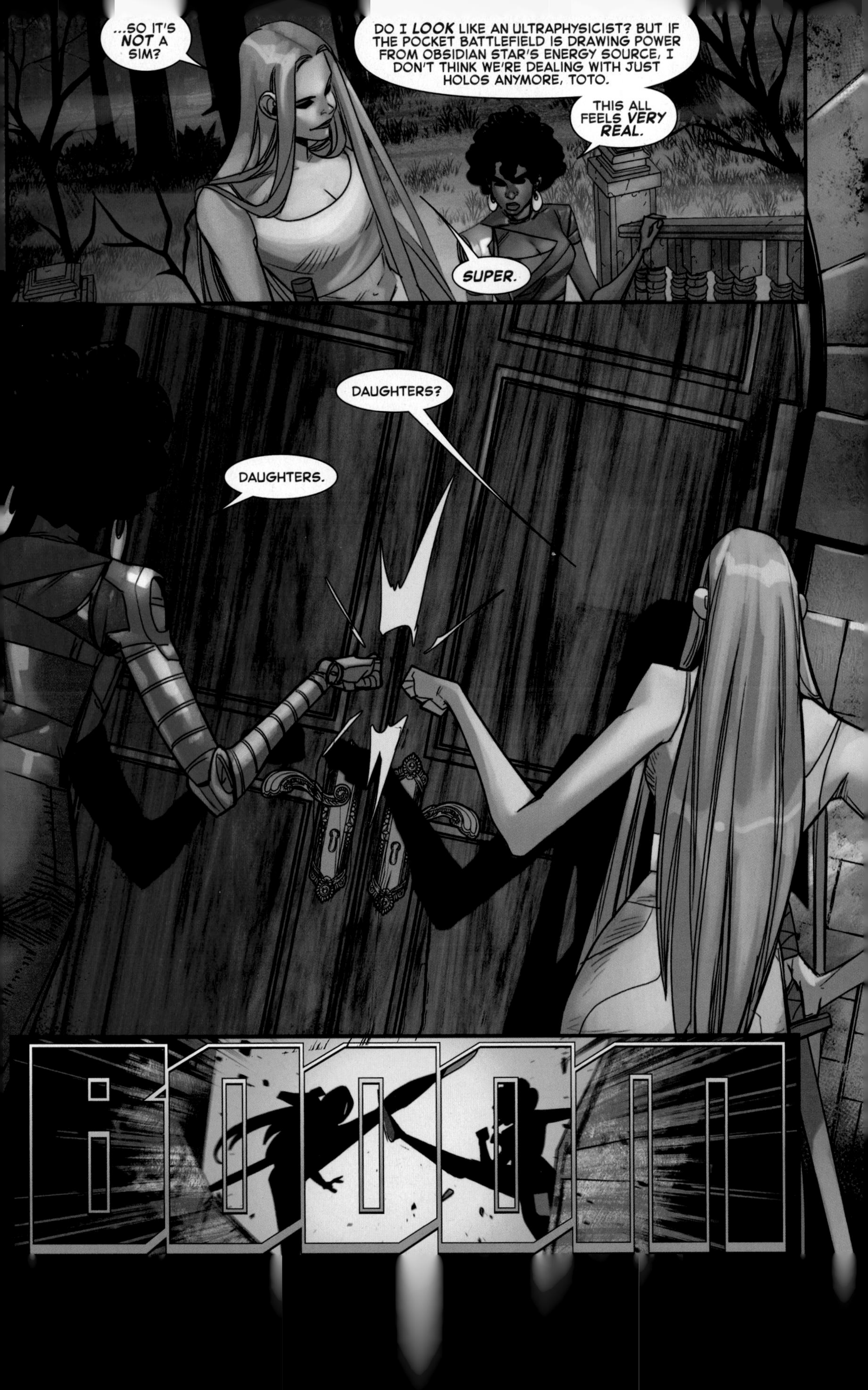

...SO IT'S NOT A SIM?
DO I LOOK LIKE AN ULTRAPHYSICIST? BUT IF THE POCKET BATTLEFIELD IS DRAWING POWER FROM OBSIDIAN STAR'S ENERGY SOURCE, I DON'T THINK WE'RE DEALING WITH JUST HOLOS ANYMORE, TOTO.
THIS ALL FEELS VERY REAL.
SUPER.
DAUGHTERS?
DAUGHTERS.

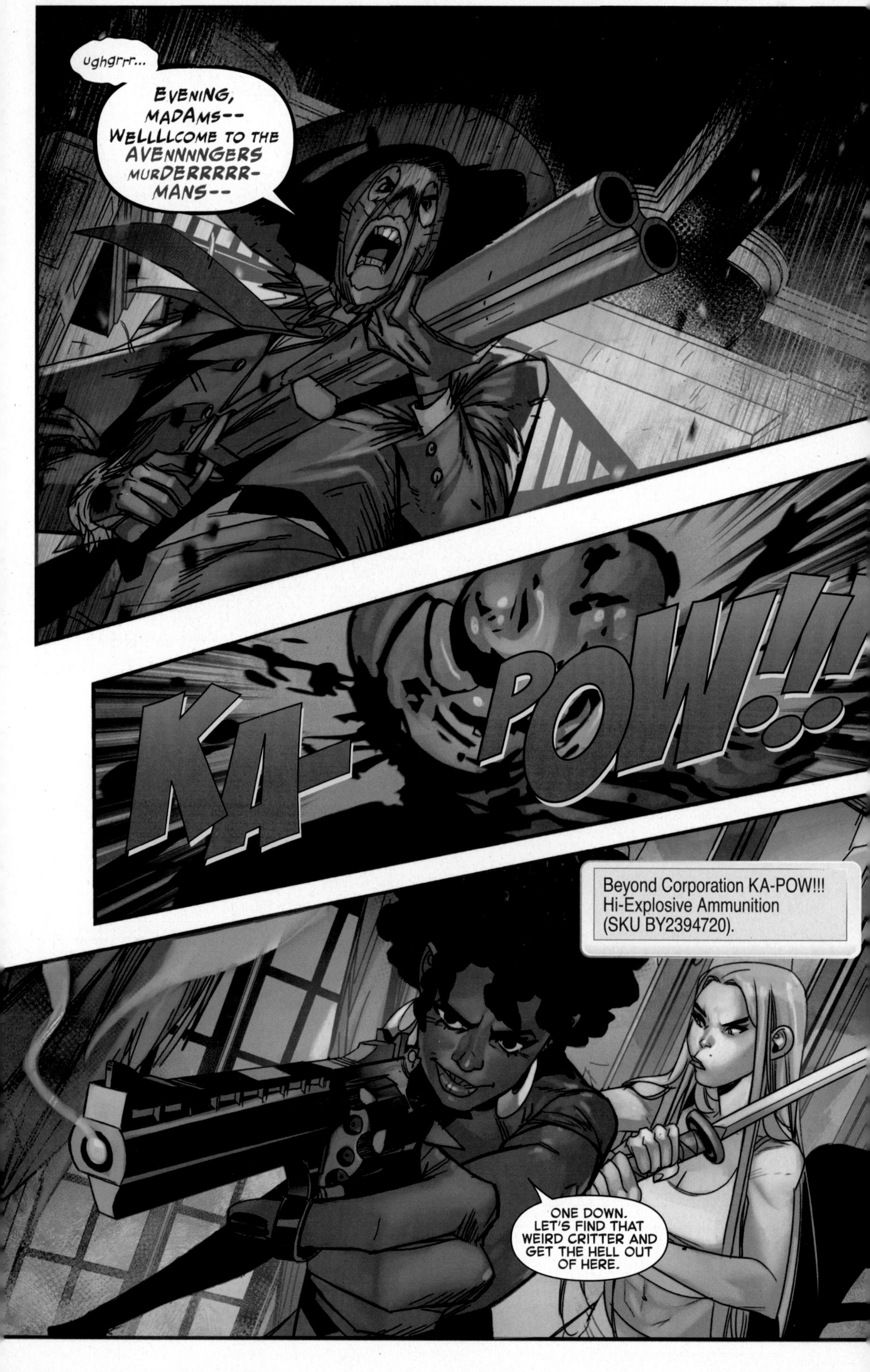
ughgrrr...
EVENING, MADAMS-- WELLLLCOME TO THE AVENNNNGERS MURDERRRRR-MANS--
KA-POW!!!
Beyond Corporation KA-POW!!! Hi-Explosive Ammunition (SKU BY2394720).
ONE DOWN. LET'S FIND THAT WEIRD CRITTER AND GET THE HELL OUT OF HERE.

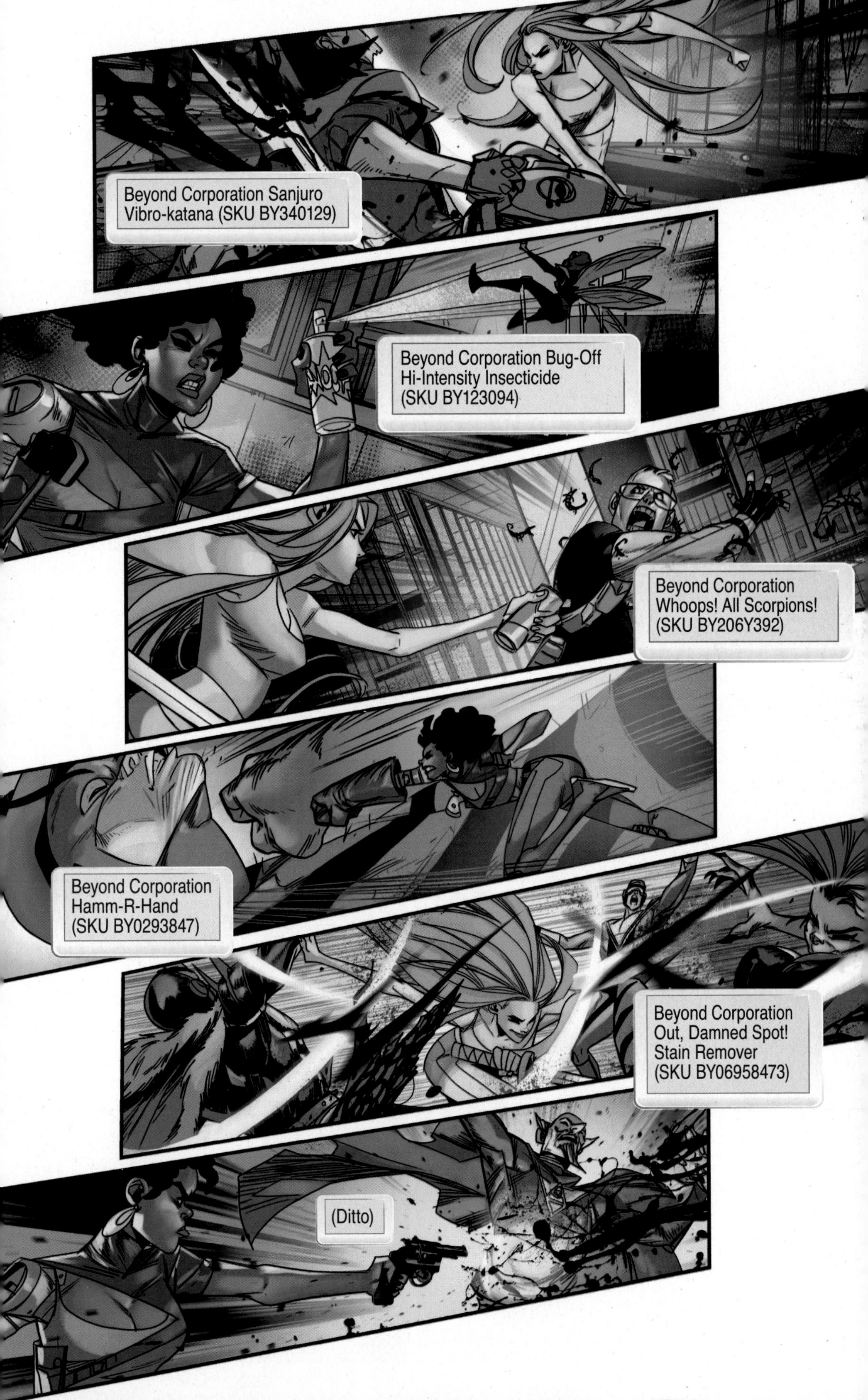
Beyond Corporation Sanjuro
Vibro-katana (SKU BY340129)
Beyond Corporation Bug-Off
Hi-Intensity Insecticide
(SKU BY123094)
Beyond Corporation
Whoops! All Scorpions!
(SKU BY206Y392)
Beyond Corporation
Hamm-R-Hand
(SKU BY0293847)
Beyond Corporation
Out, Damned Spot!
Stain Remover
(SKU BY06958473)
(Ditto)

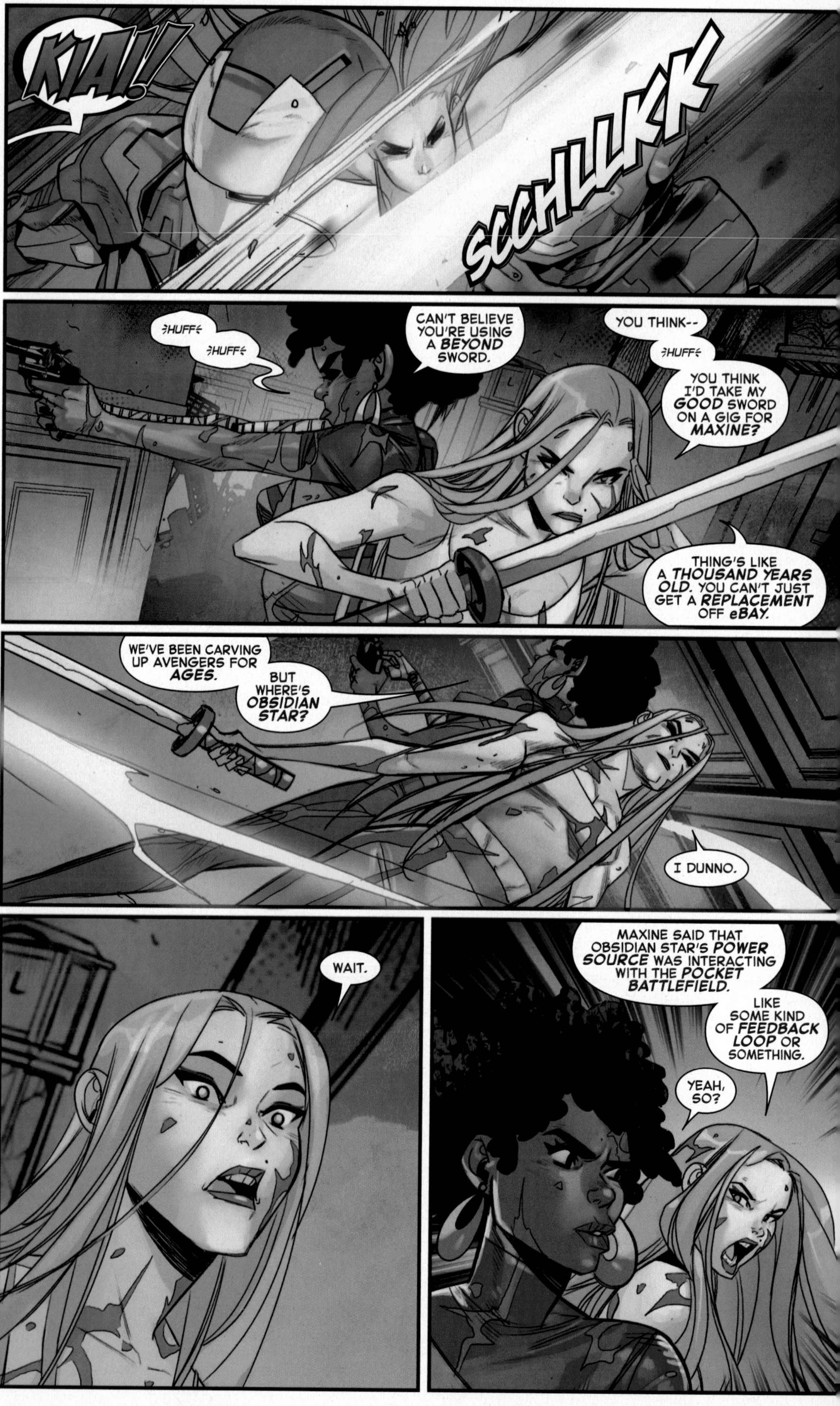
KIAI!!
SCCHLLLKK
≯HUFF≮
≯HUFF≮
CAN'T BELIEVE YOU'RE USING A BEYOND SWORD.
YOU THINK--
≯HUFF≮
YOU THINK I'D TAKE MY GOOD SWORD ON A GIG FOR MAXINE?
THING'S LIKE A THOUSAND YEARS OLD. YOU CAN'T JUST GET A REPLACEMENT OFF eBAY.
WE'VE BEEN CARVING UP AVENGERS FOR AGES.
BUT WHERE'S OBSIDIAN STAR?
I DUNNO.
WAIT.
MAXINE SAID THAT OBSIDIAN STAR'S POWER SOURCE WAS INTERACTING WITH THE POCKET BATTLEFIELD.
LIKE SOME KIND OF FEEDBACK LOOP OR SOMETHING.
YEAH, SO?

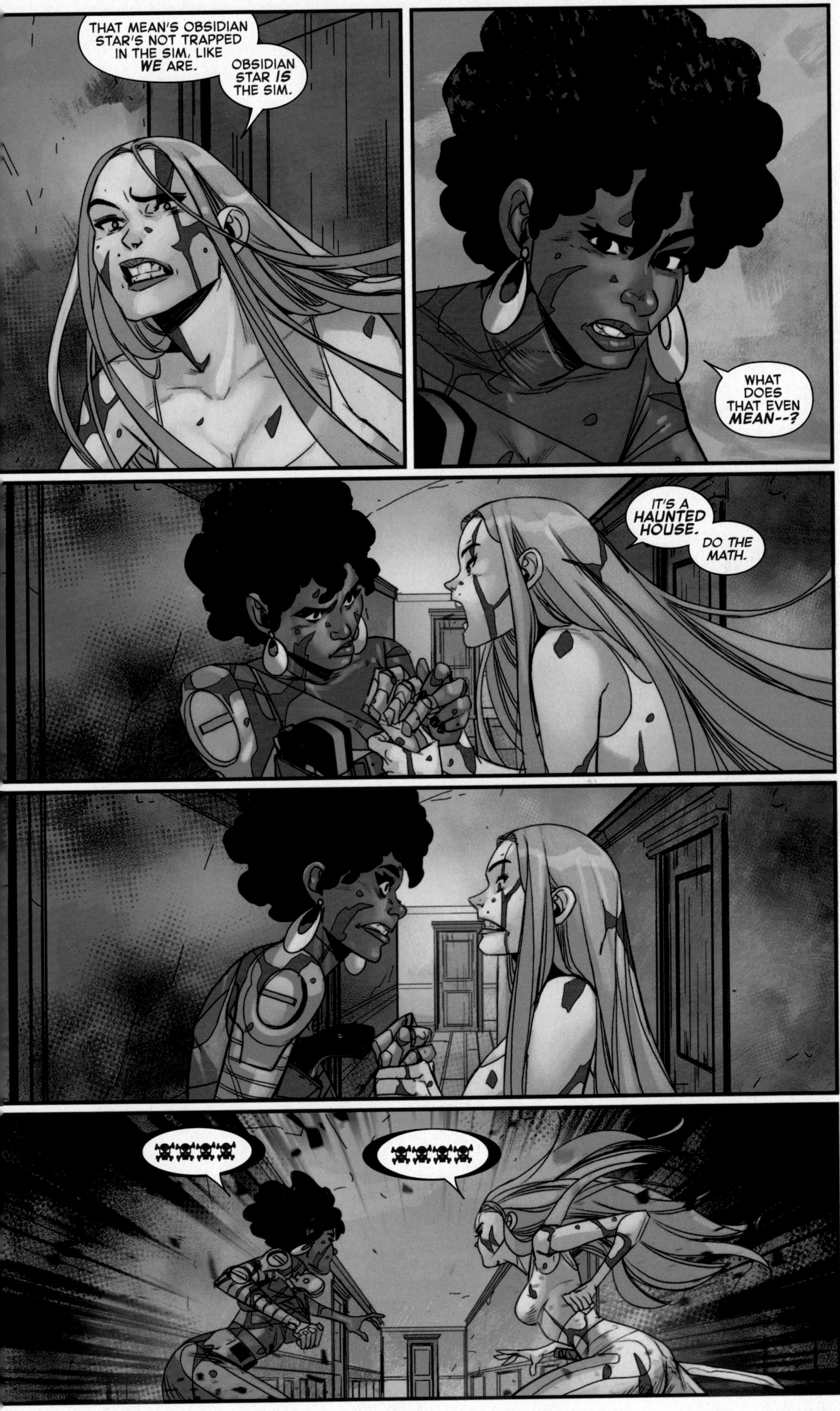
THAT MEAN'S OBSIDIAN STAR'S NOT TRAPPED IN THE SIM, LIKE *WE* ARE.
OBSIDIAN STAR *IS* THE SIM.
WHAT DOES THAT EVEN *MEAN--?*
IT'S A **HAUNTED HOUSE.**
DO THE MATH.

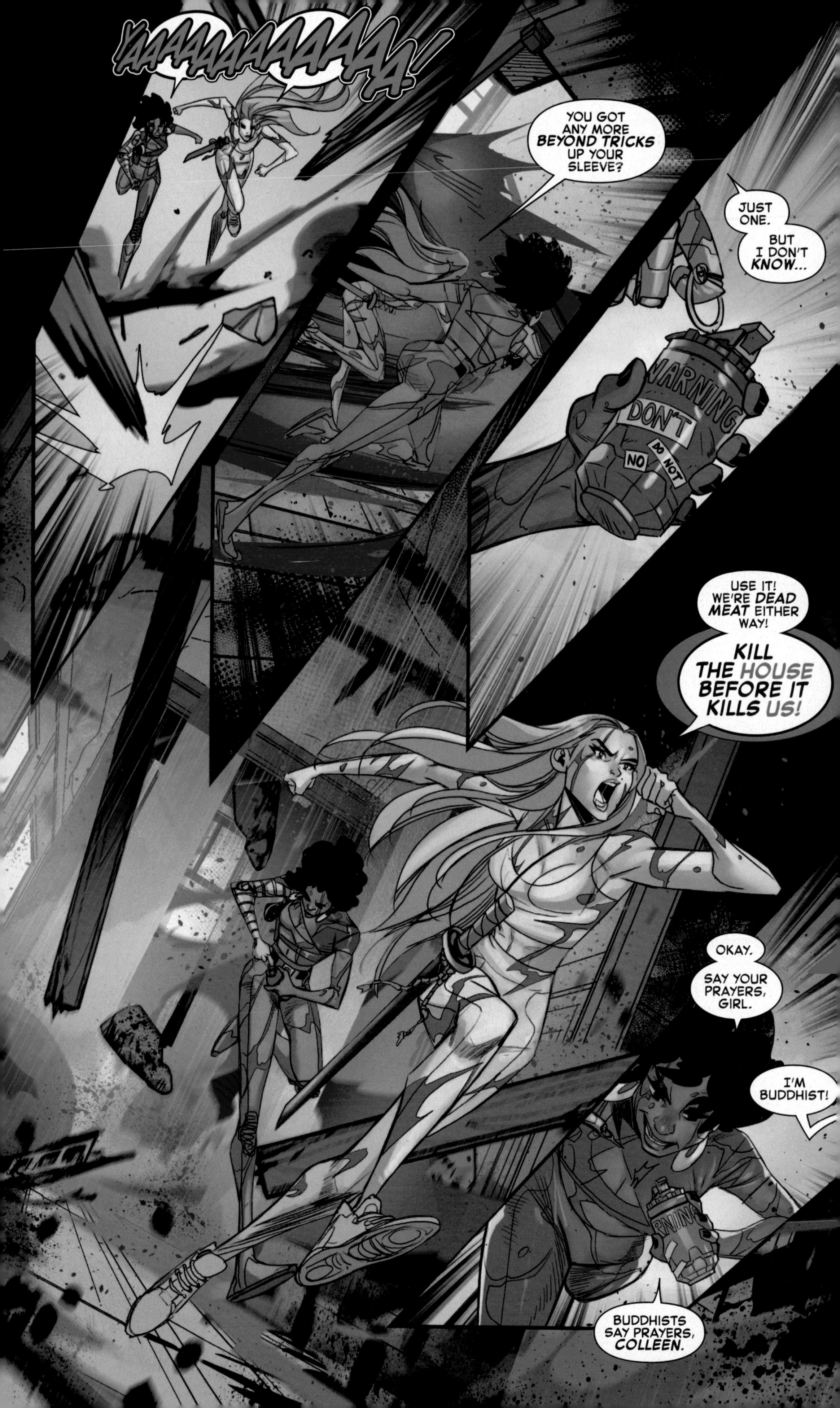
YAAAAAAAAAAAA!
YOU GOT ANY MORE BEYOND TRICKS UP YOUR SLEEVE?
JUST ONE.
BUT I DON'T KNOW...
WARNING
DON'T
NO
DO NOT
USE IT! WE'RE DEAD MEAT EITHER WAY!
KILL THE HOUSE BEFORE IT KILLS US!
OKAY.
SAY YOUR PRAYERS, GIRL.
I'M BUDDHIST!
BUDDHISTS SAY PRAYERS, COLLEEN.

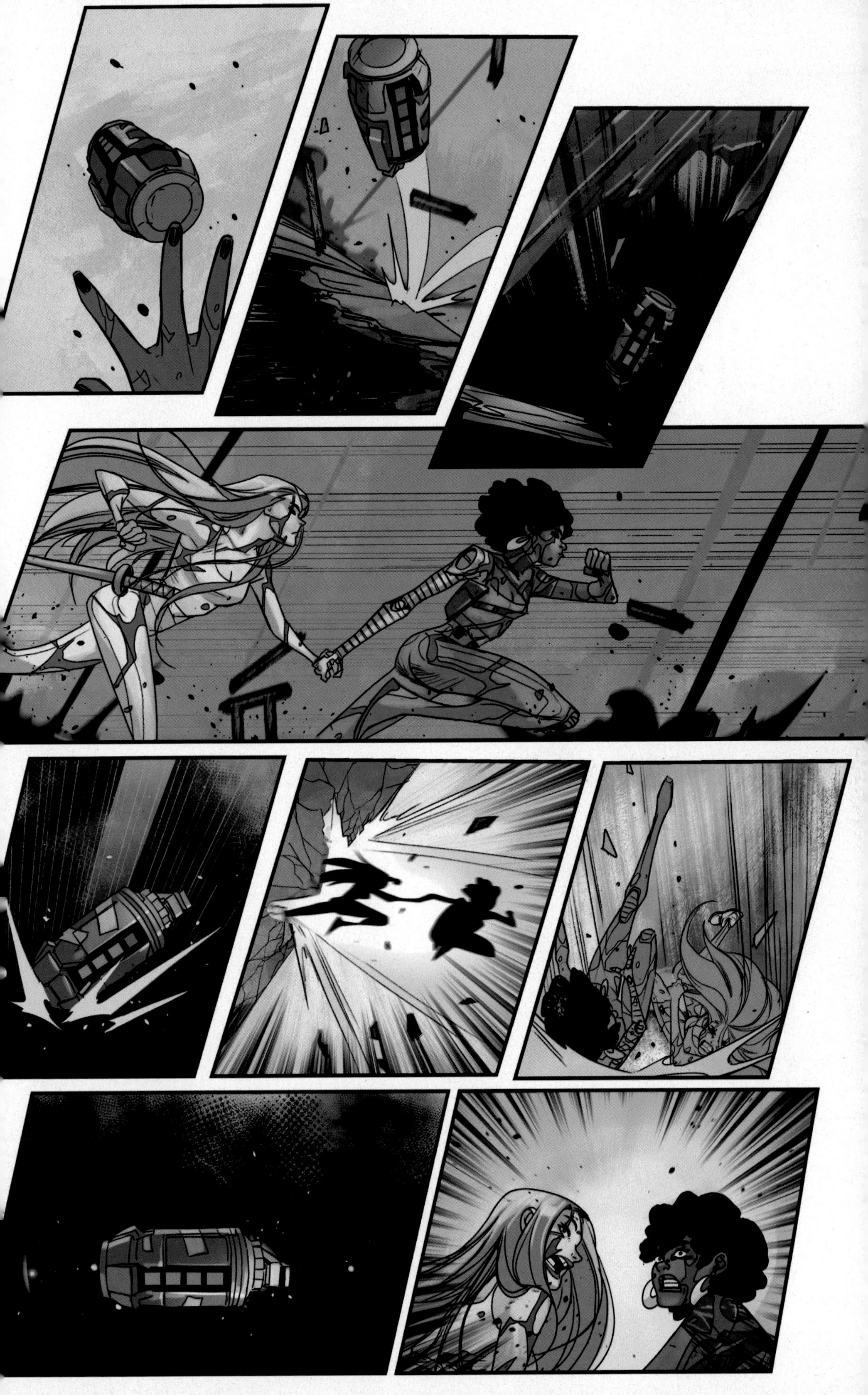

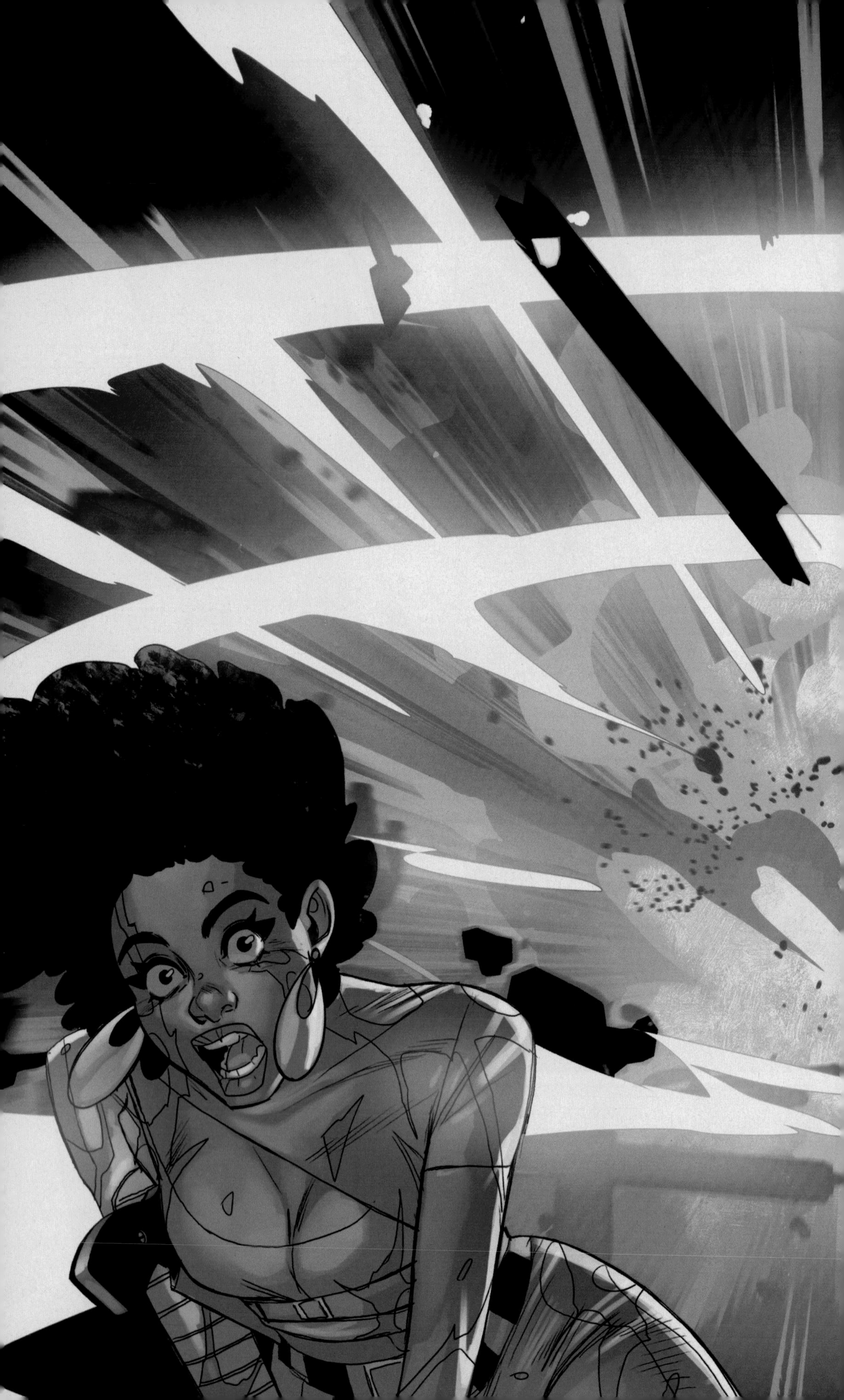

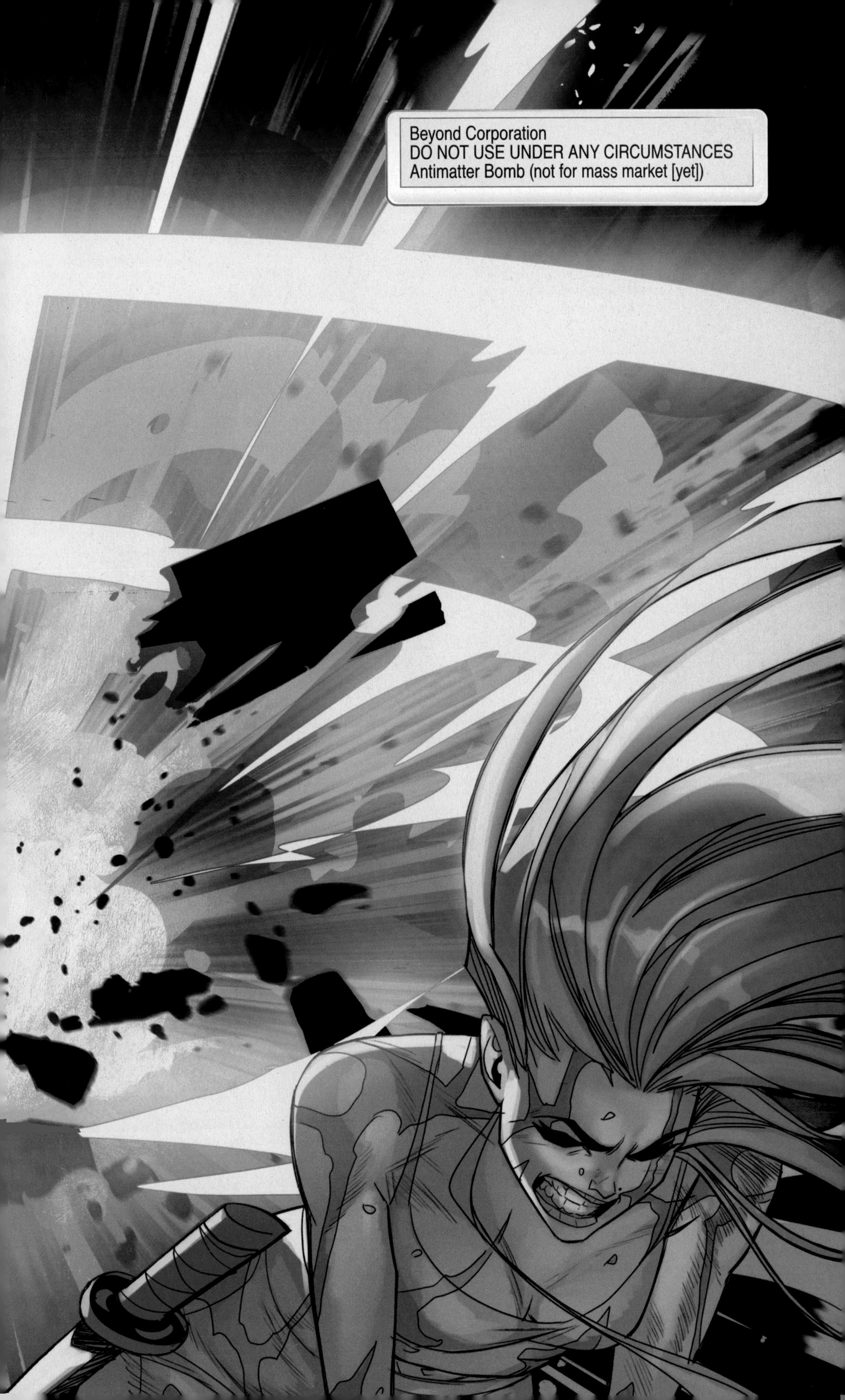
Beyond Corporation
DO NOT USE UNDER ANY CIRCUMSTANCES
Antimatter Bomb (not for mass market [yet])

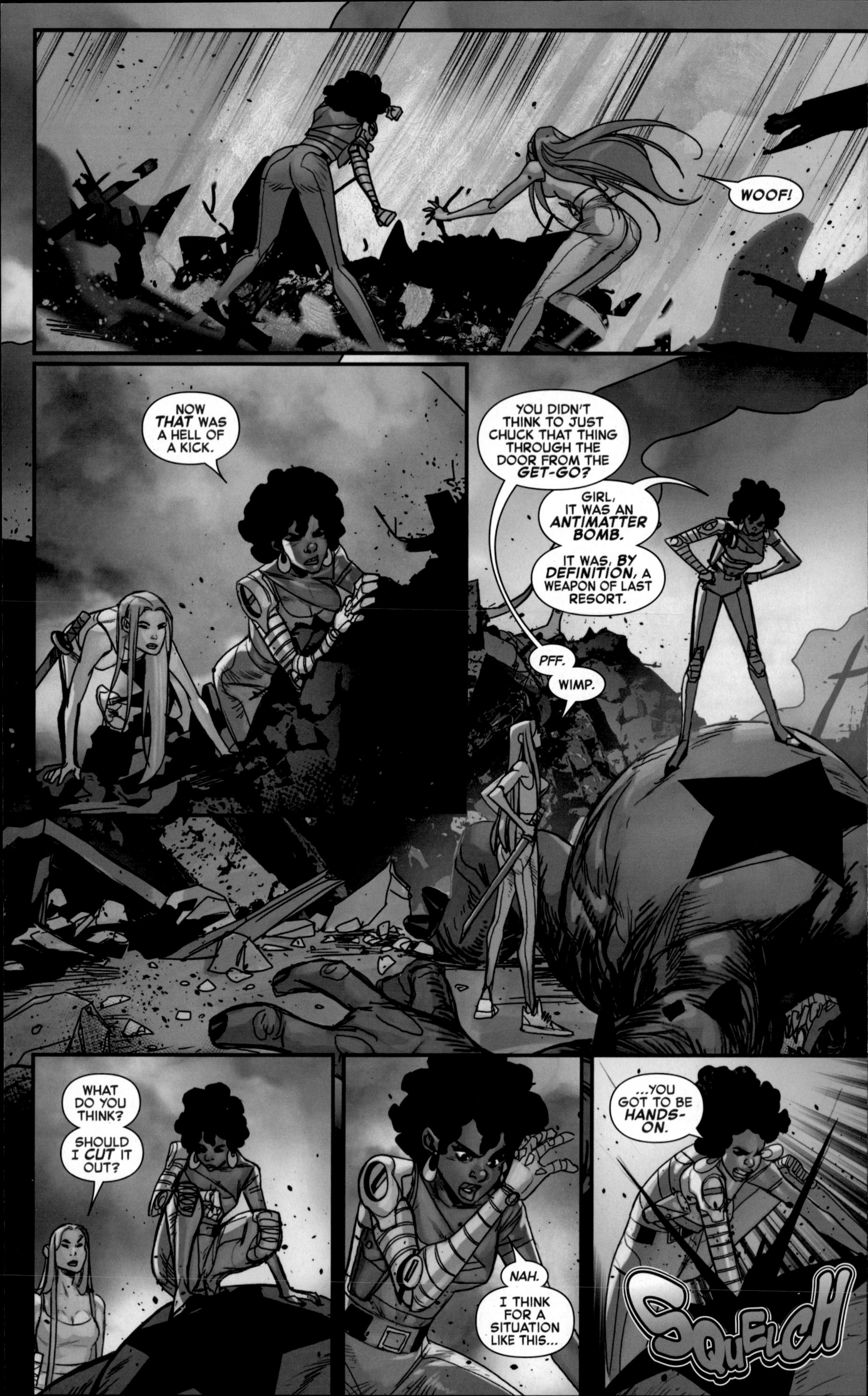

WOOF!
NOW THAT WAS A HELL OF A KICK.
YOU DIDN'T THINK TO JUST CHUCK THAT THING THROUGH THE DOOR FROM THE GET-GO?
GIRL, IT WAS AN ANTIMATTER BOMB.
IT WAS, BY DEFINITION, A WEAPON OF LAST RESORT.
PFF.
WIMP.
WHAT DO YOU THINK?
SHOULD I CUT IT OUT?
NAH.
I THINK FOR A SITUATION LIKE THIS...
...YOU GOT TO BE HANDS-ON.
SQUELCH

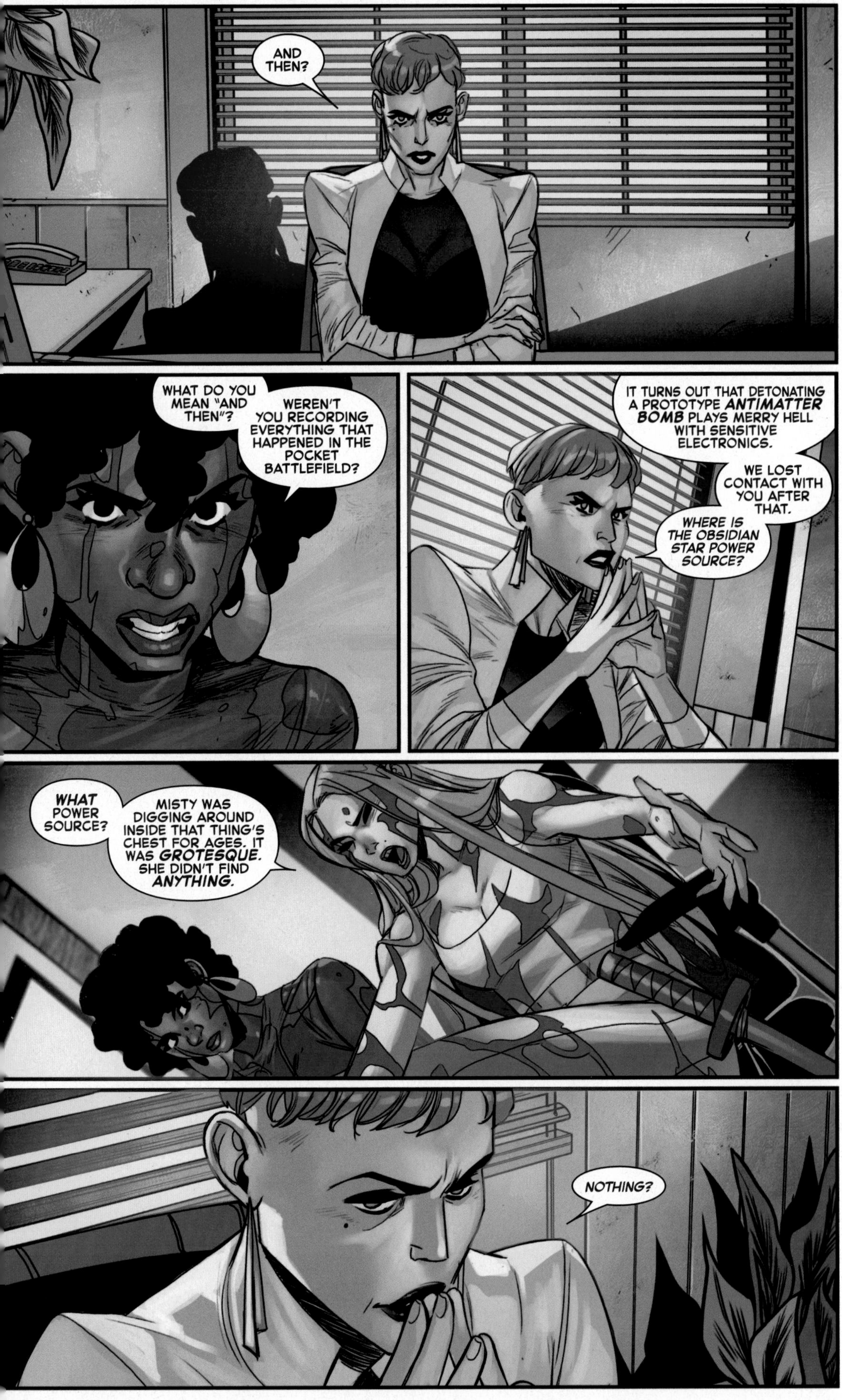

AND THEN?
WHAT DO YOU MEAN "AND THEN"?
WEREN'T YOU RECORDING EVERYTHING THAT HAPPENED IN THE POCKET BATTLEFIELD?
IT TURNS OUT THAT DETONATING A PROTOTYPE ANTIMATTER BOMB PLAYS MERRY HELL WITH SENSITIVE ELECTRONICS.
WE LOST CONTACT WITH YOU AFTER THAT.
WHERE IS THE OBSIDIAN STAR POWER SOURCE?
WHAT POWER SOURCE?
MISTY WAS DIGGING AROUND INSIDE THAT THING'S CHEST FOR AGES. IT WAS GROTESQUE. SHE DIDN'T FIND ANYTHING.
NOTHING?

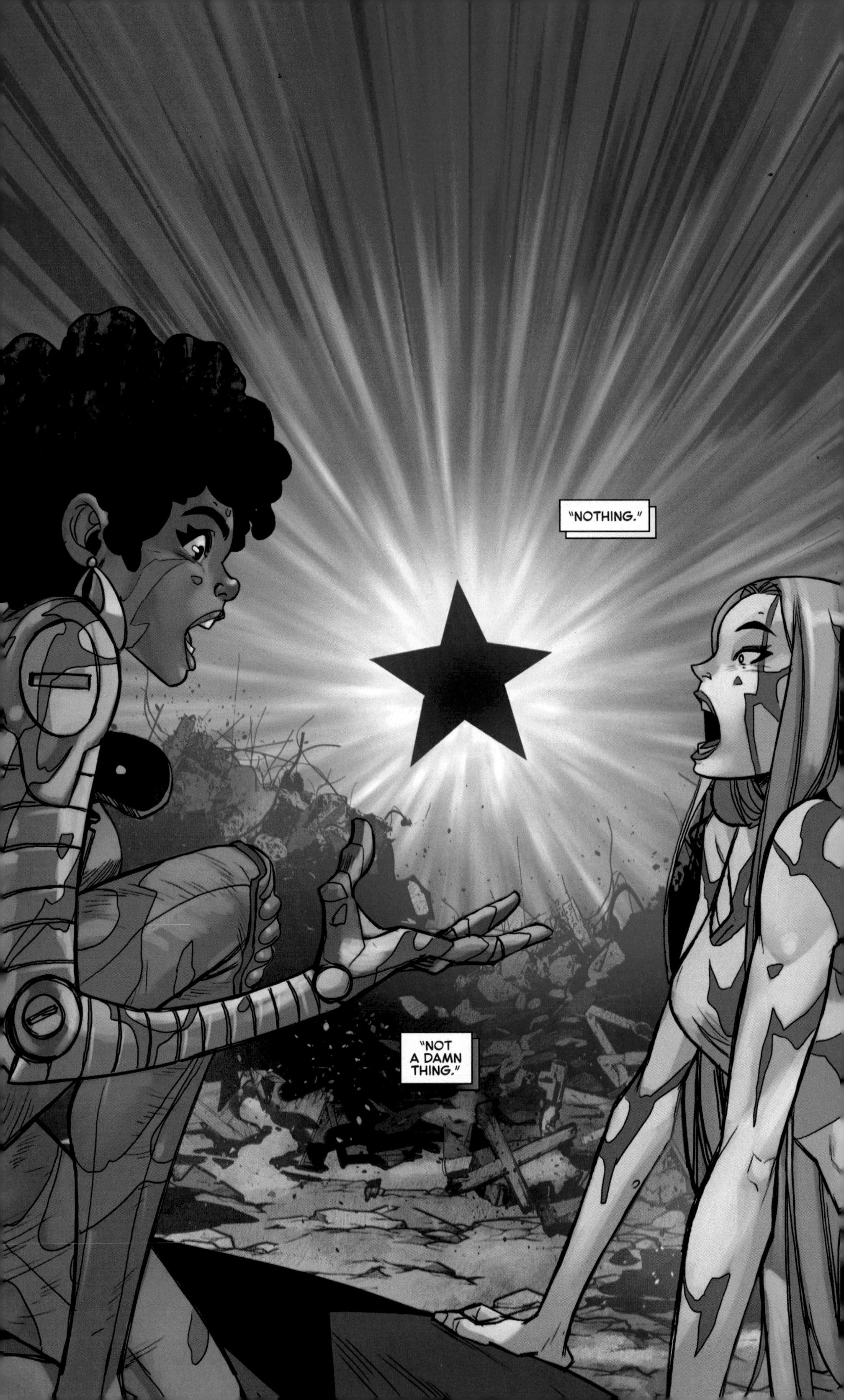
"NOTHING."
"NOT A DAMN THING."

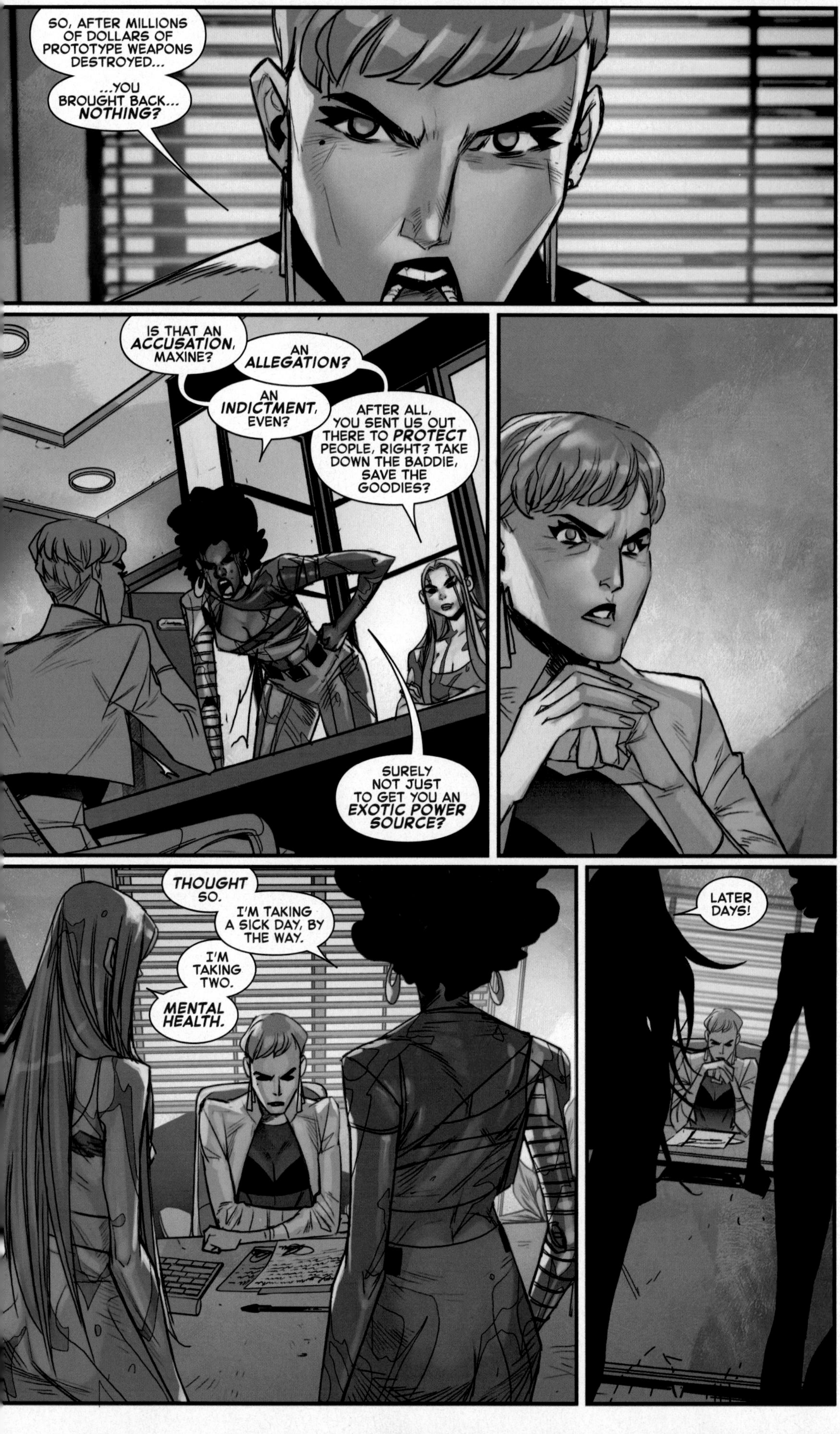

SO, AFTER MILLIONS OF DOLLARS OF PROTOTYPE WEAPONS DESTROYED...
...YOU BROUGHT BACK... NOTHING?
IS THAT AN ACCUSATION, MAXINE?
AN ALLEGATION?
AN INDICTMENT, EVEN?
AFTER ALL, YOU SENT US OUT THERE TO PROTECT PEOPLE, RIGHT? TAKE DOWN THE BADDIE, SAVE THE GOODIES?
SURELY NOT JUST TO GET YOU AN EXOTIC POWER SOURCE?
THOUGHT SO.
I'M TAKING A SICK DAY, BY THE WAY.
I'M TAKING TWO.
MENTAL HEALTH.
LATER DAYS!

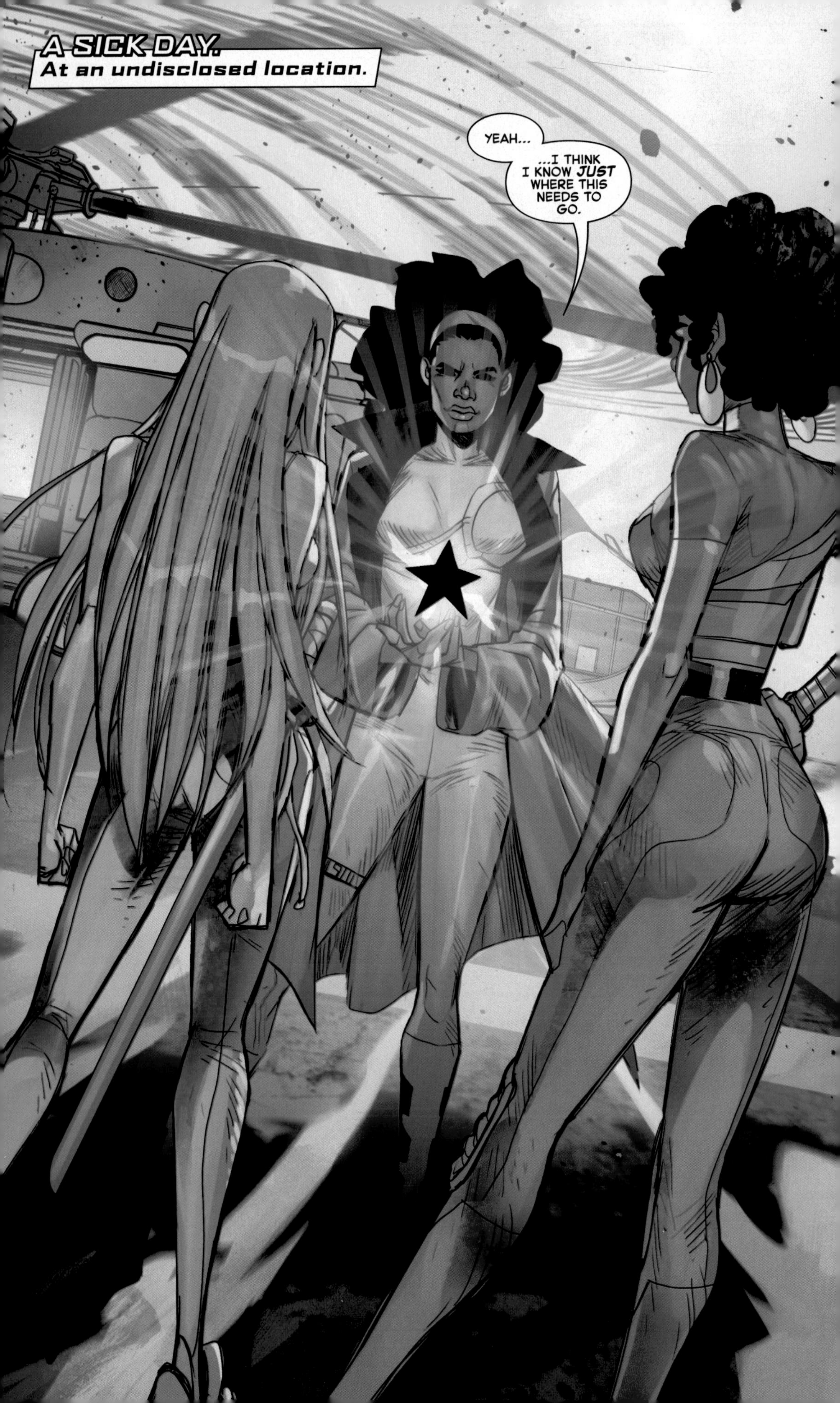
A SICK DAY.
At an undisclosed location.
YEAH...
...I THINK I KNOW JUST WHERE THIS NEEDS TO GO.

#75 WEBHEAD VARIANT BY
PATRICK GLEASON

BEYOND
CORPORATION

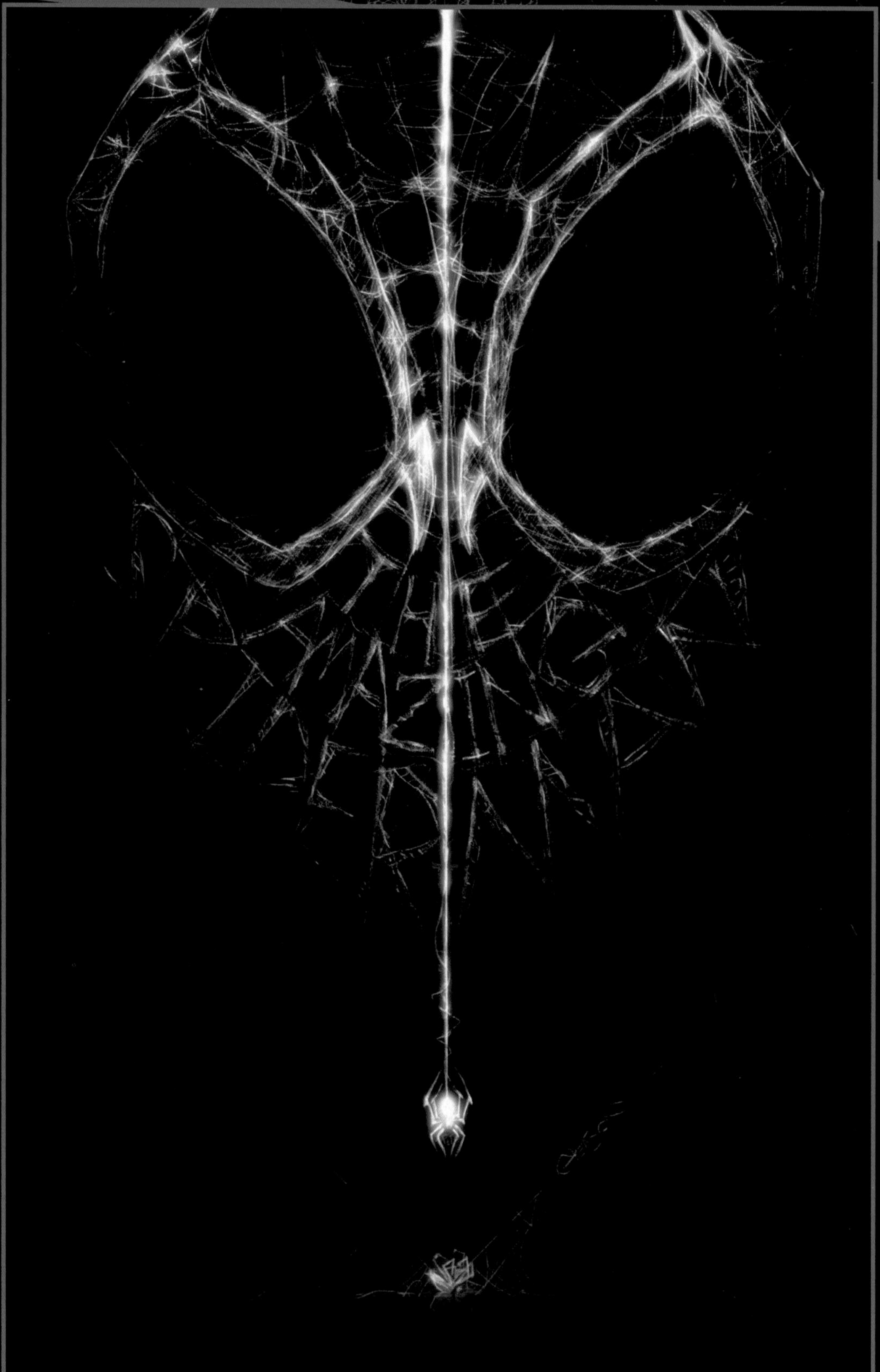

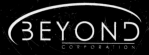

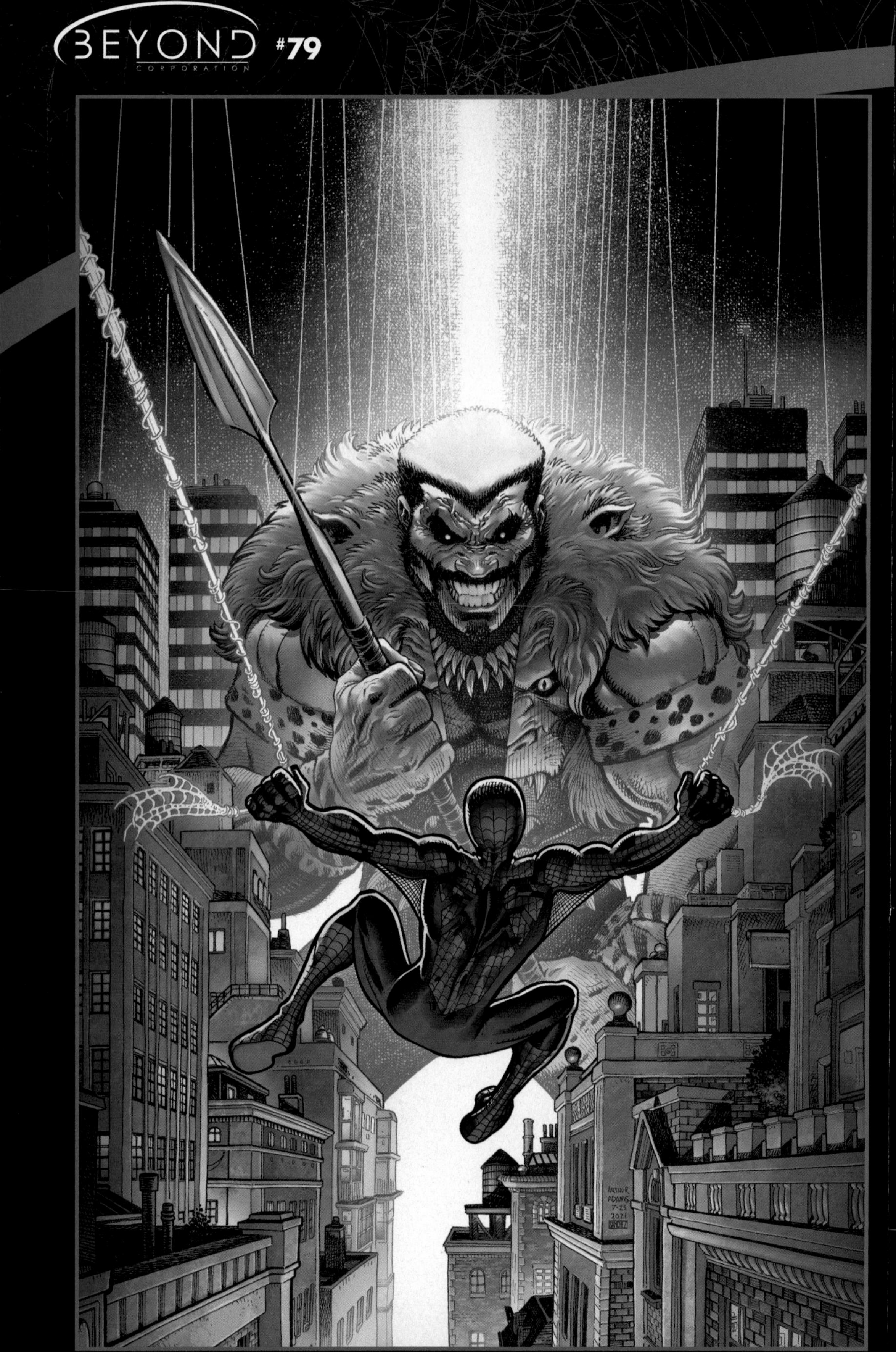
BEYOND
CORPORATION
#79

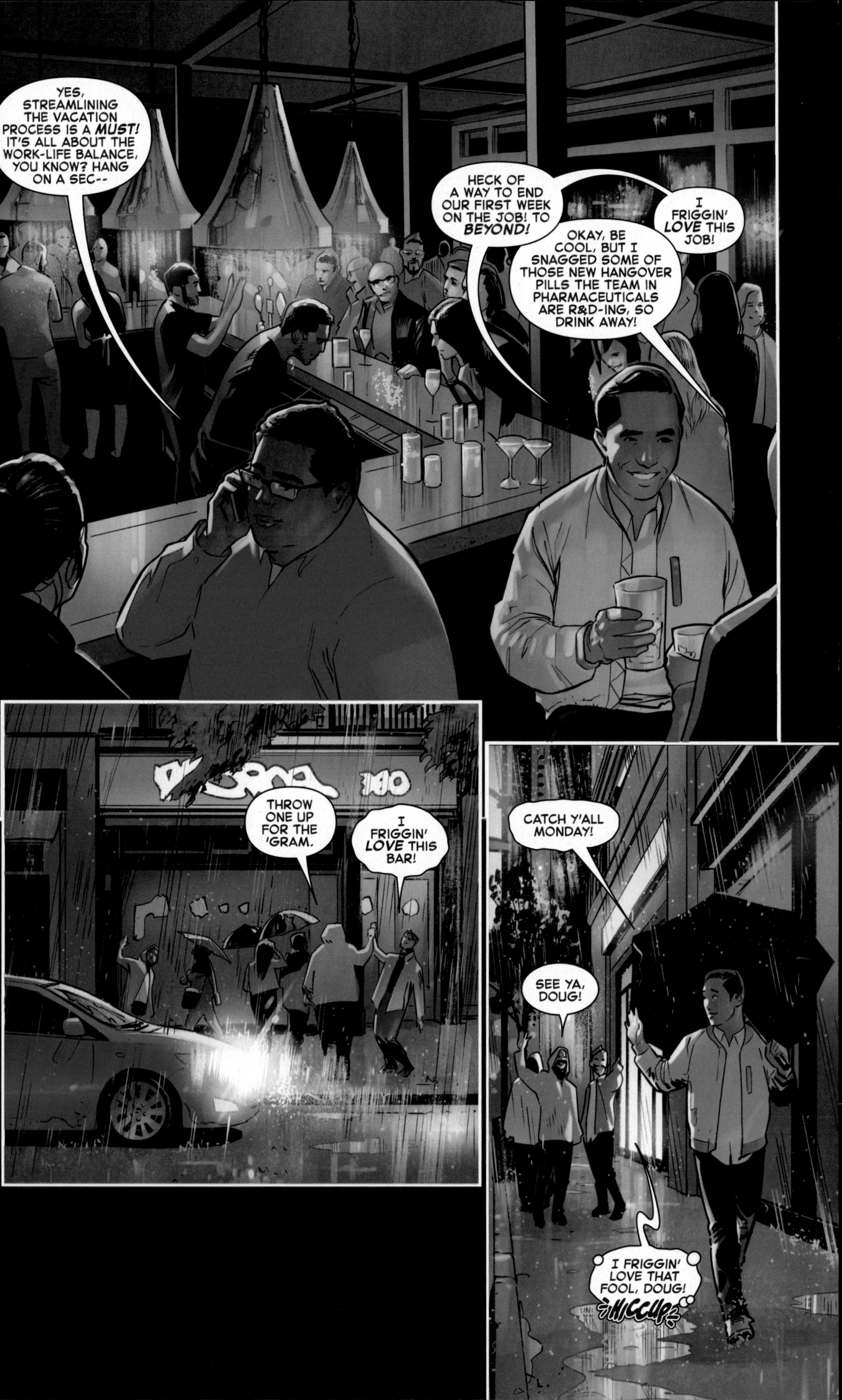
YES, STREAMLINING THE VACATION PROCESS IS A MUST! IT'S ALL ABOUT THE WORK-LIFE BALANCE, YOU KNOW? HANG ON A SEC--
HECK OF A WAY TO END OUR FIRST WEEK ON THE JOB! TO BEYOND!
I FRIGGIN' LOVE THIS JOB!
OKAY, BE COOL, BUT I SNAGGED SOME OF THOSE NEW HANGOVER PILLS THE TEAM IN PHARMACEUTICALS ARE R&D-ING, SO DRINK AWAY!
THROW ONE UP FOR THE 'GRAM.
I FRIGGIN' LOVE THIS BAR!
CATCH Y'ALL MONDAY!
SEE YA, DOUG!
I FRIGGIN' LOVE THAT FOOL, DOUG!
HICCUP

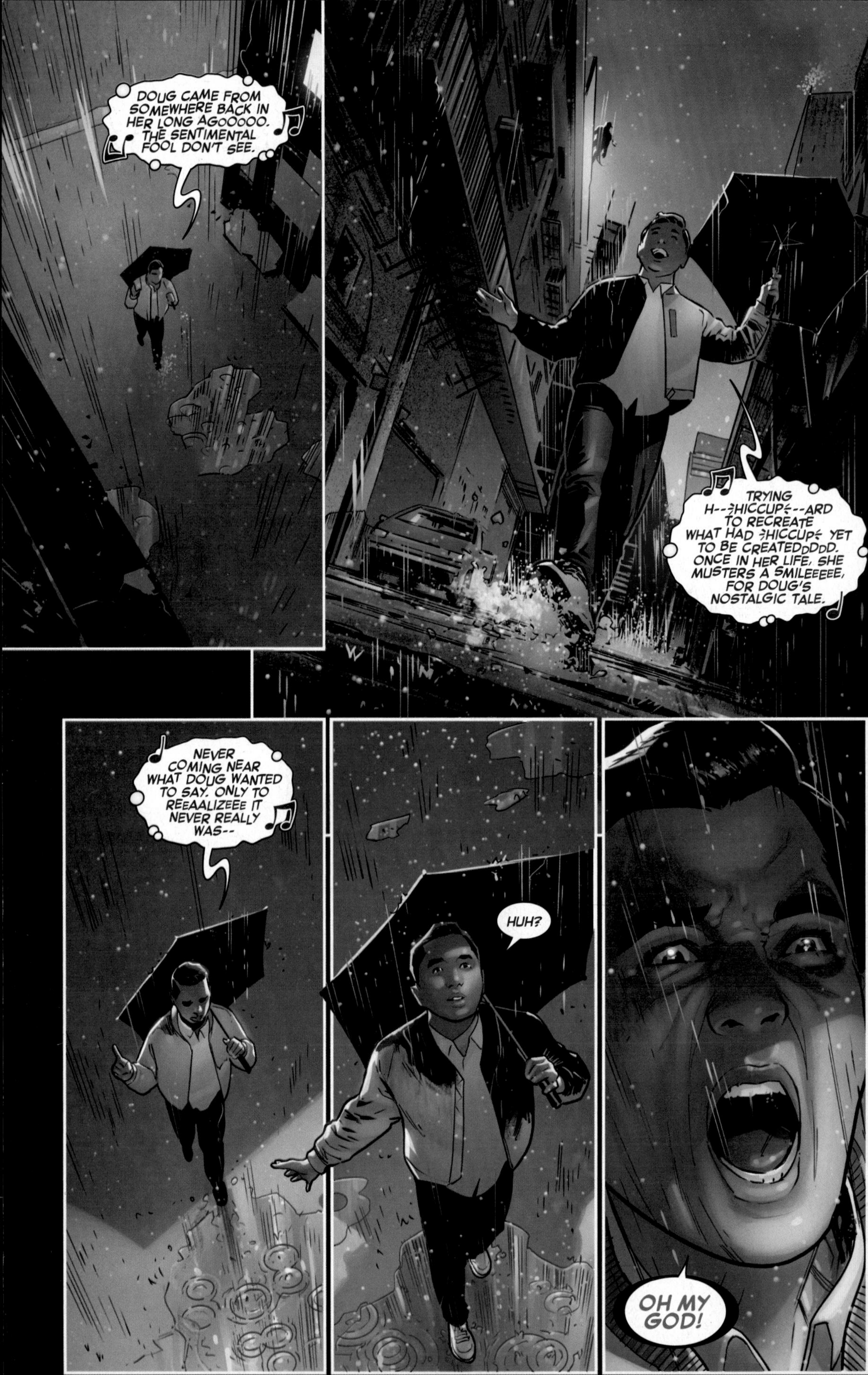
DOUG CAME FROM SOMEWHERE BACK IN HER LONG AGOOOOO. THE SENTIMENTAL FOOL DON'T SEE.
TRYING H--HICCUP--ARD TO RECREATE WHAT HAD HICCUP YET TO BE CREATEDDDD. ONCE IN HER LIFE, SHE MUSTERS A SMILEEEEE, FOR DOUG'S NOSTALGIC TALE.
NEVER COMING NEAR WHAT DOUG WANTED TO SAY. ONLY TO REEAALIZEEE IT NEVER REALLY WAS--
HUH?
OH MY GOD!

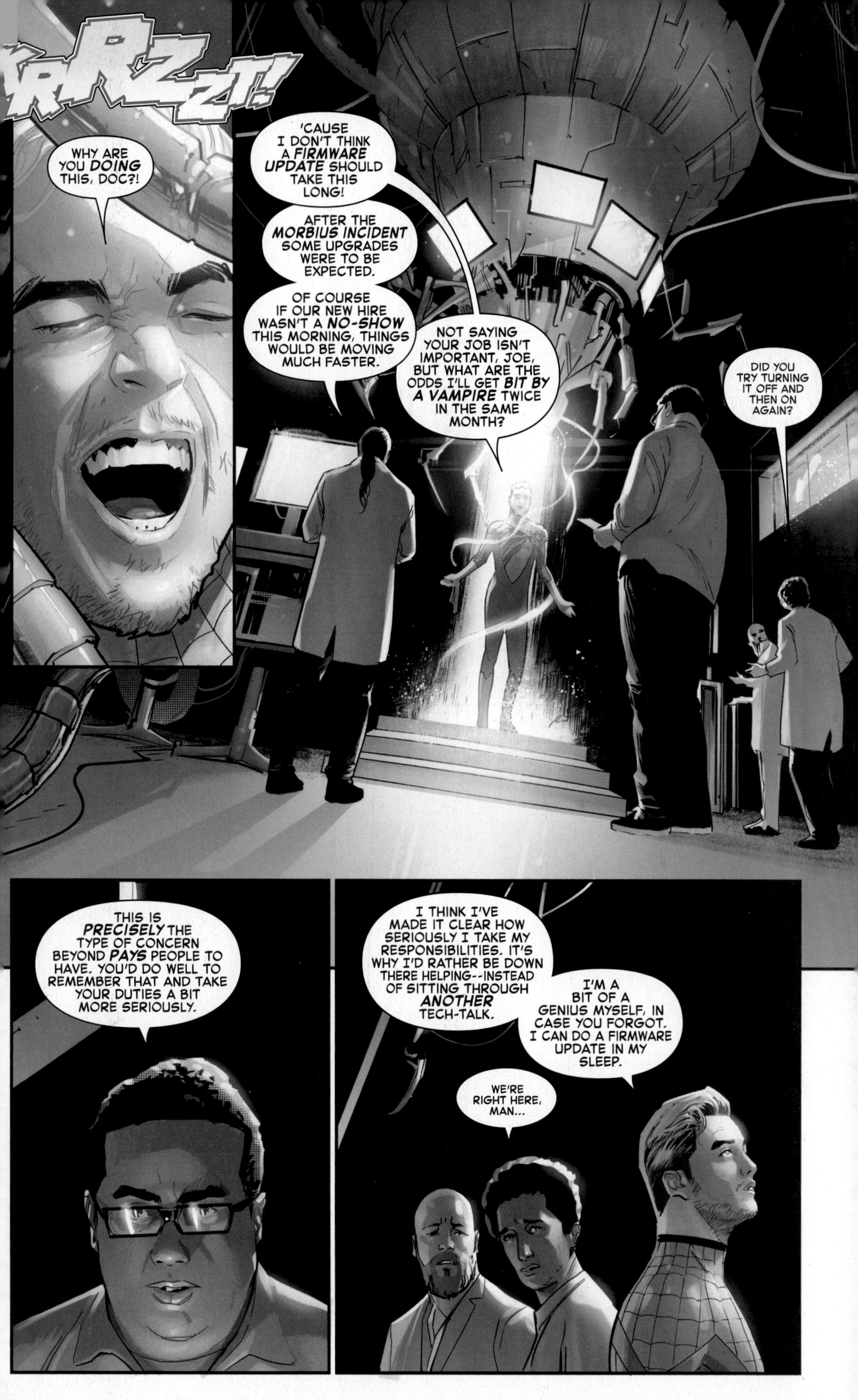

KRRZZT!
WHY ARE YOU DOING THIS, DOC?!
'CAUSE I DON'T THINK A FIRMWARE UPDATE SHOULD TAKE THIS LONG!
AFTER THE MORBIUS INCIDENT SOME UPGRADES WERE TO BE EXPECTED.
OF COURSE IF OUR NEW HIRE WASN'T A NO-SHOW THIS MORNING, THINGS WOULD BE MOVING MUCH FASTER.
NOT SAYING YOUR JOB ISN'T IMPORTANT, JOE, BUT WHAT ARE THE ODDS I'LL GET BIT BY A VAMPIRE TWICE IN THE SAME MONTH?
DID YOU TRY TURNING IT OFF AND THEN ON AGAIN?
THIS IS PRECISELY THE TYPE OF CONCERN BEYOND PAYS PEOPLE TO HAVE. YOU'D DO WELL TO REMEMBER THAT AND TAKE YOUR DUTIES A BIT MORE SERIOUSLY.
I THINK I'VE MADE IT CLEAR HOW SERIOUSLY I TAKE MY RESPONSIBILITIES. IT'S WHY I'D RATHER BE DOWN THERE HELPING--INSTEAD OF SITTING THROUGH ANOTHER TECH-TALK.
I'M A BIT OF A GENIUS MYSELF, IN CASE YOU FORGOT. I CAN DO A FIRMWARE UPDATE IN MY SLEEP.
WE'RE RIGHT HERE, MAN...

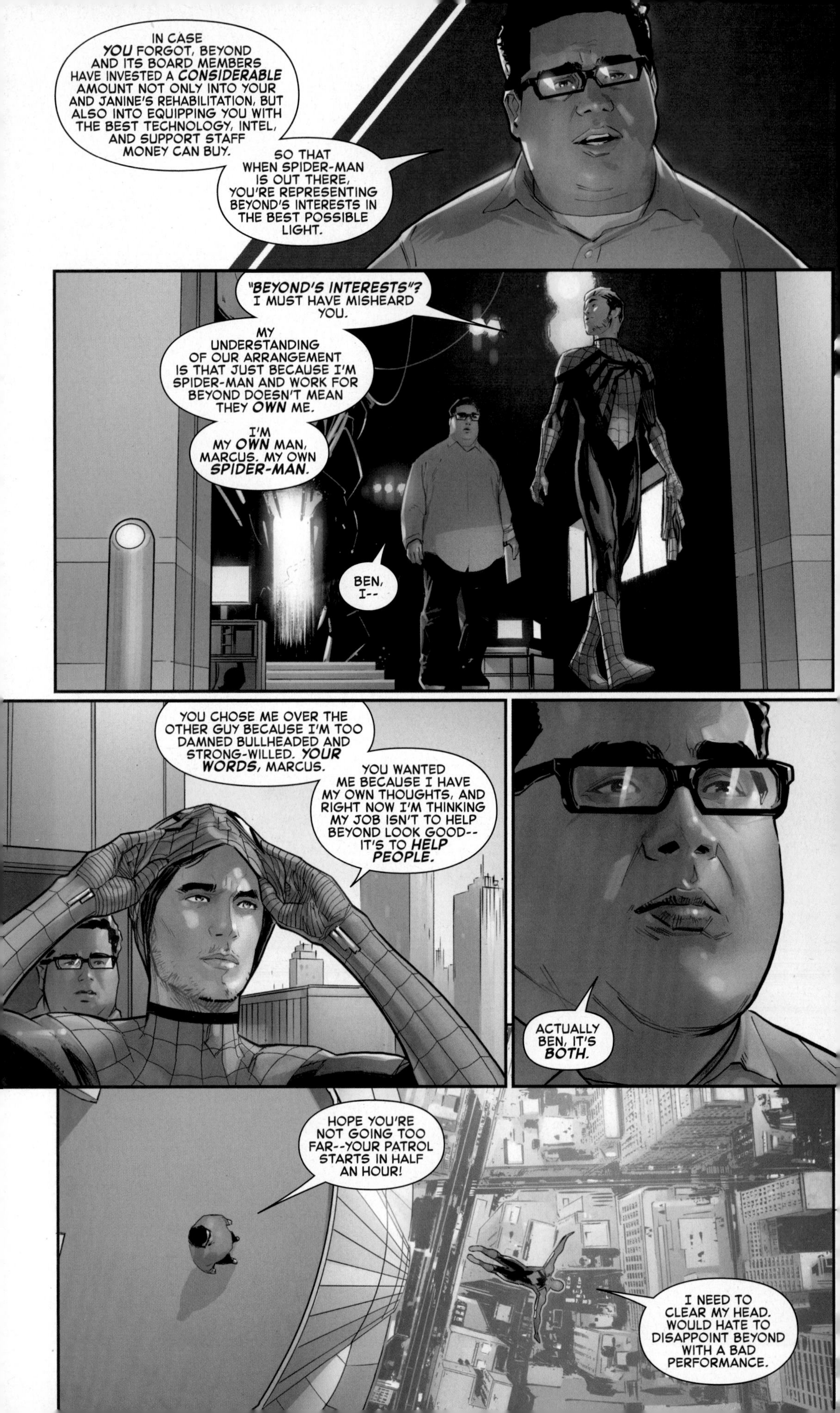
IN CASE YOU FORGOT, BEYOND AND ITS BOARD MEMBERS HAVE INVESTED A CONSIDERABLE AMOUNT NOT ONLY INTO YOUR AND JANINE'S REHABILITATION, BUT ALSO INTO EQUIPPING YOU WITH THE BEST TECHNOLOGY, INTEL, AND SUPPORT STAFF MONEY CAN BUY.
SO THAT WHEN SPIDER-MAN IS OUT THERE, YOU'RE REPRESENTING BEYOND'S INTERESTS IN THE BEST POSSIBLE LIGHT.
"BEYOND'S INTERESTS"? I MUST HAVE MISHEARD YOU.
MY UNDERSTANDING OF OUR ARRANGEMENT IS THAT JUST BECAUSE I'M SPIDER-MAN AND WORK FOR BEYOND DOESN'T MEAN THEY OWN ME.
I'M MY OWN MAN, MARCUS. MY OWN SPIDER-MAN.
BEN, I--
YOU CHOSE ME OVER THE OTHER GUY BECAUSE I'M TOO DAMNED BULLHEADED AND STRONG-WILLED. YOUR WORDS, MARCUS.
YOU WANTED ME BECAUSE I HAVE MY OWN THOUGHTS, AND RIGHT NOW I'M THINKING MY JOB ISN'T TO HELP BEYOND LOOK GOOD-- IT'S TO HELP PEOPLE.
ACTUALLY BEN, IT'S BOTH.
HOPE YOU'RE NOT GOING TOO FAR--YOUR PATROL STARTS IN HALF AN HOUR!
I NEED TO CLEAR MY HEAD. WOULD HATE TO DISAPPOINT BEYOND WITH A BAD PERFORMANCE.

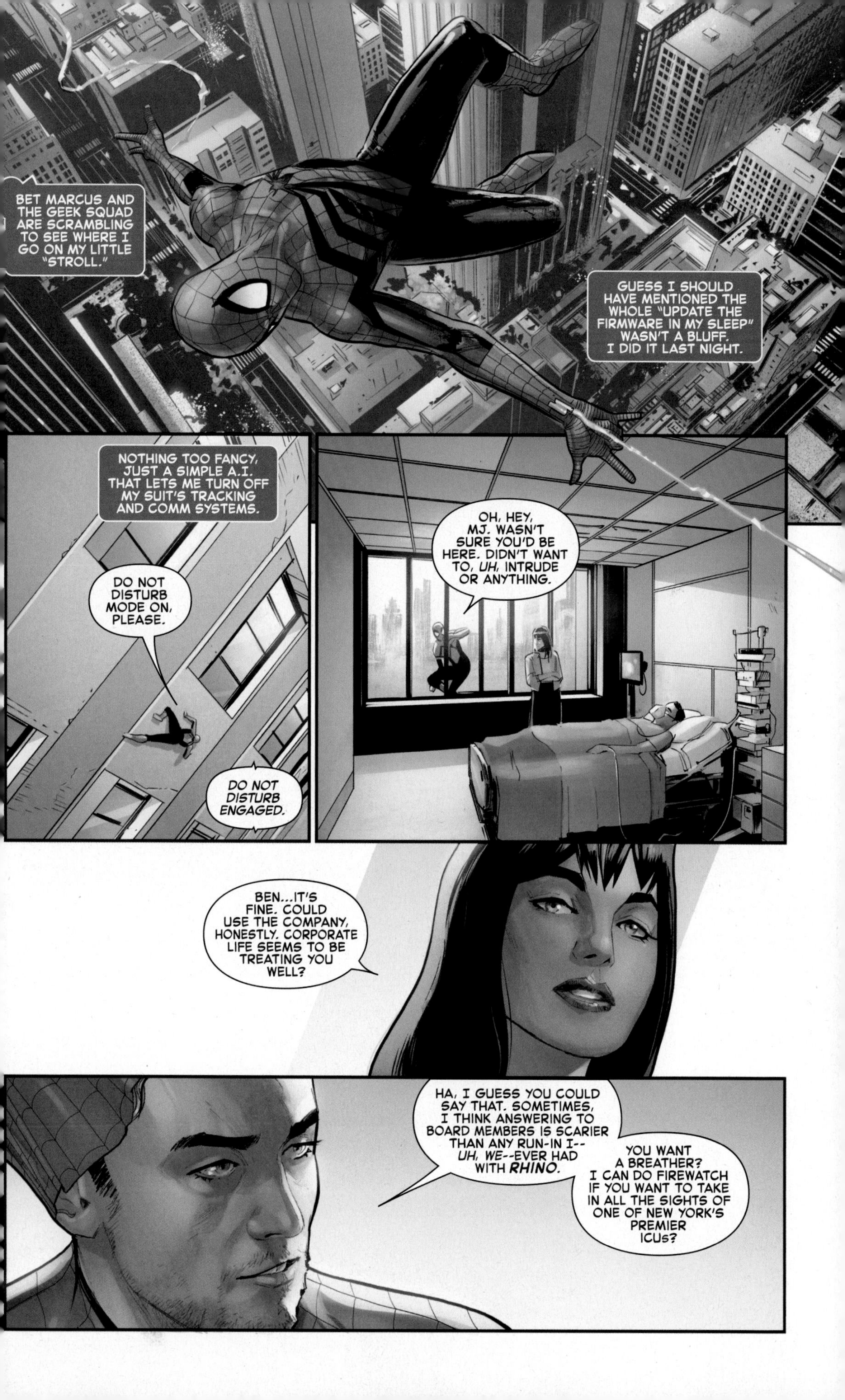
BET MARCUS AND THE GEEK SQUAD ARE SCRAMBLING TO SEE WHERE I GO ON MY LITTLE "STROLL."
GUESS I SHOULD HAVE MENTIONED THE WHOLE "UPDATE THE FIRMWARE IN MY SLEEP" WASN'T A BLUFF. I DID IT LAST NIGHT.
NOTHING TOO FANCY, JUST A SIMPLE A.I. THAT LETS ME TURN OFF MY SUIT'S TRACKING AND COMM SYSTEMS.
DO NOT DISTURB MODE ON, PLEASE.
DO NOT DISTURB ENGAGED.
OH, HEY, MJ. WASN'T SURE YOU'D BE HERE. DIDN'T WANT TO, UH, INTRUDE OR ANYTHING.
BEN...IT'S FINE. COULD USE THE COMPANY, HONESTLY. CORPORATE LIFE SEEMS TO BE TREATING YOU WELL?
HA, I GUESS YOU COULD SAY THAT. SOMETIMES, I THINK ANSWERING TO BOARD MEMBERS IS SCARIER THAN ANY RUN-IN I-- UH, WE--EVER HAD WITH RHINO.
YOU WANT A BREATHER? I CAN DO FIREWATCH IF YOU WANT TO TAKE IN ALL THE SIGHTS OF ONE OF NEW YORK'S PREMIER ICUs?

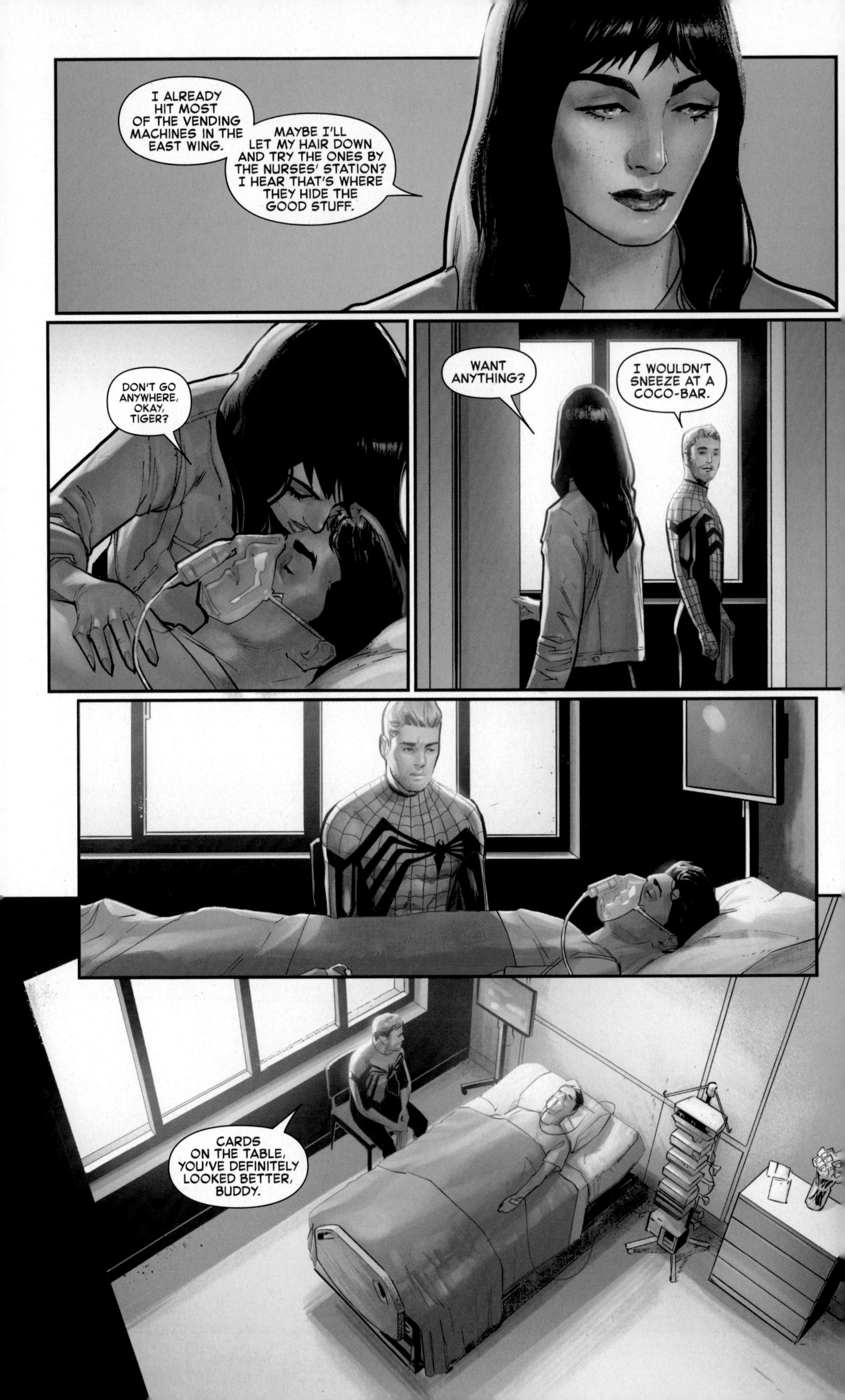

I ALREADY HIT MOST OF THE VENDING MACHINES IN THE EAST WING.
MAYBE I'LL LET MY HAIR DOWN AND TRY THE ONES BY THE NURSES' STATION? I HEAR THAT'S WHERE THEY HIDE THE GOOD STUFF.
DON'T GO ANYWHERE, OKAY, TIGER?
WANT ANYTHING?
I WOULDN'T SNEEZE AT A COCO-BAR.
CARDS ON THE TABLE, YOU'VE DEFINITELY LOOKED BETTER, BUDDY.

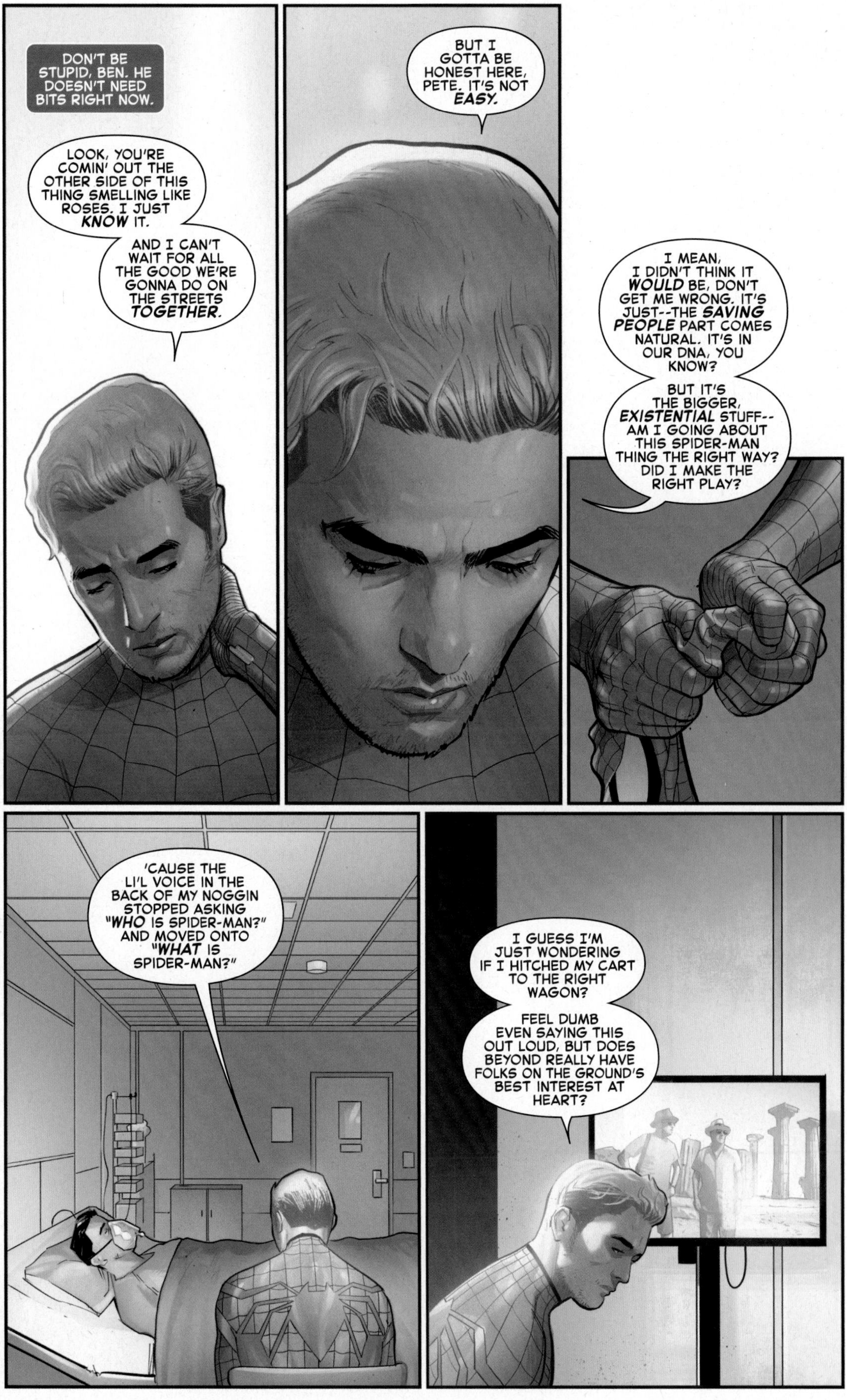
DON'T BE STUPID, BEN. HE DOESN'T NEED BITS RIGHT NOW.
LOOK, YOU'RE COMIN' OUT THE OTHER SIDE OF THIS THING SMELLING LIKE ROSES. I JUST KNOW IT.
AND I CAN'T WAIT FOR ALL THE GOOD WE'RE GONNA DO ON THE STREETS TOGETHER.
BUT I GOTTA BE HONEST HERE, PETE. IT'S NOT EASY.
I MEAN, I DIDN'T THINK IT WOULD BE, DON'T GET ME WRONG. IT'S JUST--THE SAVING PEOPLE PART COMES NATURAL. IT'S IN OUR DNA, YOU KNOW?
BUT IT'S THE BIGGER, EXISTENTIAL STUFF--AM I GOING ABOUT THIS SPIDER-MAN THING THE RIGHT WAY? DID I MAKE THE RIGHT PLAY?
'CAUSE THE LI'L VOICE IN THE BACK OF MY NOGGIN STOPPED ASKING "WHO IS SPIDER-MAN?" AND MOVED ONTO "WHAT IS SPIDER-MAN?"
I GUESS I'M JUST WONDERING IF I HITCHED MY CART TO THE RIGHT WAGON?
FEEL DUMB EVEN SAYING THIS OUT LOUD, BUT DOES BEYOND REALLY HAVE FOLKS ON THE GROUND'S BEST INTEREST AT HEART?

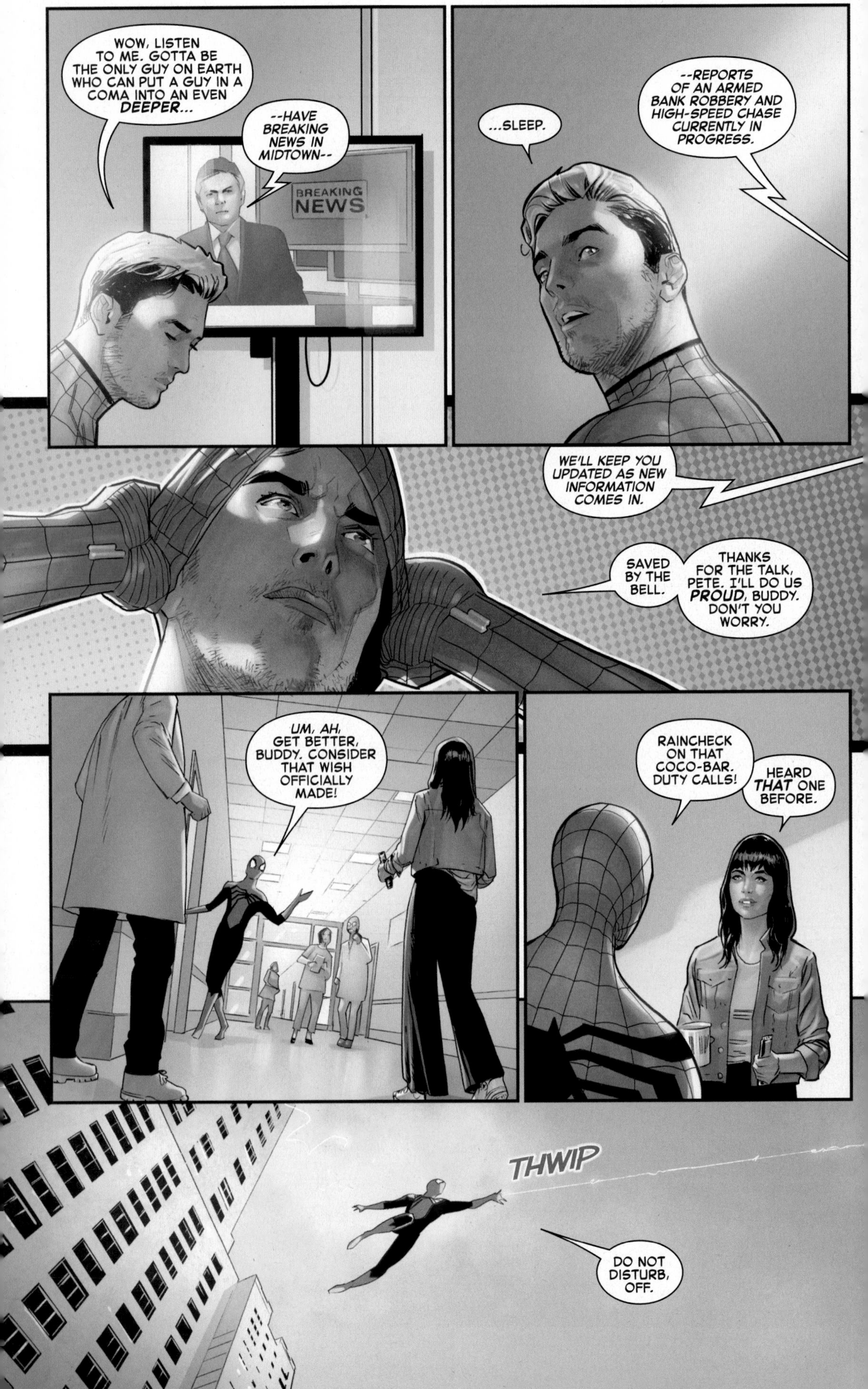
WOW, LISTEN TO ME. GOTTA BE THE ONLY GUY ON EARTH WHO CAN PUT A GUY IN A COMA INTO AN EVEN DEEPER...
--HAVE BREAKING NEWS IN MIDTOWN--
BREAKING NEWS
...SLEEP.
--REPORTS OF AN ARMED BANK ROBBERY AND HIGH-SPEED CHASE CURRENTLY IN PROGRESS.
WE'LL KEEP YOU UPDATED AS NEW INFORMATION COMES IN.
SAVED BY THE BELL.
THANKS FOR THE TALK, PETE. I'LL DO US PROUD, BUDDY. DON'T YOU WORRY.
UM, AH, GET BETTER, BUDDY. CONSIDER THAT WISH OFFICIALLY MADE!
RAINCHECK ON THAT COCO-BAR. DUTY CALLS!
HEARD THAT ONE BEFORE.
THWIP
DO NOT DISTURB, OFF.

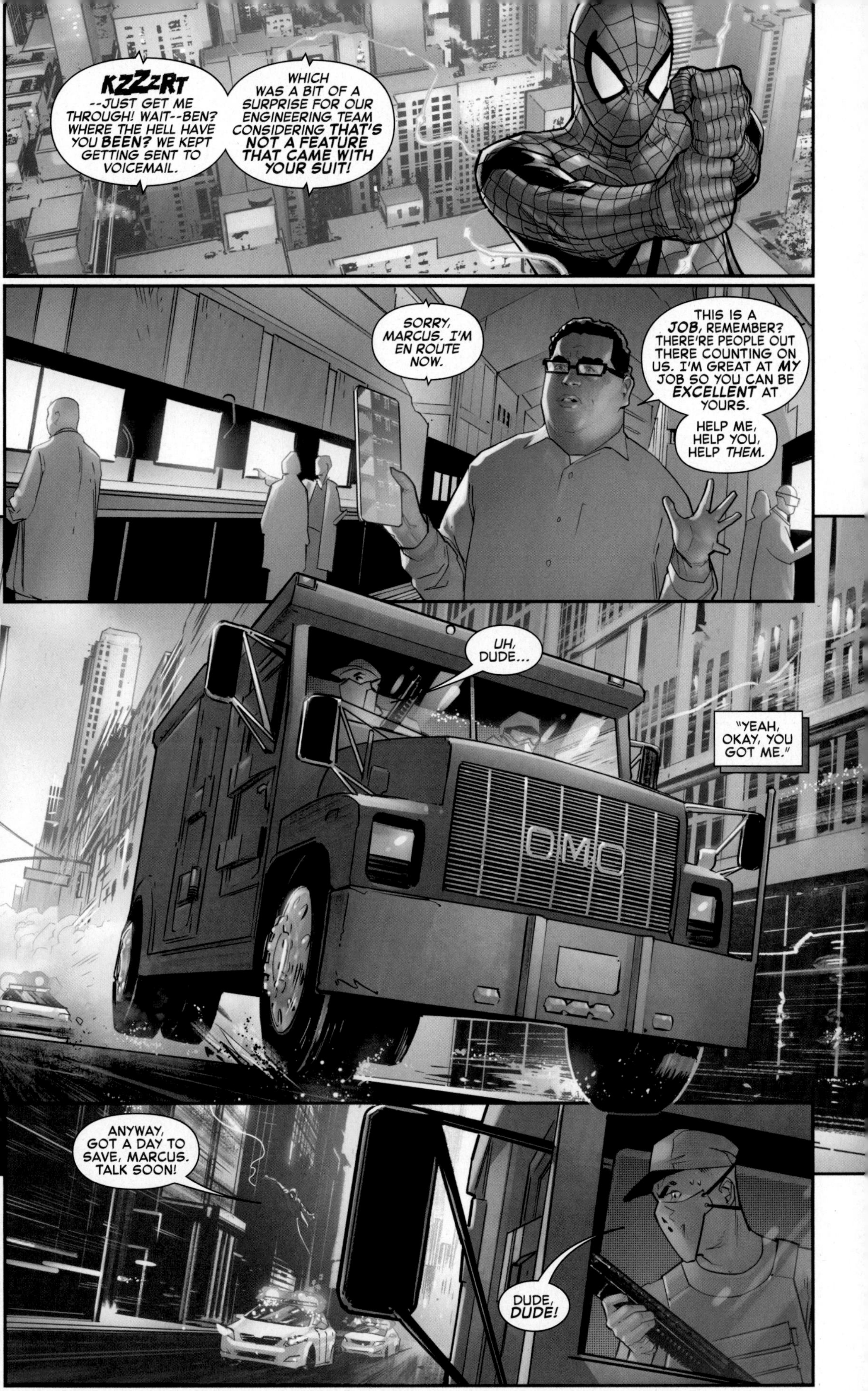
KZZZRT --JUST GET ME THROUGH! WAIT--BEN? WHERE THE HELL HAVE YOU BEEN? WE KEPT GETTING SENT TO VOICEMAIL.
WHICH WAS A BIT OF A SURPRISE FOR OUR ENGINEERING TEAM CONSIDERING THAT'S NOT A FEATURE THAT CAME WITH YOUR SUIT!
SORRY, MARCUS. I'M EN ROUTE NOW.
THIS IS A JOB, REMEMBER? THERE'RE PEOPLE OUT THERE COUNTING ON US. I'M GREAT AT MY JOB SO YOU CAN BE EXCELLENT AT YOURS.
HELP ME, HELP YOU, HELP THEM.
UH, DUDE...
"YEAH, OKAY, YOU GOT ME."
OMO
ANYWAY, GOT A DAY TO SAVE, MARCUS. TALK SOON!
DUDE, DUDE!

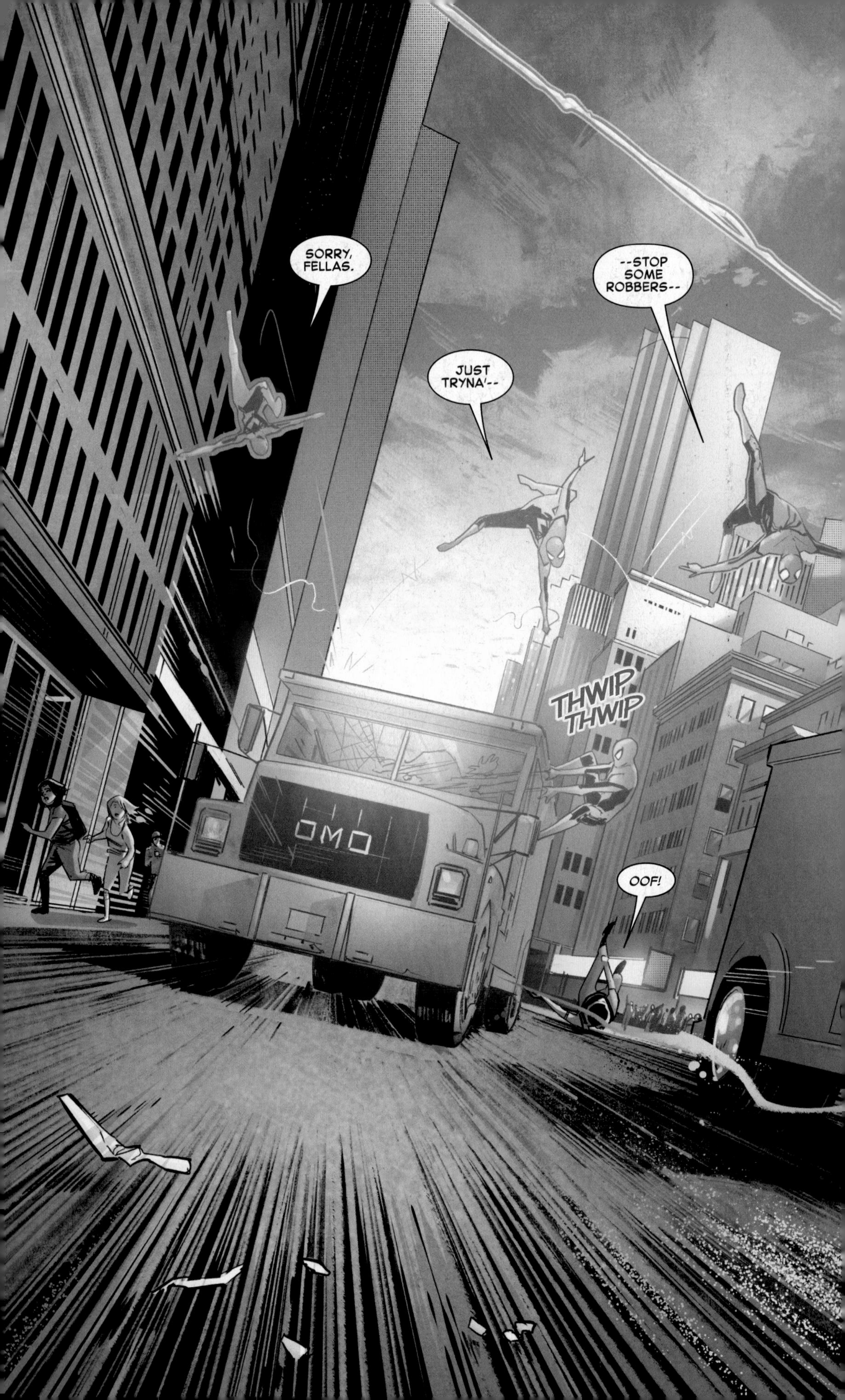
SORRY, FELLAS.
JUST TRYNA'--
--STOP SOME ROBBERS--
THWIP THWIP
OMO
OOF!

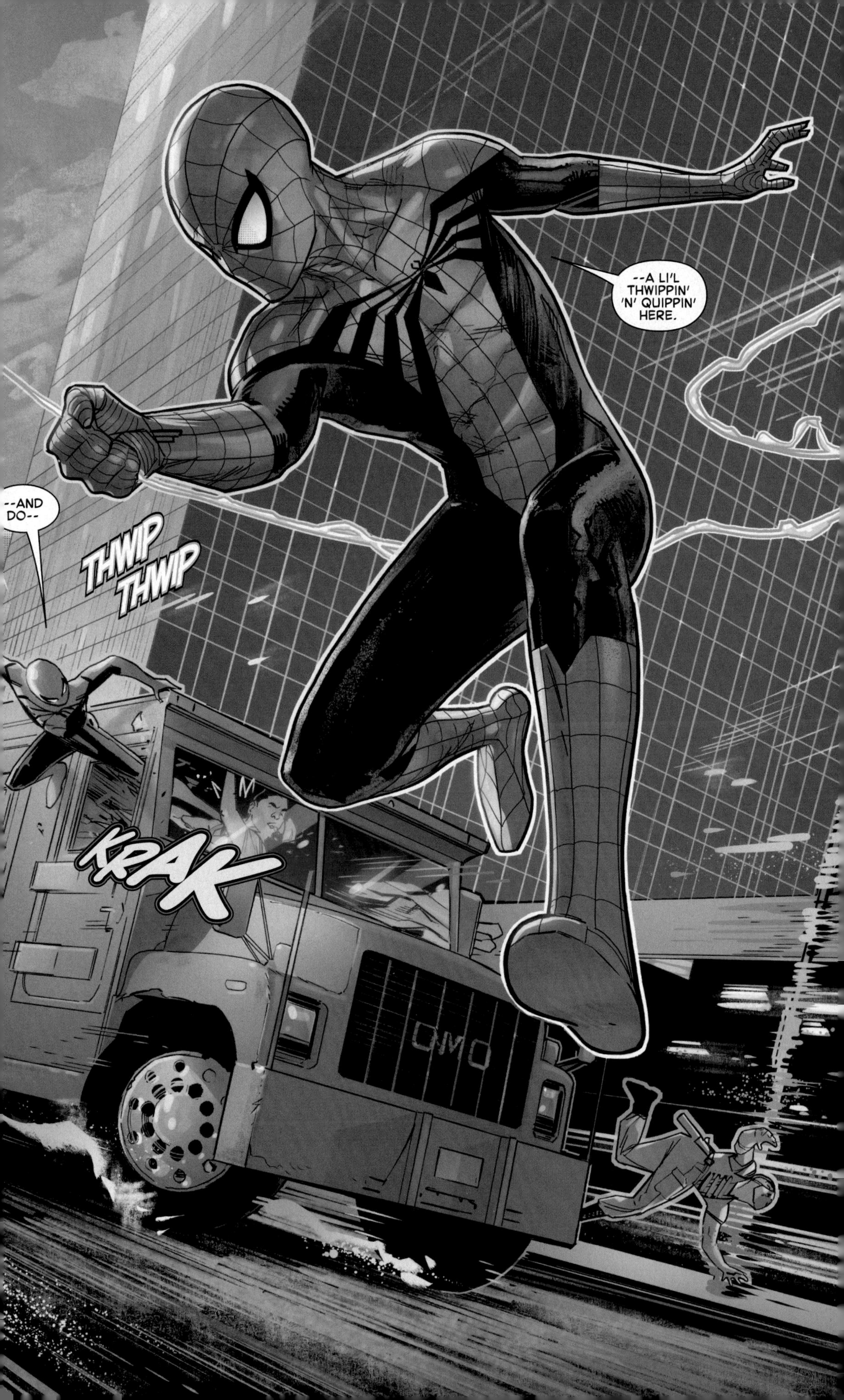
--AND DO--
THWIP THWIP
--A LI'L THWIPPIN' 'N' QUIPPIN' HERE.
KRAK

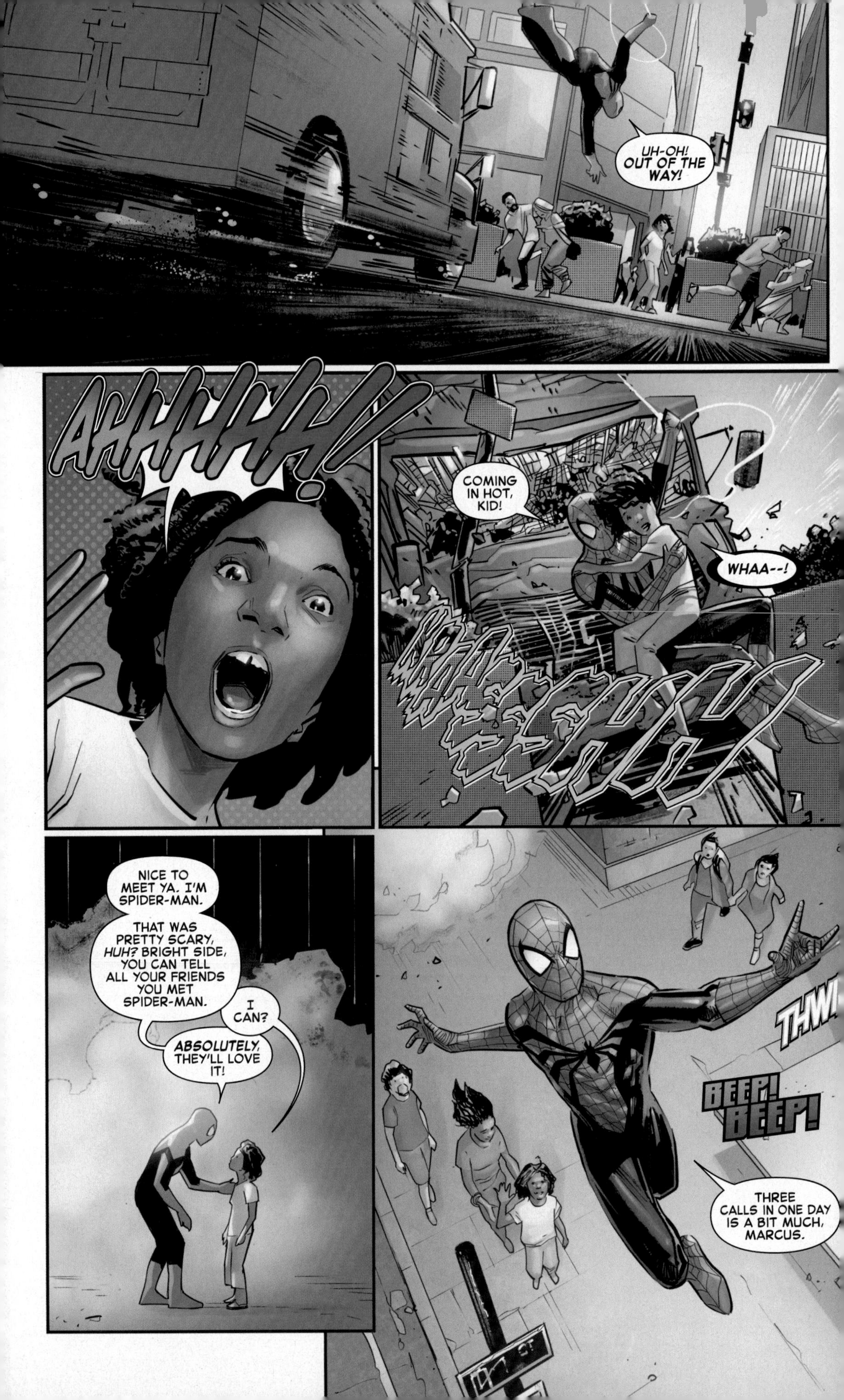
UH-OH! OUT OF THE WAY!
AHHHHH!!
COMING IN HOT, KID!
WHAA--!
NICE TO MEET YA. I'M SPIDER-MAN.
THAT WAS PRETTY SCARY, *HUH?* BRIGHT SIDE, YOU CAN TELL ALL YOUR FRIENDS YOU MET SPIDER-MAN.
I CAN?
ABSOLUTELY, THEY'LL LOVE IT!
BEEP! BEEP!
THREE CALLS IN ONE DAY IS A BIT MUCH, MARCUS.

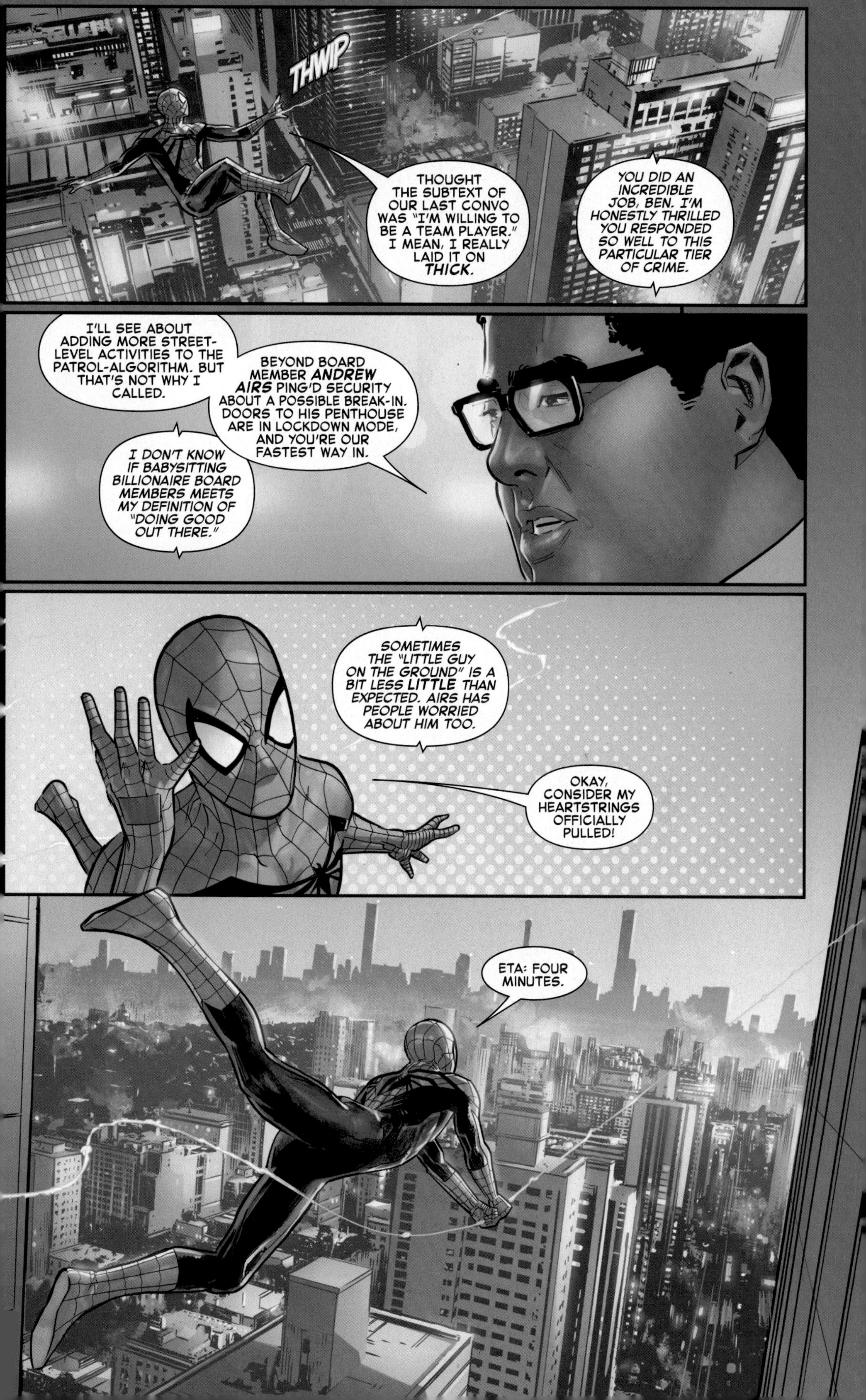
THWIP
THOUGHT THE SUBTEXT OF OUR LAST CONVO WAS "I'M WILLING TO BE A TEAM PLAYER." I MEAN, I REALLY LAID IT ON THICK.
YOU DID AN INCREDIBLE JOB, BEN. I'M HONESTLY THRILLED YOU RESPONDED SO WELL TO THIS PARTICULAR TIER OF CRIME.
I'LL SEE ABOUT ADDING MORE STREET-LEVEL ACTIVITIES TO THE PATROL-ALGORITHM. BUT THAT'S NOT WHY I CALLED.
BEYOND BOARD MEMBER ANDREW AIRS PING'D SECURITY ABOUT A POSSIBLE BREAK-IN. DOORS TO HIS PENTHOUSE ARE IN LOCKDOWN MODE, AND YOU'RE OUR FASTEST WAY IN.
I DON'T KNOW IF BABYSITTING BILLIONAIRE BOARD MEMBERS MEETS MY DEFINITION OF "DOING GOOD OUT THERE."
SOMETIMES THE "LITTLE GUY ON THE GROUND" IS A BIT LESS LITTLE THAN EXPECTED. AIRS HAS PEOPLE WORRIED ABOUT HIM TOO.
OKAY, CONSIDER MY HEARTSTRINGS OFFICIALLY PULLED!
ETA: FOUR MINUTES.

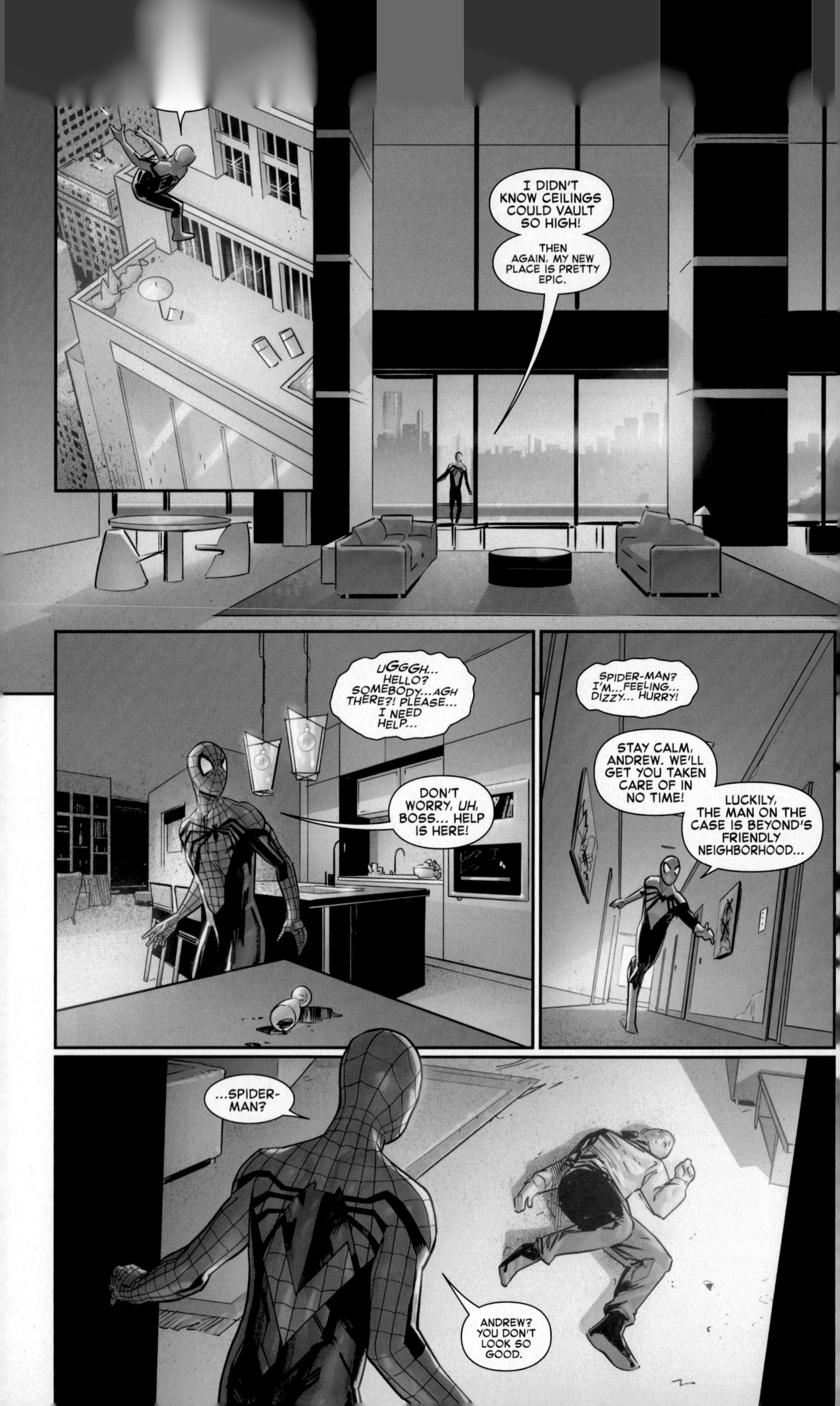

I DIDN'T KNOW CEILINGS COULD VAULT SO HIGH!
THEN AGAIN, MY NEW PLACE IS PRETTY EPIC.
UGGGH... HELLO? SOMEBODY...AGH THERE?! PLEASE... I NEED HELP...
DON'T WORRY, UH, BOSS... HELP IS HERE!
SPIDER-MAN? I'M...FEELING... DIZZY... HURRY!
STAY CALM, ANDREW. WE'LL GET YOU TAKEN CARE OF IN NO TIME!
LUCKILY, THE MAN ON THE CASE IS BEYOND'S FRIENDLY NEIGHBORHOOD...
...SPIDER-MAN?
ANDREW? YOU DON'T LOOK SO GOOD.

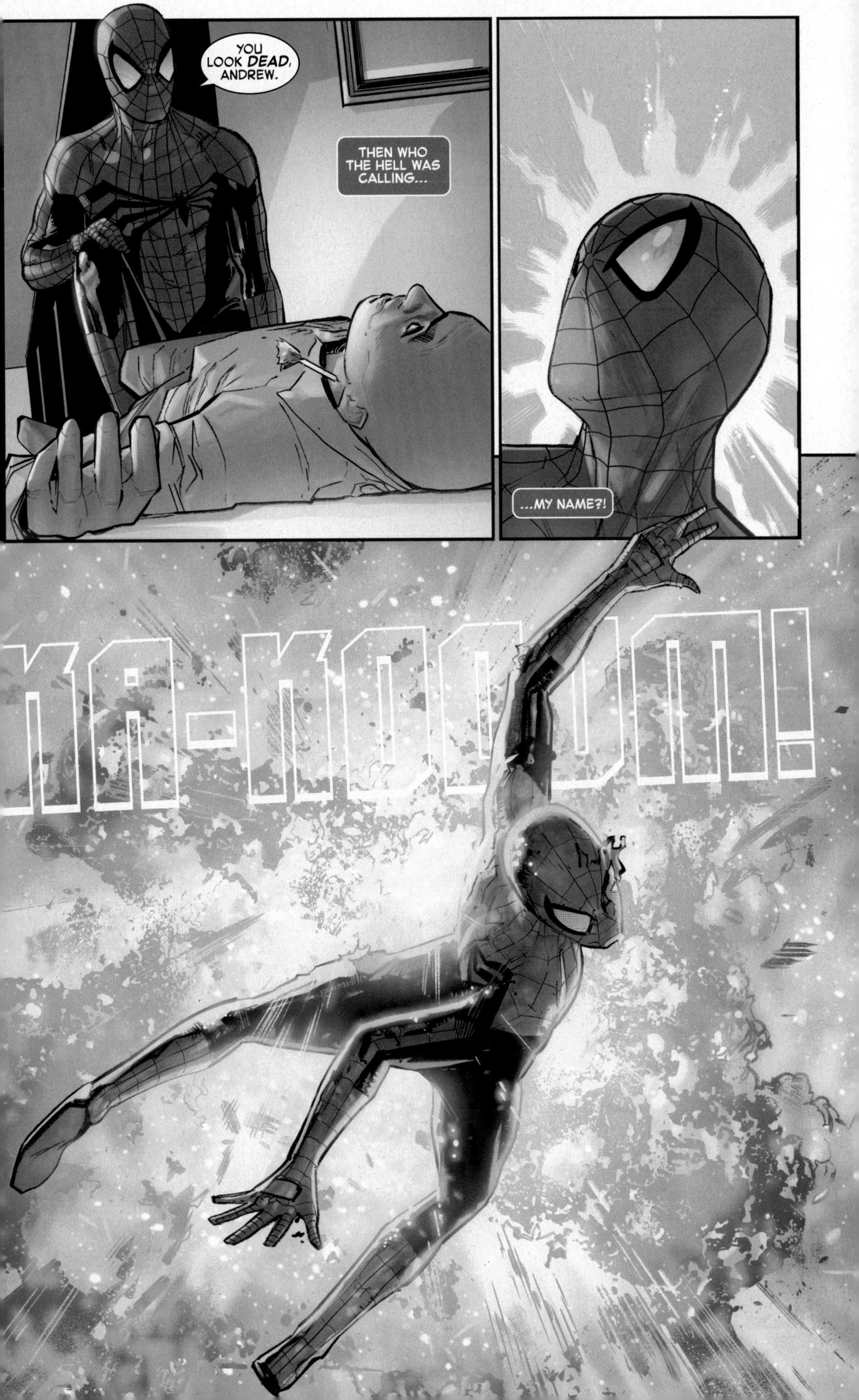
YOU LOOK DEAD, ANDREW.
THEN WHO THE HELL WAS CALLING...
...MY NAME?!
KA-BOOOM!

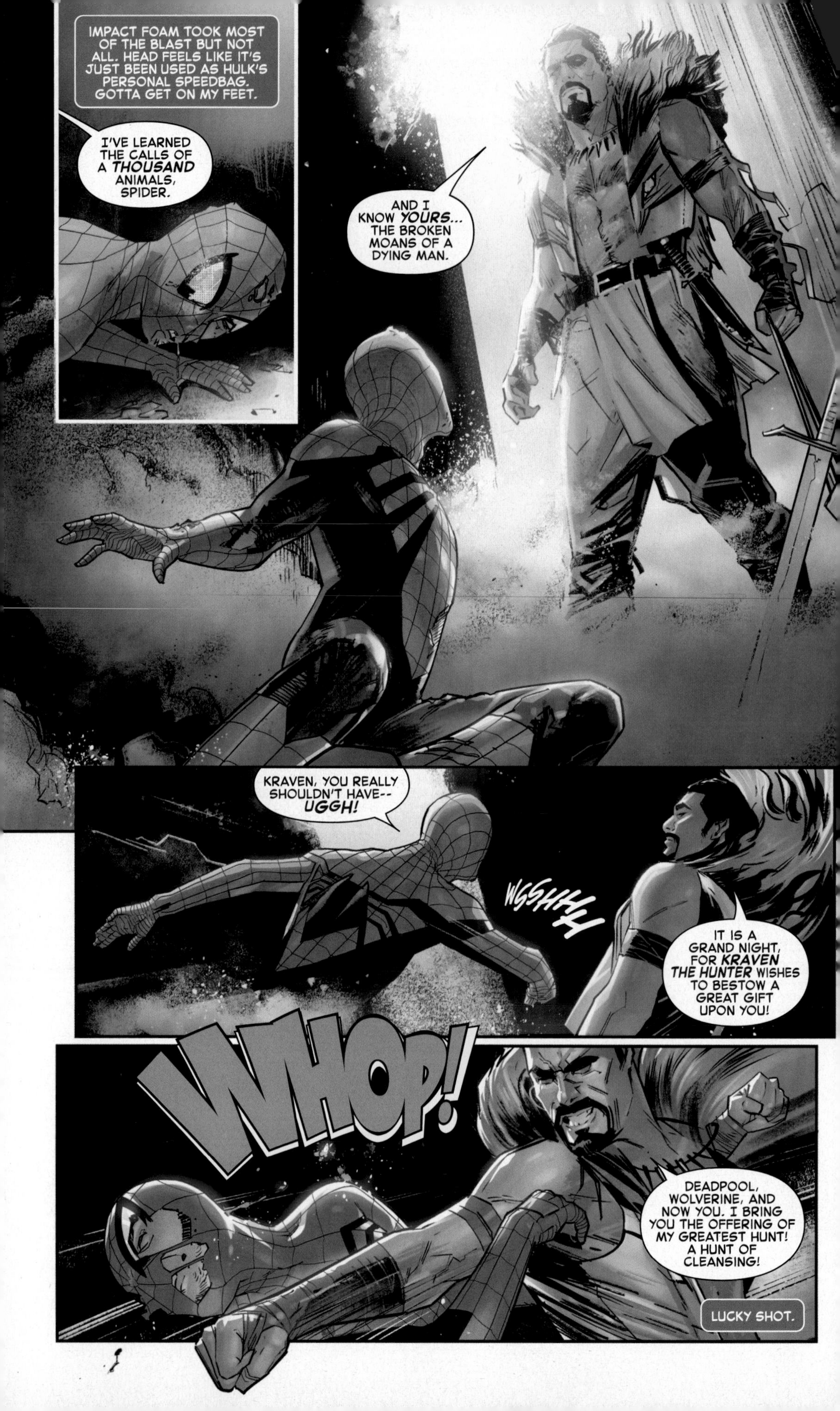

IMPACT FOAM TOOK MOST OF THE BLAST BUT NOT ALL. HEAD FEELS LIKE IT'S JUST BEEN USED AS HULK'S PERSONAL SPEEDBAG. GOTTA GET ON MY FEET.
I'VE LEARNED THE CALLS OF A THOUSAND ANIMALS, SPIDER.
AND I KNOW YOURS... THE BROKEN MOANS OF A DYING MAN.
KRAVEN, YOU REALLY SHOULDN'T HAVE-- UGGH!
WSSHHH
IT IS A GRAND NIGHT, FOR KRAVEN THE HUNTER WISHES TO BESTOW A GREAT GIFT UPON YOU!
WHOP!
DEADPOOL, WOLVERINE, AND NOW YOU. I BRING YOU THE OFFERING OF MY GREATEST HUNT! A HUNT OF CLEANSING!
LUCKY SHOT.

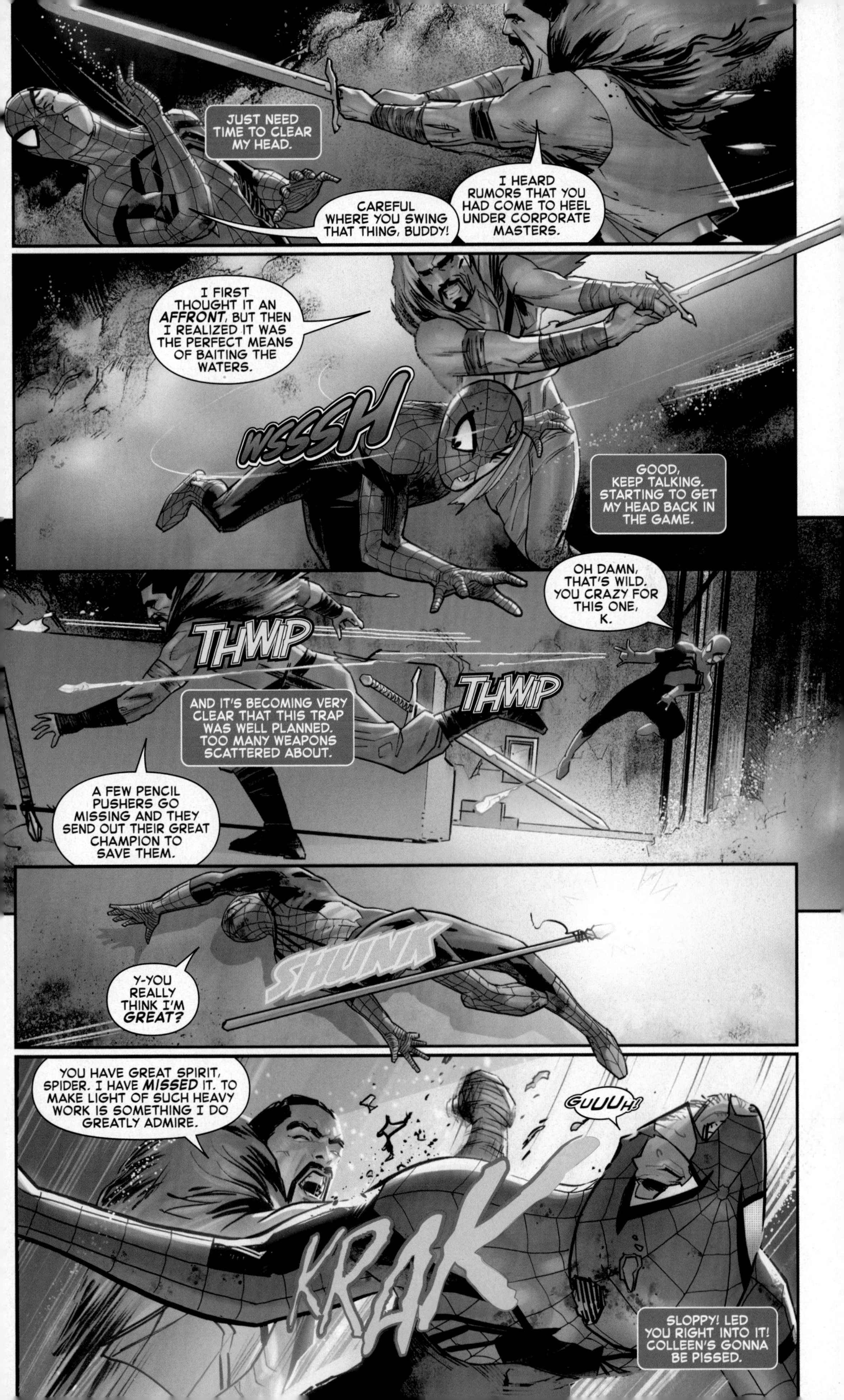
JUST NEED TIME TO CLEAR MY HEAD.
CAREFUL WHERE YOU SWING THAT THING, BUDDY!
I HEARD RUMORS THAT YOU HAD COME TO HEEL UNDER CORPORATE MASTERS.
I FIRST THOUGHT IT AN AFFRONT, BUT THEN I REALIZED IT WAS THE PERFECT MEANS OF BAITING THE WATERS.
WSSSH
GOOD, KEEP TALKING. STARTING TO GET MY HEAD BACK IN THE GAME.
OH DAMN, THAT'S WILD. YOU CRAZY FOR THIS ONE, K.
THWIP
THWIP
AND IT'S BECOMING VERY CLEAR THAT THIS TRAP WAS WELL PLANNED. TOO MANY WEAPONS SCATTERED ABOUT.
A FEW PENCIL PUSHERS GO MISSING AND THEY SEND OUT THEIR GREAT CHAMPION TO SAVE THEM.
SHUNK
Y-YOU REALLY THINK I'M GREAT?
YOU HAVE GREAT SPIRIT, SPIDER. I HAVE MISSED IT. TO MAKE LIGHT OF SUCH HEAVY WORK IS SOMETHING I DO GREATLY ADMIRE.
GUUUH!
KRAK
SLOPPY! LED YOU RIGHT INTO IT! COLLEEN'S GONNA BE PISSED.

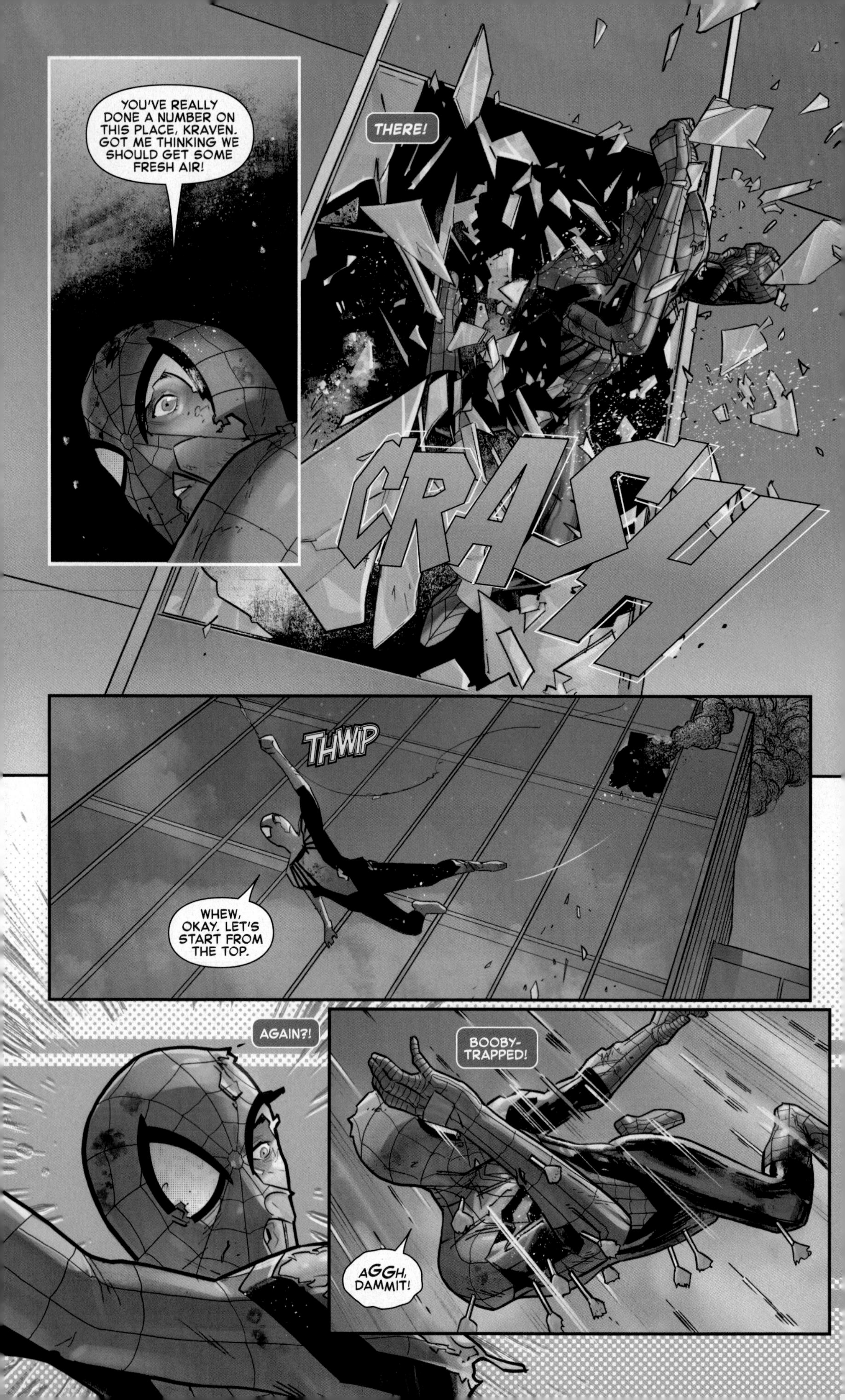
YOU'VE REALLY DONE A NUMBER ON THIS PLACE, KRAVEN. GOT ME THINKING WE SHOULD GET SOME FRESH AIR!
THERE!
CRASH
THWIP
WHEW, OKAY. LET'S START FROM THE TOP.
AGAIN?!
BOOBY-TRAPPED!
AGGH, DAMMIT!

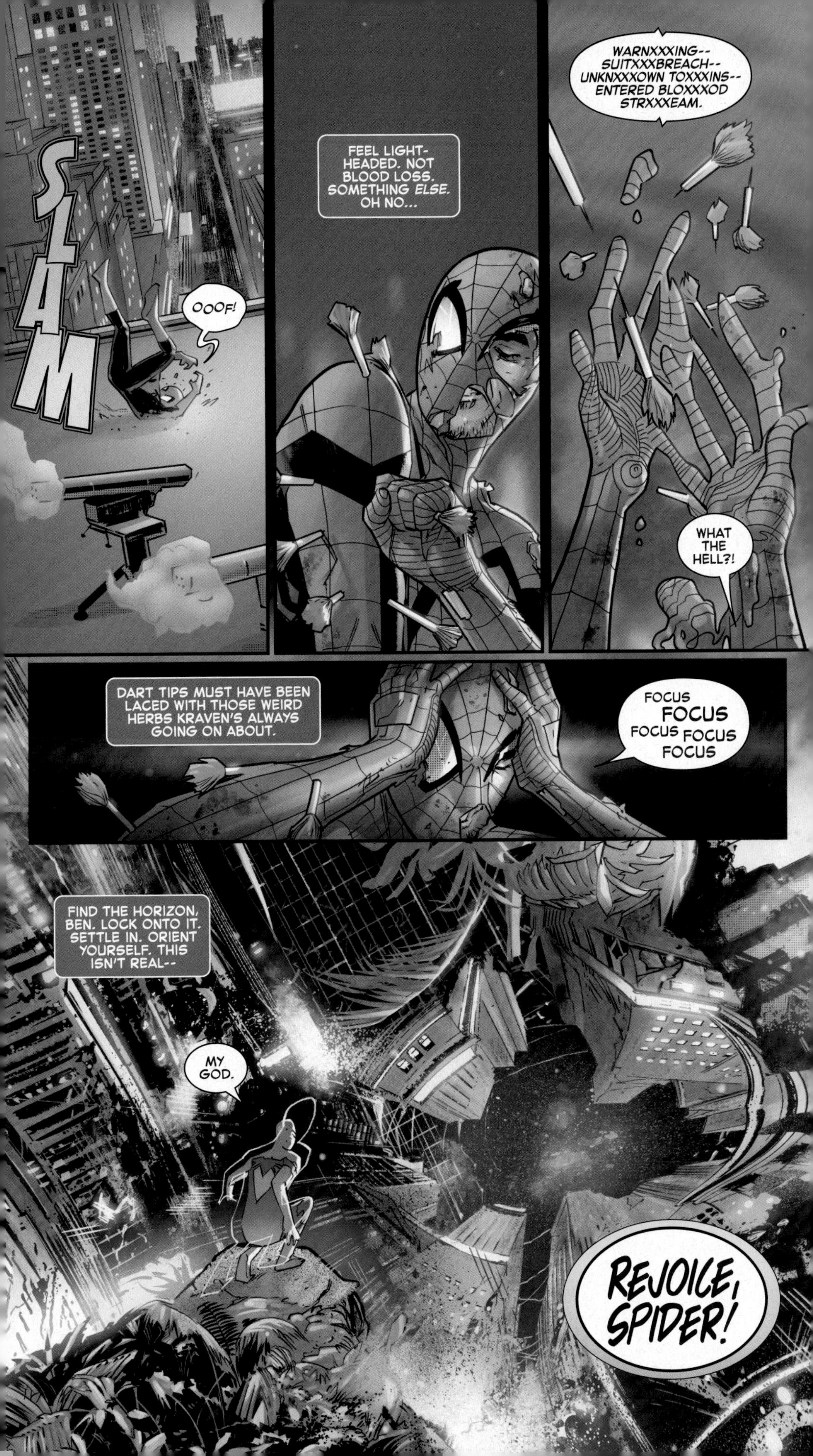
SLAM
OOOF!
FEEL LIGHT-HEADED. NOT BLOOD LOSS. SOMETHING ELSE. OH NO...
WARNXXXING-- SUITXXXBREACH-- UNKNXXXOWN TOXXXINS-- ENTERED BLOXXXOD STRXXXEAM.
WHAT THE HELL?!
DART TIPS MUST HAVE BEEN LACED WITH THOSE WEIRD HERBS KRAVEN'S ALWAYS GOING ON ABOUT.
FOCUS FOCUS FOCUS FOCUS FOCUS
FIND THE HORIZON, BEN. LOCK ONTO IT. SETTLE IN. ORIENT YOURSELF. THIS ISN'T REAL--
MY GOD.
REJOICE, SPIDER!

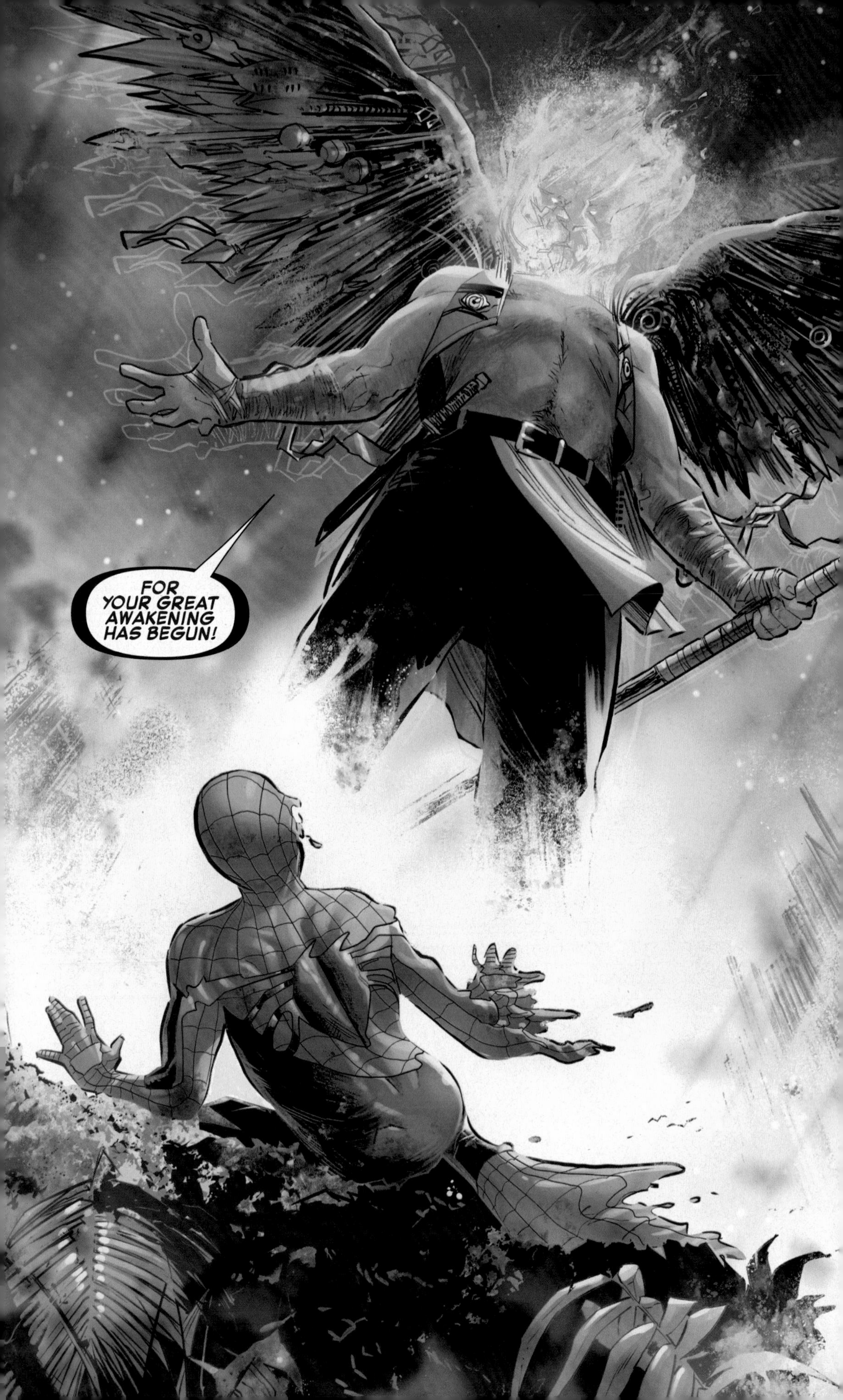
FOR YOUR GREAT AWAKENING HAS BEGUN!

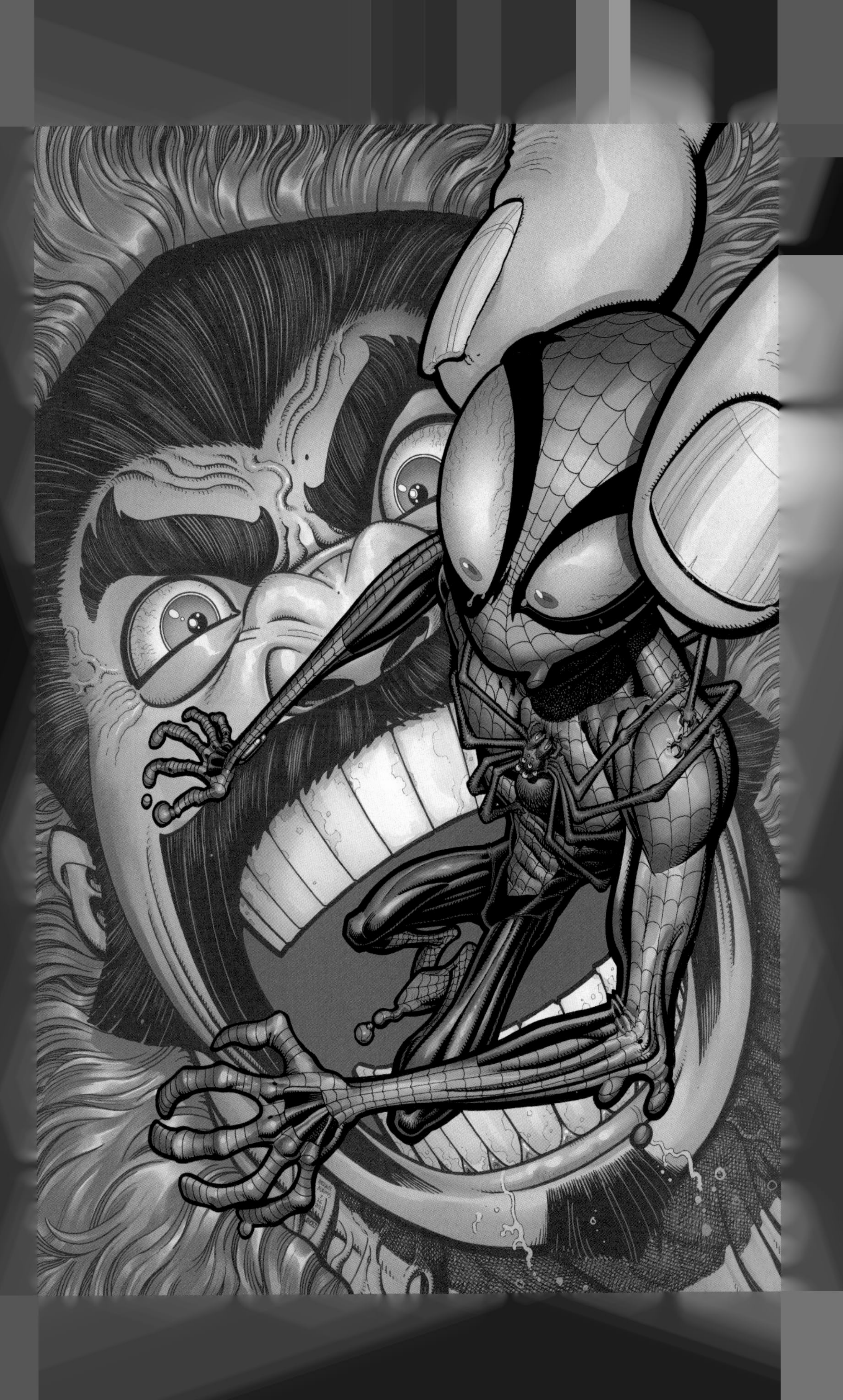

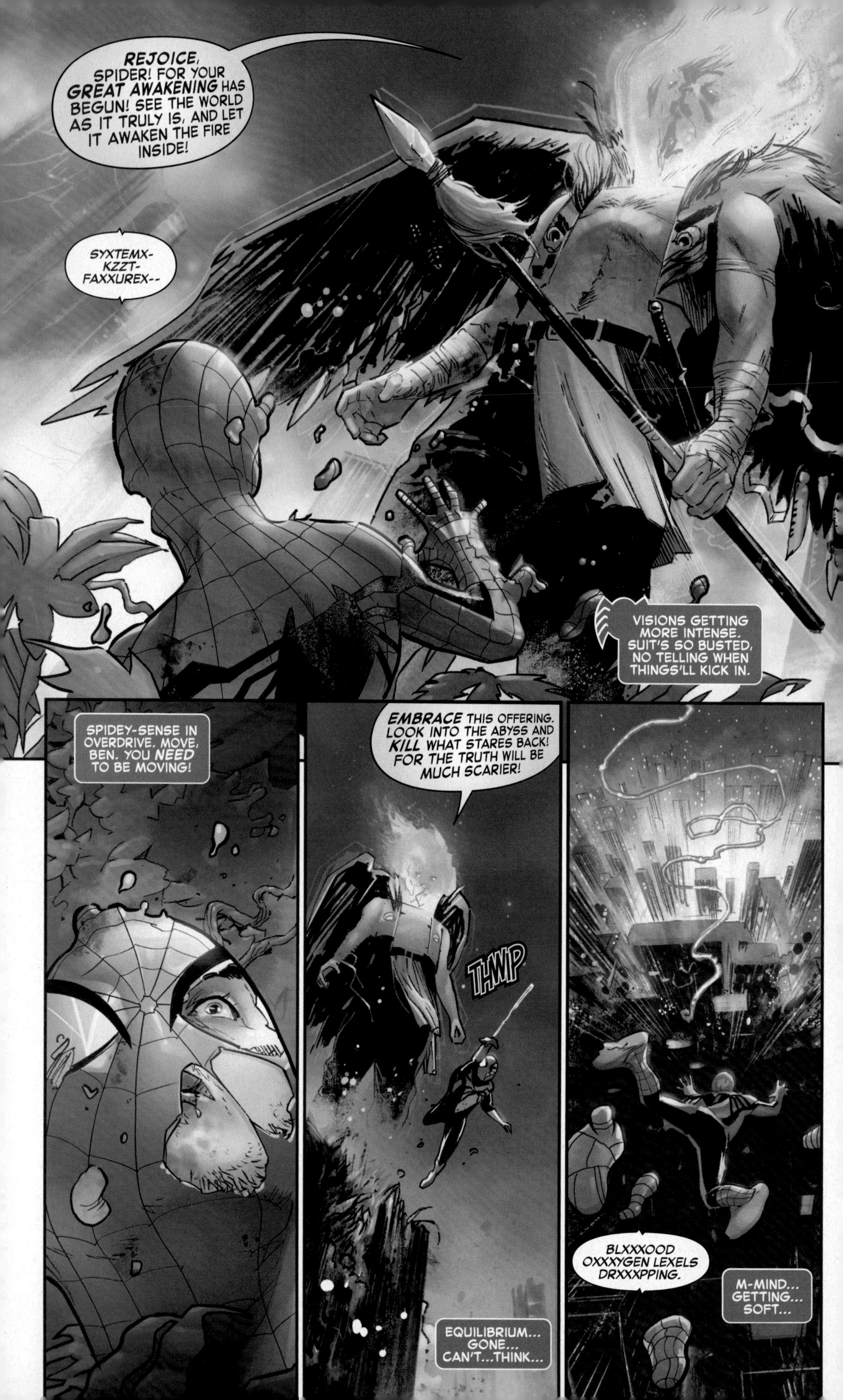
REJOICE, SPIDER! FOR YOUR GREAT AWAKENING HAS BEGUN! SEE THE WORLD AS IT TRULY IS, AND LET IT AWAKEN THE FIRE INSIDE!
SYXTEMX-KZZT-FAXXUREX--
VISIONS GETTING MORE INTENSE. SUIT'S SO BUSTED, NO TELLING WHEN THINGS'LL KICK IN.
SPIDEY-SENSE IN OVERDRIVE. MOVE, BEN. YOU NEED TO BE MOVING!
EMBRACE THIS OFFERING. LOOK INTO THE ABYSS AND KILL WHAT STARES BACK! FOR THE TRUTH WILL BE MUCH SCARIER!
THWIP
EQUILIBRIUM... GONE... CAN'T...THINK...
BLXXXOOD OXXXYGEN LEXELS DRXXXPPING.
M-MIND... GETTING... SOFT...

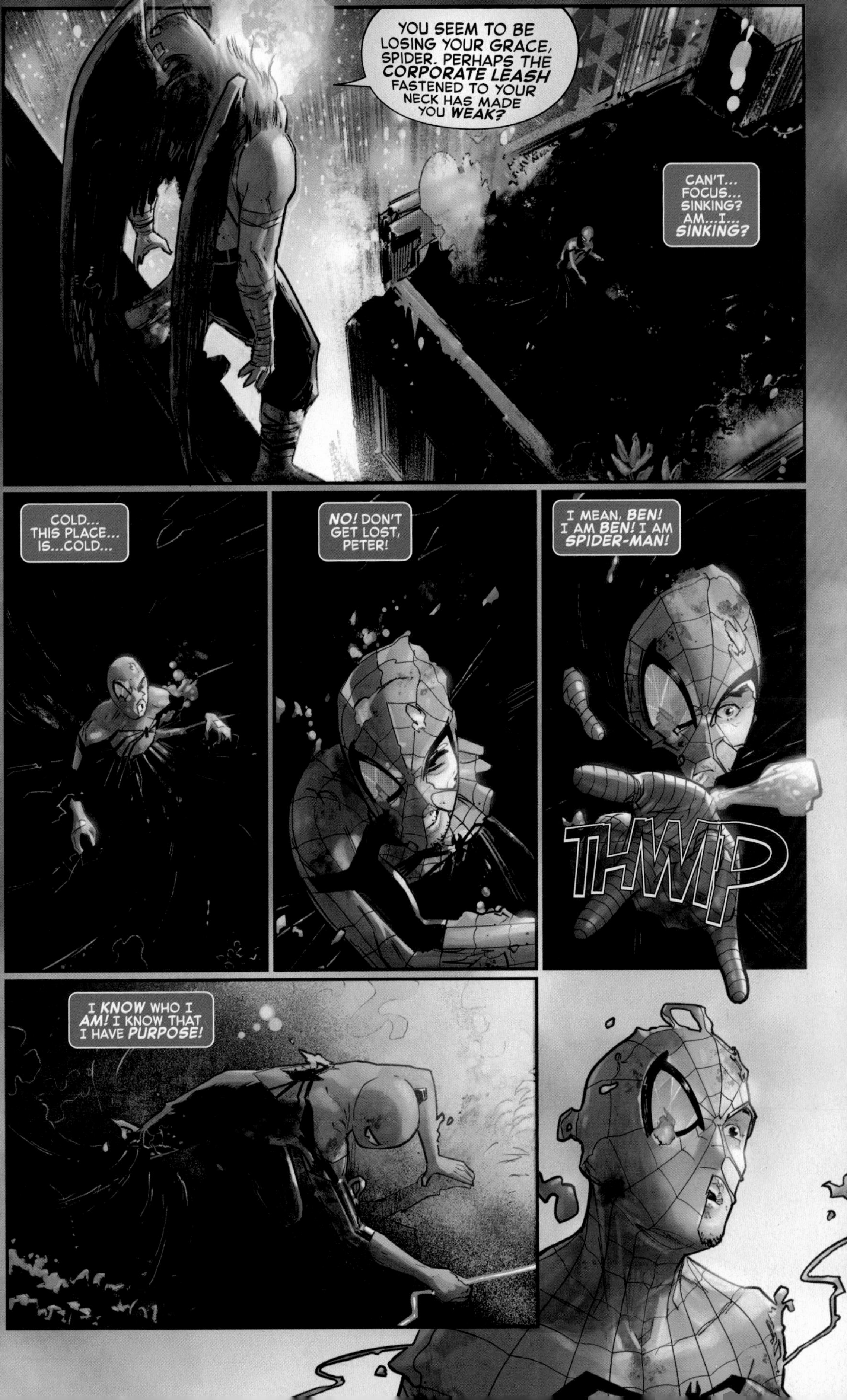
YOU SEEM TO BE LOSING YOUR GRACE, SPIDER. PERHAPS THE CORPORATE LEASH FASTENED TO YOUR NECK HAS MADE YOU WEAK?
CAN'T... FOCUS... SINKING? AM...I... SINKING?
COLD... THIS PLACE... IS...COLD...
NO! DON'T GET LOST, PETER!
I MEAN, BEN! I AM BEN! I AM SPIDER-MAN!
THWIP
I KNOW WHO I AM! I KNOW THAT I HAVE PURPOSE!

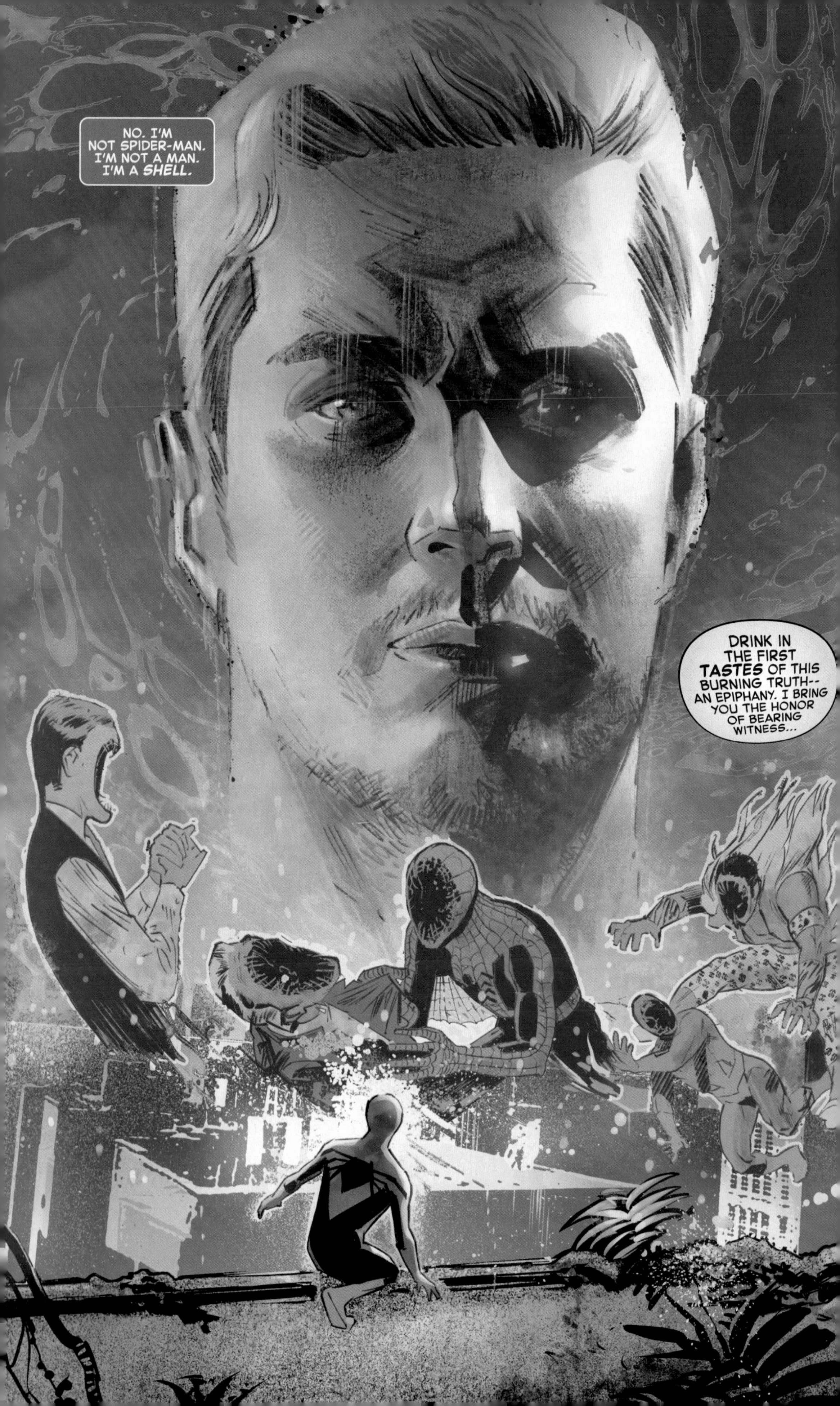
NO. I'M NOT SPIDER-MAN. I'M NOT A MAN. I'M A SHELL.
DRINK IN THE FIRST TASTES OF THIS BURNING TRUTH-- AN EPIPHANY. I BRING YOU THE HONOR OF BEARING WITNESS...

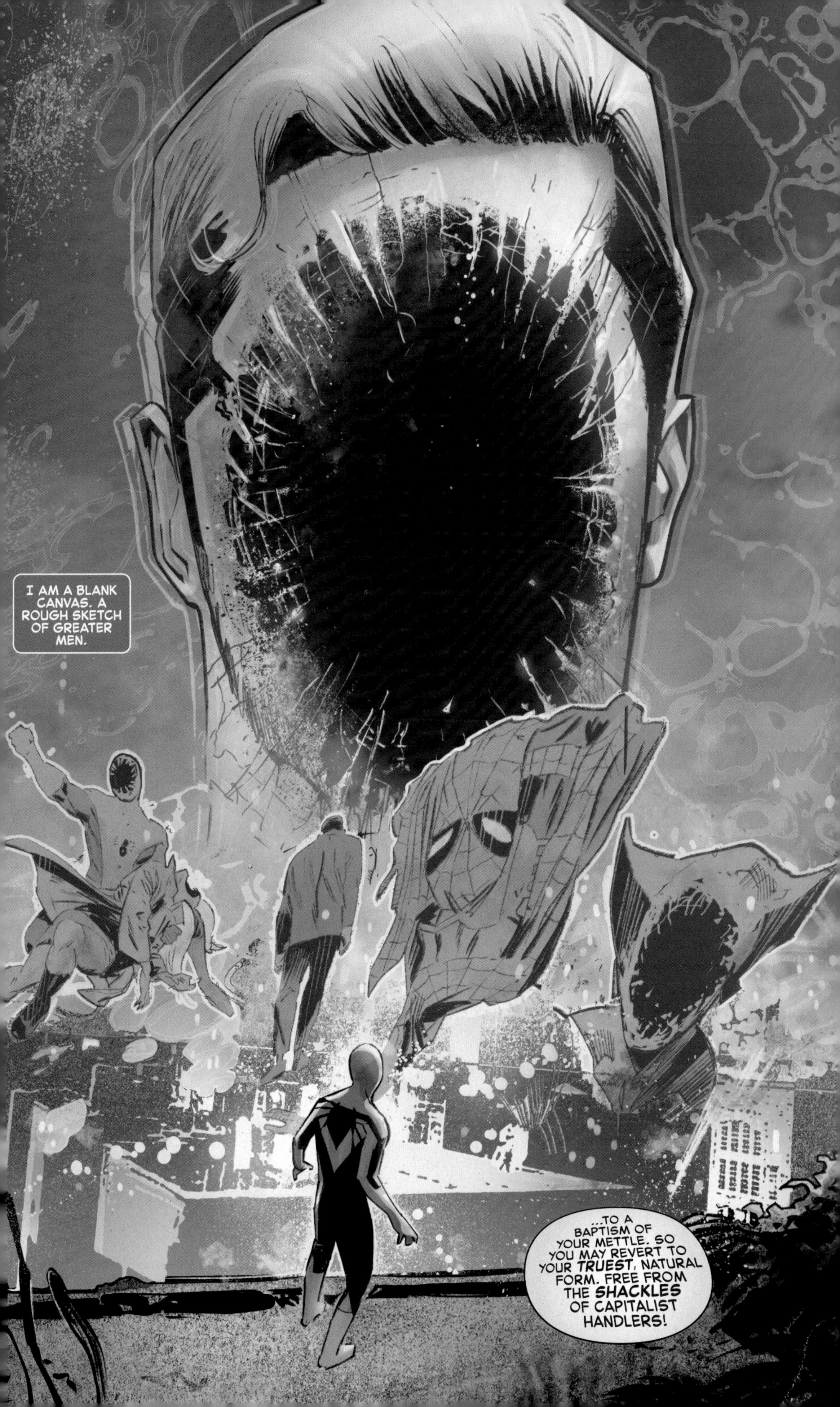
I AM A BLANK CANVAS. A ROUGH SKETCH OF GREATER MEN.
...TO A BAPTISM OF YOUR METTLE. SO YOU MAY REVERT TO YOUR TRUEST, NATURAL FORM. FREE FROM THE SHACKLES OF CAPITALIST HANDLERS!

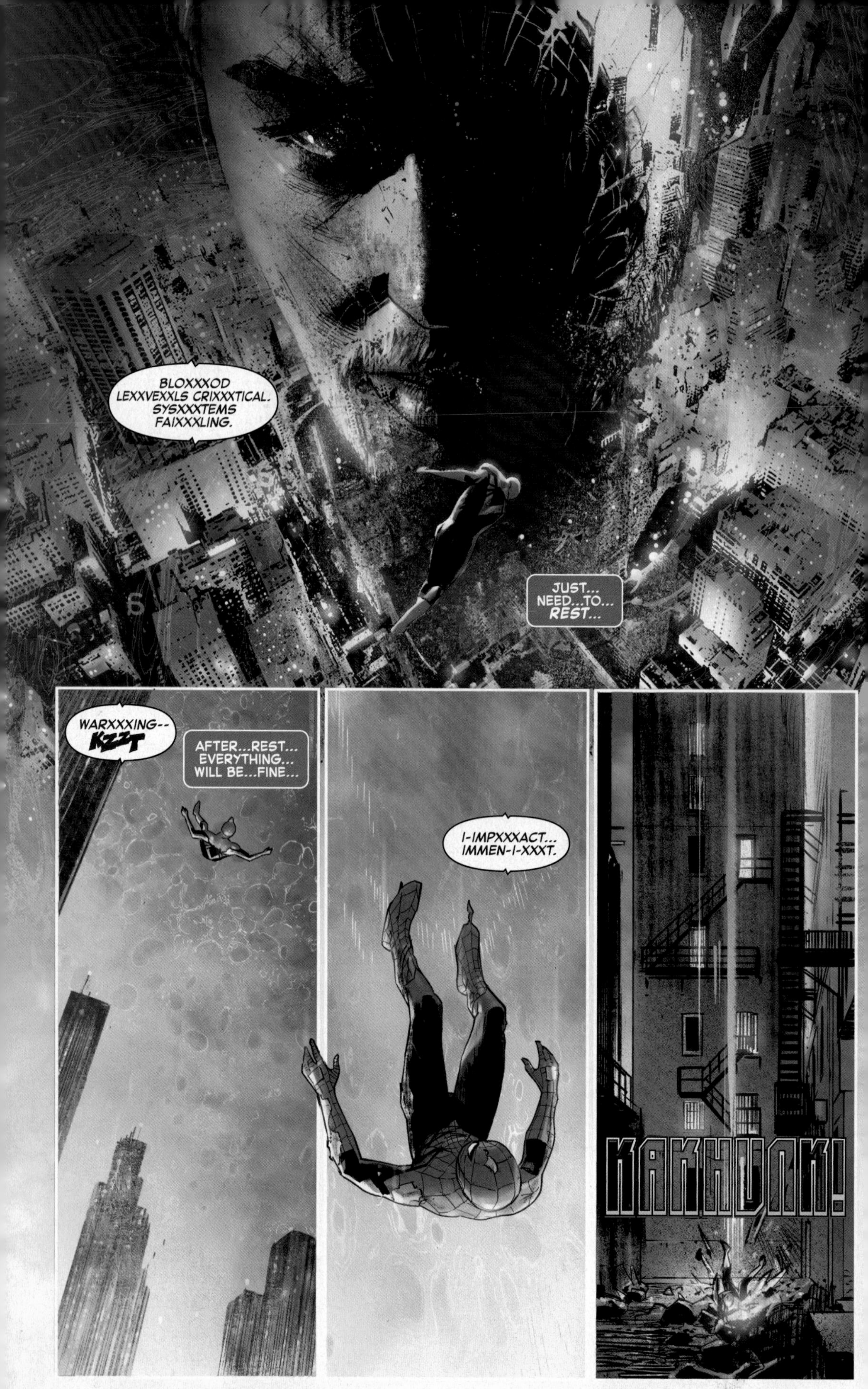
BLOXXXOD LEXXVEXXLS CRIXXXTICAL. SYSXXXTEMS FAIXXXLING.
JUST... NEED...TO... REST...
WARXXXING-- KZZT
AFTER...REST... EVERYTHING... WILL BE...FINE...
I-IMPXXXACT... IMMEN-I-XXXT.
KAKHUNK!

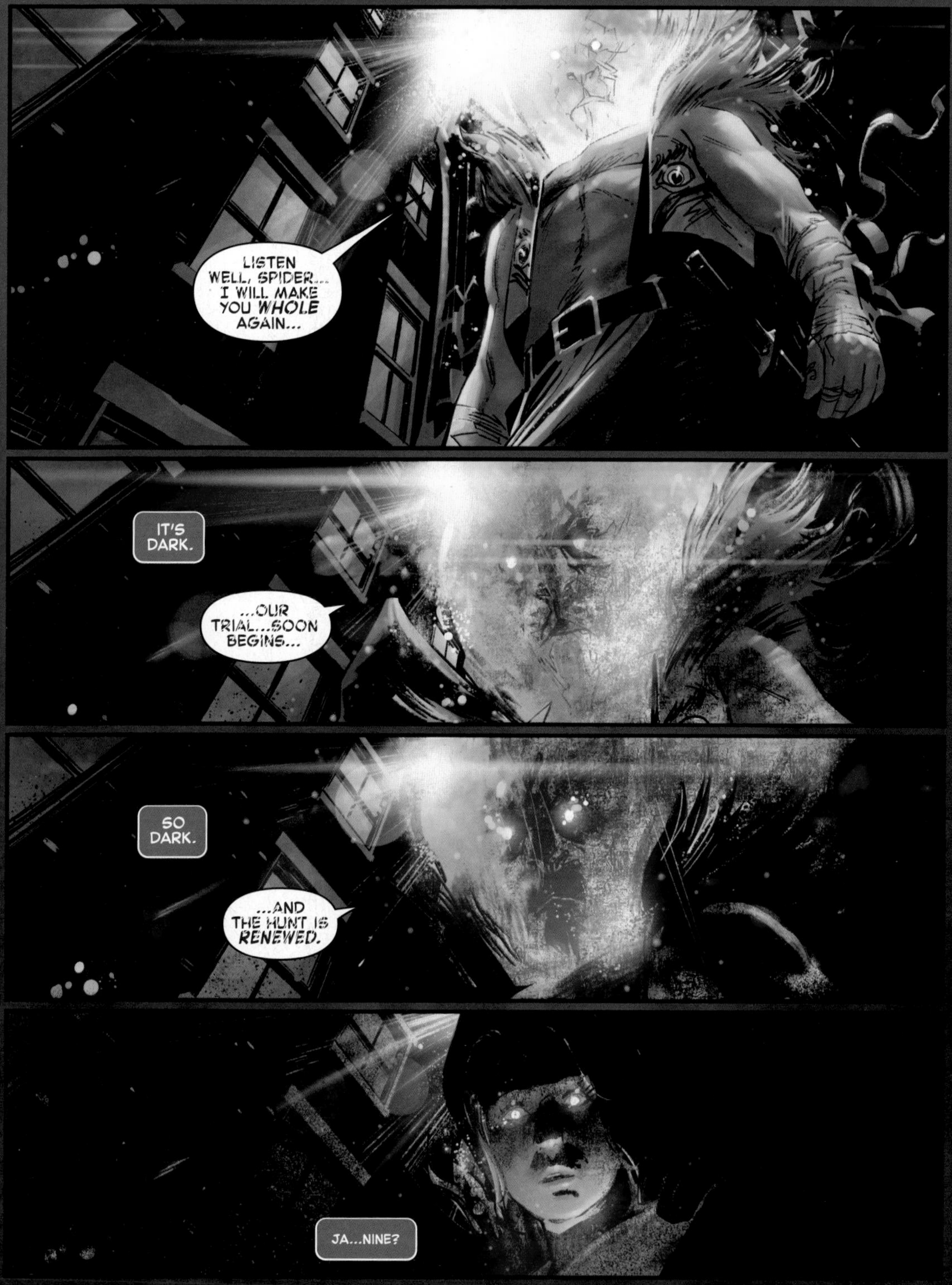
LISTEN WELL, SPIDER... I WILL MAKE YOU WHOLE AGAIN...
IT'S DARK.
...OUR TRIAL...SOON BEGINS...
SO DARK.
...AND THE HUNT IS RENEWED.
JA...NINE?

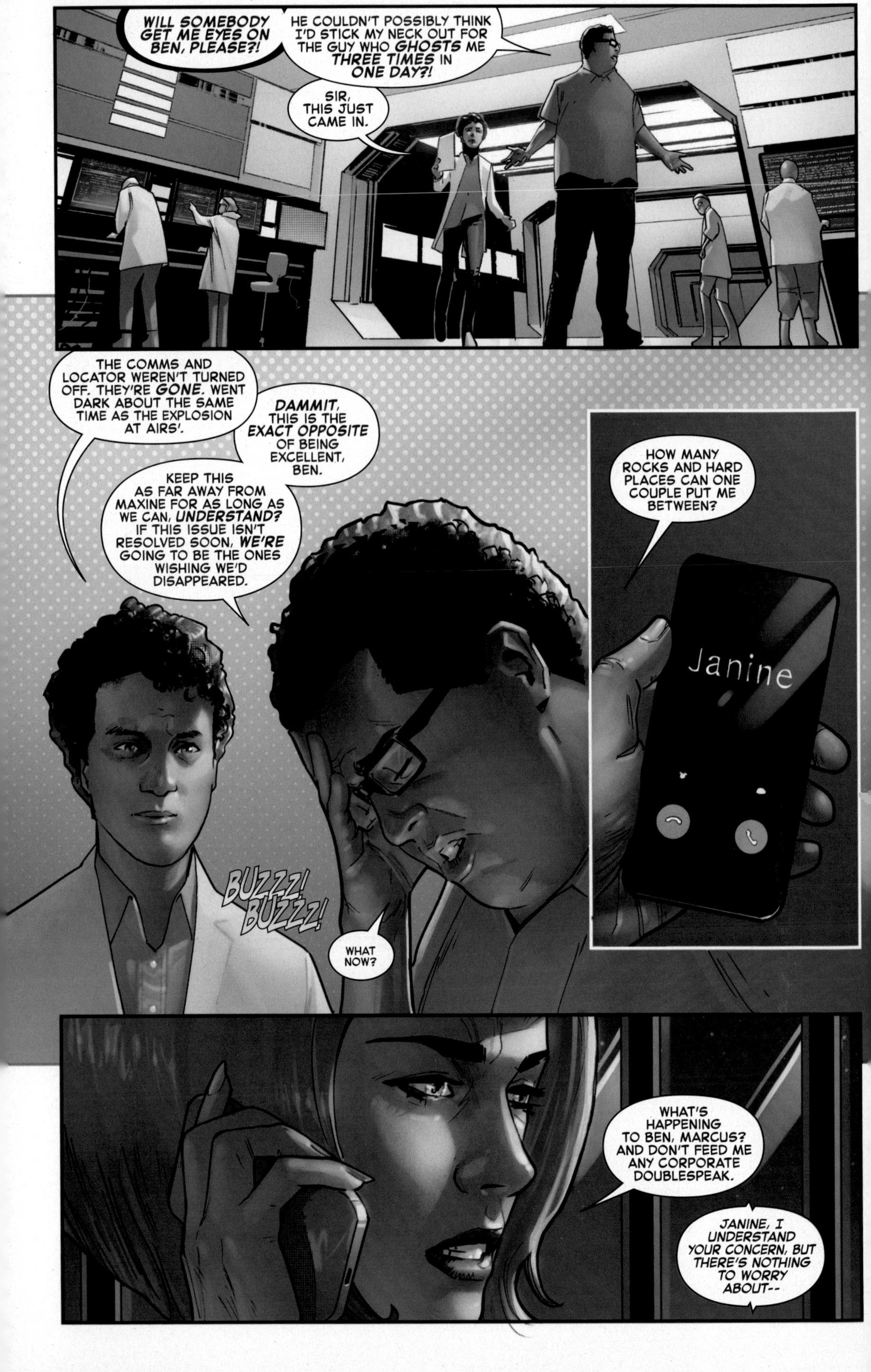
WILL SOMEBODY GET ME EYES ON BEN, PLEASE?!
HE COULDN'T POSSIBLY THINK I'D STICK MY NECK OUT FOR THE GUY WHO GHOSTS ME THREE TIMES IN ONE DAY?!
SIR, THIS JUST CAME IN.
THE COMMS AND LOCATOR WEREN'T TURNED OFF. THEY'RE GONE. WENT DARK ABOUT THE SAME TIME AS THE EXPLOSION AT AIRS'.
DAMMIT, THIS IS THE EXACT OPPOSITE OF BEING EXCELLENT, BEN.
KEEP THIS AS FAR AWAY FROM MAXINE FOR AS LONG AS WE CAN, UNDERSTAND? IF THIS ISSUE ISN'T RESOLVED SOON, WE'RE GOING TO BE THE ONES WISHING WE'D DISAPPEARED.
HOW MANY ROCKS AND HARD PLACES CAN ONE COUPLE PUT ME BETWEEN?
Janine
BUZZZ! BUZZZ!
WHAT NOW?
WHAT'S HAPPENING TO BEN, MARCUS? AND DON'T FEED ME ANY CORPORATE DOUBLESPEAK.
JANINE, I UNDERSTAND YOUR CONCERN, BUT THERE'S NOTHING TO WORRY ABOUT--

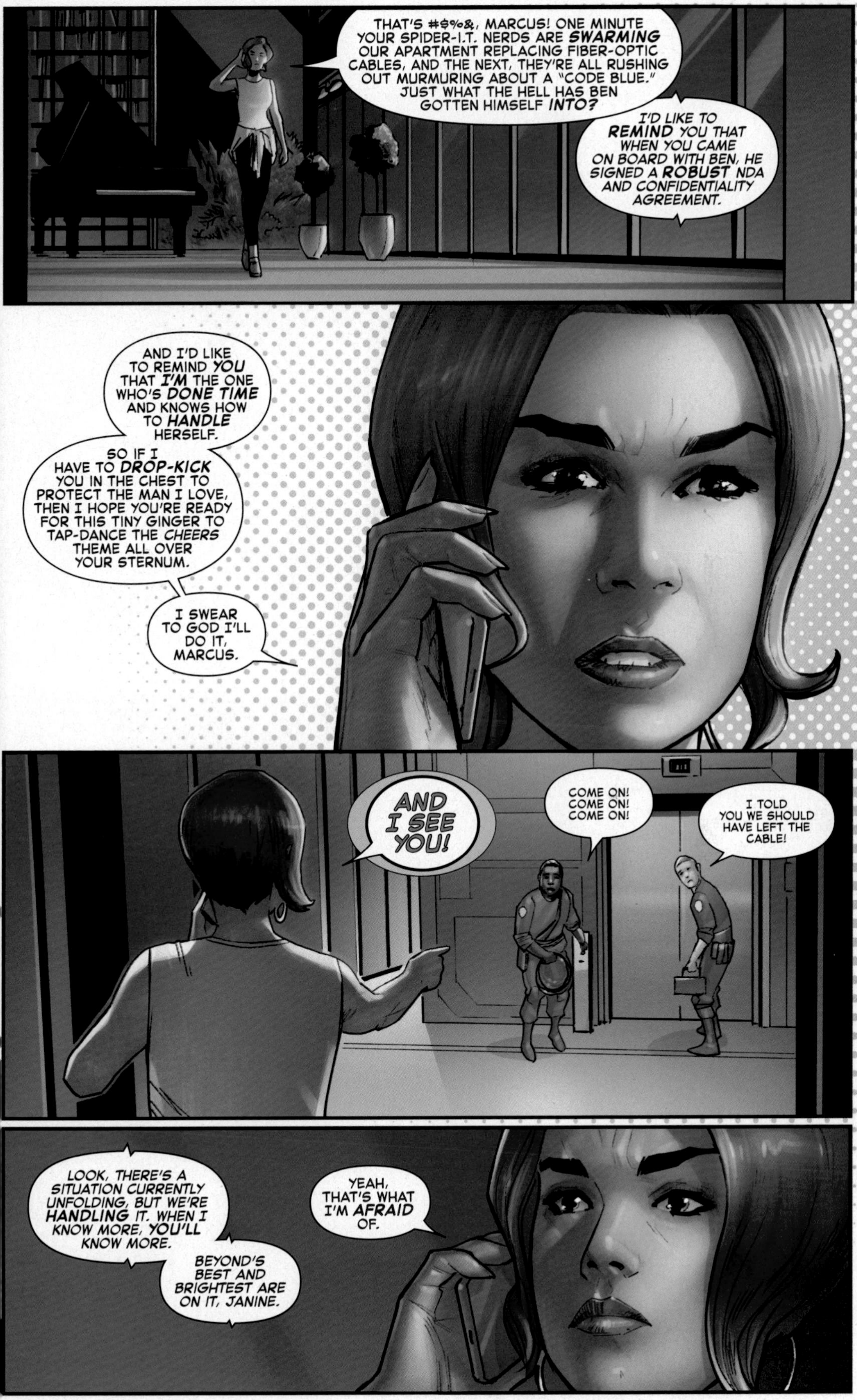

THAT'S #$%&, MARCUS! ONE MINUTE YOUR SPIDER-I.T. NERDS ARE SWARMING OUR APARTMENT REPLACING FIBER-OPTIC CABLES, AND THE NEXT, THEY'RE ALL RUSHING OUT MURMURING ABOUT A "CODE BLUE." JUST WHAT THE HELL HAS BEN GOTTEN HIMSELF INTO?
I'D LIKE TO REMIND YOU THAT WHEN YOU CAME ON BOARD WITH BEN, HE SIGNED A ROBUST NDA AND CONFIDENTIALITY AGREEMENT.
AND I'D LIKE TO REMIND YOU THAT I'M THE ONE WHO'S DONE TIME AND KNOWS HOW TO HANDLE HERSELF.
SO IF I HAVE TO DROP-KICK YOU IN THE CHEST TO PROTECT THE MAN I LOVE, THEN I HOPE YOU'RE READY FOR THIS TINY GINGER TO TAP-DANCE THE CHEERS THEME ALL OVER YOUR STERNUM.
I SWEAR TO GOD I'LL DO IT, MARCUS.
AND I SEE YOU!
COME ON! COME ON! COME ON!
I TOLD YOU WE SHOULD HAVE LEFT THE CABLE!
LOOK, THERE'S A SITUATION CURRENTLY UNFOLDING, BUT WE'RE HANDLING IT. WHEN I KNOW MORE, YOU'LL KNOW MORE.
BEYOND'S BEST AND BRIGHTEST ARE ON IT, JANINE.
YEAH, THAT'S WHAT I'M AFRAID OF.

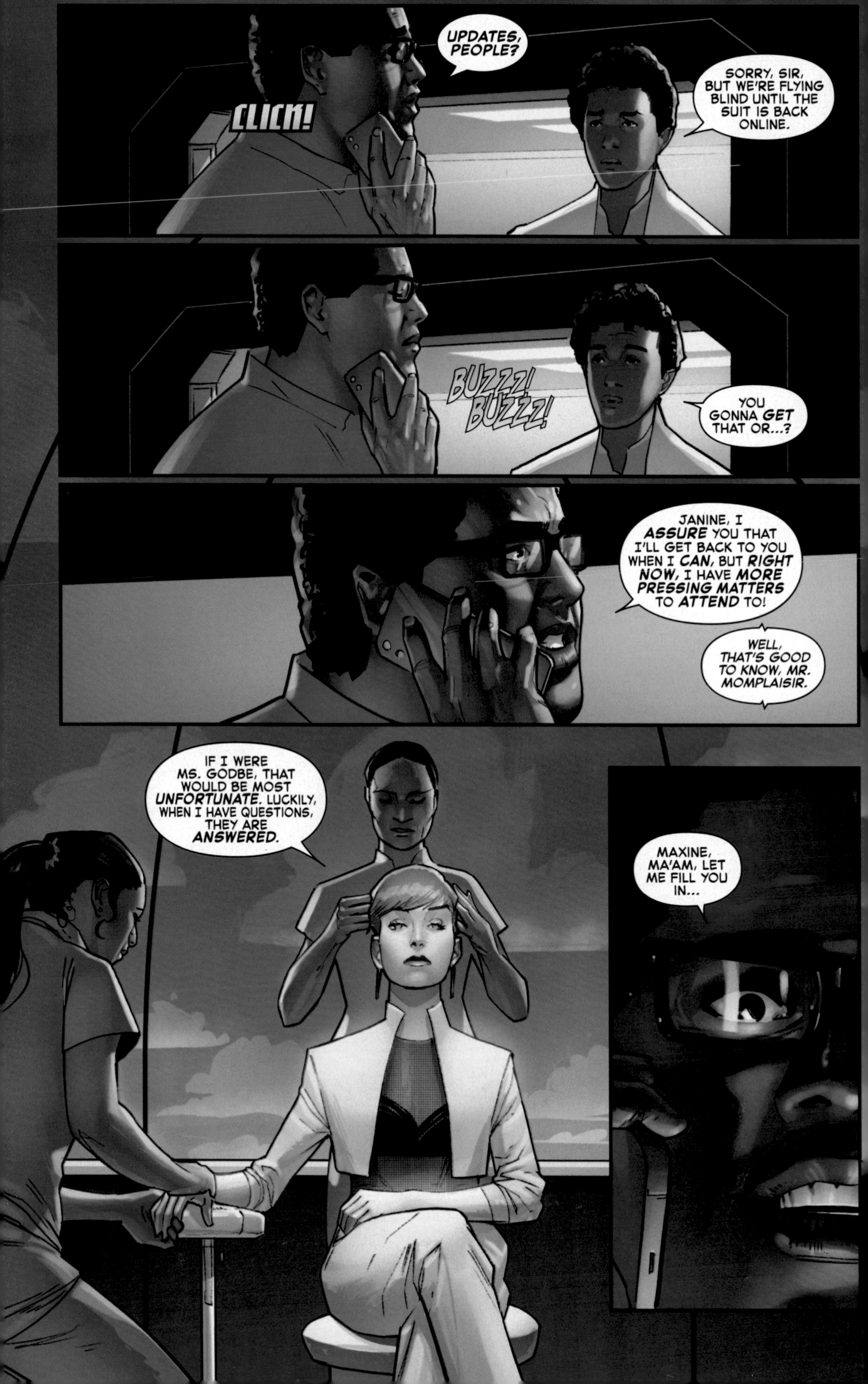
UPDATES, PEOPLE?
CLICK!
SORRY, SIR, BUT WE'RE FLYING BLIND UNTIL THE SUIT IS BACK ONLINE.
BUZZZ! BUZZZ!
YOU GONNA GET THAT OR...?
JANINE, I ASSURE YOU THAT I'LL GET BACK TO YOU WHEN I CAN, BUT RIGHT NOW, I HAVE MORE PRESSING MATTERS TO ATTEND TO!
WELL, THAT'S GOOD TO KNOW, MR. MOMPLAISIR.
IF I WERE MS. GODBE, THAT WOULD BE MOST UNFORTUNATE. LUCKILY, WHEN I HAVE QUESTIONS, THEY ARE ANSWERED.
MAXINE, MA'AM, LET ME FILL YOU IN...

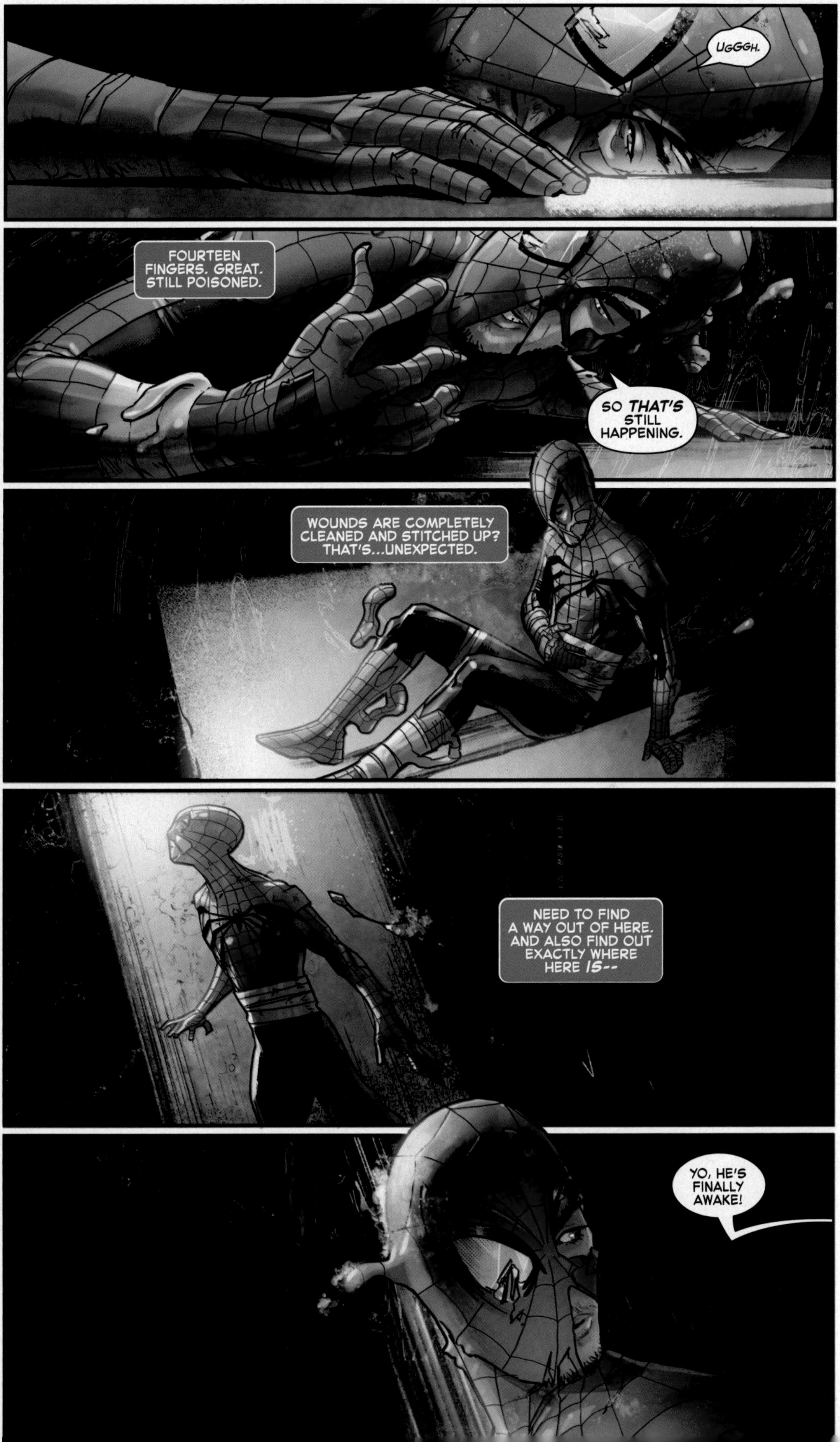
UGGGH.
FOURTEEN FINGERS. GREAT. STILL POISONED.
SO THAT'S STILL HAPPENING.
WOUNDS ARE COMPLETELY CLEANED AND STITCHED UP? THAT'S...UNEXPECTED.
NEED TO FIND A WAY OUT OF HERE. AND ALSO FIND OUT EXACTLY WHERE HERE IS--
YO, HE'S FINALLY AWAKE!

IT'S THE BIG MAN HIMSELF! THIS IS KINDA COOL!

I'M *DOUG SIRAVANTA!* THAT'S *ADAOBI* AND *BASIR.* WE'VE BEEN HELD UP HERE A FEW DAYS.

ONE MINUTE, I'M CLEANING THE ALGAE TANKS, AND THE NEXT, I'M BEING TOSSED IN HERE.

HECK OF A WAY TO START OUR FIRST WEEK.

ALGAE TANKS? WHAT ARE YOU *TALKING* ABOUT, JANINE?

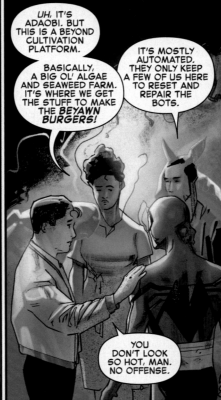

UH, IT'S ADAOBI. BUT THIS IS A BEYOND CULTIVATION PLATFORM.

BASICALLY, A BIG OL' ALGAE AND SEAWEED FARM. IT'S WHERE WE GET THE STUFF TO MAKE THE *BEYAWN BURGERS!*

IT'S MOSTLY AUTOMATED. THEY ONLY KEEP A FEW OF US HERE TO RESET AND REPAIR THE BOTS.

YOU DON'T LOOK SO HOT, MAN. NO OFFENSE.

NONE TAKEN, GIANT TURTLE. I'VE BEEN DRUGGED.

OH YEAH? ACTUALLY, I THINK I HAVE SOMETHING FOR THAT.

PUT IT IN HERE SOMEWHERE... OH, *HERE!*

FROM THE PHARMACEUTICAL DIVISION. SUPPOSED TO BE A CURE-ALL FOR MIGRAINES AND HEAD COLDS.

I USE IT FOR, UH, HANGOVERS. SAME BALLPARK.

"SAME BALLPARK" IS DOING A LOT OF HEAVY LIFTING RIGHT NOW, BUT LET'S GIVE IT A SPIN.

THE GREAT SPIDER HAS ARISEN AND FOUND MY OFFERING. PLEASE, JOIN ME TOPSIDE.

ANYONE ELSE HEAR THAT CHOIR OF COYOTES? GUESS I DON'T HAVE A CHOICE. THANKS, GIANT TURTLE!

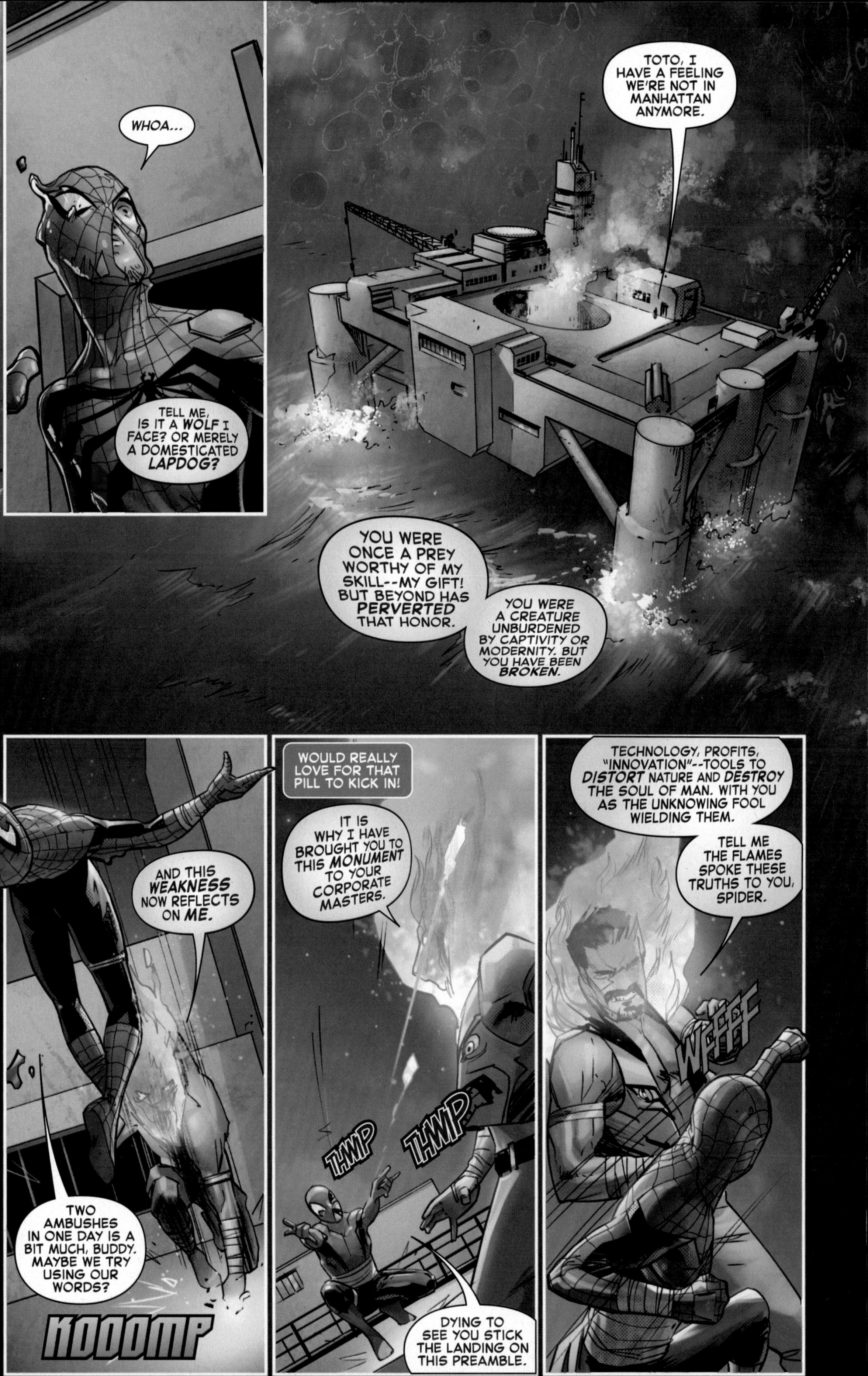
WHOA...
TELL ME, IS IT A WOLF I FACE? OR MERELY A DOMESTICATED LAPDOG?
TOTO, I HAVE A FEELING WE'RE NOT IN MANHATTAN ANYMORE.
YOU WERE ONCE A PREY WORTHY OF MY SKILL--MY GIFT! BUT BEYOND HAS PERVERTED THAT HONOR.
YOU WERE A CREATURE UNBURDENED BY CAPTIVITY OR MODERNITY. BUT YOU HAVE BEEN BROKEN.
AND THIS WEAKNESS NOW REFLECTS ON ME.
TWO AMBUSHES IN ONE DAY IS A BIT MUCH, BUDDY. MAYBE WE TRY USING OUR WORDS?
KOOOMF
WOULD REALLY LOVE FOR THAT PILL TO KICK IN!
IT IS WHY I HAVE BROUGHT YOU TO THIS MONUMENT TO YOUR CORPORATE MASTERS.
THWP
THWP
DYING TO SEE YOU STICK THE LANDING ON THIS PREAMBLE.
TECHNOLOGY, PROFITS, "INNOVATION"--TOOLS TO DISTORT NATURE AND DESTROY THE SOUL OF MAN. WITH YOU AS THE UNKNOWING FOOL WIELDING THEM.
TELL ME THE FLAMES SPOKE THESE TRUTHS TO YOU, SPIDER.
WFFF

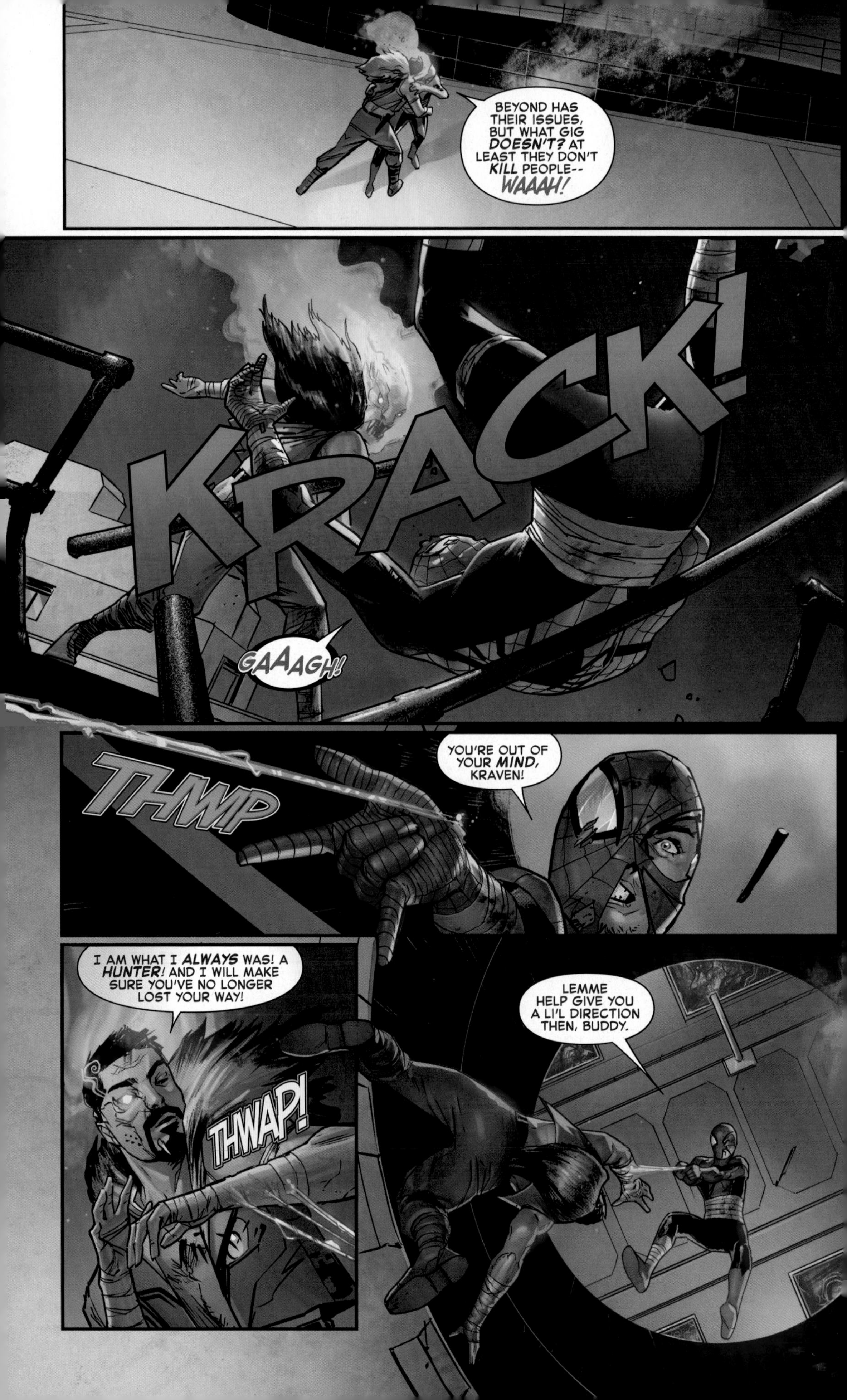
BEYOND HAS THEIR ISSUES, BUT WHAT GIG DOESN'T? AT LEAST THEY DON'T KILL PEOPLE-- WAAAH!
KRACK!
GAAAGH!
THMP
YOU'RE OUT OF YOUR MIND, KRAVEN!
I AM WHAT I ALWAYS WAS! A HUNTER! AND I WILL MAKE SURE YOU'VE NO LONGER LOST YOUR WAY!
THWAP!
LEMME HELP GIVE YOU A LI'L DIRECTION THEN, BUDDY.

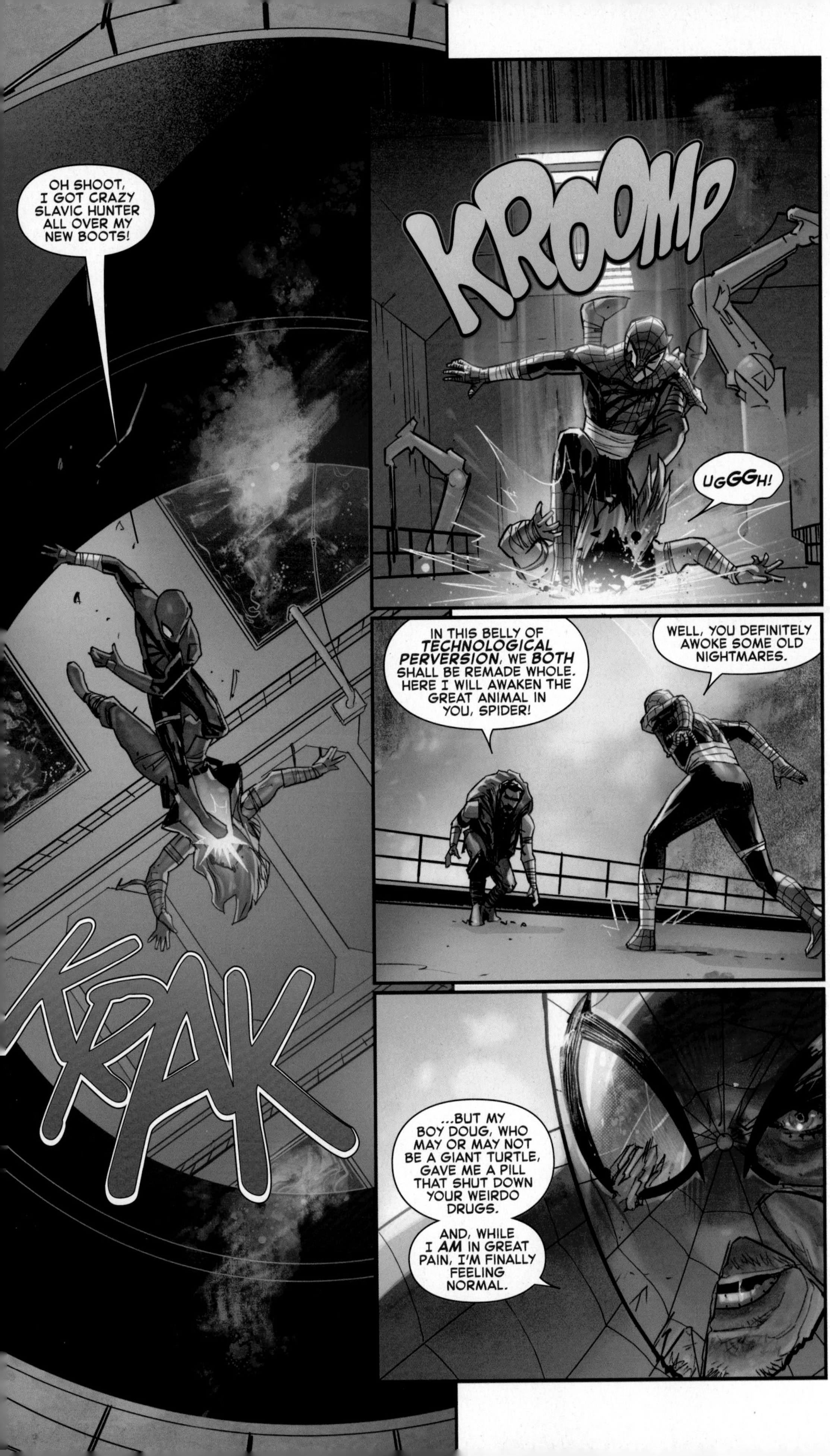
OH SHOOT, I GOT CRAZY SLAVIC HUNTER ALL OVER MY NEW BOOTS!
KRAK
KROOMP
UGGGH!
IN THIS BELLY OF TECHNOLOGICAL PERVERSION, WE BOTH SHALL BE REMADE WHOLE. HERE I WILL AWAKEN THE GREAT ANIMAL IN YOU, SPIDER!
WELL, YOU DEFINITELY AWOKE SOME OLD NIGHTMARES.
...BUT MY BOY DOUG, WHO MAY OR MAY NOT BE A GIANT TURTLE, GAVE ME A PILL THAT SHUT DOWN YOUR WEIRDO DRUGS.
AND, WHILE I AM IN GREAT PAIN, I'M FINALLY FEELING NORMAL.

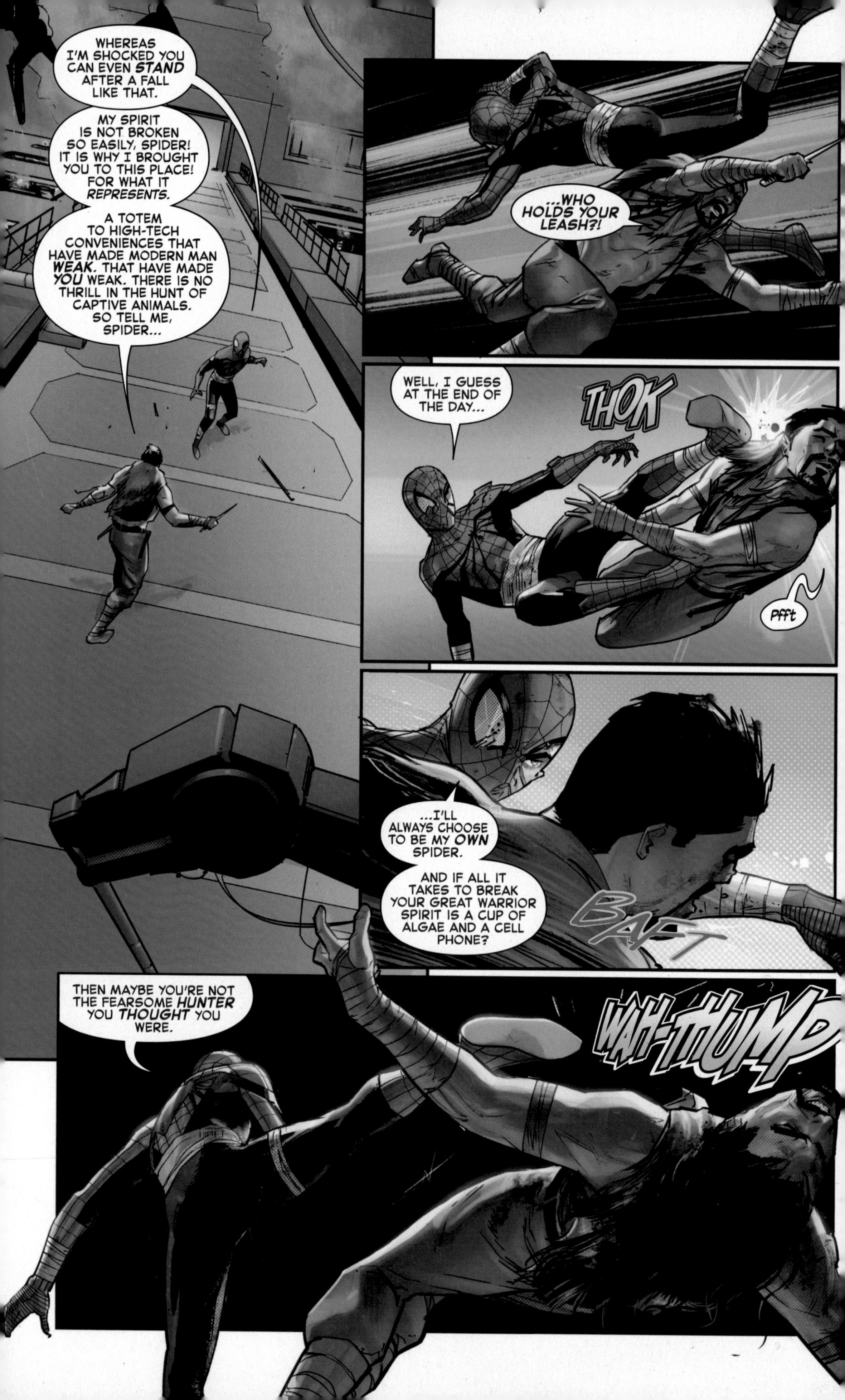
WHEREAS I'M SHOCKED YOU CAN EVEN STAND AFTER A FALL LIKE THAT.
MY SPIRIT IS NOT BROKEN SO EASILY, SPIDER! IT IS WHY I BROUGHT YOU TO THIS PLACE! FOR WHAT IT REPRESENTS.
A TOTEM TO HIGH-TECH CONVENIENCES THAT HAVE MADE MODERN MAN WEAK. THAT HAVE MADE YOU WEAK. THERE IS NO THRILL IN THE HUNT OF CAPTIVE ANIMALS. SO TELL ME, SPIDER...
...WHO HOLDS YOUR LEASH?!
WELL, I GUESS AT THE END OF THE DAY...
THOK
Pfft
...I'LL ALWAYS CHOOSE TO BE MY OWN SPIDER.
AND IF ALL IT TAKES TO BREAK YOUR GREAT WARRIOR SPIRIT IS A CUP OF ALGAE AND A CELL PHONE?
BAFT
THEN MAYBE YOU'RE NOT THE FEARSOME HUNTER YOU THOUGHT YOU WERE.
WAH-THUMP

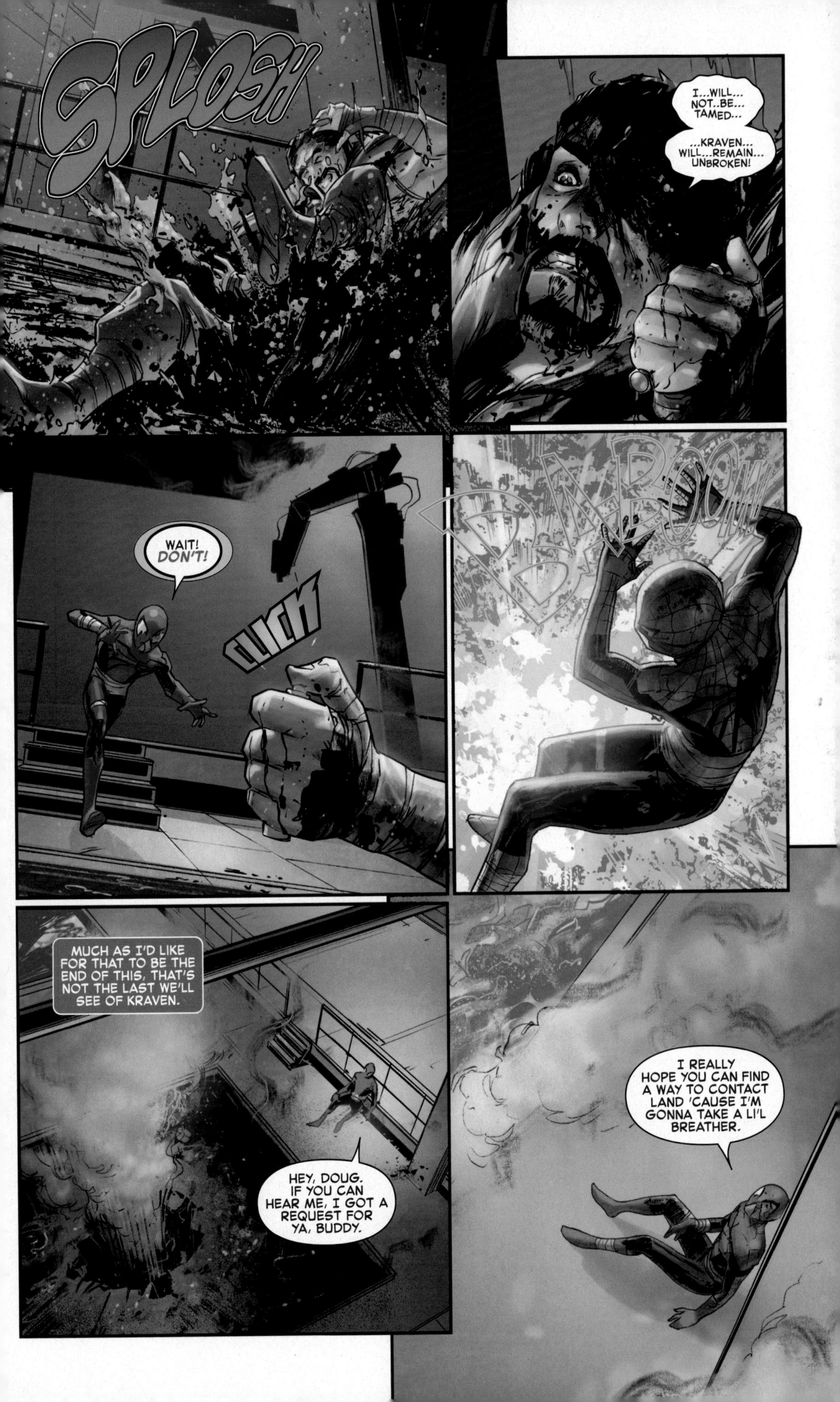
SPLOSH
I...WILL... NOT..BE... TAMED...
...KRAVEN... WILL...REMAIN... UNBROKEN!
WAIT! DON'T!
CLICK
BA-BOOM!!
MUCH AS I'D LIKE FOR THAT TO BE THE END OF THIS, THAT'S NOT THE LAST WE'LL SEE OF KRAVEN.
HEY, DOUG. IF YOU CAN HEAR ME, I GOT A REQUEST FOR YA, BUDDY.
I REALLY HOPE YOU CAN FIND A WAY TO CONTACT LAND 'CAUSE I'M GONNA TAKE A LI'L BREATHER.

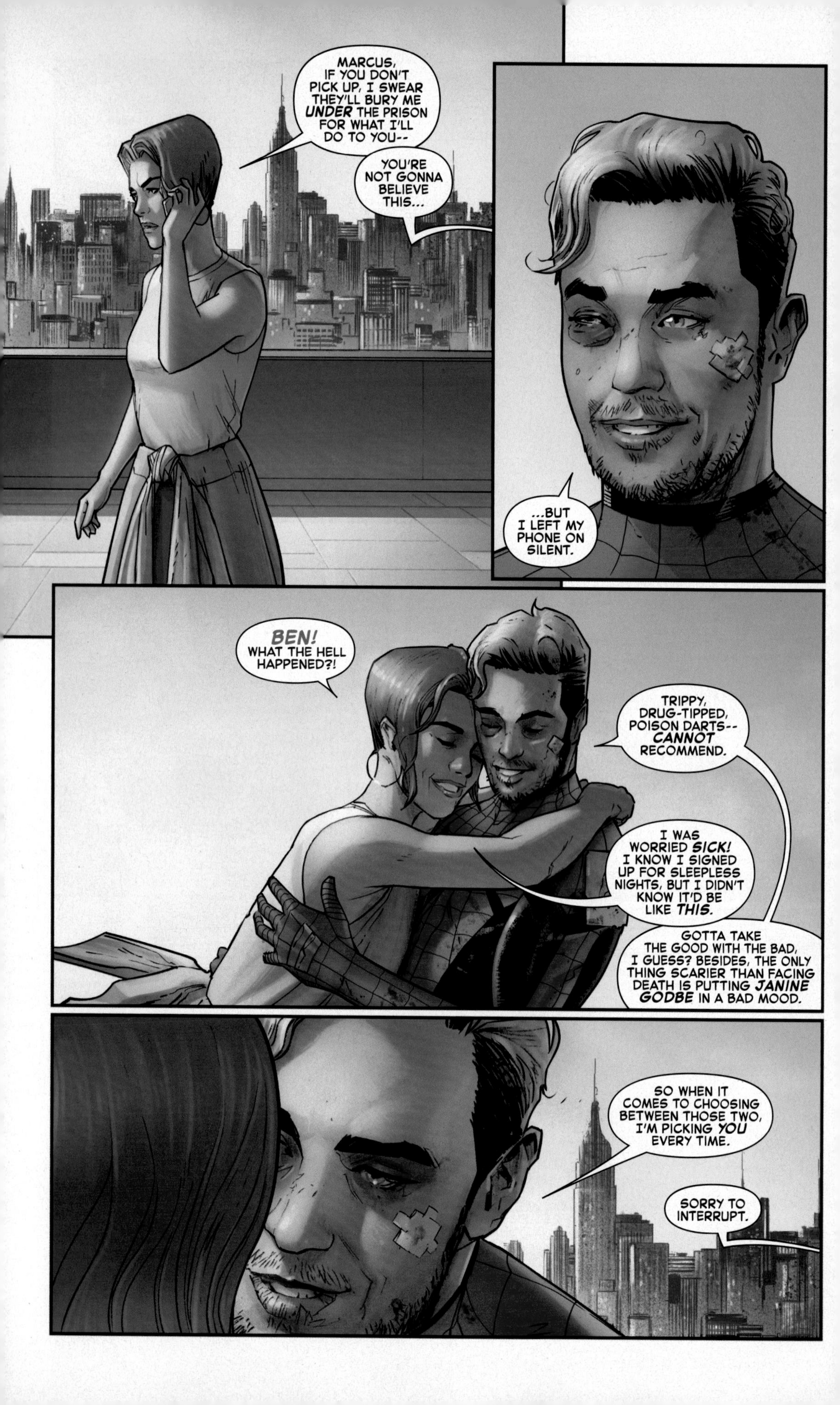
MARCUS, IF YOU DON'T PICK UP, I SWEAR THEY'LL BURY ME UNDER THE PRISON FOR WHAT I'LL DO TO YOU--
YOU'RE NOT GONNA BELIEVE THIS...
...BUT I LEFT MY PHONE ON SILENT.
BEN! WHAT THE HELL HAPPENED?!
TRIPPY, DRUG-TIPPED, POISON DARTS-- CANNOT RECOMMEND.
I WAS WORRIED SICK! I KNOW I SIGNED UP FOR SLEEPLESS NIGHTS, BUT I DIDN'T KNOW IT'D BE LIKE THIS.
GOTTA TAKE THE GOOD WITH THE BAD, I GUESS? BESIDES, THE ONLY THING SCARIER THAN FACING DEATH IS PUTTING JANINE GODBE IN A BAD MOOD.
SO WHEN IT COMES TO CHOOSING BETWEEN THOSE TWO, I'M PICKING YOU EVERY TIME.
SORRY TO INTERRUPT.

BUT WE NEED TO GET YOU OUT OF THAT SUIT AND GET THOSE WOUNDS LOOKED AT.

I NEED MED POD SIX PREPPED. SUBJECT HAS MULTIPLE ABRASIONS AND CUTS WITH POSSIBLE CONCUSSION AND BLOOD POISONING.

YES, MA'AM.

WE'LL HAVE HIM RIGHT BACK TO YOU, JANINE.

IT MAY NOT *LOOK* LIKE IT, BUT I'M *VERY* GLAD TO SEE YOU'RE IN ONE PIECE, BEN. YOU HAD A LOT OF PEOPLE LOSING A LOT OF SLEEP.

FAMILY TRAIT.

GIVE IT TO ME STRAIGHT, MARCUS, JUST HOW MUCH IS MY LIFE ABOUT TO SUCK?

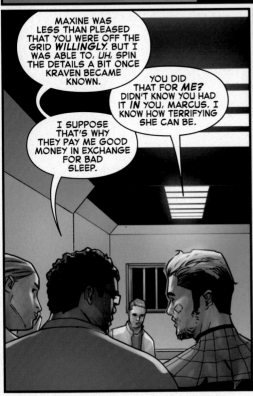

MAXINE WAS LESS THAN PLEASED THAT YOU WERE OFF THE GRID *WILLINGLY.* BUT I WAS ABLE TO, *UH,* SPIN THE DETAILS A BIT ONCE KRAVEN BECAME KNOWN.

YOU DID THAT FOR *ME?* DIDN'T KNOW YOU HAD IT *IN* YOU, MARCUS. I KNOW HOW TERRIFYING SHE CAN BE.

I SUPPOSE THAT'S WHY THEY PAY ME GOOD MONEY IN EXCHANGE FOR BAD SLEEP.

I HAVE TO MAKE A CALL, BUT WE'LL CONTINUE ONCE YOU'RE PATCHED UP. I THINK YOU'VE EARNED THE WEEK OFF.

THEY'VE BEEN USING THOSE PILLS TO DO *WHAT?!*

UH, WAS I NOT SUPPOSED TO SAY THAT?

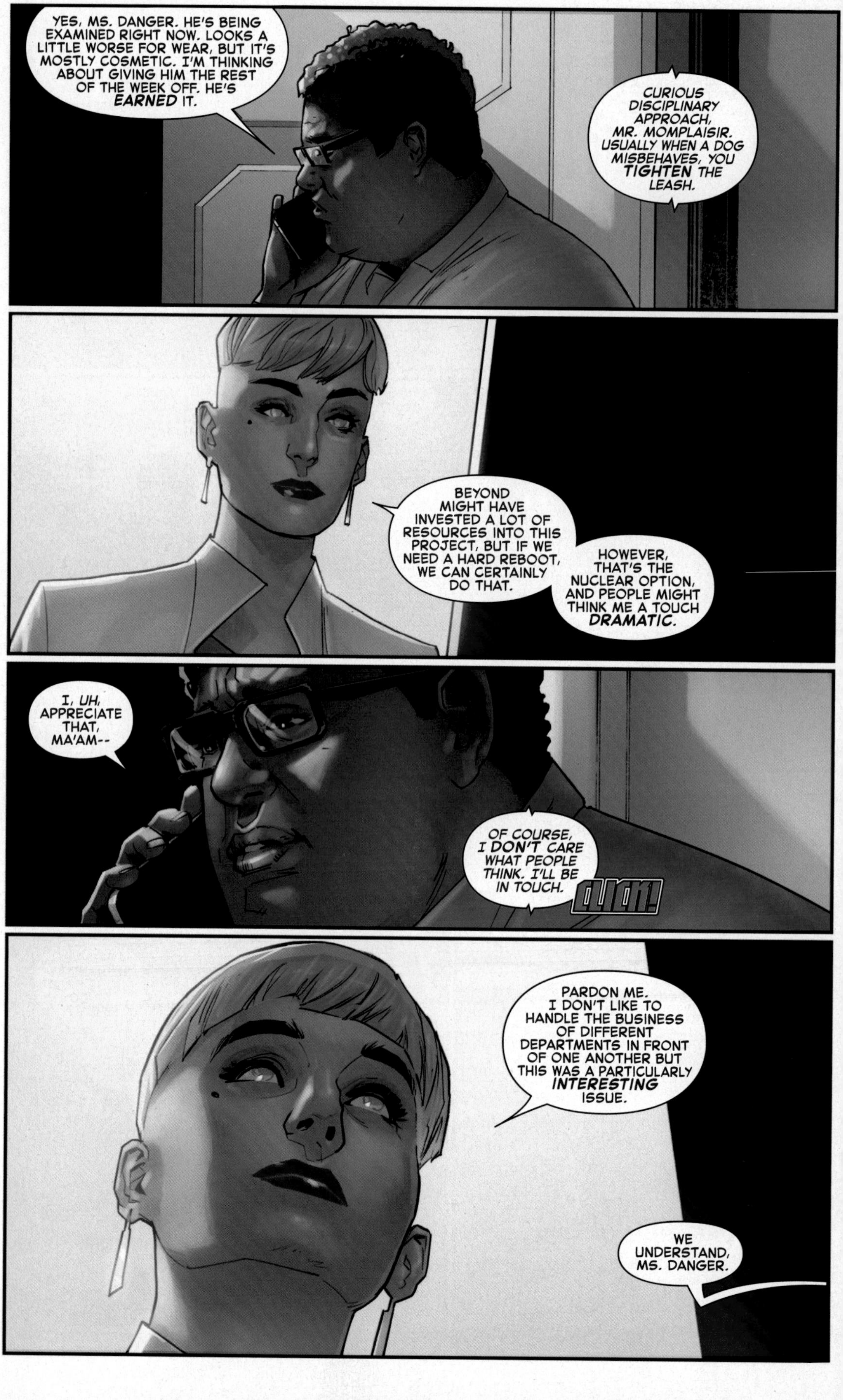
YES, MS. DANGER. HE'S BEING EXAMINED RIGHT NOW. LOOKS A LITTLE WORSE FOR WEAR, BUT IT'S MOSTLY COSMETIC. I'M THINKING ABOUT GIVING HIM THE REST OF THE WEEK OFF. HE'S EARNED IT.
CURIOUS DISCIPLINARY APPROACH, MR. MOMPLAISIR. USUALLY WHEN A DOG MISBEHAVES, YOU TIGHTEN THE LEASH.
BEYOND MIGHT HAVE INVESTED A LOT OF RESOURCES INTO THIS PROJECT, BUT IF WE NEED A HARD REBOOT, WE CAN CERTAINLY DO THAT.
HOWEVER, THAT'S THE NUCLEAR OPTION, AND PEOPLE MIGHT THINK ME A TOUCH DRAMATIC.
I, UH, APPRECIATE THAT, MA'AM--
OF COURSE, I DON'T CARE WHAT PEOPLE THINK. I'LL BE IN TOUCH.
CLICK!
PARDON ME. I DON'T LIKE TO HANDLE THE BUSINESS OF DIFFERENT DEPARTMENTS IN FRONT OF ONE ANOTHER BUT THIS WAS A PARTICULARLY INTERESTING ISSUE.
WE UNDERSTAND, MS. DANGER.

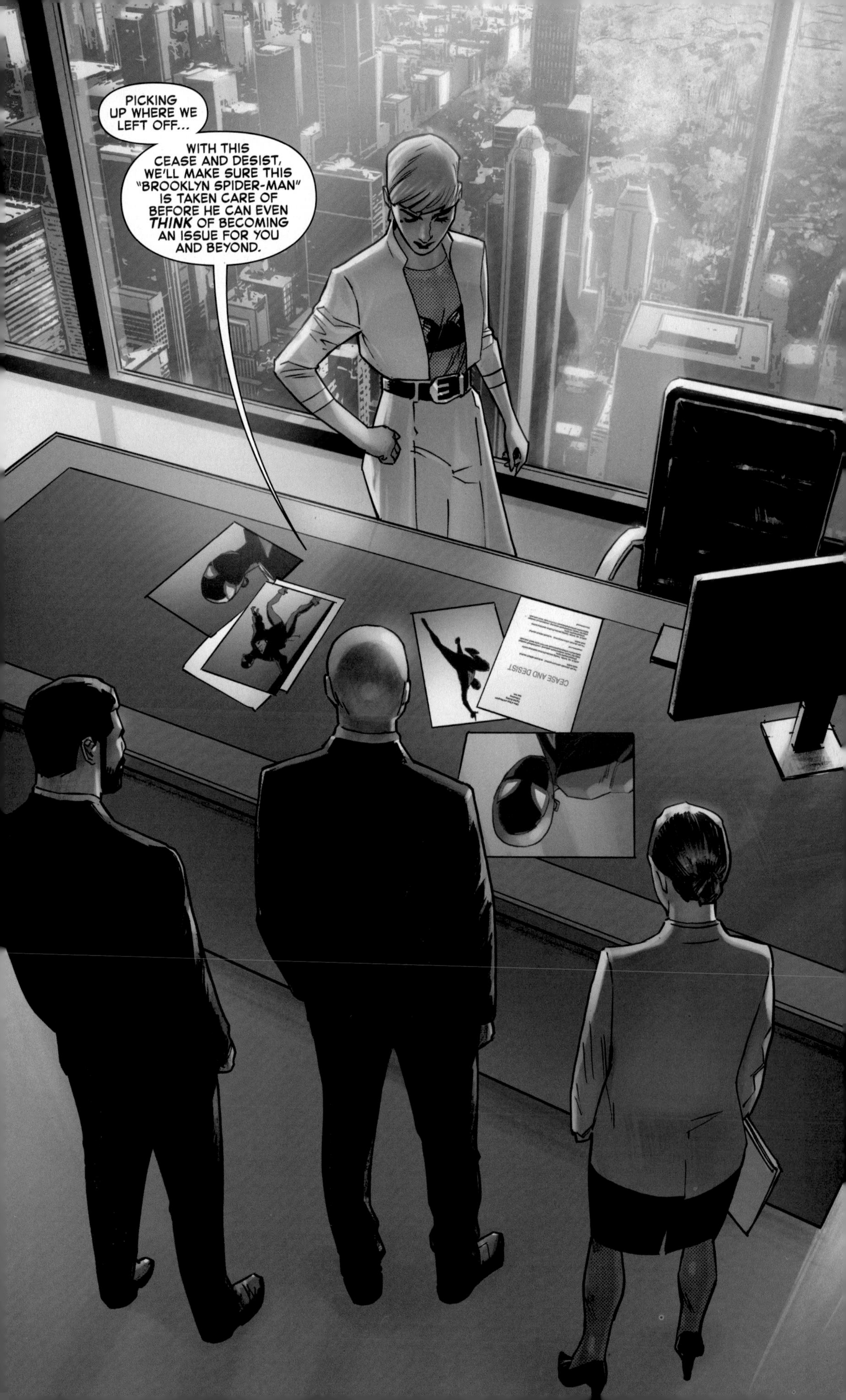
PICKING UP WHERE WE LEFT OFF...
WITH THIS CEASE AND DESIST, WE'LL MAKE SURE THIS "BROOKLYN SPIDER-MAN" IS TAKEN CARE OF BEFORE HE CAN EVEN *THINK* OF BECOMING AN ISSUE FOR YOU AND BEYOND.
CEASE AND DESIST

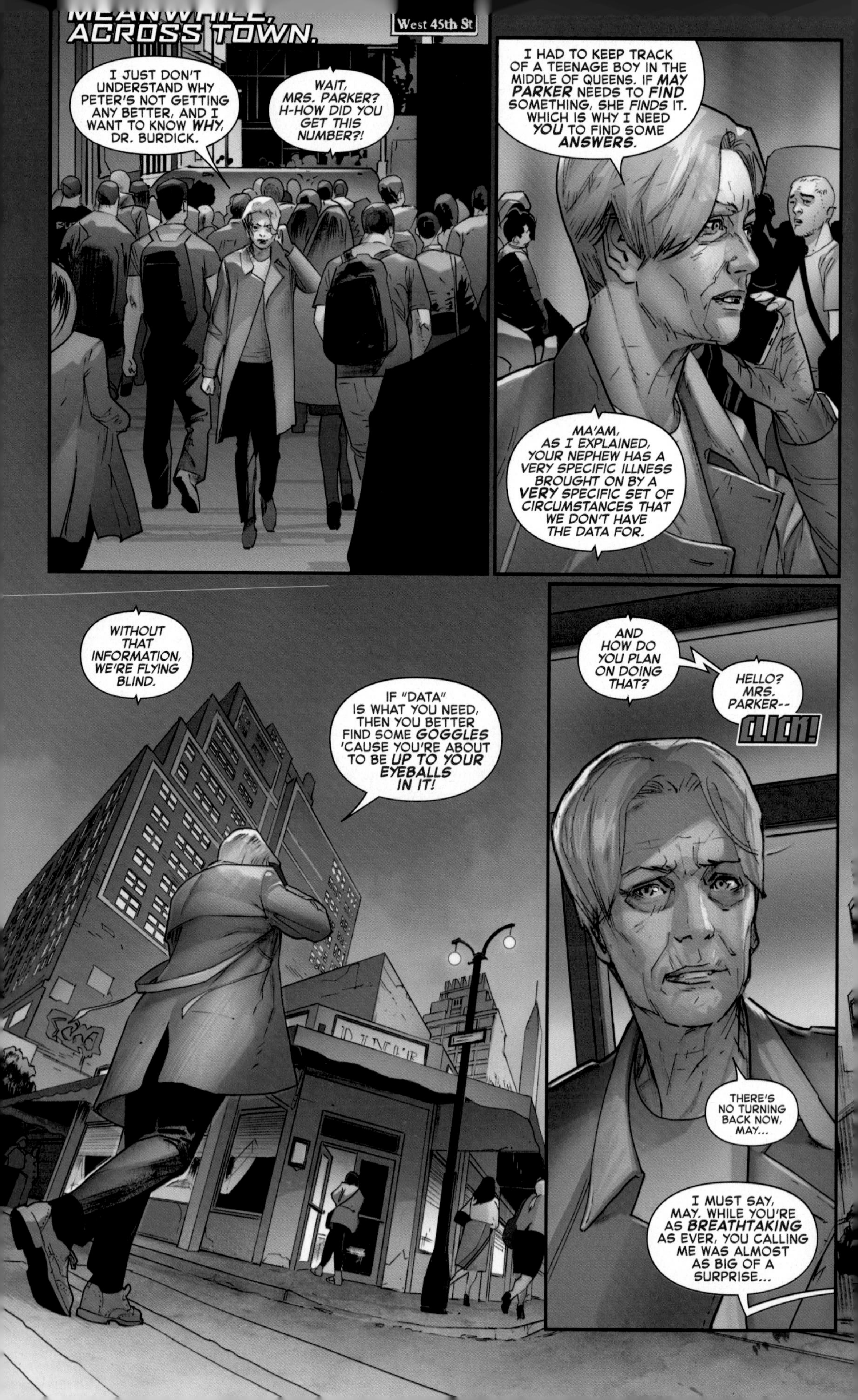
MEANWHILE, ACROSS TOWN.
West 45th St
I JUST DON'T UNDERSTAND WHY PETER'S NOT GETTING ANY BETTER, AND I WANT TO KNOW WHY, DR. BURDICK.
WAIT, MRS. PARKER? H-HOW DID YOU GET THIS NUMBER?!
I HAD TO KEEP TRACK OF A TEENAGE BOY IN THE MIDDLE OF QUEENS. IF MAY PARKER NEEDS TO FIND SOMETHING, SHE FINDS IT. WHICH IS WHY I NEED YOU TO FIND SOME ANSWERS.
MA'AM, AS I EXPLAINED, YOUR NEPHEW HAS A VERY SPECIFIC ILLNESS BROUGHT ON BY A VERY SPECIFIC SET OF CIRCUMSTANCES THAT WE DON'T HAVE THE DATA FOR.
WITHOUT THAT INFORMATION, WE'RE FLYING BLIND.
IF "DATA" IS WHAT YOU NEED, THEN YOU BETTER FIND SOME GOGGLES 'CAUSE YOU'RE ABOUT TO BE UP TO YOUR EYEBALLS IN IT!
AND HOW DO YOU PLAN ON DOING THAT?
HELLO? MRS. PARKER--
CLICK!
THERE'S NO TURNING BACK NOW, MAY...
I MUST SAY, MAY. WHILE YOU'RE AS BREATHTAKING AS EVER, YOU CALLING ME WAS ALMOST AS BIG OF A SURPRISE...

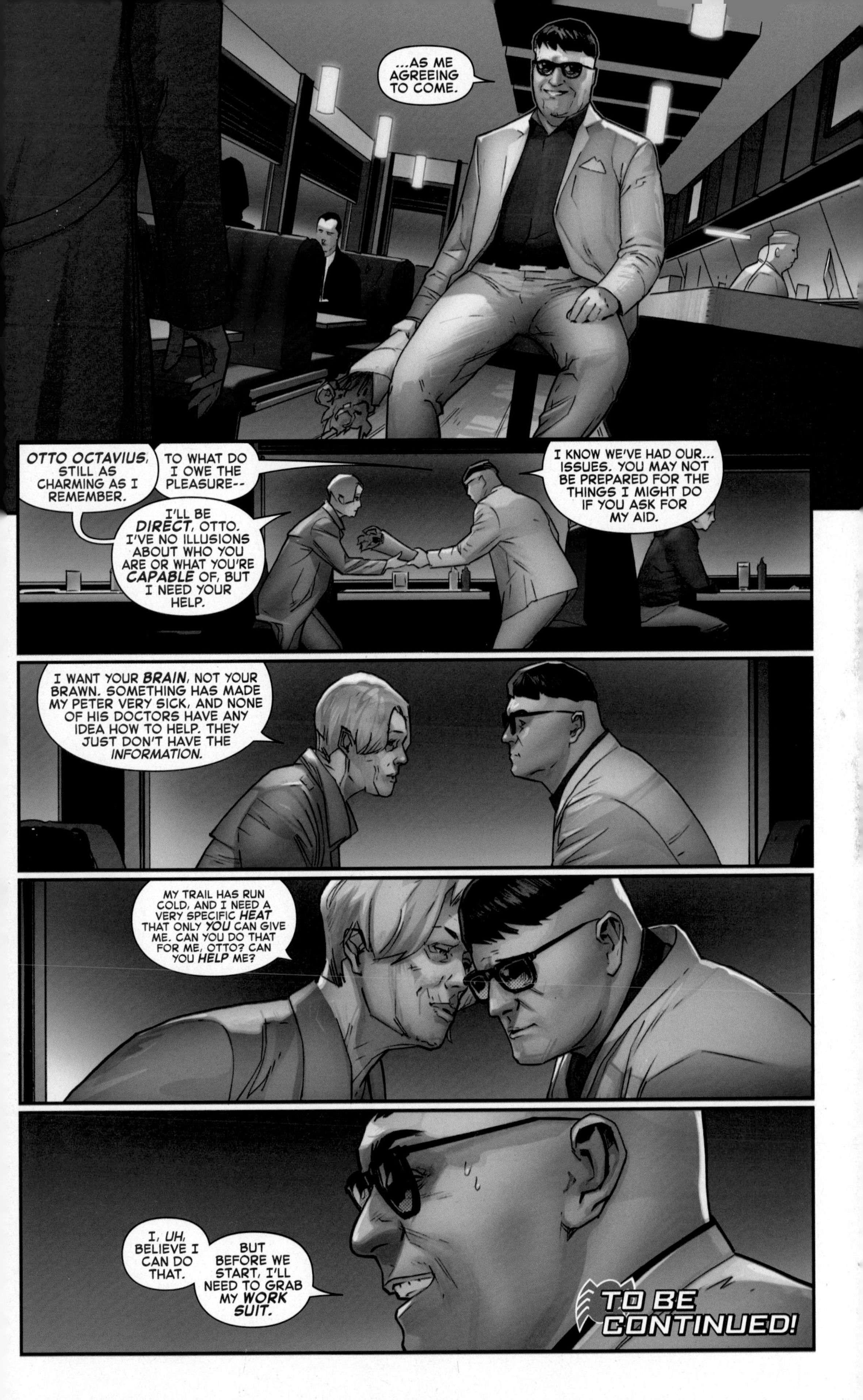
...AS ME AGREEING TO COME.
OTTO OCTAVIUS, STILL AS CHARMING AS I REMEMBER.
TO WHAT DO I OWE THE PLEASURE--
I'LL BE DIRECT, OTTO. I'VE NO ILLUSIONS ABOUT WHO YOU ARE OR WHAT YOU'RE CAPABLE OF, BUT I NEED YOUR HELP.
I KNOW WE'VE HAD OUR... ISSUES. YOU MAY NOT BE PREPARED FOR THE THINGS I MIGHT DO IF YOU ASK FOR MY AID.
I WANT YOUR BRAIN, NOT YOUR BRAWN. SOMETHING HAS MADE MY PETER VERY SICK, AND NONE OF HIS DOCTORS HAVE ANY IDEA HOW TO HELP. THEY JUST DON'T HAVE THE INFORMATION.
MY TRAIL HAS RUN COLD, AND I NEED A VERY SPECIFIC HEAT THAT ONLY YOU CAN GIVE ME. CAN YOU DO THAT FOR ME, OTTO? CAN YOU HELP ME?
I, UH, BELIEVE I CAN DO THAT.
BUT BEFORE WE START, I'LL NEED TO GRAB MY WORK SUIT.
TO BE CONTINUED!

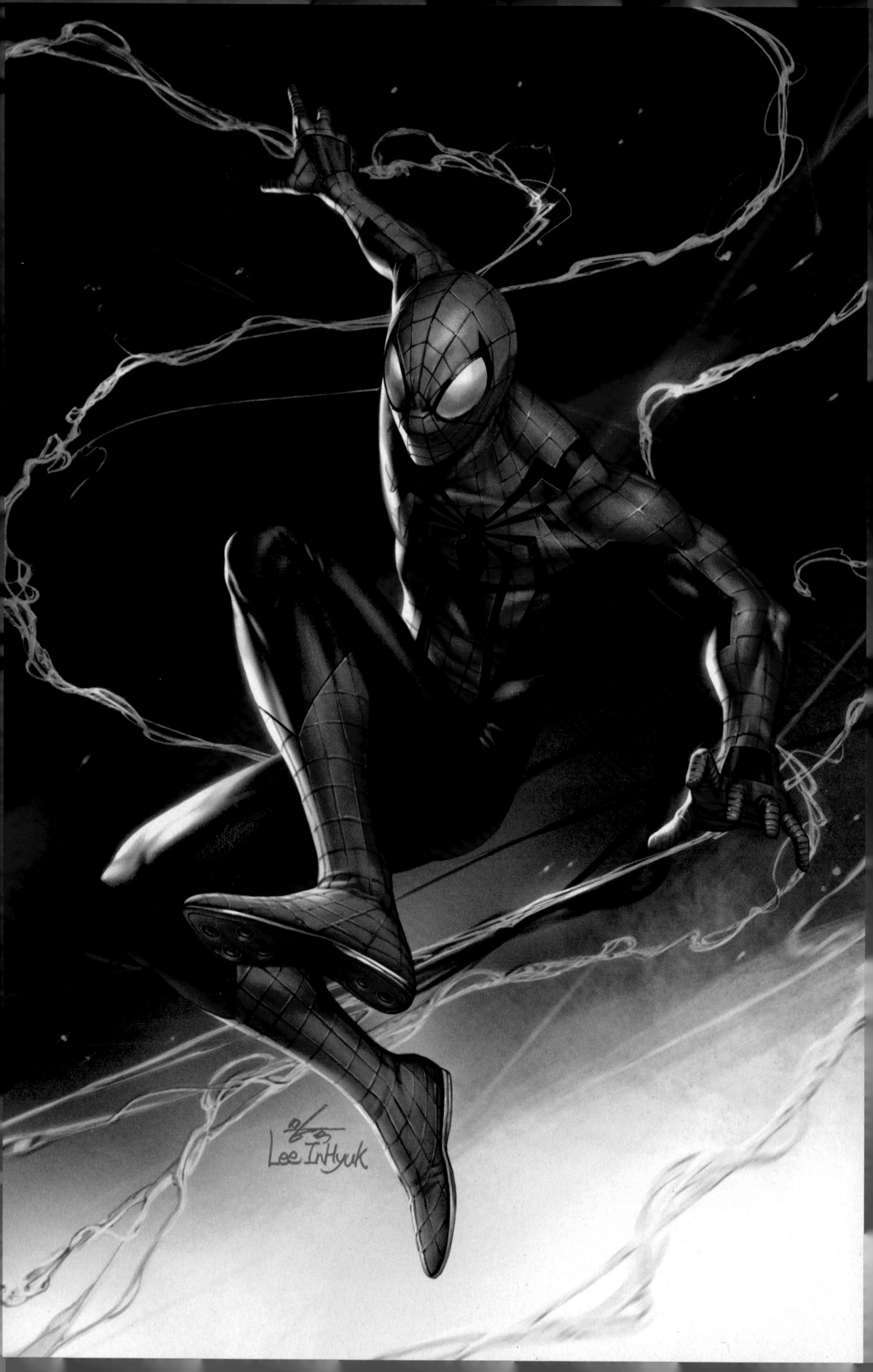
Lee InHyuk

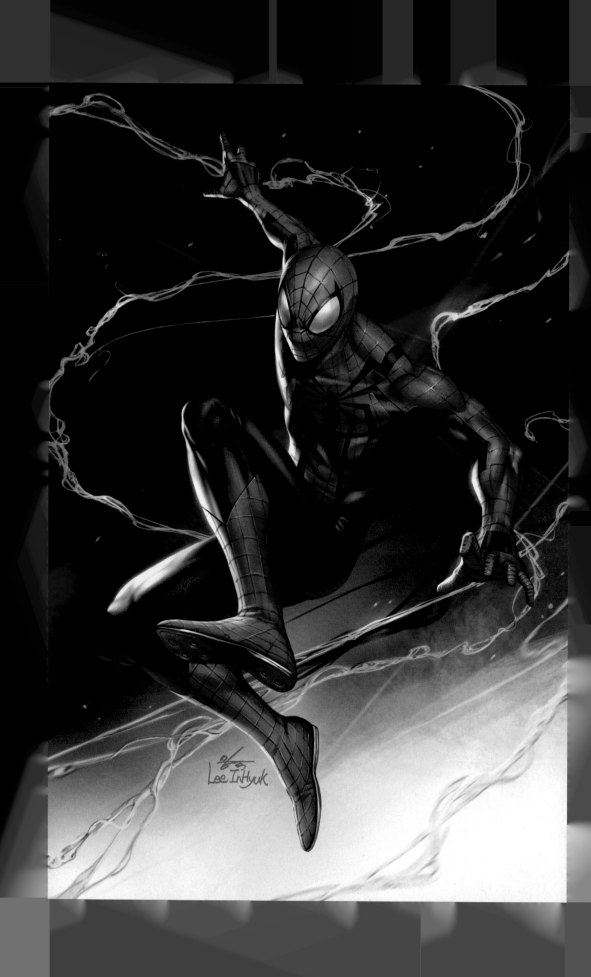

#75 VARIANT BY
ALEX OGLE

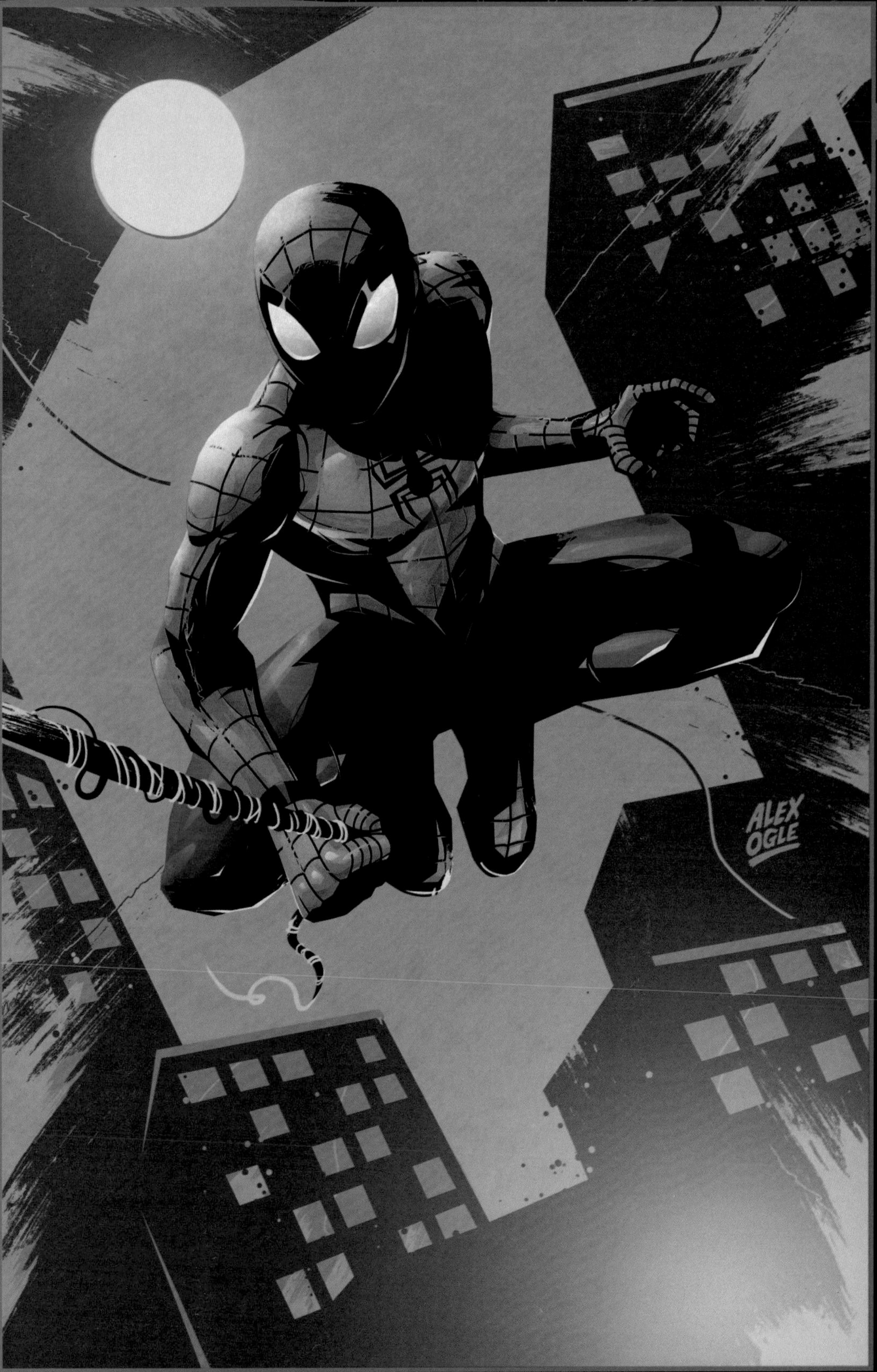
ALEX OGLE

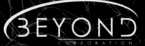

BEYOND CORPORATION

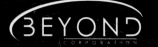

#75 VARIANT BY
SKOTTIE YOUNG

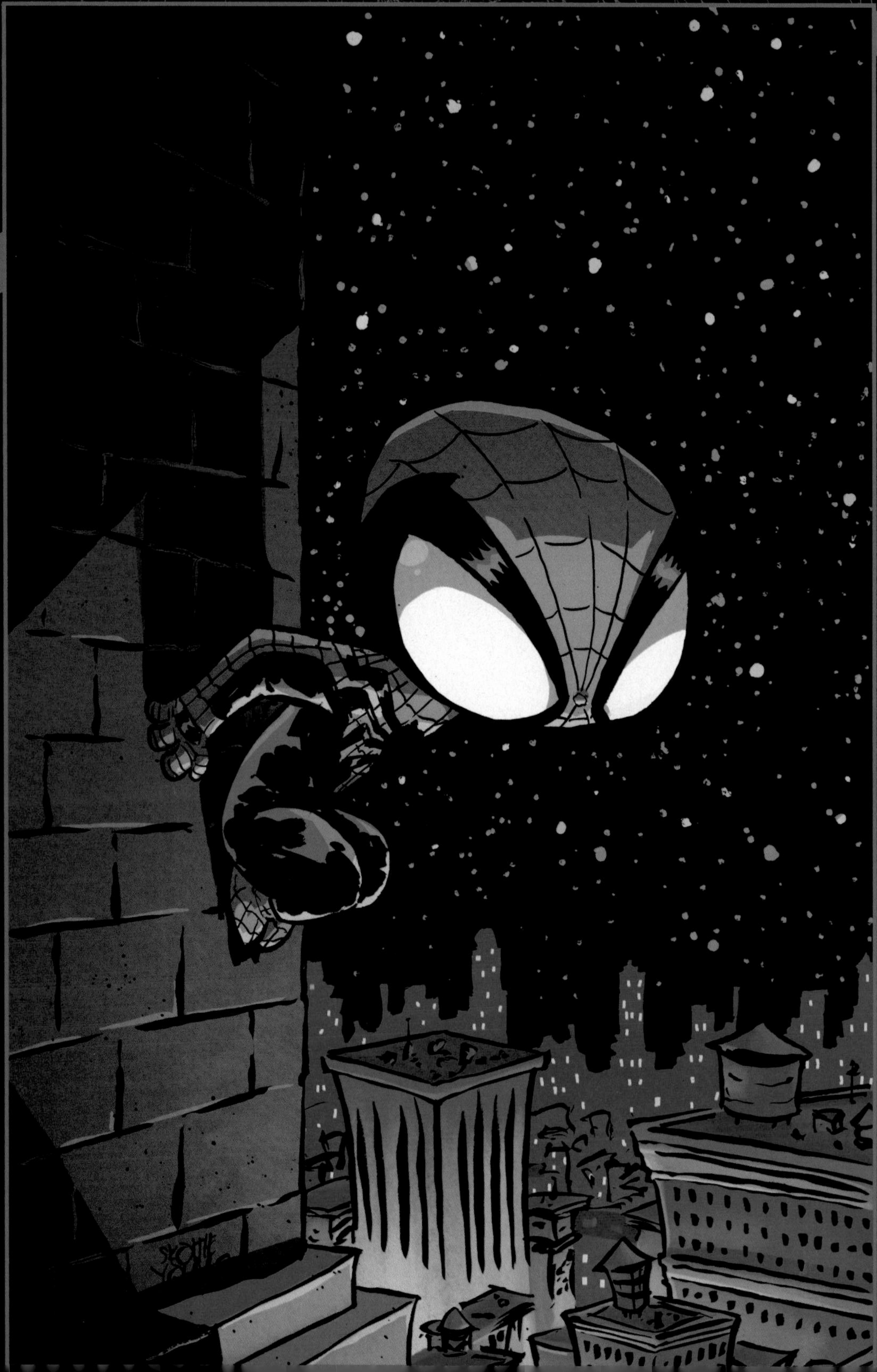

#75 STORMBREAKERS VARIANT BY
IBAN COELLO & **EDGAR DELGADO**

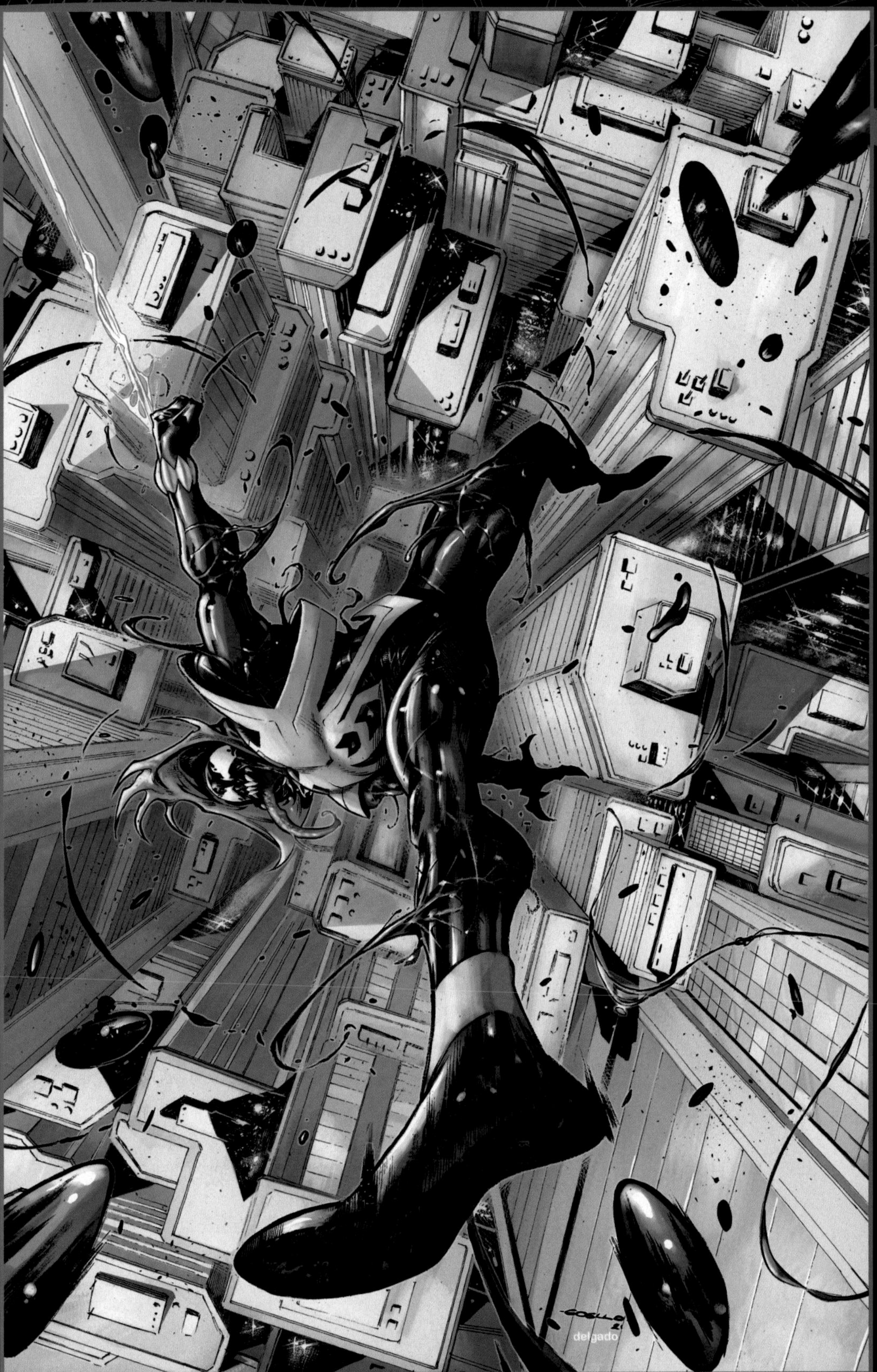

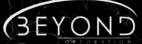

BEYOND CORPORATION

#75 VARIANT BY
RON LIM & **ISRAEL SILVA**

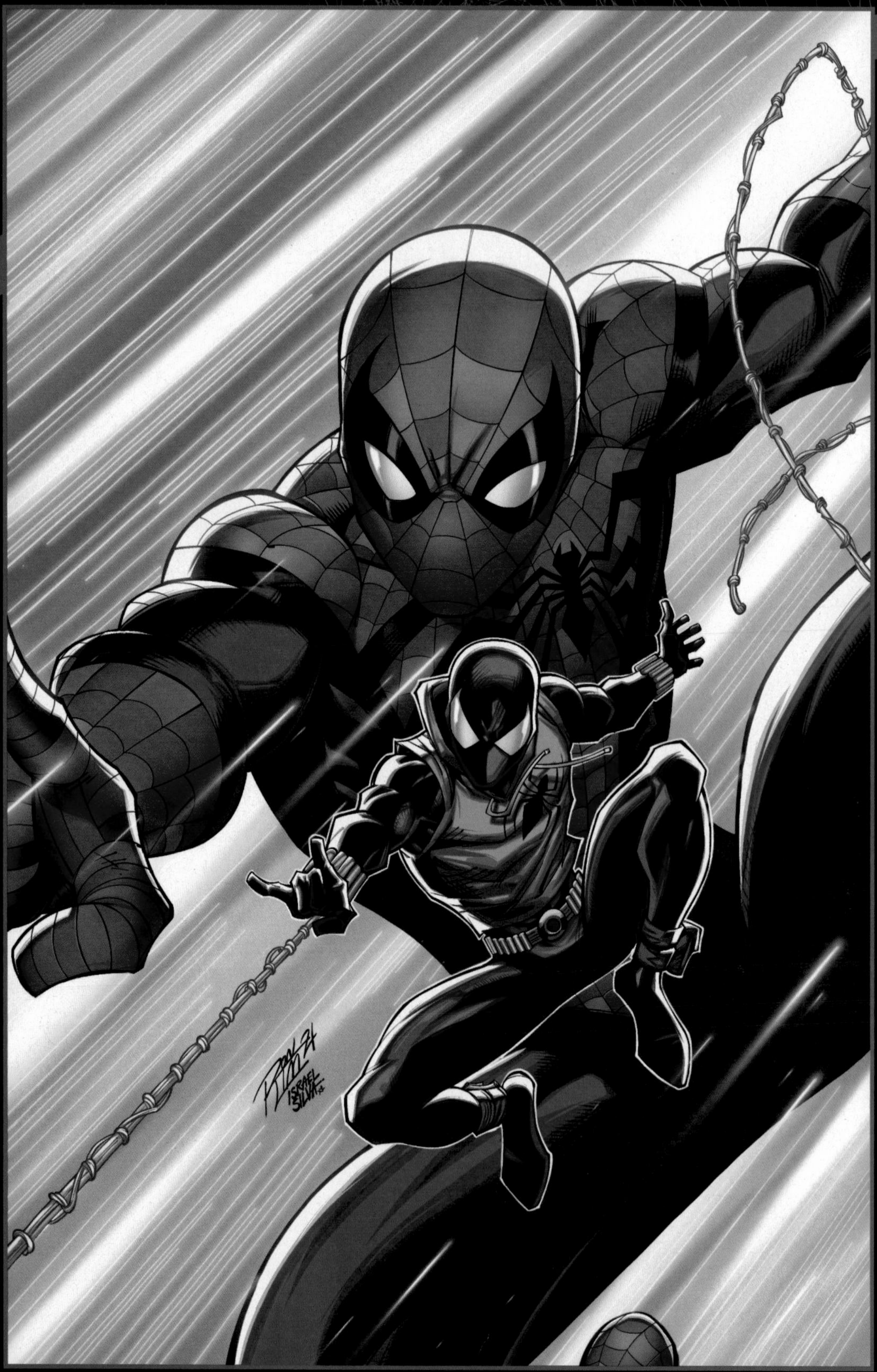

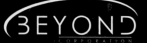

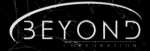

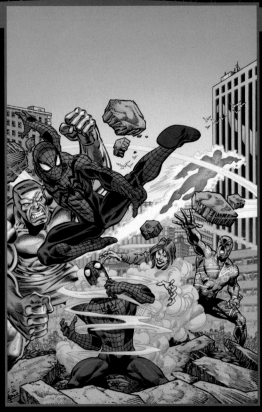

#75 VARIANT BY
RON FRENZ, BRETT BREEDING
& **NOLAN WOODARD**

from your pal, Spider-Man
X-219

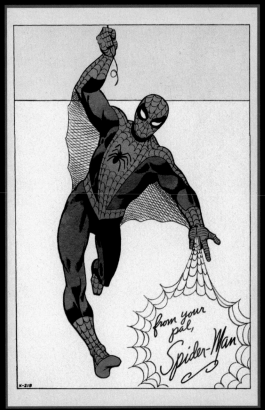

#75 HIDDEN GEM VARIANT BY
STEVE DITKO & **MORRY HOLLOWELL**

BEYOND CORPORATION

#76 VARIANT BY
PATRICK GLEASON & ALEJANDRO SÁNCHEZ

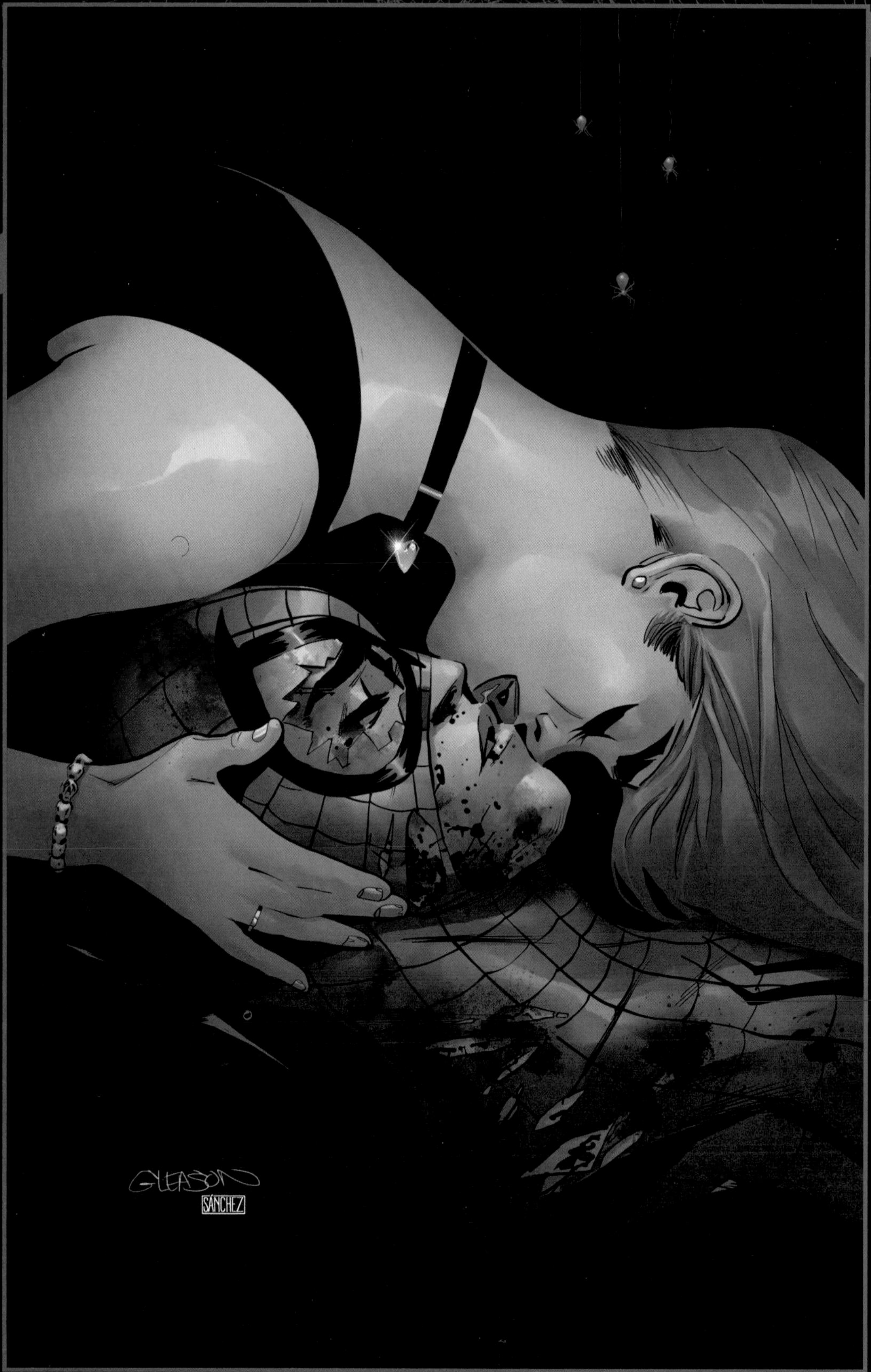
GLEASON
SÁNCHEZ

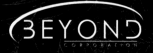

#77 VARIANT BY
DAVID AJA

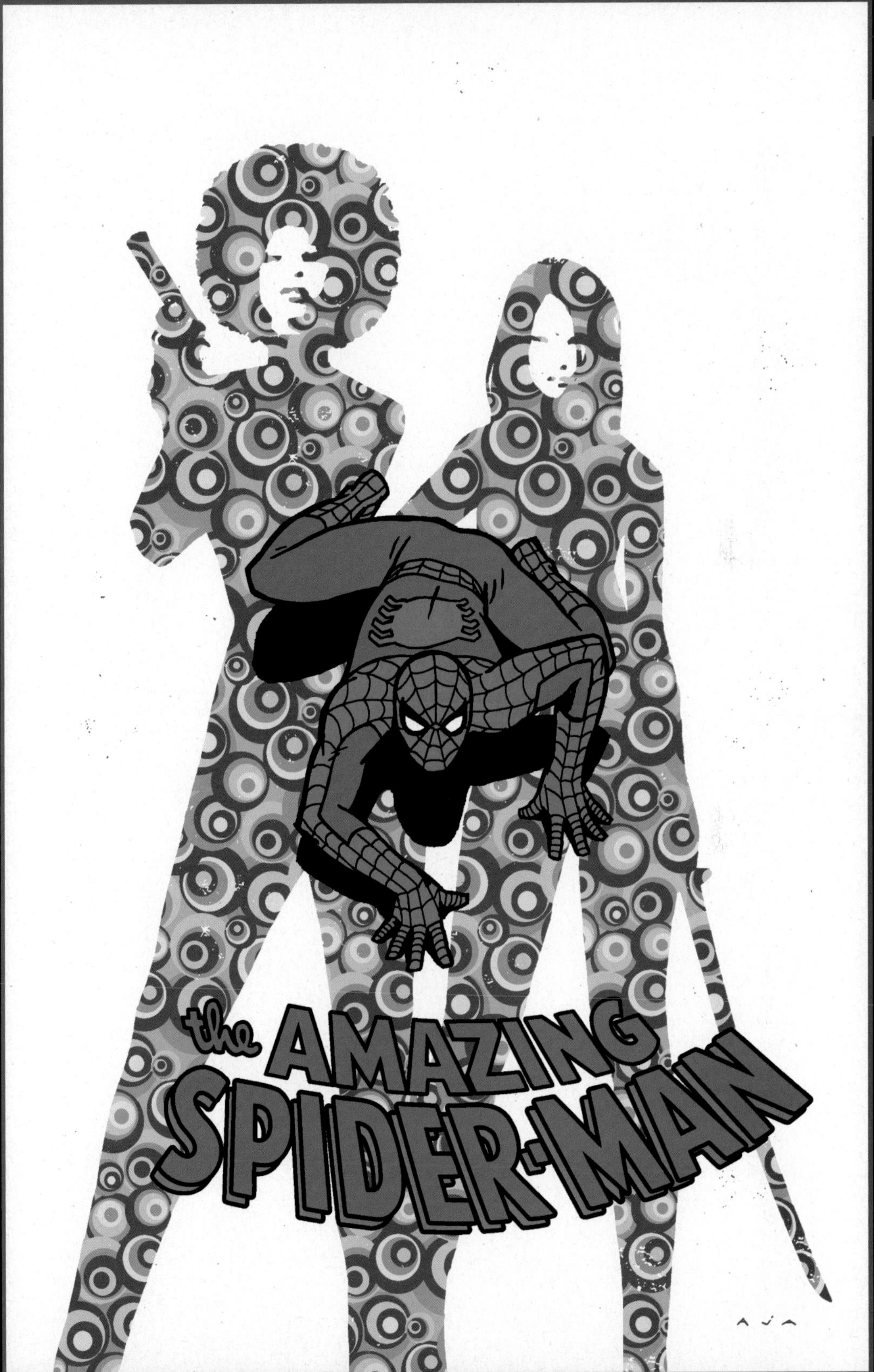
the AMAZING
SPIDER-MAN
AJA

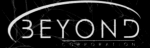

BEYOND CORPORATION

#78 DEADPOOL 30TH ANNIVERSARY VARIANT BY
ROB LIEFELD

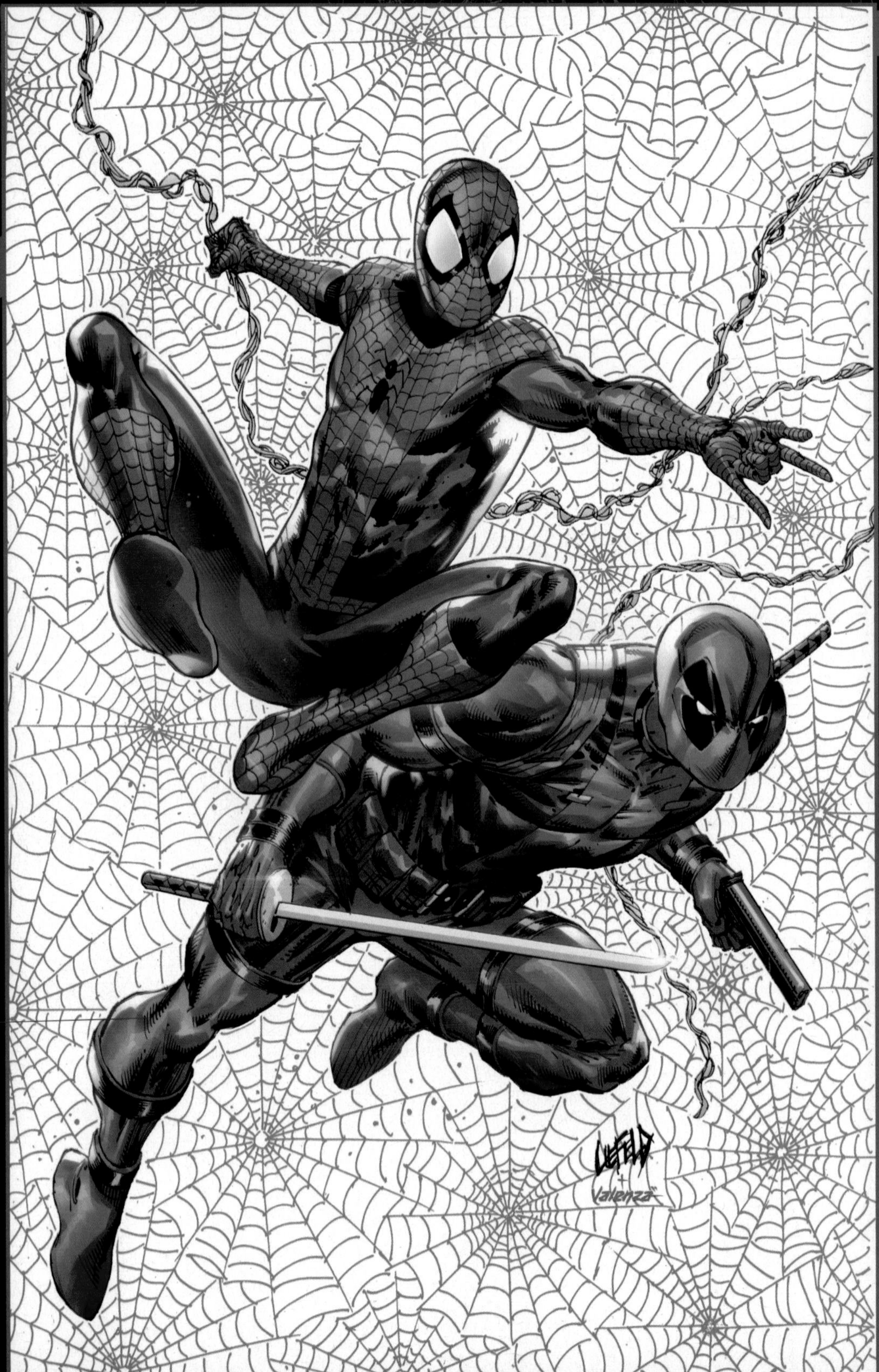

#78 MILES MORALES: SPIDER-MAN 10TH ANNIVERSARY VARIANT BY
DECLAN SHALVEY

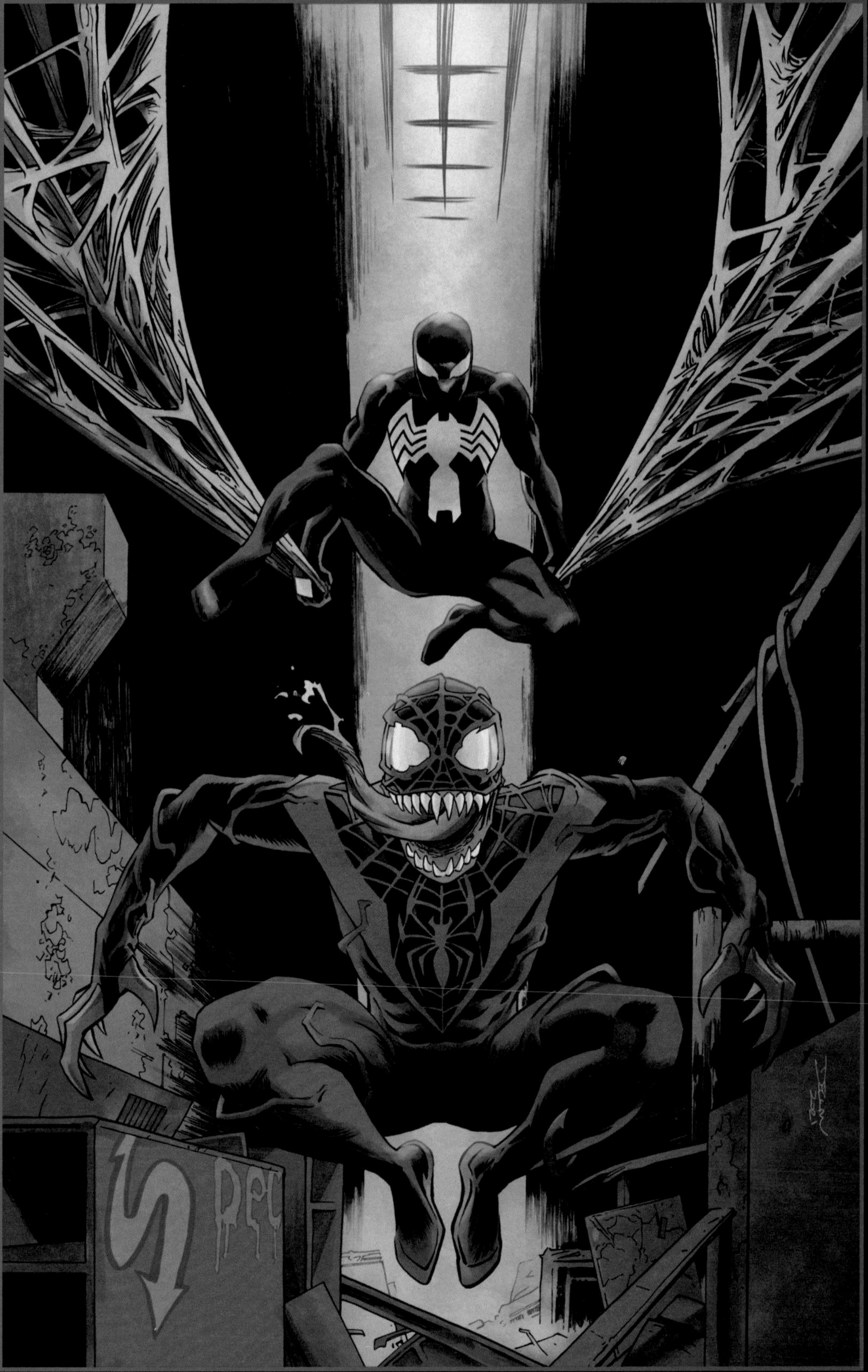

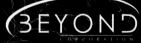

BEYOND CORPORATION

#78.BEY VARIANT BY
PEACH MOMOKO

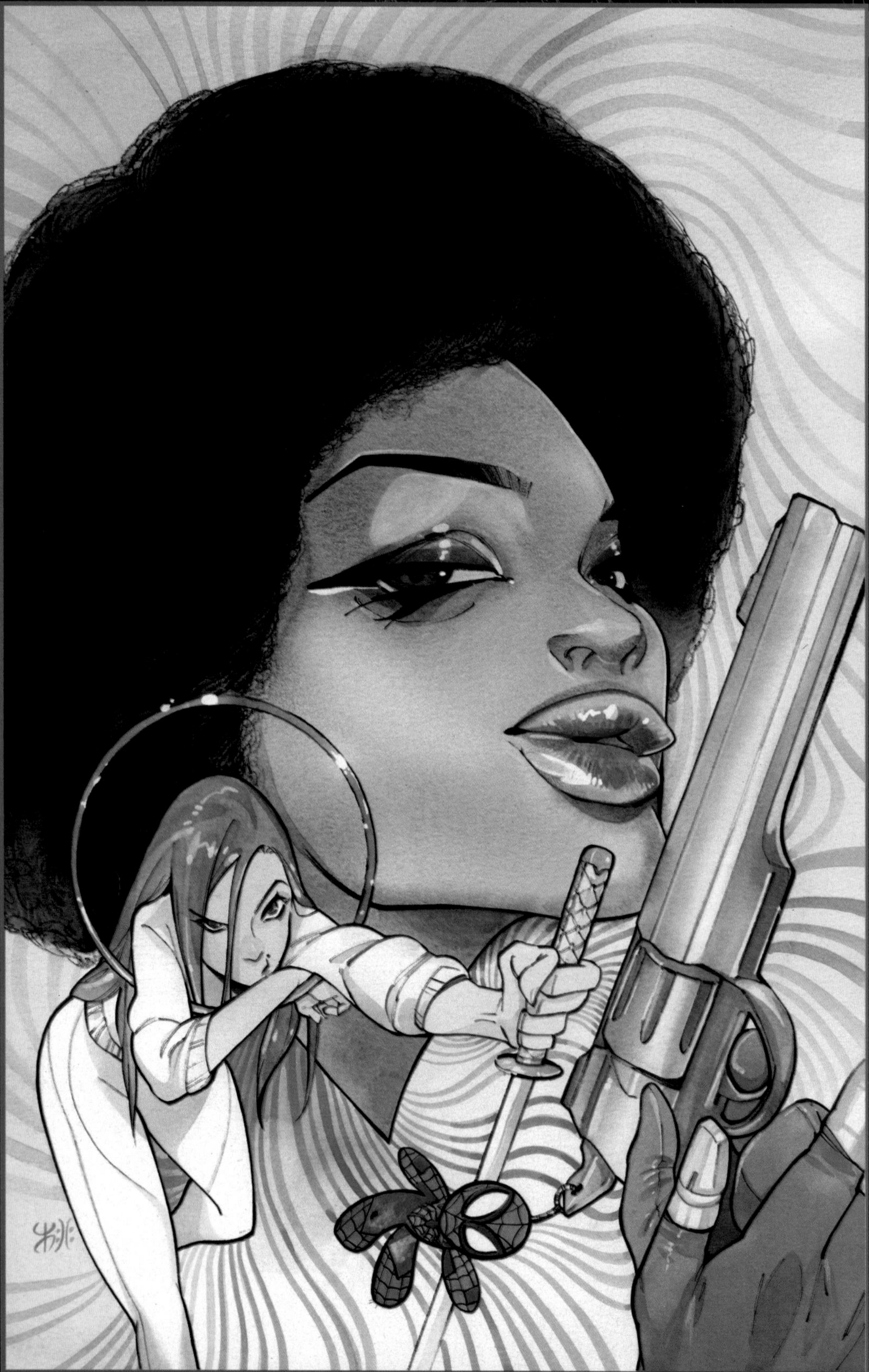

#79 VARIANT BY
SERGIO DÁVILA, SEAN PARSONS & MORRY HOLLOWELL

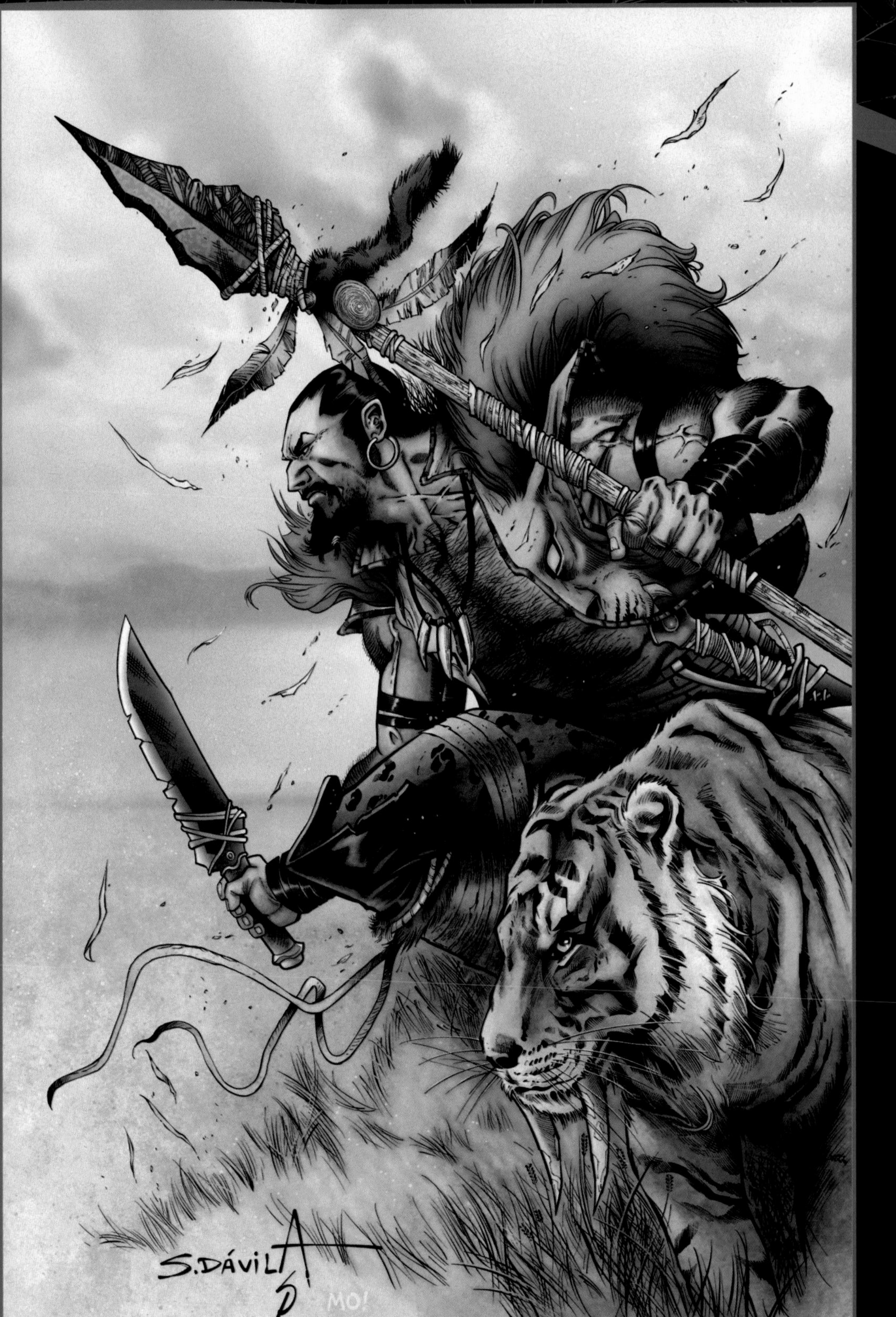

S.DÁVILA
MO!

BEYOND CORPORATION

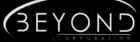

#79 VARIANT BY
DAN JURGENS, BRETT BREEDING & ALEX SINCLAIR

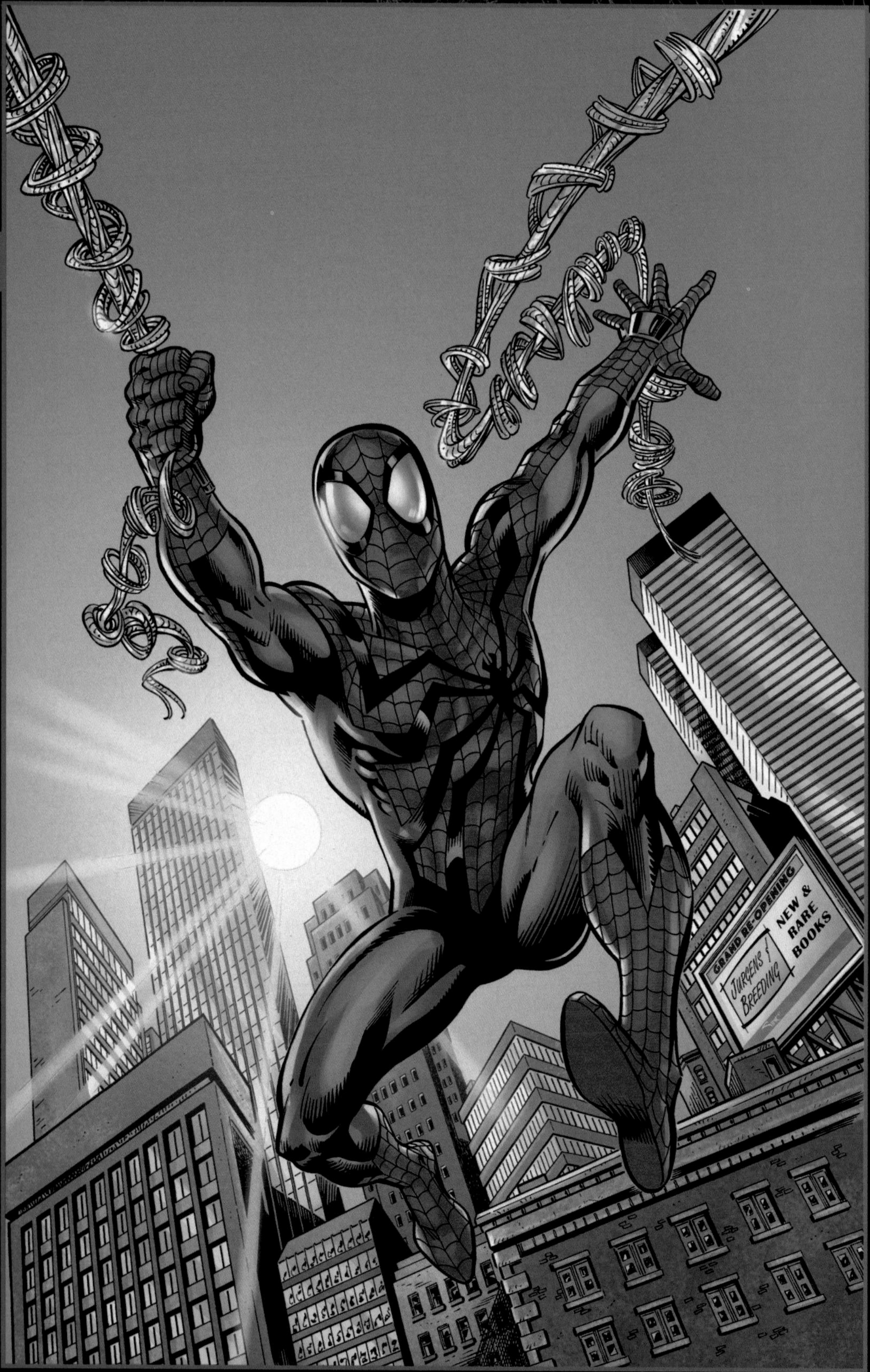
GRAND RE-OPENING
JURGENS & BREEDING
NEW & RARE BOOKS

#79 STORMBREAKERS VARIANT BY
R.B. SILVA & ALEJANDRO SÁNCHEZ

BEYOND
CORPORATION

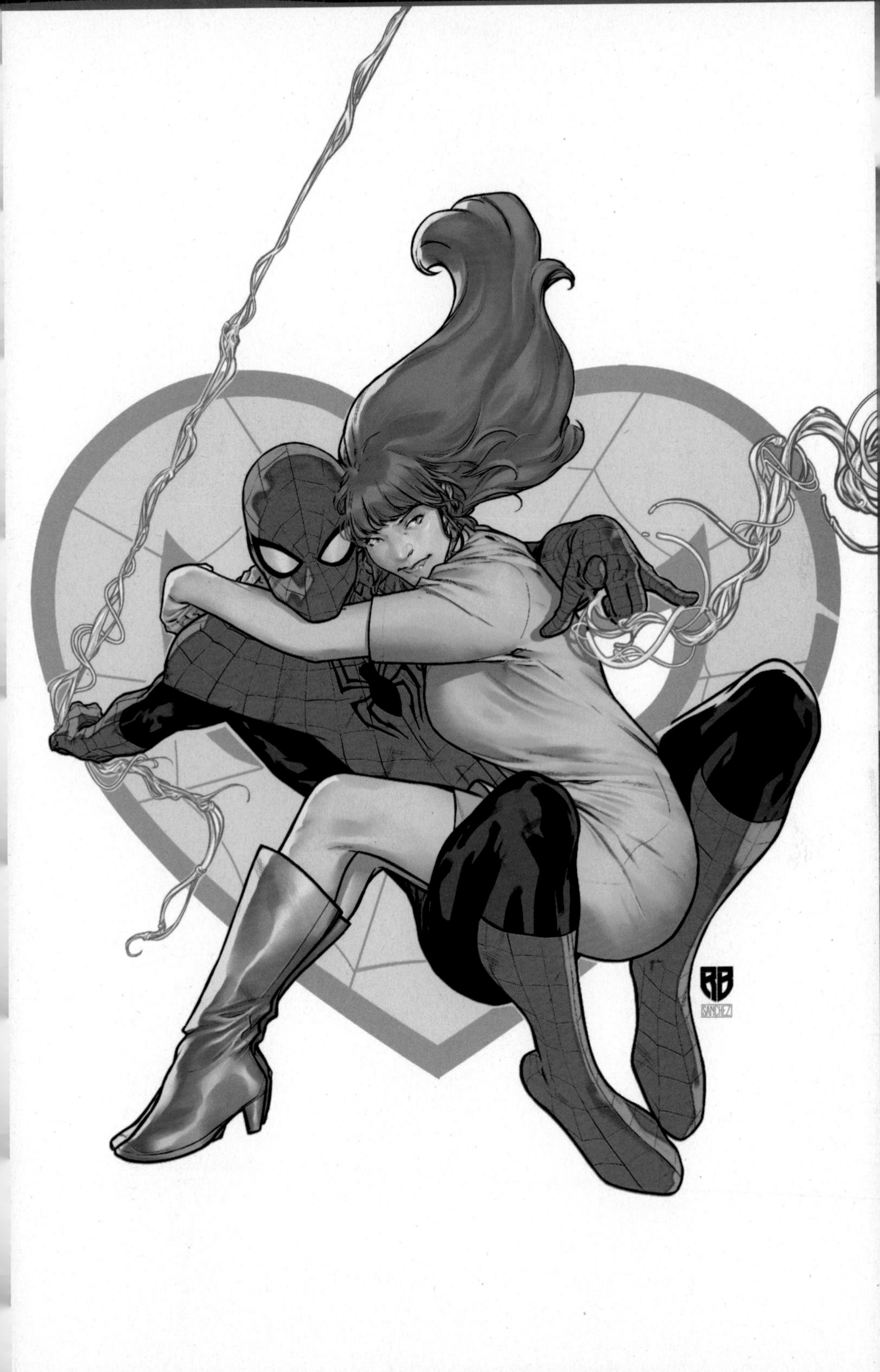
RB
SÁNCHEZ

BEYOND
CORPORATION

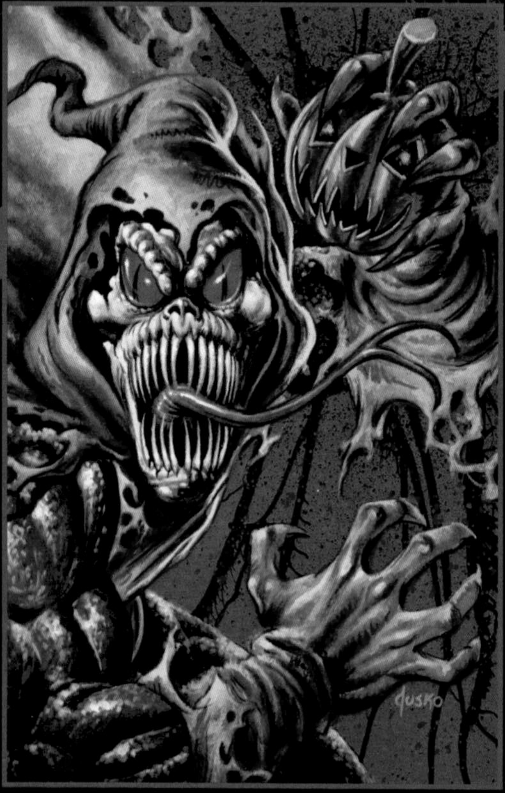

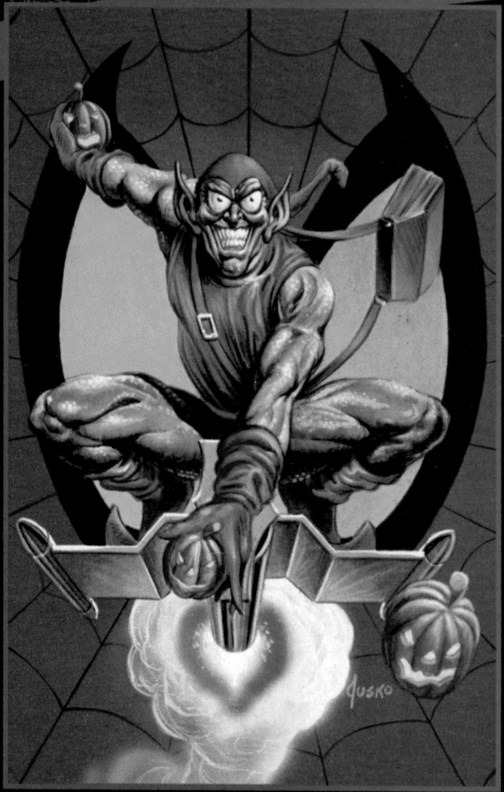

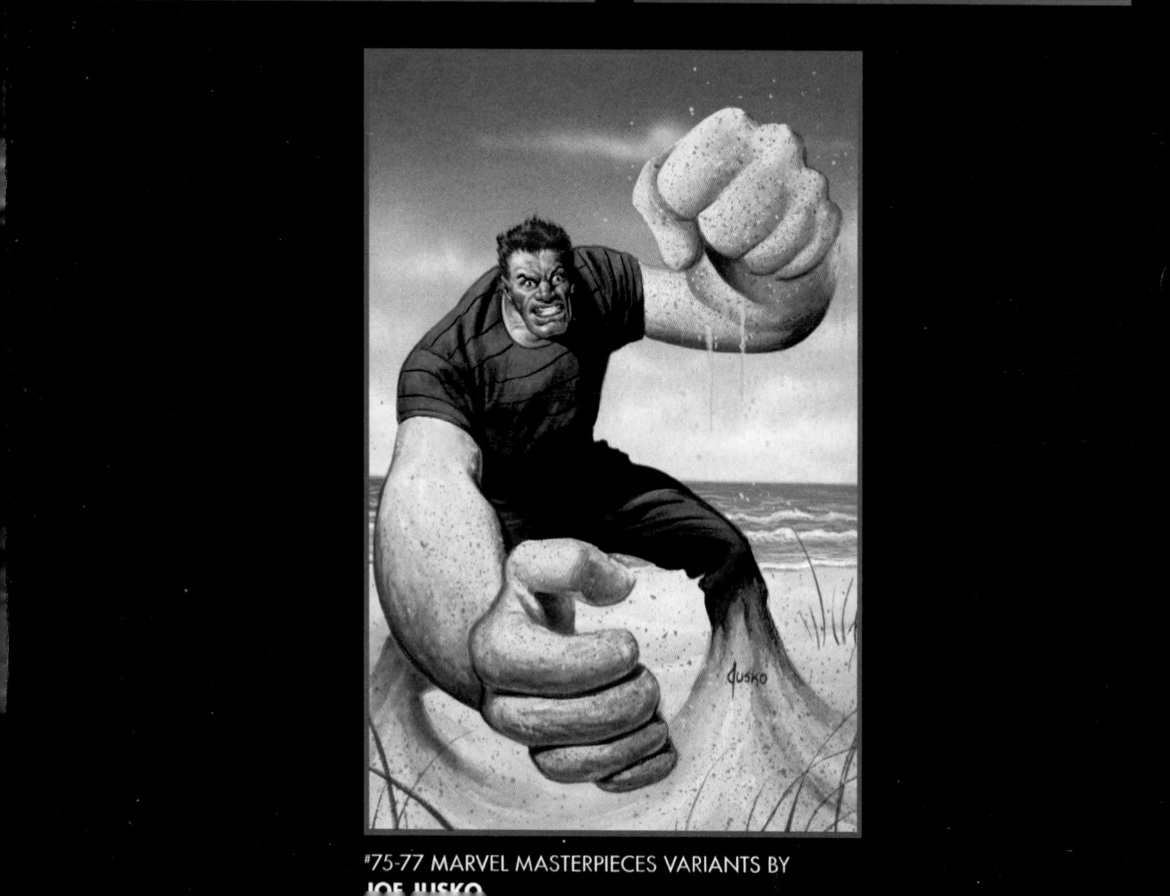

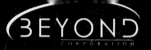

#75-77 MARVEL MASTERPIECES VARIANTS BY
JOE JUSKO